Guide to Intelligent Investing

Guide to Intelligent Investing

Jerome B. Cohen
Professor of Finance and Dean (Emeritus)
Bernard M. Baruch College
The City University of New York

Edward D. Zinbarg
Vice President
Bond and Commercial Loan Department
The Prudential Insurance Company of America

Arthur Zeikel
President and
Chief Investment Officer
Merrill Lynch Asset Management, Inc.

Dow Jones-Irwin
Homewood, Illinois 60430

ISBN 0-87094-152-6
Library of Congress Catalog Card No. 77–083590
Printed in the United States of America

3 4 5 6 7 8 9 0 K 5 4 3 2 0 9

Preface

The advice in this book has been distilled from the two largely separate worlds of theory and practice. The resulting investing strategies can be understood and applied by the general public. They combine what is *known* about *investing*, and what is *practiced*, into successful asset management techniques. Historically, there have been two types of investment books. Most offer advice with scant factual support. Other books, and the learned journals, contain a wealth of information, but typically leave the reader without practical suggestions. This book is different. It offers practical advice based on factual information. The facts have been gleaned from hundreds of scientific research studies, as well as from the experience of the authors in managing large securities portfolios.

This book is organized around three aspects of intelligent investing: Part I describes the environment in which securities transactions occur and the sources of information about that environment. Part II describes the intelligent approaches to selecting the investment vehicle most appropriate for you. Part III explains how you can determine the correct time to buy or sell your securities.

The book is written for today's investor. No special knowledge or required educational level is assumed—only an interest in building and protecting a prosperous future through intelligent investment management.

October 1977

Jerome B. Cohen
Edward D. Zinbarg
Arthur Zeikel

Contents

Part One
Introduction

To the busy doctor, dentist, lawyer, or other professional, the field of investments presents a bewildering variety of choices and alternatives. Affluence brings a need for knowledge which the busy specialist doesn't have time to acquire. Yet, even to listen to the counsel of a stockbroker or of an investment advisor, and to evaluate the advice, affluent investors need some background and information in order to judge whether the course of action suggested is logical and sensible and suitable to their goals and needs.

The objective of the first three chapters is to provide a basic orientation to the kinds of securities, markets, and information available to meet an investor's objective. Chapter 1 is devoted mainly to the varieties of stocks and bonds available in the market. Chapter 2 outlines the nature and operation of financial markets, while Chapter 3 describes the sources of basic investment information available to all literate nonprofessional investors.

Investment objectives vary with each stage in the life cycle. The young family looks for income, but more often for growth, and has time to wait out a developing situation. However, it should not be so preoccupied with growth as to risk losing its initial nest egg. Investors at midstream (age 35–55) know more, have higher earnings, and can afford more risk, but like their younger counterparts have to weigh risk against a relatively uncertain return and are thought basically to be risk averters. The third stage, the later years, of the life cycle bring a need for considerable caution and conservatism in investments. Older investors are retired or on the verge of retirement and cannot afford to lose much, if any, capital because they have limited ability to replace it. Moreover, they may no longer have the drive and concentration which are necessary for venturesome investing.

To the extent that it is possible—and as we shall see, it is difficult—older investors usually seek to combine safety and income. While even these two goals are not easy to attain, the avowed goals of most investors—high income, safety of principal, and *capital gain*—are almost impossible.

1

The Investment Setting

October. This is one of the peculiarly dangerous months to speculate in stocks. The others are July, January, September, April, November, May, March, June, December, August, and February.

Mark Twain

Investment has many facets. It may involve putting money into bonds, Treasury bills, or notes, or common stock, or paintings, or real estate, or mortgages, or oil ventures, or cattle, or the theater. It may involve speculating in bull markets or selling short in bear markets. It may involve choosing growth stocks, or blue chips, or defensive stocks, or income stocks, or even penny cats and dogs. It may involve options, straddles, rights, warrants, convertibles, margin, gold, silver, mutual funds, money market funds, index funds, tax exempt bond funds and result in accumulation of wealth or dissipation of resources. Diversity and challenge characterize the field. For the able or the lucky, the rewards may be substantial. For the uninformed, results can be disastrous.

Investment could mean buying 100 shares of IBM in 1913 for $44½ per share, and watching it appreciate, through stock dividends and stock splits, to 74,150 shares by 1977, worth about $20.6 million. Or it could have meant buying Du Pont in 1929 at $503 per share and seeing it fall to $22 per share by 1932. In the raging bull market of the 1960s one could have bought AT&T, the bluest of the blue chips, at 75 and seen it decline from 75 to 40. By contrast Houston Oil and Minerals stock rose from the equivalent of 75 cents a share following its listing in late 1972 to a high of 60⅞ in 1977, after splitting several times. This meant that the stock increased in value approximately 80 times in less than five years. An investment of $100 in the stock at its listing in 1972 would have been worth around $8,000 by early 1977.

Investment could mean buying new land or new homes. For example, new homes in Southern California have become a speculative commodity, with investment syndicates buying them when completed and selling them a year or so later in a sizzling market that often doubles or triples their money, according to the *New York Times*. When done on the leverage of mortgage debt, this may mean a return of from 50 to 250 percent of the money invested.

How Investment Alternatives Compare

How investment alternatives compare may be seen in Tables 1–1 and 1–2. All investment is a balancing of objectives and purposes. A

Table 1–1
Securities Markets of the Past 20 Years, 1957–1976

	Jan. 1 1957	Jan. 1 1962	Jan. 1 1967	Dec. 31 1976	% Change 10 Yrs. 1967-1976	% Change 15 Yrs. 1962-1976	% Change 20 Yrs. 1957-1976
Cost of Living Index	82.7	89.9	98.6	174.3	+ 77%	+ 94%	+111%
Value of the Dollar	120.9	111.2	101.4	57.4	− 43	− 48	− 53
Dow-Jones Industrial Average	499.47	731.14	785.69	1004.65	+ 28	+ 37	+101
Standard & Poor's 500 Stock Index	46.67	71.55	80.33	107.46	+ 34	+ 50	+130
New York Stock Exchange Index	24.35	38.39	43.72	57.88	+ 32	+ 51	+138
Value Line Composite Average	—	104.11	118.45	93.47	− 21	− 10	—
S. & P. Utilities	31.76	64.83	69.35	54.24	− 22	− 16	+ 71
S. & P. Railroads	31.36	33.25	41.04	50.67	+ 23	+ 52	+ 62
S. & P. High-Grade Corporate Bonds	102.8	94.50	83.13	61.97	− 25	− 34	− 40
S. & P. Municipal Bonds	108.1	107.3	103.06	80.94	− 21	− 25	− 25
S. & P. Long-Term Government Bonds	95.19	87.72	82.52	74.95	− 9	− 15	− 21
S. & P. Preferred Stocks	151.4	150.9	133.6	91.50	− 32	− 39	− 40
Savings Bank Deposit	100.0	100.0	100.0	100.0	0	0	0
Johnson Growth Fund Average	94.09	164.86	228.01	309.99	+ 28	+ 77	+210
Johnson Growth & Income Fund Average	92.00	143.15	169.21	256.07	+ 39	+ 65	+156
Johnson Income Fund Average	93.90	116.77	125.70	135.58	+ 1	+ 9	+ 36
Johnson Balanced Fund Average	95.13	138.64	146.05	168.43	+ 10	+ 16	+ 68

Source: Johnson's Investment Company Charts, 1977 edition.

very safe investment may not provide protection against inflation. An inflation-resistant investment may not provide liquidity. And there is and has been an ongoing debate over the risk-return trade-off. It has

Table 1–2
How Investment Alternatives Compare

	Risk or Safety of Capital	Current Yield	Inflation Resistance	Liquidity	Additional Expense Involved
U.S. savings bonds:					
First year	Excellent	Poor	Poor	Excellent	None
Held to maturity	Excellent	Fair	Poor	Excellent	
Insured savings accounts	Excellent	Poor	Poor	Excellent	None
Savings certificates	Excellent	Fair to good	Poor	*Good*	None
Government securities:					
Treasury bills	Excellent	Fair	Good	*Excellent*	May be a sales commission *or bank charge*
Medium-term notes	Excellent	Good	Fair	Good	
Long-term bonds	Excellent	Excellent	Poor	Good	
Common stocks	Fair	Poor	Good	Good	Sales commission
Preferred stocks	*Fair*	Excellent	Poor	Good	Sales commission
High-grade corporate bonds	Good	Excellent	Poor	Good	Sales commission *or bank charge*
Tax-exempt bonds	*Good*	*Good*	*Fair*	*Fair*	*Sales commission or bank charge*
Mutual funds:					
Growth stock funds	Fair	Poor	Good	Good	Management fee, may be a sales commission
Bond funds	Fair	Excellent	Poor	Good	
Money market funds	Good	Fair to good	Good	Good to excellent	Management fee, may be a sales commission
Real estate:					
Land	Good	None	Good	Poor	Maintenance and management costs (rental), taxes and interest
Rental property	Good	Varies	Good	Poor	
Gold:					
Bullion	Fair	None	Good	Poor	Sales commission, storage fees, insurance
Coins	Good	None	Good	Poor	
Art works	*Good*	*None*	*Excellent*	*Good*	*Sales charge*

Italics indicate our adaptations from *Changing Times* original.

Source: Adapted and reprinted from *Changing Times: The Kiplinger Magazine,* February 1976, p. 14. Copyright 1976 by the Kiplinger Washington Editors, 1729 H Street, N. W., Washington, D.C. 20006.

been widely assumed that the higher the risk undertaken, the more ample the return and, conversely, the lower the risk, the more modest the return. But recent research has shown that this is often not the case. Different investment media fit different investment objectives but the fit is seldom perfect.

The average investor seeks a safe, inflation-resistant investment, which provides a good return, with capital gains opportunities, but which can be liquidated quickly if necessary. As the following pages make clear, there is no such animal.

Risk and Return: Objectives in Conflict

Generally speaking, all rational investors would like to:

1. Preserve principal and have it available at any time (that is, maintain liquidity).
2. Maximize the rate of return on investment, net of taxes and inflation.

Unfortunately, these admirable twin objectives conflict with each other. It is a central tenet of finance that the greater the assurance that principal will be preserved from loss, the lower the *anticipated* rate of return. Conversely, the higher the *expected* return, the greater the possibility of loss.

There is substantial evidence documenting a *long-run* tendency for actual returns on investment and anticipated risk of principal to vary directly. But the data also show that over shorter periods of time there is frequently an inverse relationship, with less risky investments actually earning more than risky ones. Therein lies the dilemma. The undertaking of increased investment risk does not inherently guarantee a higher return than a less risky position.

Thus, in both the setting of their objectives and the making of actual portfolio decisions, investors must engage in a compromise, or trade-off, between the desire to preserve capital and maintain liquidity on the one hand, and to maximize anticipated total return on the other.

In order to grapple with the concept of a risk-return trade-off more effectively, investors should view their alternatives as being represented by a spectrum such as that shown in Figure 1–1. At one extreme are the "safest" investments with the lowest anticipated returns available in the marketplace. These include U.S. Treasury bills, bank certificates of deposit, commercial paper, and the like. At the other extreme lie the high risks and highest anticipated returns, usually associated with venture capital, real estate development activities,

Figure 1–1
The Spectrum of Anticipated Investment Returns and Risks

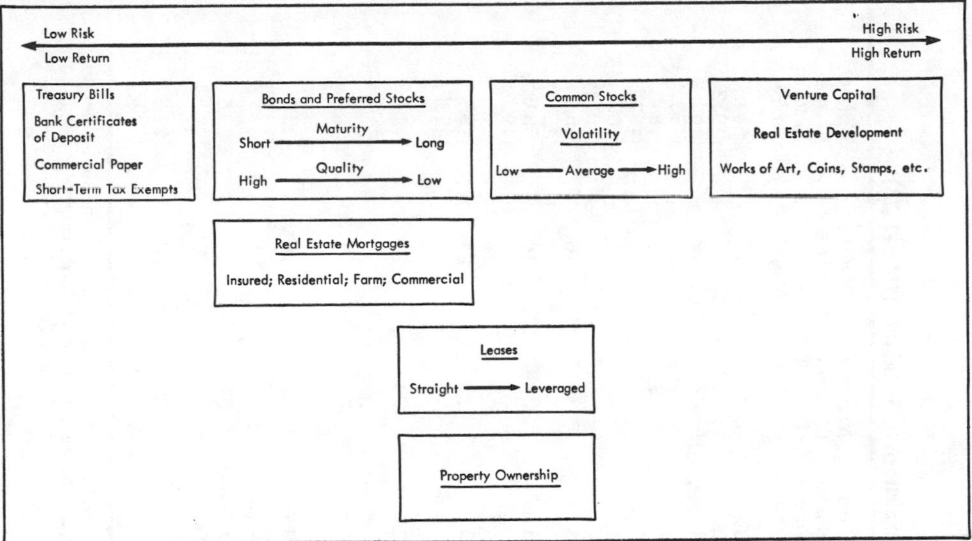

works of art, stamps, and coins. In between, where most investors operate most of the time, are fixed-income securities, real estate mortgages, common stocks, and other media. Of course, anticipated returns vary within each asset category. It is not unlikely that a particular security in a relatively low-risk investment category could provide a higher anticipated return than another particular security in a higher risk, category. A low-quality bond, for example, might provide a higher total return than a high-quality common stock.

Stocks versus Bonds. The investor's risk-return trade-off is usually discussed in terms of the relative rates of return provided by the stock market versus fixed-income securities. Over the years, extensive research efforts have documented the proposition that stocks, over the *long run,* do in fact provide higher total returns. In other words, higher actual returns are related to higher anticipated risk.

"For the long-haul, stocks invariably outperform both bills and bonds," was the way *Barron's* summed up a recent most important study. This extensive study for the period (1926–74) showed that common stocks returned an arithmetic average annual rate of 10.9 percent, compared with 3.7 percent for corporate bonds and 2.3 percent for Treasury bills. The difference between the rate of return on stocks and T-bills, 8.6 percent, is sometimes considered as the *risk* premium earned from the decision to invest in common stocks. The study

Table 1–3
Rates of Return on Comparative Investment Media: Basic and Derived Series: Historical Highlights (1926–1974)

Series	*Annual Geometric Mean Rate of Return*	*Arithmetic Mean of Annual Returns*	*Standard Deviation of Annual Returns*	*Number of Years Returns Are Positive*	*Number of Years Returns Are Negative*	*Highest Annual Return (and Year)*	*Lowest Annual Return (and Year)*
Common stocks	8.5%*	10.9%	22.5%	32	17	54.0% (1933)	−43.3 (1931)
Long-term government bonds	3.2	3.4	5.4	37	12	16.8 (1932)	−9.2 (1967)
Long-term corporate bonds	3.6	3.7	5.1	39	10	18.4 (1970)	−8.1 (1969)
U.S. Treasury bills	2.2	2.3	2.1	48	1	8.0 (1974)	−0.0 (1940)
Consumer price index	2.2	2.3	4.8	39	10	18.2 (1946)	−10.3 (1932)
Risk premiums on common stocks	6.1	8.8	23.5	31	18	53.5 (1933)	−43.7 (1931)
Maturity premiums on long-term government bonds	1.0	1.1	5.6	25	24	15.7 (1932)	−12.8 (1967)
Default premium on long-term corporate bonds	0.3	.4	3.2	28	21	10.5 (1933)	−7.2 (1974)
Common stocks—inflation adjusted	6.1	8.8	23.5	31	18	53.3 (1954)	−37.4 (1931)
Long-term government bonds—inflation adjusted	1.0	1.3	8.0	29	20	30.2 (1932)	−15.5 (1946)
Long-term corporate bonds—inflation adjusted	1.4	1.7	7.7	31	18	23.5 (1932)	−13.9 (1946)
U.S. Treasury bills—inflation adjusted	0.1	0.2	4.6	29	20	12.6 (1932)	−15.1 (1946)

* The annual geometric mean rate of return for capital appreciation exclusive of dividends was 3.5 percent over the entire period.

Source: Robert G. Ibbotson and Rex A. Sinquefield, "Stocks, Bonds, Bills, and Inflation: Year-by-Year Historical Returns (1926–1974)," *Journal of Business*, University of Chicago, vol. 49, no. 1, January 1976, p. 40.

showed that the risk premium was positive in 31 of the past 48 years. The average annual return on long-term bonds over short-term Treasury bills, was 1.4 percent. Other significant findings are summarized in Table 1–3.

The annual study by Dreher, Rogers & Associates, pension actuarial consultants, covering the ten years from January 1, 1967 through December 31, 1976 shows the S&P 425 Stock Index with a yield of 6.97 percent, 100 basis points more than the 90-day Treasury bill yield of 5.97 percent and 160 basis points more than high grade corporate bonds, which averaged 5.35 over the ten year period. See Table 1–4.

Table 1–4
Annualized Time-Weighted Rates of Return for Market Indicators

	Cumulative Periods through December 31, 1976			
	1 Year since 1/1/76	*3 Years since 1/1/74*	*5 Years since 1/1/72*	*10 Years since 1/1/67*
S&P 500 Stock Index*	23.97	7.82	4.94	6.66
S&P 425 Stock Index*	22.89	7.17	4.72	6.97
New York Stock Exchange Index*	26.24	8.21	4.27	6.40
Dow Jones Industrial Average*	22.90	10.77	6.90	6.63
American Stock Exchange Index	31.58	6.74	−0.27	6.31
Value Line Average	32.22	8.28	−3.72	−2.34
Salomon Bros. High Grade Corporate Bond Index*	18.65	9.66	7.42	5.35
Kuhn Loeb Bond Index*	19.61	9.61	—	—
90 Day Treasury Bill Portfolio	5.42	6.65	6.24	5.97

* Including dividends or interest.
Source: Dreher, Rogers & Associates, New York, 1977.

If however we examined the previous year's study it would be seen that the return on the 90-day Treasury bills exceeded the returns from both stocks and bonds over the ten-year period from January 1, 1966 to December 31, 1975. The annualized rates of return on Treasury bills were 5.66 percent compared to 3.63 percent from Standard & Poor's Industrial Stock Index and 1.34 percent from Standard & Poor's High Grade Corporate Bond Index. Extending the statistics for an additional year put bonds in a better light because a decline in interest rates from 1975 to 1976 caused the prices of bonds to rise. Thus it is clear that comparison of rates of return must obviously include an awareness of the significance of data changes due to the different time periods used.

Other Assets

Unfortunately, there has been little research conducted on the relative rates of return from assets other than stocks and bonds.

For several years, the Prudential Insurance Company has offered retirement funds an opportunity to invest in the equity ownership of real property on a commingled basis. This unique vehicle, known as PRISA (Prudential Real Estate Investment Separate Account) is actually a mutual fund devoted to diversified real estate equity investment. Table 1–5 compares the value of PRISA units, reflecting the

Table 1–5
Real Estate Equity versus Stocks through December 31, 1976

Date	*PRISA Unit Value*	*S&P 500*
July 31, 1970	$1,012.60	78.05
September 30, 1970	1,026.86	84.21
December 31, 1970	1,047.20	92.15
March 31, 1971	1,057.58	100.31
June 30, 1971	1,066.94	99.70
September 30, 1971	1,080.60	98.34
December 31, 1971	1,102.35	102.09
March 31, 1972	1,114.52	107.20
June 30, 1972	1,129.96	107.14
September 30, 1972	1,149.36	110.55
December 31, 1972	1,167.69	118.05
March 31, 1973	1,184.76	111.52
June 30, 1973	1,208.61	104.26
September 30, 1973	1,251.16	108.43
December 31, 1973	1,275.17	97.55
March 31, 1974	1,298.30	93.98
June 30, 1974	1,328.12	86.00
September 30, 1974	1,360.32	63.54
December 31, 1974	1,387.79	68.56
March 30, 1975	1,409.62	83.36
June 30, 1975	1,447.84	95.19
September 30, 1975	1,477.63	83.87
December 31, 1975	1,502.45	90.19
March 30, 1976	1,529.38	102.77
June 30, 1976	1,562.13	104.28
September 30, 1976	1,598.05	105.24
December 31, 1976	1,629.87	107.46
Percent change July 31, 1970 through December 31, 1976	61.0%	37.7%
Dividend adjustment (3% per year)		20.0
Total		57.7%

Source: The Prudential Insurance Co. of America and Standard & Poor's Corporation.

appraised value of property held, with a stock index, for the period July 31, 1970 to December 31, 1976.

Before making any comparison of rates of return, it is important to point out that the S&P 500 Price Index does not include any dividend return for the measurement period. Therefore, to make comparisons more meaningful, we have arbitrarily added approximately 3 percent a year to the change in stock prices in order to gain a better perspective of relative "total" returns.

It is apparent from Table 1–5 that equity real estate investment, as measured by PRISA unit value changes, was about the same as stock market rewards over the measurement period. However, an interesting feature of PRISA unit value changes is the constant period-to-period increase exhibited since inception. In no period was the unit value lower than in the preceding one.

Whether stock returns will be higher than bond or other investment returns in the future depends, of course, on a wide variety of factors. Even if they are, after the fact, investors must decide whether the before-the-fact *risk* is justified by whatever higher returns are expected. This *risk-return* decision is a difficult one. The starting point is, or at least should be, a careful understanding of the needs and constraints of a portfolio. Therefore, we now turn our attention to the specific objectives of the individual investor.

THE INDIVIDUAL AS AN INVESTOR

Portfolio objectives of the individual investor are influenced by a wide variety of factors but the two most important are (*a*) stage in the life cycle, and (*b*) psychological makeup or capacity to withstand the stress and tensions of risk.

Consider three key stages in the life cycle: (*a*) *the young family;* (*b*) *the family at midstream;* (*c*) *on the verge of retirement—the older family.*

The Young Family

"Thrift is a wonderful virtue, especially in an ancestor," someone once said. Naturally *a young family* which has inherited a substantial estate has no financial problem. It has merely an investment problem, probably requiring investment counseling. But for the average family, Mark Twain's quip holds true: "The first half of life consists of the capacity to enjoy without the chance; the last half consists of the chance without the capacity."

The head of the average family between 25 and 30 years of age is married and has one child. Income ranges from $8,000 to $20,000 per annum approximately. The largest single expenditure for the young American family is on housing. For many families it may be the largest single purchase and the biggest investment of a lifetime. How much to pay for a house and how to finance it are likely to be the first major investment problems for the young family. Generally, experts suggest that one should pay between two and two-and-one-half times annual take-home pay for a house. Thus, if take-home pay is about $15,000 per year, the family can pay from $30,000 to $37,500 for a house, according to this rule of thumb. (Unfortunately, the dilemma of the modern young family is that the average cost of a new house is now about $47,500.) Another useful concept for quick calculation is the "1 percent" rule. Total monthly operating costs will approximate 1 percent of the purchase price of the house. Thus a $40,000 home will absorb and require a $400-a-month housing expense. But in recent inflationary years the single best hedge against inflation has been real estate—especially the single family home.

Most young families go into debt to finance a house, car, furniture. But even these families manage to accumulate some assets—the equity in paying off the mortgage, contributions to a retirement or pension plan. While debts usually exceed assets at first, in time, with financial progress, this position tends to reverse, with assets exceeding debts. Some young families are, however, able to accumulate small surpluses from the outset. When this is the case they usually are utilized in the following order of priority: (*a*) savings account, (*b*) life insurance, and (*c*) investments.

Every young family needs an emergency fund to fall back upon in the event of trouble such as loss of job or serious illness in the family. A good rule of thumb to follow is that the emergency fund, the savings account, should be built up until it amounts to at least three and preferably six months take-home pay.

After savings, family protection through life insurance is next in order. The quickest way for a young family to build an estate is by means of life insurance.

There are only three basic types of policies: (*a*) *term,* which is temporary protection, (*b*) *whole life,* which is lifetime protection with some savings, (*c*) *endowment,* which is mostly savings with protection until the endowment matures.

The initial need for the young family usually is for maximum protection at minimum cost. This is provided by term insurance. Term insurance provides temporary protection for a given period of time.

It pays off only if you die within the given period which may be one year, five years, ten years. Term insurance is the lowest premium life insurance because it provides only temporary protection. It may not require any payment by the insurance company and does not as a rule build any cash value. For an expenditure of $125–$150 a year, a young head of family can build an immediate estate of $25,000 for the protection of dependents.

If the young family can achieve an additional surplus for investment, what are its alternatives? Two considerations tend to predominate. First, the family can look forward to 40 or 50 years of ability to earn income, accumulate surpluses, and invest them. This prospect provides it with a risk-taking capacity that otherwise would be absent. Second, if the past is any indicator of the future, the purchasing power of the dollar will continue to decline. Both of these considerations suggest investment in common stocks for the young family, since stock investment, has, over the long run, in this century, been an effective hedge against inflation and it tends to provide a substantial total return, combining dividend accumulation and capital gain.

A high degree of speculative risk is usually unwise for the young family since it is new at investment and probably would be quite distressed by the loss of a significant share of its hard-earned initial accumulation. But the overall risk of common stocks is tolerable. Over time, there will, of course, be setbacks either in corporate earnings or in the securities market as a whole, but, in the longer run, quality shares tend to rise, as dividends and earnings grow. At this stage of life, time is the one thing the family has in abundance!

Young investors usually build a portfolio one stock at a time or buy mutual fund shares. Generally, individual stocks are selected from a list of blue chips, or established growth stocks, provided by many brokerage firms.

The Investor at Midstream

The average business or professional person is probably moving into the prime of life from age 40 to 50. Although earnings are perhaps not at the highest level that will be attained, such persons find themselves in these years with greater financial mobility than previously. Generally the house is paid for, or almost so, insurance programs are well under way, and a comfortable cash balance is available in the bank for any emergency which may arise. The investor is financially more mature and sophisticated. It is during this period that funds can be used more aggressively. The whole gamut of investment possibilities may be considered. These include a speculative capital gains portfolio, or trading in performance stocks—the market favorites of the time—or moving into cyclical stocks at the appropriate stage of the business cycle. The investor can buy on margin to enhance profitability, sell short, look into special situations, consider convertible bonds or warrants, or trade in options. The switching from stocks to bonds to take advantage of interest rate trends can also be undertaken. In light of their tax position, these investors can consider tax-exempt state and municipal bonds, tax-sheltered investments, oil and gas royalties, real estate, or stock gifts to children. "Born Again: Tax Shelters '77," was the way *Dun's Review* in April 1977 described the tax shelter changes embodied in the Tax Reform Act of 1976. "Movies, equipment leasing, cattle, coal, and all the other familiar tax shelters are still around and thriving, but they've changed. Investors must now assume new risks and get in early."

Investors are also in a better position to know their own psychological makeup at this stage of their career. The capacity to take risks varies among individuals. Some, aiming at preservation of capital, perhaps painfully accumulated, are content with a low-anticipated return involving little risk. Others, confident of their earning capacity and their ability to replace any losses, will aim at higher returns commensurate with higher risks.

Unfortunately, we know very little about the actual investment behavior and portfolio activity of individuals. One recent study found that U.S. individuals owned over $700 billion in stock. Of this total, $460 billion was held in listed stock, $50 billion in mutual fund shares, $35 billion in unlisted bank and insurance company stock, and $190 billion in direct holdings of other traded and privately held unlisted stock. The holdings were quite concentrated. The 1 percent of U.S. families (including single individuals) with the largest personal income accounted for 47 percent of dividend income received and 51 percent of the market value of stock owned by all families, while the 10 percent of families with the largest income accounted for 71 percent of dividend income and 74 percent of market value.

This study found that "a surprisingly high proportion of the portfolios held by individuals was dominated by a very small number of issues; thus the portfolios were not well diversified. This finding applies to all income groups." The implication of lack of diversification is explored in a later chapter.

Other studies have portrayed the individual investor as, primarily, a "fundamental analyst" who perceives himself or herself to hold a well-balanced and diversified portfolio. He or she invests predominantly for the long run, and capital appreciation is the primary concern. Amusingly, the responses to questionnaires suggest that roughly half of all investors spend less than five hours a month, and less than $15 a year, on collecting the information for and making the decisions about the securities in their portfolios.

The Older Investor

As the individual investor moves along in years to the verge of retirement, we would expect the desire for risk aversion to become greater. For the investor between 55 and 65 it makes less sense to take speculative chances in the pursuit of capital gains and high returns. Since the prime earning years are about over, there is no time left to rebuild capital and recoup possible speculative losses. Presumably, then, the investor on the eve of retirement will want to shift the portfolio to provide income to augment social security and other possible retirement benefits. The objective becomes mainly the highest income commensurate with safety, rather than speculative or even long-term capital gains.

Of course, individuals differ greatly in financial status, especially at this stage of life. In some cases financial planning undertaken in productive years will now pay off by adequately supplementing social security, insurance, and pension income. Previous success in achieving substantial capital appreciation may make the difference between a lean retirement and an ample one. Recipients of substantial deferred compensation and large pensions may face no problem at all. In fact, in some cases, because of a change in tax and insurance status, a person may be as well off in retirement as he or she was when actively employed.

But for the average older family the most pressing investment problem is having an accumulation which does not yield enough to live on comfortably, especially in an inflationary environment. This presents a very difficult investment dilemma. An accumulation of $100,000 or $200,000 which seemed ample when the family was living on the salary of the breadwinner, becomes much less adequate when one has to rely on the income from the fund to live on for 15 or more years of retirement, with an inflation rate of 5 to 6 percent per annum. This is the preeminent problem of investing for retirement.

Many experts believe that the only way to resolve the problem is to cannibalize the accumulated fund. The retired family should not plan to leave an estate. It should plan to use up its accumulated resources over its remaining lifetime. It can do this by means of annuities, fixed, variable, or balanced, or by a mutual fund withdrawal plan. These programs have merit for yet another reason. With age comes a certain weariness of attention to investment trends and detail. In all probability, investing at this stage of the life cycle is better turned over to the institutional professional, who devotes full time and attention to these matters.

COMMON STOCK INVESTMENT

Common Stock and Inflation

To most individuals investment has meant buying common stock. The 1976 study, by Ibbotson and Sinquefield, found that over the 1926–74 period, common stocks far outperformed corporate and government bonds and Treasury bills, whether in current dollars, or adjusted for inflation. See Table 1–3 previously discussed. Not only did they study the past, they also provided a startling forecast for the next quarter century. In their own words:

> The compounded inflation rate is expected to be 6.4 percent per year over the period 1976–2000 compared to the historical compounded inflation rate of only 2.3 percent over the period 1926–75.
>
> The expected compounded return on common stocks for the period 1976–2000 is 13.0 percent per year. . . . Stocks are expected to have a compounded return of 6.3 percent after adjustment for inflation. . . . The nominal compounded annual returns from maintaining either a 20-year maturity government bond or a 20-year maturity corporate bond portfolio are expected to be 8.0 percent and 8.2 percent, respectively, from 1976 to 2000. . . . The inflation-adjusted returns are expected to be 1.5 percent per year for long-term government bonds and 1.8 percent per year for long-term corporate bonds. . . . The nominal Treasury bill rate is expected to be 6.8 percent per year, compared to the expected 6.4 percent compounded inflation rate, thus producing a very low inflation adjusted Treasury bill return (real interest rate).

Looking backward, the value of the dollar has fallen steadily since the turn of the century and investment in common stock has appeared to be a good, *long-run* hedge against inflation. As Figure 1–2 shows, over the past 79 years, the value of the dollar fell by 85 percent while the Dow Jones Industrial Stock Average rose by 1,979 percent.

Types of Common Stock

There is a diversity in common stock which extends not only to industry and to company but to type of stock as well. In the loose and

Figure 1–2
Common Stocks and the Cost of Living, 1897–1976

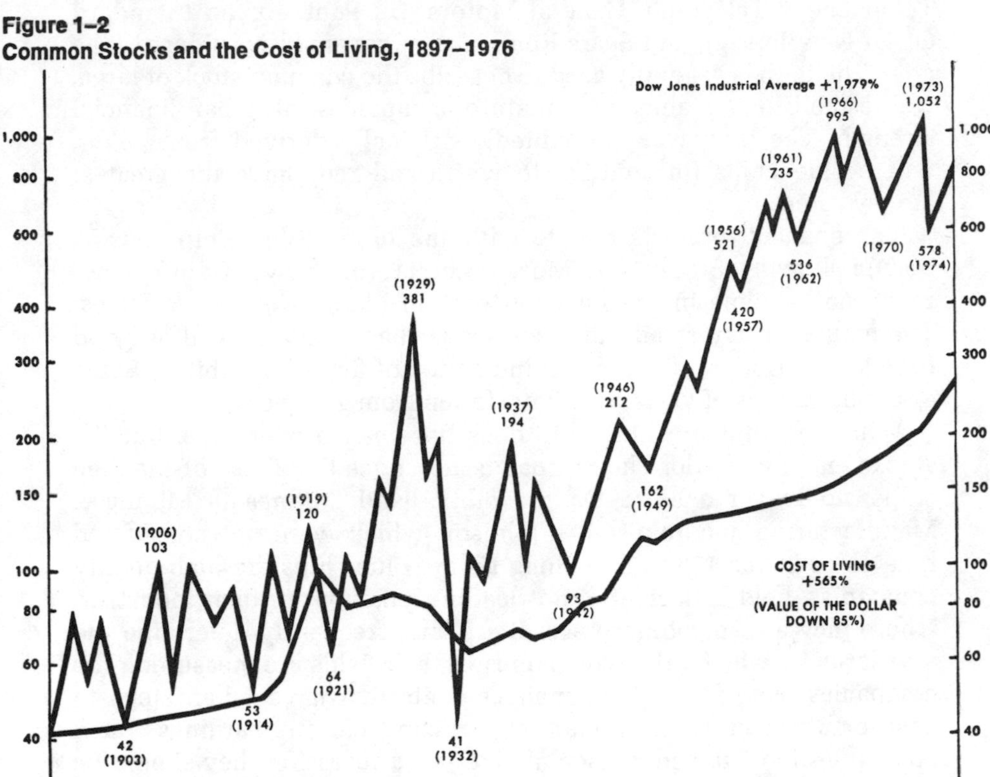

During this period of 80 years, common stocks as measured by the history of the Dow Jones Industrial Average increased 2,350%, while the Cost of Living, as measured by the Consumers' Price Index of the Bureau of Labor Statistics, was up 597%. Over the very long term, common stocks provided an effective hedge against inflation, but there were shorter periods, during sharp declines in the market, where the opposite was true (1906–1914, 1937–1942, 1946–1949, 1966–1974).

Source: Johnson's Investment Company Charts.

flexible language of the Street, it is customary to speak of blue chip stocks, of growth stocks, of cyclical (or smokestack) stocks, of income stocks, of defensive stocks, and of speculative stocks—both high flyers and low-priced issues. Lines of demarcation between types are not precise and clear, but investors have a general notion of what is meant by each of these imprecise categories.

Blue Chip Stocks. Blue chip stocks are high grade investment quality issues of major companies which have long and unbroken records of earnings and dividend payments. Stocks such as American

Telephone & Telegraph, General Motors, Du Pont, Exxon (Standard Oil of New Jersey), and Sears Roebuck are generally considered *blue chip*. The term is generally used to describe the common stock of large, well-established, stable, and mature companies of great financial strength. The term was undoubtedly originally derived from poker, where blue chips (in contrast to white and red) have the greatest money value.

The financial press is replete with the term. "Blue Chips Losing Some Following. Stocks with More Potential for Growth Gain Favor," read one headline in the financial section of the *New York Times*. The ability to pay steady dividends over bad years as well as good for a long period is, of course, an indication of financial stability. Some of the *blue chips* of yesteryear have fallen from greatness.

What constitutes a blue chip does not change over time, but the stocks that qualify do. The railroad issues, once the bluest of the blue chips, no longer qualify. On the other hand, Minnesota Mining & Manufacturing and Johnson & Johnson which were not considered blue chips in the 1950s, do belong today. Blue chips are high-quality companies, hold important, if not leading, positions in their industries where they are sometimes pacesetters, and frequently determine the standards by which other companies in their fields are measured. The companies have foresighted managements that have taken steps to ensure future growth without jeopardizing current earnings. Such companies have the advantage of size—in a recession they should be able to hold their own and then record strong earnings gains in an economic upswing because they have the resources to capitalize on a recovery. By and large, however, investors who seek safety and stability and are conservative in their approach to the market turn to the blue chips.

Growth Stocks. Many of the blue chips may also be considered growth stocks. A *growth stock* is one of a company whose sales and earnings are expanding faster than the general economy and faster than the average for the industry. The company is usually aggressive, research minded, plowing back earnings to facilitate expansion. For this reason growth companies, intent on financing their own expansion from retained earnings, pay relatively small dividends and their yield is generally low. Over time, however, substantial capital gains may accrue from the appreciation of the value of the common as a result of the plowback and expansion.

Growth stocks are usually quite volatile. They go up faster and farther than other stocks, but at the first hint that the high rate of earnings is either leveling off or not being sustained, prices can come tumbling down. For example, Texas Instruments, a high-flying growth company of the late 1950s saw earnings fall from some $15 million in 1960 to about $9 million in 1961. The common price fell from $256 a share in 1960 to $95 a share in 1961. In 1966 Fairchild Camera fell from a high of 144½ to 64½; and after recovering somewhat in the 1967–68 boom fell to 18 in 1970. Polaroid fell from a high of 149½ to 14. From a high of 172½ Itek Corporation fell to a low of 4⅞ in 1974. Over the 1960–70 decade, IBM ranged from a high of 387 to a low of 72½ and in 1971–75 ran from a high of 426¾ to a low of 150½.

Declines in leading growth stocks are usually due more to a collapse in the price/earnings ratio than to major actual decrease in earnings themselves. For example, from its 1973 high of 91⅝, Minnesota Mining & Manufacturing which was then selling at 36.2 times earnings, fell to 50¾ in early 1977 when its price/earnings ratio dropped to 17.3. Johnson & Johnson fell from a 1973 high of 132¼ with a price/earnings ratio of 61.5 to a price of 66 in February 1977 and a price/earnings ratio of 19.1. Eastman Kodak fell from a 1973 high of 151¾ at a time when its P/E ratio was 44.8, to 71 in early 1977 when its price/earnings ratio had dropped to 17.8. The leading growth stocks suffered a sharp deflation of price/earnings ratios between 1973 and 1977. Perhaps the best example is Polaroid whose P/E ratio dropped from 101.8 in 1973 to 14.7 in early 1977.

In an effort to define the term *growth* stock with more precision, several services have developed statistical tests to identify and select growth stocks. Standard & Poor's, for example, has developed a list of "140 Rapid Growth Stocks" by screening over 6,000 issues by electronic data processing methods. The resultant list of 140 stocks, obtained by a purely mechanical process, is not to be regarded as a "buy list." The major criteria employed in selection are (*a*) if the growth in the share earnings over the previous five years is steady, it must have amounted to at least 7 percent per annum compounded; (*b*) if the trend had been interrupted in only one year and the decline was less than 5 percent, annual growth must have been at least 10 percent; (*c*) if growth had been interrupted in more than one year, or in one year the decline was more than 5 percent, annual growth rate must have been at least 12 percent. Selections are limited to issues with more than 750,000 shares outstanding and to those with earnings of at least 25 cents a share in the last full year. The screening is reported monthly. Thus the composition of the list changes from time to time as some stocks are added and others removed. At times companies are removed from the list even though they still qualify, if other firms with more desirable characteristics such as better marketability and/or better earnings records are unearthed.

The larger brokerage houses also publish lists of growth stocks from time to time. They do not always, however, explicitly indicate the statistical basis for their selection. Merrill Lynch, Pierce, Fenner & Smith, Inc., once issued an elaborate study of "101 Growth Stocks" and from time to time publishes select lists of growth stocks. An example may be seen in Table 1–6. By and large the Merrill Lynch growth stock selections are of the larger, more mature, and more conservative growth companies, whereas some other lists such as those of "America's Fastest Growing Companies" tend more to newer, smaller, and more obscure companies.

Table 1–6
How Growth Stocks Grow*

	Mid-1953	*Mid-1963*	*End 1966*	*End 1971*	*Mid-1976*	*March 31 1977*
American Cyanamid	$1,000	$ 2,610	$ 2,726	$ 3,038.82	$ 2,279	$ 2,279
Bristol-Myers	1,000	15,671	34,727	36,857.96	50,196	39,226
Caterpillar Tractor	1,000	5,356	8,694	11,736.89	22,682	20,353
Corning Glass Works	1,000	5,548	10,033	6,023.04	6,089	5,084
General Electric	1,000	3,320	3,720	10,529.49	9,605	8,260
Grumman Aircraft	1,000	2,540	5,619	2,504.12	2,956	3,180
Gulf Life Holding	1,000	4,336	2,695	5,067.23	3,263	4,059
Honeywell, Inc.	1,000	3,500	4,658	9,359.86	3,483	3,281
International Business Machines	1,000	14,557	23,256	86,366.37	88,790	88,709
Minnesota Mining & Manufacturing	1,000	7,235	9,879	34,196.53	28,181	25,394
Pacific Gas & Electric	1,000	2,601	2,929	2,652.49	1,669	1,905
Pitney Bowes	1,000	7,557	7,442	15,154.61	10,361	11,211
Polaroid	1,000	33,777	137,700	308,795.00	140,953	117,967
Procter & Gamble	1,000	5,071	4,887	21,020.79	25,406	21,155
RCA	1,000	3,106	6,478	5,625.63	4,394	4,319
Safeway Stores	1,000	4,857	4,070	6,021.08	6,839	7,573
Texaco	1,000	5,646	6,012	11,561.53	9,460	8,913

* The table shows how a $1,000 cash investment in any of the above stocks regarded as growth stocks in 1953 would have grown since mid-1953. Full adjustment has been made in this tabulation for splits and stock dividends. But no account has been taken of cash dividends or rights offerings, and no allowance has been made for brokerage fees.

Source: Merrill Lynch, Pierce, Fenner & Smith, Inc.

Two leading, large no-load growth stock funds present an interesting contrast in growth stock investing. T. Rowe Price Growth Stock Fund, the larger, more mature fund, listed as its ten largest growth stock holdings, IBM, Coca-Cola, Minnesota Mining & Manufacturing, S. S. Kresge, Avon Products, Merck, Burroughs, Johnson & Johnson, NCR, and Texas Instruments. On the other hand the ten largest growth stock investments of the newer, more volatile Rowe Price New Horizons Fund included Alexander & Alexander Services, American International Reinsurance Co., Millipore, Petric Stores, Lowe's Companies, Intel, Tropicana Products, W. W. Grainger, Leaseway Transportation, and Wal-Mart Stores. Thus growth stocks can mean different things to different people, and it makes a big difference whether psychologically you take a conservative or adventurous view of the market.

Income Stocks. Some people, particularly the elderly and retired, buy stock for current income. While in recent years stocks have yielded less, on the average, on current dividends, than bonds or the return on savings accounts, there are some stocks which may be classed as *income stocks* because they pay a higher than average return. Income stocks are those that yield generous current returns. They are often sought by trust funds, pension funds, university and college endowment funds, charitable, educational, and health foundations. Selecting income stocks can be a very tricky business. The stock may be paying a high return because price has fallen due to the fact that there is considerable uncertainty as to whether the dividend can be maintained in the light of declining earnings. Or the stock may be that of a lackluster company in an unpopular industry, with little future. Or the company may be located in a foreign area where there is a large risk due to political instability. On the other hand, there may be perfectly good overlooked stocks which are paying high yields because the public has not bid them up due to lack of knowledge. Some examples may be cited. Free State Geduld ADR, a South African gold producer, has a yield of 12.9 percent. Blyvoor Gold Mining ADR, another South African gold and uranium producer has a yield of 10.5 percent; West Dreifontein ADR, 11.7 percent; and Telephonos de Mexico ADR provides a yield of 13.2 percent. These reflect the political factor of a foreign location.

Some real estate investment trusts provide a current return of 9 percent or better: for example, Realty Income Trust 14.5 percent, Fraser Mortgage Investors 10.3 percent, First Continental Reit SBI 10.4 percent, M&T Mortgage Investment SBI 11.1 percent, Hotel Investors SBI 9.9 percent, and Florida Gulf Realty SBI 9.5 percent. There are large elements of risk involved.

On the other hand, for the conservative investor a number of utility preferred stocks are available yielding 9 percent or more. These include Boston Edison 9.2 percent, Consumers Power 9 percent, Philadelphia Electric 9.1 percent, Detroit Edison Cm Pfd 9.5 percent, and Consolidated Edison 9.2 percent as of March 1977.

Focusing investment attention on *current income* is, of course, an inadequate approach in common stock selection. More properly, attention should center on *total return,* which is the addition of dividend income and capital appreciation over the holding period. Straining for maximum current return in stocks rather than for total return over time often involves greater risk and less capital appreciation. Often companies have high yields because their shares sell at low prices due to poor prospects and to doubts about continuation of dividends at the then current rate.

"Do 'Income' Stocks Provide a Higher 'Total Return'?", David L. Babson & Co., Inc., asked. Every so often the question is raised as to whether *growth* or *income* stocks produce the greater investment return over a period of years. Most shareowners assume that growth stocks create more in the way of capital gains. But some believe that income stocks—despite their more moderate appreciation—provide a higher "total return" when dividend income is added to the rise in market value.

Babson set out to find the answer. In 1951 its staff put together two $10,000 portfolios. Both contained ten issues with a market value of $1,000 each. One list consisted wholly of what Babson at the time considered to be *growth* stocks, the other solely of *income* stocks. At that time, the growth stock idea was new, seldom discussed, and misunderstood by many investors. At the time of selection, the average yield of the *income* stocks was 30 percent higher than that of the growth list. Large companies were picked for both lists so that the subsequent difference in results was not due to the selection of small, fast-growing firms in one case and large, mature companies in the other.

Selections were as shown in Table 1–7.

Table 1–7
***Income* and *Growth* Portfolios, December 31, 1950**

"Income" Stocks	*Industry Rank*	*Amount Invested*	*"Growth" Stocks*	*Industry Rank*	*Amount Invested*
American Chicle*	Second	$ 1,000	Abbott Laboratories	Third	$ 1,000
American Telephone	Largest	1,000	Celanese	Second	1,000
American Tobacco	Largest	1,000	Corning	Largest	1,000
Beneficial Loan†	Largest	1,000	Dow	Fourth	1,000
Consolidated Edison	Largest	1,000	Eastman Kodak	Largest	1,000
Corn Products‡	Largest	1,000	Gulf Oil	Third	1,000
General American Transport	Largest	1,000	IBM	Largest	1,000
General Foods	Largest	1,000	Minnesota Mining	Largest	1,000
International Shoe§	Largest	1,000	Standard Oil (N.J.)#	Largest	1,000
Woolworth	Largest	1,000	Union Carbide	Second	1,000
Total		$10,000	Total		$10,000

Now: * Warner-Lambert. † Beneficial Corp. ‡ CPC International. § Interco. # Exxon.
Source: David L. Babson & Co.

Obviously were the selections made today the choices would be different in many cases. However, no change was made in either list since 1951 in order to rule out the factor of hindsight.

As most investors would assume, the growth portfolio has shown more capital appreciation. Against the original $10,000 commitment, its market value by June 30, 1976 was $158,114. In contrast, the income list was worth $37,855. Over the same period, a $10,000 investment in the Dow Jones Industrial Average would have increased to $46,533.

Equally strking is the difference in the present income-paying ability of the two portfolios. The ten growth stocks, which back in 1950 yielded less, now provide an annual return on cost of 42.1 percent—over twice the 19.8 percent yield at cost of the income shares. Table 1–8 shows the investment progress of each list over the past 26 years.

Table 1–8
Comparative Performance of *Growth* versus *Income* Portfolios

	Market Value		*Annual Income*		*Yield at Market*		*Yield at Cost*	
Year-End	*Growth*	*Income*	*Growth*	*Income*	*Growth*	*Income*	*Growth*	*Income*
1976* ...	$158,114	$37,855	$4,212†	$1,940†	2.7%	5.1%	42.1%	19.4%
1975....	138,599	36,162	4,084	1,785	2.9	4.9	40.8	17.8
1974....	98,200	26,800	3,556	1,686	3.6	6.3	35.6	16.9
1973....	152,400	40,300	3,046	1,667	2.0	4.1	30.5	16.7
1972....	186,700	51,100	2,858	1,587	1.5	3.1	28.6	15.9
1971....	147,500	50,200	2,809	1,569	1.9	3.1	28.1	15.7
1970....	129,800	45,600	2,681	1,514	2.1	3.3	26.8	15.1
1969....	146,300	42,500	2,425	1,481	1.7	3.5	24.3	14.8
1968....	140,400	45,200	2,196	1,449	1.6	3.2	22.0	14.5
1967....	139,400	35,900	1,989	1,398	1.4	3.9	19.9	14.0
1966....	104,300	35,400	1,907	1,376	1.8	3.9	19.1	13.8
1965....	96,500	43,700	1,795	1,334	1.9	3.1	18.0	13.3
1960....	65,600	29,500	982	968	1.5	3.3	9.8	9.7
1955....	26,700	15,900	611	734	2.3	4.6	6.1	7.3
1950....	10,000	10,000	447	581	4.5	5.8	4.5	5.8

* As of June 30, 1976.
† Annual rate.
Source: David L. Babson & Co.

Since 1950, the growth portfolio has provided a total investment return of $192,212 ($148,114 in capital appreciation and $44,098 in dividends). This is over three times the income portfolio's overall return of $58,383 ($27,855 in appreciation and $30,528 in dividends). Thus growth stocks over time may well outperform income stocks in both total return and dividend yield at cost.

Cyclical Stocks. *Cyclical shares,* or smokestack stocks in Wall Street terminology, refer to stocks of companies in basic industries whose earnings fluctuate with the business cycle and are accentuated by it. When business conditions improve, the company's profitability is restored and enhanced. The common stock price rises. When conditions deteriorate, business for the cyclical company falls off sharply, and its profits are greatly diminished.

Industries which may be regarded as cyclical include steel, cement, aluminum, chemicals, paper, machinery and machine tools, airlines, railroads and railroad equipment, and automobiles. Commenting on the so-called two-tiered market, which placed growth stocks on one level and cyclical or smokestack shares on a lower level, *Forbes* commented:

> Probably never before in history has Wall Street had such a split personality. Call a stock a Growth stock and it sells for 40, 50, or even 60 times earnings. Call it Cyclical . . . and it sells for 10 times earnings or less. The market is saying that if General Motors earns $1, that $1 should be capitalized at only $10.90, but if, say, Johnson and Johnson earns $1, it is worth $64. This kind of disparity can go on for a long time, of course, but it can't go on forever.

For example at a time when Ford was selling at 9 times earnings, Chrysler at 10 times earnings, Bethlehem Steel at 9.5 times earnings, U.S. Steel at 12 times earnings, Copperweld Steel at 8 times earnings, Kennecott Copper at 10 times earnings, Giant Portland Cement at 9.4 times earnings, Crane at 9.3 times earnings, Norfolk & Western Railway, at 10 times earnings, and Mesta Machine at 9.9 times earnings, Simplicity Pattern was selling at 51 times earnings, Winnebago Industries at 73 times earnings, Tropicana Products at 54 times earnings, Levitz Furniture at 86 times earnings, Walt Disney Productions at 78 times earnings, and McDonald's at 70 times earnings, to contrast a few.

In the 1973–74 bear market the two-tiered market came apart as former favorites plunged. Polaroid fell from 149½ to 14, Avon Products from 140 to 18⅝, Xerox from 171⅞ to 49, Disney from 119 to 17, ARA Services from 187 to 46. But cyclical issues moved up as the economic recovery unfolded. U.S. Steel went from 25 to 89, International Paper rose from 28½ to 78¾, Du Pont from 84 to 161, General Motors from 28 to 70¼. *Cyclicals* surge in the early stages of recovery, tend to top out prior to the business cycle peak, and yield market leadership to the newly annointed *concept* stocks or *performance* issues of the period. Basic industry stocks led the market in its sharp recovery in 1975–76.

Defensive Stocks. At the opposite pole from cyclical stocks are the so-called *defensive* stocks; by *defensive stocks* are meant shares of a company which is likely to do better than average, from an earnings and dividend point of view, in a period of deteriorating business. If a recession is anticipated, a growing interest tends to develop in certain recession-resistant companies. While such stocks lack the glamour of the fallen market leaders, they are characterized by a degree of stability desirable when the economy faces a period of uncertainty and decline.

Utility stocks are generally regarded as defensive issues, since their slow (5 to 7 percent) but steady growth rate tends to hold up in recession years as well as in boom years. They are, however, very sensitive to interest rate changes, falling in price if interest rates rise sharply, and increasing in price if interest rates decline. In addition to the electric and gas utilities, the shares of gold mining companies have tended to be effective defensive issues. The price of gold either rises or remains stable during recessions, while the cost of mining may decrease due to lower costs. Also the market demand for gold seems to hold up or even increase. Other defensive issues are found among companies whose products suffer relatively little in recession periods. These include shares in companies producing tobacco, snuff, soft drinks, gum, candy bars, and other staples. Companies that provide the essentials of life, particularly food and drugs tend to be stable. Packaged foods and grocery chain companies are examples.

Speculative Stocks. Webster defines *speculation* as a "transaction or venture the profits of which are conjectural." In this sense all common stock investment is speculative. When you buy shares you have no promise, no certainty that the funds you receive ultimately when you sell the stock will be more, less, or the same as the dollars you originally paid. Since they provide a variable rather than a fixed dollar outcome, common shares are speculative in Webster's sense. Yet in the accepted parlance of the Street, *speculative* shares or *speculative* stock has a more limited meaning. High-flying glamour stocks are speculative. Likewise, hot new issues and penny mining stocks are speculative. Other types could be identified as they come and go from time to time. Some are easy to spot, some more difficult. The high-flying glamour stocks can usually be identified by their very high price/earnings ratios. Speculative buying of these shares would appear to be discounting the future quite far ahead. As a famous Dow Theory disciple, William P. Hamilton, wrote back in the 1920s: "A bull market runs until it outruns values: in the final stage it is discounting possibilities only."

There usually comes a point in a bull market when small, hitherto unknown companies go public, or little new companies are formed, and the offering of their low-priced shares finds a fierce speculative demand. Prices double, triple, or even quadruple within a few days after issuance. Dynatronics issued at 7½, went to 25 overnight. Cove Vitamin soared from 3⅛ to 60. Simulmatics, a two-year-old company with a net worth of minus $21,000 offered stock to the public at 2, and within a few hours it was quoted at 9. While stocks in companies with names ending in "tron" or "ics" were particularly coveted, even prosaically named issues like Leaseway Transportation and Mother's Cookie Company leaped 50 percent or more in price.

Playboy Enterprises came out at $23.50, but in a matter of weeks,

Table 1–9
Klinker Index

	Recent Price	*High*	*Percent Decline*	*Former Business*
Acme Missiles & Constr.	.06	25	−100.0	Missile launching sites
AITS	0	93	−100.0	Travel agency
Airlift Int.	.19	12	− 98.4	Airfreight carrier
Alphanumeric	.10	84	−100.0	Computer peripheral equipment
Astrodata	.25	36	− 99.3	Electronic data equipment
Beck Indust.	.01	42	−100.0	Leased shoe departments
Bermec*	.05	31	−100.0	Truck leasing
Borne Chem.	1.12	27	− 96.0	Textile oils
Cognitronics	1.12	39	− 97.1	Optical scanning
Commonwealth United† ..	.25	25	− 99.0	Conglomerate/theaters
Corporation S	.38	64	− 99.4	Data services
Dolly Madison*	.13	47	−100.0	Ice cream, furniture
Elcor Chem.	3.38	80	− 96.0	New sulphur process
Energy Conver. Devices ...	4.25	155	− 97.2	Electronic breakthrough
FAS Int.	.38	63	− 99.4	Famous artist schools
Farrington*	0	66	−100.0	Optical scanning
Fotochrome	.06	25	−100.0	Film processing
Four Seasons Equity	0	49	−100.0	Financing nursing homes
Four Seasons Nursing‡ ...	3.38	91	− 96.3	Nursing homes
Gale Indust.	.50	26	− 98.1	Heat conductive windowpanes
R. Hoe	.06	60	−100.0	Printing presses
King Resources	.08	34	−100.0	Computerized oil development
Liquidonics	.06	155	−100.0	Magnetic door locks
Management Assistance ..	.50	46	− 99.0	Leasing data equipment
Nat'l Student Marketing ..	.30	36	− 99.1	Still trying to determine
Omega Equities	.05	36	−100.0	Questionable ventures
Panacolor	.06	40	−100.0	Color film processing
Performance Systems .... (i.e., Minnie Pearl)	.05	24	−100.0	Greasy chicken franchiser
Transitron	.50	60	− 99.0	Semiconductors
Viatron*	.10	62	−100.0	Computer systems

* In bankruptcy or receivership.
† Name change 1/73—Iota Industries.
‡ Name change 11/72—Anta Corp.
Source: Spencer Trask & Co., Incorporated, May 5, 1975.

like an aging "bunny," sagged to a price of 15½. National Video was issued at 3¾, soared to 120 and then went into bankruptcy. Four Seasons Nursing Homes was a hot new issue when it went public at $11 a share on May 10, 1968. It rose to more than $100 a share the same year. After a two-for-one split, this stock shot up again to $90.75 in 1969. It went into receivership in 1970 and in 1972 a number of those associated with the stock issue were indicated for alleged fraud. Other examples of speculative issues which have had a sad demise are shown in Table 1–9.

Perhaps the lowest level of speculative stocks are the penny mining and oil shares. A broker specializing in such shares circulated his market report and offers extensively by mail, and his combination packets read almost like a stamp dealer's. In one report he plugged Trans-Mountain Uranium Company, Globe Hill Mining Company, and Santa Fe International.

The mail-order broker's packet offer read:

Combination Offer—Following combination orders will be filled for whatever number combinations desired while can locate stock in above 3 companies to fill at price shown below: (bonus 1,000 United Empire Gold with each combination order)

1,000 Trans-Mountain, 1,000 Santa Fe and 5,000 Globe Hill Mining, $63.75.

Thus common stock investment can range from buying shares in the staid and stable Bank of New York which has paid dividends uninterruptedly for the past 193 years, to buying Trans-Mountain Uranium at 2 cents per share. Obviously, with so wide a diversity in common stock, generalizations are both difficult and hazardous.

Styles in Stocks

Fads and enthusiasms can be either very costly or very profitable to investors, or both, depending on their footwork. Or, as one Wall Street pundit put it, "If you want to make your pile, you got to be in style." Styles in common stocks, Eldon Grimm pointed out, change almost as rapidly as women's fashions. Reviewing past enthusiasms (which in due course faded), one can go back as far as World World I, during the course of which Bethlehem Steel was in high fashion. It jumped from $10 a share in 1914 to $200 in one year. In the 1920s talking pictures and radio swept the country. Warner Bros. Pictures soared from 9¾ in 1927 to 138 in 1928. RCA skyrocketed from 12½ in 1922 to 573 in 1929. Bank stocks took off in the mid-1920s. The ordinarily conservative First National City Bank of New York (now Citibank), for example, jumped from the equivalent of 131 in 1926 to 580 in 1929. In the ensuing collapse the bluest of the blue chips fell dismally. (See Table 1–10.) Even in the Great Depression there were fads and fancies. With the repeal of Prohibition, National Distillers became a magic word,

Table 1–10
A Dozen Good Common Stocks, 1929–1932

Company	*1929*	*1932*
Anaconda Copper	174⅞	3
AT&T	310¼	70¼
Chrysler Corporation	87	5
Du Pont	503	22
General Motors	224	7⅝
Montgomery Ward	156⅞	3½
New York Central	256½	8¾
Sears, Roebuck	197½	9⅞
Standard Oil of California	81⅞	15⅛
Standard Oil of New Jersey	83	19⅞
U.S. Steel	261¾	21¼
Western Union	272¼	12⅜

Source: Jerome B. Cohen, *Personal Finance,* 5th ed. (Homewood, Ill.: Richard D. Irwin, 1975), p. 641.

and the stock jumped from 13 in 1932 to a peak of 124⅞ one year later and then went out of style.

Aluminum stocks were very much in style in the early 1950s. Alcoa went from 46 in 1949 to the equivalent of 352 in 1955. Reynolds Metals rose from 19 to the equivalent of 300 over the same period. As a group, the aluminum stocks rose some 430 percent in the early 1950s and then fell out of bed in 1957, declining by more than 50 percent. The advent of the computers helped push IBM from 40 to over 600 and Control Data from 2 to over 100. The ephemeral popularity of Metrecal as a dieting fad sent Mead Johnson shares up by 230 percent, but when the style changed and sales fell 31 percent in 1962, net fell 90 percent to just 3 cents a share, and Mead Johnson stock went down to its 1958 pre-Metrecal level.

Electronics shares boomed in the late 1950s. For example, when Lehman Bros. decided to back Litton Industries and raise the $1.5 million needed, they created a unique financial package. They divided the sum into 52 units requiring a cash investment of $29,200 each. The makeup of each unit was:

20 bonds at $1,200 per bond	$24,000
50 shares of 5% preferred	5,000
2,000 shares of common stock (10 cents par)	200
	$29,200

The bonds were subsequently converted into common stock at $10.75 per share. The preferred shares were converted into common at $1 per share. There followed, after conversion, a 2½ percent stock dividend, a 2 for 1 stock split, and another 2½ percent stock dividend. When LIT common hit a high of $143 per share by 1961, each $29,200 unit had grown to 29,416 shares of common worth $4.2 million.

Other investors were not so fortunate. Toward the end of 1961 *Business Week* reported "Glamour industry takes its lumps. Shakeout among electronics companies is starting as industry matures after a decade of fast, youthful growth. To survive, a company will need sharp management." The *Wall Street Journal* headed its story "Fading Glamour. Sales Growth Slows, Competition Tightens for Electronics Firms. Transistor Prices Drop 44%." Transitron Electronic Corporation shares fell from 60 to 4. Fairchild Camera, which had risen from 13¾ (adjusted) to 144½ per share, fell to 64½, though if investors held on during the deep gloom, the stock rose again during 1967 from 73 to 134. Then Fairchild ran into rough weather and by 1970 its stock reached a low of 18.

Conglomerates were all the rage in the late 1960s. Ling-Temco-Vought peaked in August 1967, selling at 169½. By 1970 it was down to 7. Litton hit a high of 120 in 1967, but was down to 10 in 1972. Monogram Industries reached a high of 81¾ in 1967, then fell to a low of 8½ in 1970. Gulf & Western peaked at 66⅛ in 1968 but then dropped to 11¾ in 1970. Comparable peaks and lows could be detailed for other conglomerates such as Fuqua Industries, National General, Bangor Punta, Whittaker, Ogden, AMK, Walter Kidde, and Northwest Industries. The average decline of the conglomerates from their 1967–68 highs to their 1970–71 lows was 85 percent.

Food franchisers captured the market's attention for a time in the late 60s. Minnie Pearl (fried chicken), changed its name to Performance Systems, soared to a high of 67 in 1967, but by 1970 was selling for 50 cents a share. Other popular issues were Denny's Restaurants, Kentucky Fried Chicken, Lum's, Marriott, and McDonald's. Some survived and prospered, others fell by the roadside.

Pollution control stocks waxed and waned. Buffalo Forge went to a high of 57 in 1970 then fell to 25 in 1972. Research-Cottrell rose from 4¾ to a peak of 84½ in 1972, then fell off to 54. Other companies in this volatile field, which surged and then faded, are Zurn Industries, Wheelabrator-Frye, Peabody-Galion, Marley, Joy Manufacturing, American Air Filter, Aqua-Chem, and Ecological Science.

Computer equipment and technology stocks rose spectacularly and some of them dropped sharply. For example, University Computing rose to a peak of 186 in 1967–68, but by 1970–71 was down to 12¾. Control Data went to 163½ and then fell to 28¾, but has since come back part way. Memorex reached a bull market high of 173⅞ and then fell to 14⅞. Telex ranged from a high of 159½ to a low of 20¾. Wall Street's penchant for stocks that end in an "x"—Xerox, Syntex, Ampex, Tampax, Tektronix, and so on, at least in the ascending phase—seemed to work for a time in the case of Memorex and Telex. The average decline of the computer stocks from their 1967–68 highs to their 1970–71 lows was 85 percent and the same was true of the so-called technology stocks.

When the dollar was devalued in 1971 and again in 1973, and the de facto price of gold rose from $42 an ounce to a high of $198 an ounce, gold shares zoomed. Dome Mines rose from a low of 17⅞ in the 1960s to 73 in 1971 and to 155 in 1973 and then fell back to 30 in 1975. Campbell Red Lake shot up from 9⅝ to 35 in 1971 and to 79 in 1973 and then fell to 17½ in 1975. Homestake Mining jumped from 8 to 31 in 1971 and then to 70⅞ in 1973, declining to 31 in 1975.

After the oil embargo and the OPEC cartel price action in sharply raising oil prices, the spotlight in the United States turned onto coal, of which the United States has enormous reserves, totaling some 10,313,200 trillion BTUs, as compared to 277,500 trillion BTUs of oil and a mere 237 trillion BTUs of natural gas. Investors bid up the coal stocks rapidly, in 1975–77. North American Coal rose from 24¼ to 55¼; Pittston Co. from 17⅞ to 47⅛; Eastern Gas & Fuel from 15¾ to 28⅛; Westmoreland Coal from 18⅛ to 65¾; and St. Joe Minerals from 17⅛ to 50.

In recent years the term *concept stock* has become popular. If Wall Street believes the story behind the stock, it will go up—even if the *concept* ultimately proves to have been just puffery.

Keeping up with styles in stocks is, then, in many cases, an important part of the selection process. There has never been a time when some stocks were not advancing against a declining market. Spotting these stocks early and getting out before the usual collapse should be a goal of every investor who can afford the risk of being wrong. Sometimes riding *concepts* through their upswing is worth more in total return than fundamental analysis.

Fundamental Analysis

The heart of the investment process is choosing what to buy and when to buy it, deciding what to sell and when to sell it. Coal and steel—seemingly both basic industries—why buy one and not buy the other? The choice to the casual investor may not have appeared very crucial or complicated, but if you will look at Figure 1–3, you will see that over a recent decade coal shares were among the best performers of 50 industries while steel shares were below average performers. If you had bought Eastern Gas & Fuel you would have a 398 percent gain. The Pittston Co. shares rose 782 percent. On the other hand, Allegheny Ludlum Steel fell 33 percent, while Republic Steel declined 16 percent. By and large, investments in utilities, aerospace, air transport, apparel, copper, machine tools, life insurance, and aluminum would likely have had poor results, while, on the other hand, coal, gold mining, beverages (soft drinks), restaurants, savings & loan, business equipment, and drugs would have done well.

Even within a given industry selectivity was important and necessary. For example business equipment shares, on the average, performed well, but whereas Burroughs rose 318 percent, Addressograph–Multigraph fell 73 percent. In cameras, Eastman Kodak rose 35 percent while Polaroid fell 51 percent. In oil, Phillips Petroleum rose 167 percent while Texaco fell 22 percent. In chain stores, Kresge rose 371 percent while W. T. Grant fell 100 percent. In automobiles, Ford rose 59 percent while American Motors fell 39 percent. In agricultural equipment, International Harvester fell 12 percent, while Deere & Co. rose 86 percent. And in something as basic as chemicals, Dow rose 323 percent, while Du Pont fell 6 percent. The need for security analysis should be clear.

By security analysis we mean, of course, fundamental analysis. This is the basic process of the evaluation of common stock by studying earnings, dividends, price-earnings multiples, economic outlook for the industry, financial prospects for the company, sales penetration, market share, and quality of management. Selecting the industry or industries which are likely to do best over the next three to five years and then choosing the company or companies within the selected industries which are likely to outperform their competitors—this is the essence of fundamental analysis.

In general terms there are four aspects of any complete and concise analysis: (*a*) the sales analysis and forecast, (*b*) the earnings analysis and forecast, (*c*) the multiplier analysis and forecast, and (*d*) the analysis of management, a qualitative consideration.

Basic to any estimate of earning power is a sales analysis and forecast. Growth of demand for a company's products is essential for common stock appreciation. While expanding production and sales do not

Figure 1–3
Stocks of 50 Industries, January 1, 1967—December 31, 1976

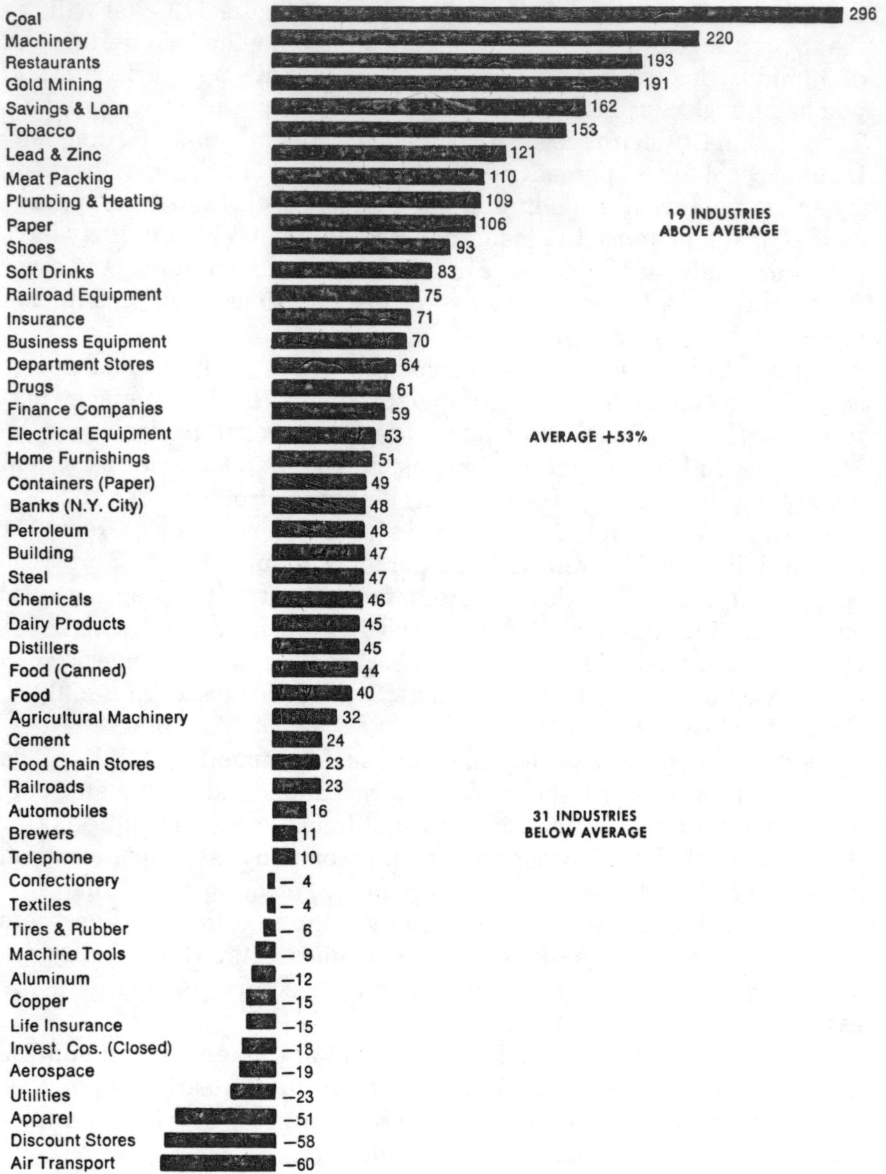

Source: Johnson's Investment Company Charts.

guarantee rising profits, rising demand, or the introduction of new products, at least gives a company an opportunity to earn a rising profit.

What the analyst is seeking is a working forecast of sales in order to determine the profit implications of the sales forecast. But just as a sales forecast is essential to an effective profits forecast, an economic forecast is a preliminary prerequisite to the sales forecast. The starting point of an effective industry and company forecast may be a GNP forecast, with a breakdown of components. For example, a forecast of sales for the automobile industry may be tied to the growth of real GNP by using historic figures on the number of cars sold per billion dollar increase in real GNP. Or, the analyst may use estimates of prospective consumer durable goods expenditures, derived from an econometric model of the composite economy and use this to forecast automobile sales. Or, the estimate may begin with a forecast of personal disposable income for either the coming year or longer. Since expenditures on automobiles are a relatively stable percentage of disposable personal income, a reasonable estimate of expenditures for automobiles may be made. Since this will be an estimate for the entire industry, market shares must be allocated to companies.

Having obtained an estimate or range of estimates of prospective sales growth rates, the next step is to proceed to obtain an estimate, or range of estimates, of prospective earnings growth rates. To achieve this an analysis of earnings is necessary. One approach is to start with the GNP forecast and derive from it a prospective corporate profits trend for all industry. Then factor out a profits trend for the particular industry under review, making such adjustments as special industry characteristics may suggest a greater or lesser rate of growth than that of the total corporate profits series. From this, develop a company estimate, again making adjustment for special company characteristics.

Or, one can start with the sales forecast developed earlier and relate this to the company's profit margin, operating income, equity turnover, rate of return on equity, earnings before interest and taxes, net income after interest and taxes, return on total capital, and net earnings per share. By dissecting the anatomical character of a corporation's profitability and measuring the impact of prospective changes on each element, it is possible to derive an estimate of a range of earnings from one to three years ahead.

Once an earnings forecast, or a range of forecasts, is derived, it remains to develop and apply a multiplier, the price-earnings ratio. A variety of factors impinge upon and help determine a price-earnings ratio. Among these are the growth rate of earnings, actual and anticipated, the dividend payment, the marketability and volatility of the stock, the stability or volatility of earnings, and the quality of earnings and of management. Of these, perhaps, the growth rate of earnings is the most significant. In general, there seems to be a consensus that the higher the growth rate of earnings, the higher the P/E ratio.

From this brief summary of fundamental analysis, it should be clear that the modern approach to common stock evaluation centers on a two-part question. What is the potential growth of earnings and dividends of a company whose stock is being analyzed and what is a reasonable price to pay for that potential?

Investment Timing

Perhaps as important as the choice of what stocks to buy is the decision as to when to buy—and when to sell. Investment timing is possibly even more difficult a task than investment choice. But the competent investor must constantly make a judgment as to the trend and level of the market as a whole to provide the appropriate environmental setting for portfolio additions or deletions. The level and trend of the market may be considered in three time dimensions: the secular, the cyclical, and the seasonal.

As described earlier, the secular trend is the long-run course of the market over a 20-, 25-, 40-, or 50-year period. Generally the trend has been upward because of the continuing decline in the purchasing power of the dollar, the gradual inflation in the economy, the rise in demand for common stock as compared to a relatively limited supply, and the relatively steady growth in gross national product and corporate profits. The rising secular trend in common stock prices may be seen in Table 1–11.

In 1898 the Dow Jones Industrials registered a low of 42 and a high of 60.97. By 1903 the high was 103; in 1916 it reached 110.15 and in 1919, 119.62. There followed a postwar setback but from 81.50 in 1921 the DJIA rose to a peak of 381.17 in 1929. The Great Depression saw the index fall to a low of 41.22 in 1932, back to the 1898 level. It then recovered to a peak of 194 in 1937, fell thereafter, and did not regain this level again until it reached 195 in 1945. Thereafter it rose sharply to a peak of 995 in 1966. This postwar bull market far outshadowed anything in our history. Then the market remained on a plateau until a sharp setback in 1969–70, the DJIA falling to a low of 631 in May 1970. The years 1971 and particularly 1972 saw a resurgence with the DJIA piercing the 1,000 level in 1972, hitting a peak of 1,051 in January

Table 1–11
Dow Jones Industrial Average 42-Year Performance, 1935–1976

	Market						Yield		P/E Multiple			Consumer Price Index (Annual Average) 1967=100
Year	High	Low	Close	Yearly Change	Earn-ings	Divi-dends	High	Low	High	Low	Book Value	
1935	148.44	96.71	144.13	38.5	6.34	4.55	4.7%	3.1%	23½	15	80.42	41.1
1936	184.90	143.11	179.90	24.8	10.07	7.05	4.9	3.8	18	14	83.20	41.5
1937	194.40	113.64	120.85	−32.8	11.49	8.78	7.7	4.5	17	10	86.48	43.0
1938	158.41	98.95	154.76	28.1	6.01	4.98	5.0	3.1	26	16½	87.38	42.2
1939	155.92	121.44	150.24	− 2.9	9.11	6.11	5.0	3.9	17	13	90.20	41.6
1940	152.80	111.84	131.13	−12.7	10.92	7.06	6.3	4.6	14	10	92.39	42.0
1941	133.59	106.34	110.96	−15.4	11.64	7.59	7.1	5.7	11½	9	95.45	44.1
1942	119.71	92.92	119.40	7.6	9.22	6.40	6.9	5.3	13	10	97.94	48.8
1943	145.82	119.26	135.89	13.8	9.74	6.30	5.3	4.3	15	12	101.68	51.8
1944	152.53	134.22	152.32	12.1	10.07	6.57	4.9	4.3	15	13	105.40	52.7
1945	195.82	151.35	192.91	26.6	10.56	6.69	4.4	3.4	18½	14	110.29	53.9
1946	212.50	163.12	177.20	− 8.1	13.63	7.50	4.6	3.5	15½	12	119.22	58.5
1947	186.85	163.21	181.16	2.2	18.80	9.21	5.6	4.9	10	9	126.65	66.9
1948	193.16	165.39	177.30	− 2.1	23.07	11.50	7.0	6.0	8	7	148.12	72.1
1949	200.52	161.60	200.13	12.9	23.54	12.79	7.9	6.4	8½	7	160.33	71.4
1950	235.47	196.81	235.41	17.6	30.70	16.13	8.2	6.9	7½	6½	186.11	72.1
1951	276.37	238.99	269.23	14.4	26.59	16.34	6.8	5.9	10½	9	197.05	77.8
1952	292.00	256.35	291.90	8.4	24.78	15.48	6.0	5.3	12	10	207.50	79.5
1953	293.79	255.49	289.90	− 3.8	27.23	16.11	6.3	5.5	11	9½	218.76	80.1
1954	404.39	279.87	404.39	44.0	28.18	17.47	6.2	4.3	14½	10	232.38	80.5
1955	488.40	388.20	488.40	20.8	35.78	21.58	5.6	4.4	13½	11	258.92	80.2
1956	521.05	462.35	499.47	2.3	33.34	22.99	5.0	4.4	15½	14	276.19	81.4
1957	520.77	419.79	435.69	−12.8	36.08	21.61	5.1	4.2	14½	11½	283.49	84.3
1958	583.65	436.89	583.65	34.0	27.95	20.00	4.6	3.4	21	15½	292.45	86.6
1959	679.36	574.46	679.36	16.4	34.31	19.38	3.4	2.9	20	17	308.50	87.3
1960	685.47	566.05	615.89	− 9.3	32.21	20.46	3.6	3.0	21	17½	343.00	88.7
1961	734.91	610.25	731.14	18.7	31.91	21.28	3.5	2.9	23	19	356.96	89.6
1962	726.01	535.76	652.10	−10.8	36.43	22.09	4.1	3.0	20	15	372.48	90.6
1963	767.21	646.79	762.95	17.0	41.21	23.20	3.6	3.0	18½	15½	377.10	91.7
1964	891.71	766.08	874.13	14.6	46.43	25.38	3.3	2.8	19	16½	405.98	92.9
1965	969.26	840.59	969.26	10.9	53.67	28.61	3.4	2.9	18	15½	446.23	94.5
1966	995.15	744.32	785.69	−18.9	57.68	31.89	4.0	3.0	17	13	464.20	97.2
1967	943.08	786.41	905.11	15.2	53.87	30.19	3.8	3.2	17½	14½	467.12	100.0
1968	985.21	825.13	943.75	4.3	57.89	31.34	3.8	3.2	17	14	511.75	104.2
1969	968.85	769.93	800.36	−15.2	57.02	33.90	4.2	3.3	17	13½	553.06	109.8
1970	842.00	631.16	838.92	4.8	51.02	31.53	5.0	3.7	16½	12½	584.54	116.3
1971	950.82	797.97	890.20	6.1	55.09	30.86	3.9	3.2	17	14½	600.28	121.3
1972	1,036.27	889.15	1,020.02	14.6	67.11	32.27	3.6	3.1	15½	13	634.32	125.3
1973	1,051.70	788.31	850.86	−16.6	86.17	35.33	4.5	3.4	12	9	677.82	133.1
1974	891.66	577.60	616.24	−27.6	99.04	37.72	6.5	4.2	9	5.8	730.00	147.7
1975	881.81	632.00	852.41	38.3	75.66	37.46	5.9	4.2	12	8	746.95	161.2
1976	1,014.79	858.70	1,004.65	17.9	97.00E	41.40	4.8	4.1	10½	9	783.61	170.5
Increase from 1935 to 1976	+584%	+788%	+597%	–	+1,430%	+810%	–	–	–	–	+847%	+315%

Note: Book values are based on net tangible assets per share. All data are adjusted to a basis consistent with the average.
Source: Johnson's Investment Company Charts.

1973. Then the market fell about 45 percent, touching a low at 577 in December 1974. Anticipating the economic recovery of 1975–76, the market rose sharply and reached 1,014 in September 1976.

Cyclical Trends

The problem of investment timing, as opposed to selection, is mostly concerned with the *cyclical* dimension of the stock market. Ideally, the investor who can buy stocks when prices are cyclically low and sell when they are cyclically high, will, of course, greatly enhance profits. Traditional value analysts approach the timing question in exactly the same way as they approach the selection process. They hold that in due course, despite possible temporary deviations or psychological pulls, stock prices anticipate and reflect basic economic trends and anticipate or respond to corporate profits, earnings per share, and dividends. Analysis of these fundamentals guides them in their judgment as to whether the market is in a buying (low) or selling (high) range. But they do not attempt to *forecast* when a bull market will turn into a bear market or vice versa.

Common stock prices are one of the 12 leading indicators developed during the course of years of business cycle study by the National Bureau of Economic Research (NBER). Leading indicators are those economic series, such as new orders for durable goods, commercial and industrial building contracts, and business failures, basic changes in whose trend or direction tend, on the average, to precede and signal basic cyclical changes in business activity as a whole. Based on a study of past business cycles from 1873 to date, it has been found that basic cyclical changes in common stock prices tend to precede cyclical changes in business as a whole by about five to nine months.

In a scoring plan developed by the NBER in evaluating indicators, the stock price series scored 81, on a scale of 100, compared to 78 for the series on new orders for durable goods, its closest competitor as a leading indicator. In the NBER study the record of stock prices since 1873 was compared with peaks and troughs in general business conditions. During 43 expansions and recessions over this 100-year period, the movements of stock prices conformed in 33 instances, or 77 percent of the time. The same study showed that stock prices anticipated 33 out of 44, or 75 percent, of the business cycle turning points.

If the business cycle concept is broadened to include slowdowns in growth that did not qualify as recessions, then the record is even stronger. Thus, since 1948 stock prices show a one-to-one match at every peak and trough. They led at every turning point. They did not lag at any and they gave no false leading signals.

The designation of common stock prices as a leading indicator was based on performance on the average over preceding business cycles. It does not mean that common stock price trends by *themselves* forecast business changes, nor does it mean that a downtrend in stock prices preceded every recession since 1873. But the relationship between stock price cycles and business cycles has been close enough frequently enough to encourage investors to utilize the relationship for forecasting purposes. This effort will be examined at length in a later chapter.

Seasonal Trends

There is considerable debate as to whether there is a discernible seasonal pattern in the market. Financial writers speak of the traditional "summer rally" and "year-end rally." To a lesser extent there is a widespread impression that February and September are generally—but not always—poor months in the market. These impressions of financial writers and observers of the market are based upon tabulations of advances and declines, by months, of long past periods of time. A recent study, covering the 23-year period (May 1951–April 1974), found pronounced seasonal strength in January, March–April, July–August, and November–December, with weakness in February, May, June, and October (Figure 1–4).

Figure 1–4
Market Performance Each Month of the Year (May 1951–April 1974)*

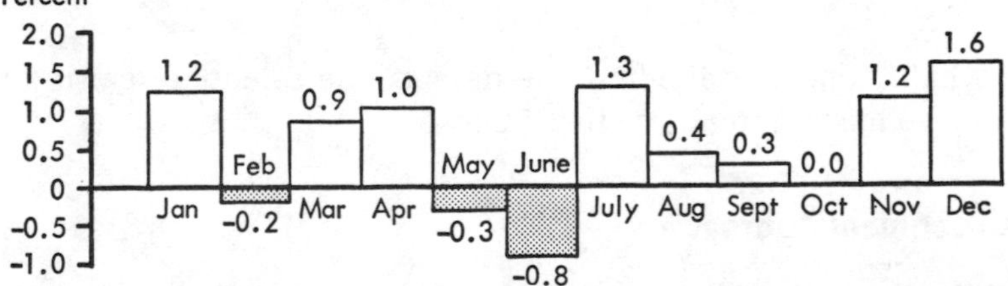

* Average month-to-month change in Standard & Poor's Composite Index (monthly average).

Source: The Hirsch Organization. *The 1976 Stock Trader's Almanac,* Old Tappan, N.J.

Statistical analysts have taken issue with these conclusions on seasonality. Using a sophisticated technique, called spectral analysis, for examining economic time series, two experts found very little evidence of a seasonal pattern. They declared: "In general, the seasonal components, although just observable, are of no financial significance."

The folklore of the market refuses to die, however, and any practitioner will tell you that the professors are wrong—that there usually is a summer and end-of-year rally. Some will go even further and tell you that Friday morning trading is the strongest of the week; that Fridays rise 54 percent more than Mondays, that when the market is down on Fridays, chances are three to one that it will be down on Monday as well.

The market rises more often (64.5 percent) on the second trading day of the month than on any other. And a period of five consecutive trading days, the last, first, second, third, and fourth, distinctly outperforms the rest of the days of the month. In a 276-month study (May 1952–April 1975) the market was up 59.1 percent of the time on these five bullish days. (See Figure 1–5.) Perhaps most bizarre is the notion

Figure 1–5
Market Performance Each Day of the Month (May 1952–April 1975)*

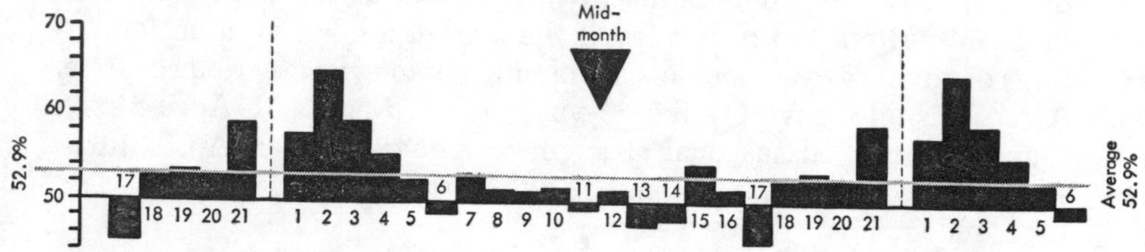

* Based on number of times S&P composite index closed higher than previous day.
Note: Trading days (excluding Saturdays, Sundays, and holidays).
Source: The Hirsch Organization. *The 1976 Stock Trader's Almanac,* Old Tappan, N.J.

that what happens in the first five days of the calendar year is predictive of the market trend for that year.

The Technical Approach

Some analysts do attempt to forecast changes in stock prices, including turning points in the market. They study the movements of stock prices themselves, past and present, and other technical data such as trading volume, number of stocks advancing and declining. They are the "technical analysts."

The tools of the technical analyst are numerous, and an elaborate and exotic jargon has been evolved. Technical factors examined and interpreted include odd-lot trading, the short interest, volume of trading indicators, breadth-of-market analysis, advance-decline lines, ratios and indexes, disparity measures, high-low indexes and ratios, moving average lines, the confidence index, and so on. The complete market technician's kit would also have to include chart jargon involving support and resistance, heads and shoulders, double tops and bottoms, line and saucer formations, V formations, measured move, first leg, the corrective phase, second leg, the coil or triangle, continuation patterns, reversal days, gaps, islands, bear traps, bull traps, fulcrums, duplex horizontals, inverse fulcrums, delayed endings, saucers, inverse saucers, compound fulcrums, and so on.

An example from a market letter reads as follows:

> The question is, of course, what we are to make of this phenomenon. The lows of mid-February and late February are, in all cases, close enough to each other so that if a rally were to continue from these levels, we would have a potential for a so-called "double bottom." The upside implications of that double-bottom base formation are not, at the moment, too terribly exciting, and we, for one, would prefer to see backing and filling around current levels so that a base suggesting a meaningful advance might be formed. The likelihood of such an event is strengthened by the fact that most of the averages have now moved above the downtrend channels projected from the year-end highs to their lows of last month.

A *Fortune* article on "The Mystique of Point-and-Figure" began "Question: Does this look like reaccumulation preparatory to a new upthrust? Answer: No—because fulcrum characteristics are not present."

This sort of jargon has convinced many observers that technical analysis is sheer rubbish. Indeed, as we will see, a group of academicians has given prominence to a theory that short-term stock price movements are *random,* and that no amount of analysis of historical data on prices, volume, and the like can enable one to forecast future stock price swings around their long-term trends. On the other hand, large numbers of Wall Street practitioners are equally convinced that price movements are not random and that technical analysis can improve one's chances of making correct timing decisions. One leading expert commented:

> It is hard to find a practitioner, no matter how sophisticated, who does not believe that by looking at the past history of prices one can learn something about their prospective behavior, while it is almost as difficult to find an academician who believes that such a backward look is of any substantial value.

It should be noted that scholars holding the random-walk view usually qualify it by observing that the random movement takes place within the framework of a long-term *drift*—that is, over long periods of time, stock prices do move higher; hence a belief in randomness is not inconsistent with a "buy and hold" policy for stocks.

No one analyst uses all of the technical approach methods. If he did he would be more confused than a psychiatrist. He becomes intrigued with several and comes to rely upon them. A more interesting approach, however, is that of the indicator consensus technique. Since individual technical indicators have given false signals from time to time in the past, the idea occurred to use a consensus of indicators for greater reliability. A number of services now use this technique. One of the more widely known is the *Indicator Digest,* which achieved some prominence as a result of the "sell" signal which it gave in January 1962, thereby correctly anticipating the subsequent sharp drop in the market in the spring of 1962. It also signaled the bear market of 1969–1970, 1973–74, and the upturn in 1975.

Indicator Digest, Inc., uses a composite index consisting of 12 technical indicators at any one time, varying several of them depending on whether a bull or a bear market is under way. These are then given weights of 1½, 1, or ½ for a total weight of 10. Whenever the composite total is 6 or more a favorable signal is given. If the score sinks to 4 or less, it is unfavorable. The 40 percent to 60 percent range is regarded as neutral. (See Figure 1–6.)

Mechanical Timing Techniques

The limitations of the technical approach cause some investors to use mechanical timing techniques. Not only do the technical methods have varying degrees of effectiveness from time to time but they are often in conflict with respect to the signals they are exuding. Even the composite techniques, of which there are several, are not always in agreement. At such times an investor can well become confused.

Three varieties of mechanical timing techniques can be distinguished. There is dollar-cost averaging; there are formula plans, either constant dollar, constant ratio, or variable ratio; and there is automatic trend following. The broad purpose of these automatic techniques is to induce caution in bull markets and bravery in bear markets, to achieve the investor's long-sought but seldom achieved goal of buying low and selling high.

Dollar-cost averaging involves the regular purchase of securities—monthly or quarterly—in equal dollar amounts. The very obvious fact that the same amount of money will buy a greater number of shares of any stock when the price is low than it will when the price is high is the basis of the success of dollar averaging. You put the same fixed amount of money periodically into the same stock or stocks regardless of the price of the stock. Your fixed amount of money buys more

Figure 1–6
Indicator Digest Composite Index

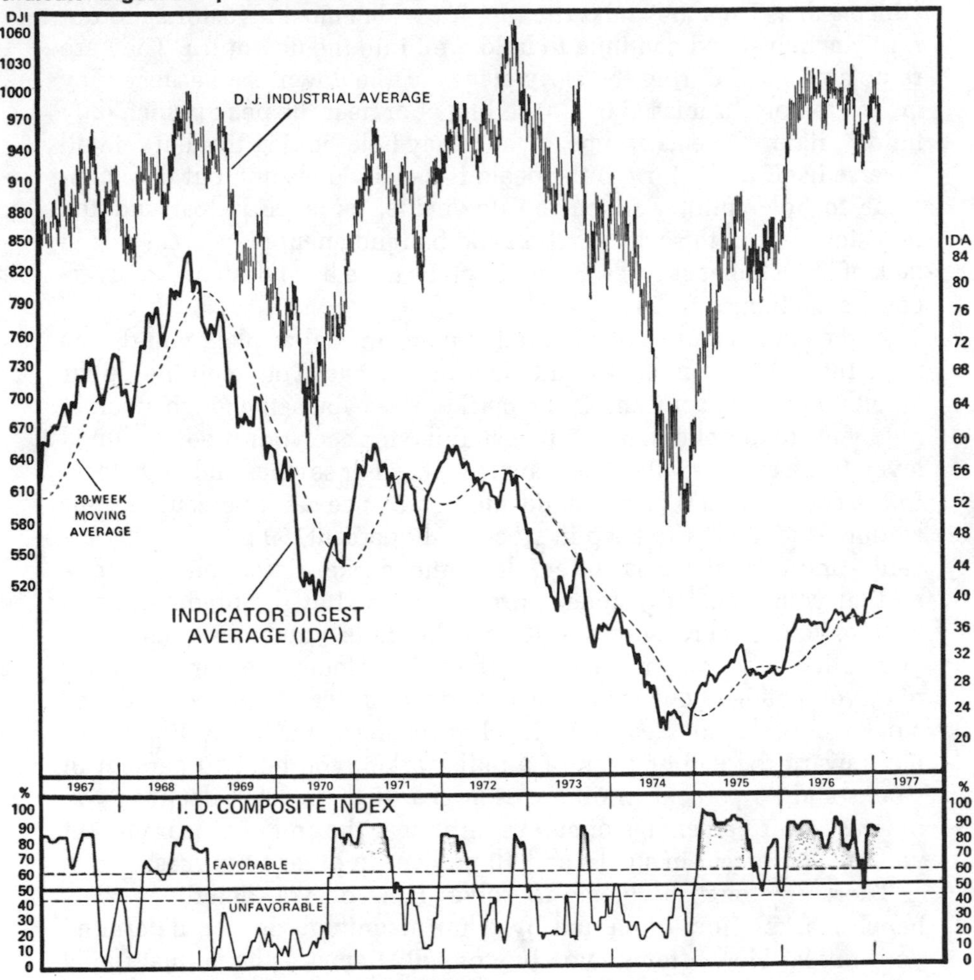

Source: *Indicator Digest*, Palisades Park, N.J.

shares when the stock is low, less shares when it is high. The important thing is to stick to your schedule—to buy, even though the price keeps falling, which, psychologically, is usually hard to do. This brings your average cost down, and any subsequent rise will yield a significant capital gain. To engage in dollar-cost averaging successfully, you must have both the funds and the courage to continue buying in a declining market when prospects may seem bleak.

In a bull market investors hate to sell and take a profit both because they do not want to pay the capital gains tax and because they are afraid the market will continue to rise and they will, by selling, forego added gains. Thus they miss the top, for which most investors aim but rarely achieve, and continue to hold well into the downturn. They are reluctant to sell during the early stages of the downturn because they mourn the profits missed by not selling at or near the peak (which only hindsight now reveals as a peak), and they hold hoping the market will reverse itself and return to the peak. It usually does not, but they continue to hold until, well on the downside, patience is lost and the investors sell. In this way emotion and bad judgment play a real role in lack of investment success. Formula plans have been designed to overcome such human failing.

In the simple and somewhat naive constant dollar plan, you divide your funds between stocks and cash or savings. You keep the dollar amount in stocks constant. If the market rises you sell enough stock to hold your total dollar amount invested in stock to your predetermined level. If the market falls, you draw from cash or savings and buy stock. In the constant ratio plan you decide in advance what percent of your resources you want to keep in stocks—40 percent, 50 percent, 60 percent—and then at regular intervals, if the market rises, you sell stock so that your stock investments are maintained at the predetermined ratio to your total resources. If the market falls, you buy stocks out of your other resources to maintain the ratio. Under the variable ratio plan you change your ratio of stocks to cash, or stocks to bonds, or stocks to total resources as the level of the market changes. For example, toward the end or peak of a bull market, you hold 10 percent in stocks and 90 percent in other resources. If the market declines you increase your percentage of stocks until near the end of a bear market you are 90 percent in stocks and 10 percent in other resources.

There are tough problems to solve. How do you determine your bench marks? How often and by what magnitude do you determine your ratios? How often do you buy or sell? Some of the mutual funds have tried the variable ratio plan and have come up with different answers, which have been changed from time to time. One thing is obvious, however. The variable ratio plan can provide better results than the constant ratio plan because under the variable ratio plan you buy significantly more stock at low prices and sell substantially more at high prices than under a constant ratio plan. If you have the resources, can cope with the intricacies and problems of a variable ratio plan, can bring yourself to buy as the market slides, you can get close to the objective of buying low and selling high.

Of Random Walks and Efficient Markets

Before attempting to plumb the depths of common stock analysis, the aspiring investor must navigate the twin Scylla and Charybdis perils of two widely held academic concepts—the efficient market and the random walk. Both combined imply that the security analyst and the portfolio manager are engaged in futile exercises for their services can avail little.

According to one terse glossary, "an efficient market is one in which prices always fully reflect all available relevant information. Adjustment to new information is virtually instantaneous," while "a random walk implies that there is no discernible pattern of travel [of a drunk wandering in the woods—or of stock prices]. The size and direction of the next step cannot be predicted from the size and direction of the last or even from all the previous steps. . . . Random walk is a term used in mathematics and statistics to describe a process in which successive changes are statistically independent."[1]

In the words of another authority, "There are two forms of random walk—narrow and broad. Thus, an accurate statement of the narrow form of the random-walk hypothesis goes as follows: The history of stock price movements contains no useful information that will enable an investor consistently to outperform a buy and hold strategy in managing a portfolio."[2] If this is correct then technical analysis (predicting future stock prices based on analysis of past stock prices and other internal market factors such as volume, breadth, highs, and lows) is about as scientific and useful as astrology.

Nor does fundamental analysis escape and survive. It is demolished by the broad form. Malkiel says:

> The broad form states that fundamental analysis is not helpful either. It says that all that is known concerning the expected growth of the company's earnings and dividends, all of the possible favorable and unfavorable developments affecting the company that might be studied by the fundamental analyst, are already reflected in the price of the company's stock. Thus throwing darts at the financial page will produce a portfolio that can be expected to do as well as any managed by professinal security analysts. In a nutshell, the broad form of the random-walk theory states: Fundamental

---

[1] See James H. Lorie and Mary T. Hamilton, *The Stock Market: Theories and Evidence* (Homewood, Ill.: Richard D. Irwin, 1973), pp. 270, 273.

[2] Burton G. Malkiel, *A Random Walk down Wall Street* (New York: W. W. Norton & Co., 1973), p. 121.

analysis of publicly available information cannot produce investment recommendations that will enable an investor consistently to outperform a buy-and-hold strategy in managing a portfolio. The random-walk theory does not, as some critics have proclaimed, state that stock prices move aimlessly and erratically and are insensitive to changes in fundamental information. On the contrary, the point of the random-walk theory is just the opposite: The market is so efficient—prices move so quickly when new information does arise—that no one can consistently buy or sell quickly enough to benefit.[3]

And still another expert, Prof. Fischer Black, has said:

My position has generally been even more extreme than the strong form of the random walk hypothesis. I have said that attempts to pick stocks that do better than others are not successful. Actively managed portfolios do not do better than buy-and-hold portfolios gross of expenses; and do worse than buy-and-hold portfolios when transactions and administrative costs are taken into consideration. This is particularly true when you adjust the performance of actively managed portfolios for the extra risk that they incur, because they tend to concentrate their investments in a relatively small list of stocks. Thus, I have said that it is better to buy a well diversified portfolio of stocks at a chosen risk level and hold it. An investor should change his list of stocks only to compensate for changes in the risk of stocks that he holds and to keep his portfolio well diversified.[4]

What does all this theory mean for the investor who wants to really study the market? To many it may suggest that he or she is pursuing a program that has no real purpose or function. Why? Because in an efficient market buyers and sellers factor into their buying and selling decisions all known influences and knowledge, both public and private that have, are, or will impact on the price of a security. Since the current price reflects all the knowable, and since prices reflect swiftly any new developments, all the digging by an investor can add little or nothing to the body of knowledge, which has itself determined the current price of a security. In its strongest form the random-walk, efficient market hypothesis maintains that past stock prices or earnings cannot be used to forecast future prices or earnings since both series behave randomly and already reflect all knowable facts and information about the market, an industry, a company, stock prices, or the price of a single stock.

As noted in *Barron's* an "A. G. Becker study found that the S&P 500

[3] Ibid., p. 168. In fact there are three forms of the efficient market-random walk hypothesis: the weak, the semistrong, and the strong. See Charles D. Kuehner, "Efficient Markets and Random Walk," *Financial Analyst's Handbook,* vol. I (Homewood, Ill.: Dow Jones-Irwin, 1975), chap. 43, pp. 1226–95.

[4] Quoted in Arnold Bernhard, *How to Invest in Common Stocks* (New York: 1975), p. 61.

outperformed 87 percent of the 3,000 largest pension funds in the country over the 1962–75 period—a timespan embracing no fewer than four complete market cycles. Their underperformance cannot be solely explained by the commissions and advisory fees charged to (and by) the money managers, for the funds were said to be running $13 billion behind the S&P Index during this period, before debiting such deductions."[5] The idea is that since the average money manager can't do as well as the averages, the way to be sure of at least keeping up with the averages is via the index fund approach. This has the added advantage of doing away with so-called analytical judgment and attendant investment fees. The portfolio manager is in essence replaced by a computer. In the process brokerage fees are held down since these funds have low portfolio turnover rates. We will consider the pros and cons of these ideas in the final chapter of this book.

BOND INVESTMENT

When a bull market begins to near its peak, when blue chips begin to sag, when speculative high flyers and low-priced cats and dogs begin to get the play, when stock yields fall to 3 percent or less and the yield spread between stocks and high-grade bonds widens to 4 percent in favor of bonds, when business is booming and interest rates are tight, the shrewd institutional investment manager who has choice and flexibility will quietly withhold funds from new common stock commitments and place the funds in high-grade bonds.

When prosperity tops out into recession, when business and common stock prices begin to slide, high-grade bonds come into favor. As interest rates decline high-grade bond prices rise. High-grade bond prices tend to vary inversely with interest rates and with common stock prices. As recession turns into recovery, reverse trends set in. Interest rates and common stock prices which have fallen start to rise and high-grade bond prices tend to weaken. Generally speaking, by high-grade bonds are meant those rated AAA or AA by the rating services.

The primary investment interest in bonds comes from institutions such as banks and insurance companies which must pay obligations in fixed number of dollars. If you have a $50,000 life insurance policy, for example, at some point in the future—whether 5 years or 35 years hence—the company will have to pay $50,000. If it invests in securities —bonds—which will return it a fixed number of dollars—it is in a

[5] See "Must Be a Beta Way: Random Walk, An Analyst Argues, Is an Idea Whose Time Has Gone," *Barron's*, April 18, 1977.

position to meet its obligation. It does not matter in this case whether the dollars it gets back buy half as little as when they were invested. It has a fixed dollar obligation, not a purchasing power obligation. The individual investor may shy away from high-grade bonds because of the purchasing power risk, but most institutional investors have less need to worry about this problem. Individual investors, particularly wealthier ones, find a special interest in several types of bonds, particularly tax-exempts and convertibles. As a hedge against recession and deflation, however, switching from common stock to highgrade bonds as a boom tops out may be an excellent, profitable move for any investor.

Bond Price and Interest Rates

The principal price risk in high-grade bonds is related to the trend of interest rates. If a commercial bank holds high-grade bonds, and interest rates, which had been low, start to rise, and the bank must sell its bonds because funds are needed for some other purpose, such as expanding business loans, then a capital loss results. Why? If the bonds carry a coupon rate of interest of, say 6 percent, and similar quality bonds now are being issued with coupons of 7½ percent or higher, no one will be willing to purchase the 6 percent bond at par value. The unwillingness of buyers to pay the previously prevailing prices, coupled with the actual selling pressure of investors who are seeking to raise funds for other investments, forces the price of the old 6 percent issue down, and it will fall to the point where its price in the market yields the new purchaser approximately the same rate of return as the average new, higher level of rates in the market. Thus, as the boom moves ahead, the demand for funds expands, and interest rates rise, high-grade bond prices will fall as stock prices rise.

At the peak of the expansion, when the central banking authorities are pursuing a tight money policy, which has driven interest rates up, bond prices down, the institutional investment manager may start switching from common stocks to high-grade bonds. As expansion turns to recession, tight money will be relaxed, interest rates will be allowed to fall, and they will go down because the demand for funds slackens, and high-grade bond prices will rise. In fact, the deeper the recession, the higher will go the prices of high-grade bonds as institutional investment demand switches to them and thus bids up their prices. However, if inflation accelerates during a recession, as in 1973–74, interest rates will rise since lenders will demand a premium to cover the inflation. (See Figure 1–7.)

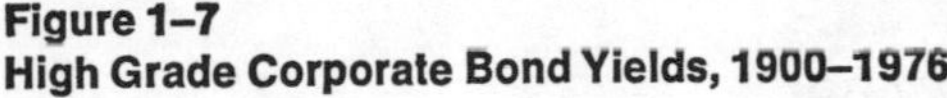

Figure 1–7
High Grade Corporate Bond Yields, 1900–1976

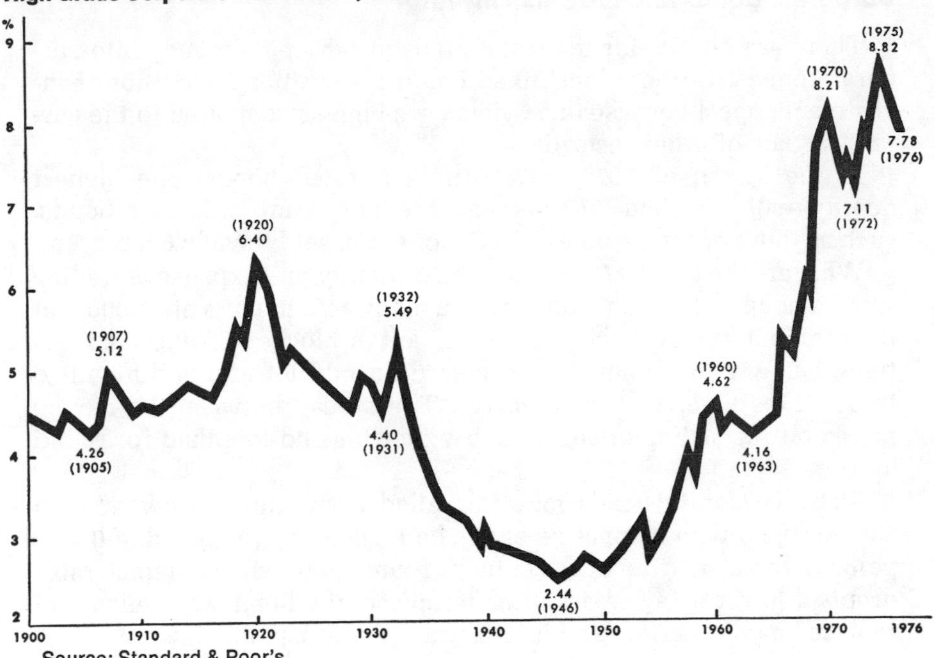

Source: Standard & Poor's.

Bond yields in 1975 were the highest of the 20th century as shown by the chart. They were very likely the highest in our history, although Standard and Poor's Corporate Bond Yield Indexes only go back to 1900. Since bond prices fluctuate in inverse proportion to yields, high grade bond prices in 1975 were the lowest on record. Many Bond Funds and Balanced Funds have been taking advantage of these low bond prices and commensurate high yields in 1974, 1975, and 1976. The following table shows major high and low points of bond yields and prices over the past 77 years.

Year	*Yield*	*Price Index*
1902	4.29%	96.13
1907	5.12	86.09
1920	6.40	73.14
1931	4.40	94.72
1932	5.49	82.05
1946	2.44	124.60

Year	*Yield*	*Price Index*
1960	4.62%	91.97
1963	4.16	97.79
1970	8.21	59.00
1972	7.11	67.10
1975	8.82	55.53
1976	7.78	61.31

Corporate Bonds and the Small Investor

There are pitfalls for the small investor who puts money into corporate bonds. Corporations' fixed income securities have a lot of investment appeal because their yields are high as compared to the current income of other securities.

In the spring of 1977 AT&T triple-A rated bonds—the highest quality—sold to yield 8.17 percent. Medium grade corporate bonds, such as those of the Standard Oil Co. of Ohio, sold to yield 8.5 percent.

What are the pitfalls? There are the difficulty and expense of trading small amounts. Corporate bonds are usually sold in units of $1,000, but they trade in the over-the-counter market in blocks of $100,000. Anything below this amount is considered an odd lot and is difficult to trade, takes time, and is expensive. The spread between the buying price and the selling price is much wider for odd lots than for round lots.

Many corporate bonds may be called early and the owner of a 25-year bond who thought he or she had nailed down a yield of 8–8½ percent for a quarter of a century, found that when interest rates dropped lower a few years after purchase, the bond was called and replaced by one carrying an interest rate 1½ or 2 points lower.

Types of Bonds

Bonds may be either secured or unsecured and may range from first-mortgage bonds on the one hand to subordinated debentures on the other. The security behind a bond, while important, is not crucial. The earning power, financial condition, and quality of management are vital. Because of this, one company's unsecured bonds may be rated higher than another company's secured obligations. For example, the debentures of AT&T are rated higher than the first-mortgage bonds of Indianapolis Power and Light. The debentures of Southern Bell Telephone have a higher rating than the first-mortgage bonds of Missouri Power and Light Company.

Mortgage bonds are secured by a conditional lien on part or all of a company's property. If the company defaults (fails to pay interest or repay principal), the bondholders, through the trustee appointed to represent them and look after their rights, may foreclose the mortgage and take over the pledged property. Some corporate mortgages have what is known as an *after-acquired property* clause, which provides that all property thereafter acquired will become subject to the mortgage and automatically be pledged to secure the bond issue.

While this is not widely found, it is very favorable to the investor, and where it exists, if the company wishes to float another bond issue secured by a mortgage on its property, this *second* mortgage will be a *junior lien*, subordinate to the first mortgage or *senior lien* on the property.

Usually, when companies float junior issues, secured by junior liens, they do not clearly label them as such. They call them "general" or "consolidated," or some other ambiguous name, and the only way an investor can determine the security status of the bonds exactly is to read the *indenture*. The *indenture* is the formal, and usually lengthy, legal contract between the borrowing company and the creditor bondholders, spelling out all the detailed terms and conditions of the loan. The indenture will also indicate whether more bonds may be issued with the same security or under the same mortgage. If so, the mortgage is said to be *open-end*. Additional issues of bonds under an *open-end* mortgage will naturally dilute the security available for earlier issues. If the mortgage is *closed-end*, no additional bonds may be issued under the same mortgage, and the issue therefore has better protection.

A bond secured by a pledge of specific securities is known as a *collateral trust bond*. These are issued mainly by holding companies, closed-end investment companies, and finance companies. They have not been popular in recent years, particularly after the passage of the Public Utility Holding Company Act in 1935. The *equipment trust bond or certificate* is usually used to finance the purchase of rolling stock by railroads. Under the Philadelphia Plan, title to equipment (freight cars, locomotives, passenger cars, and so on) being bought by a railroad rests in a trustee who holds it for the benefit of certificate holders. The railroad makes a down payment (perhaps 20 percent), and the trustee issues equipment trust certfiicates to cover the balance of the purchase price of the equipment. The trustee then leases the equipment to the railroad under an agreement whereby the railroad obtains title to the equipment only when all obligations have been met. Since the rolling stock can be moved anywhere in the country, should the railroad default, the equipment may be sold or leased to another railroad. Defaults have therefore been very rare in the case of equipment trust certificates.

Debentures are unsecured bonds protected only by the general credit of the borrowing corporation. They may contain a *covenant of equal coverage* which means that if any mortgage bond is issued in the future, which ordinarily would take precedence over the debentures, the issuer agrees to secure the debentures equally. In some states the law requires that this be done. All direct domestic obligations of federal, state, and municipal governments in the United States are debentures. This type of security is protected only by the general promise to pay; in the event of default, the debenture holder is merely a general creditor. The value of a debenture must be judged wholly in terms of the earning power and overall financial status and outlook of the issuer, which is the best basis for evaluating any bond. *Subordinated* debentures are very junior issues ranking after other unsecured debt, as a result of explicit provisions in the indenture. Finance companies have made extensive use of subordinated debentures. Because of these companies' high liquidity and their need for large sums of capital, they have tended to develop layers of debt of which subordinated debentures are the lowest. There are sometimes two layers of subordination.

Convertible bonds are bonds which may be exchanged, at the option of the holder, for a specified amount of other securities, customarily common stock. Usually the bond is convertible into a fixed number of shares of common. For example, the Occidental Petroleum 7.5s of 1996 are convertible into 50 shares of common per $1,000 bond. The conversion price of the common is thus $20 per share. When the common sold above this price, the convertible bond would move up with the common. When the common sold below the conversion parity of $20 per share, the bond would rest upon its investment value as a bond without reference to the conversion feature.

An *income bond* is a debt instrument whose distingishing characteristic is that interest need be paid only if earned. Originally many income bonds arose out of railroad reorganizations and reflected the effort to reduce the burden of fixed charges to manageable proportions. Most income bonds require sinking funds; interest must be paid if earned, in contrast to preferred stock dividends; and interest is often cumulative for three years or longer, depending on the terms of the individual bond issue. Income bonds as an alternative to preferred stock have been taken up and utilized by some industrial companies. Interest payments are a deductible expense for corporate income tax purposes. The Atchison, Topeka, and Santa Fe Railroad adjustment 4s of 1995, issued in the railroad's reorganization of 1895, are rated A. This issue is an exception, however. Most income bonds are rated in the C category because as a group they are regarded as speculative.

Tax-exempt bonds are of special interest to wealthy investors and to certain institutional investors. The income from state and municipal bonds is not subject to the U.S. federal income tax. This may mean that a nontaxable yield of 3.5 percent on a state or municipal bond may be equivalent to twice or three times as much as on a taxable security, depending on the investor's income tax bracket. Rules of analysis for bonds, which will be explored later, vary somewhat for state and municipal issues. There is, however, a simple formula which will show an investor the percentage yield which a bond or other security with fully taxable income must give in order to provide an after-tax yield equivalent to a given tax-exempt yield. The formula is as follows:

$$\frac{\text{Tax-exempt yield}}{(100\% - \text{Tax bracket }\%)} = \text{Taxable equivalent yield}$$

Assume that an investor is in the 60 percent tax bracket. If he can buy a 5 percent tax-exempt, what would an alternate investment with fully taxable income have to yield to provide 5 percent after taxes?

$$5\% \div (100\% - 60\%) = ?$$

$$\frac{5\%}{40\%} = 12.50\%$$

A fully taxable investment would have to yield 12.50 percent to give an after-tax return of 5 percent for an investor in the 60 percent tax bracket.

Since trading costs are high and liquidity just fair, tax-exempts are usually bought by the individual investor for the long pull. Occasionally, shrewd investors will abandon a speculative stock commitment and seek the safety of municipals. *Fortune* cited the case of the Bakalar Brothers, original owners of Transitron Electronic Corporation. "After selling over $75 million of Transitron stock in 1959 and 1960, at around $34 a share, they put much of the money into municipal bonds; since Transitron later sold under $6 a share, and their bonds are intact, this surely rates as one of the great investment switches in history."

United States government securities include bills, notes, and bonds. Treasury bills have the shortest maturities—usually three-month or six-month bills. They are sold at weekly auctions by the Treasury. The smallest amount that can be purchased is $10,000. They are sold at a discount from par, the discount determining the yield, and are redeemed at par. Notes have a maturity of from one to seven years, and are thus an intermediate term security. Bonds generally have a range of maturity of from 7 to 25 years. Both notes and bonds can be purchased in denominations as low as $1,000. All these types of U.S. government securities are subject to federal income and capital gains taxes but not to state and local income or property taxes. When you buy Treasury bills, at say 96, and redeem them six months later at 100, the appreciation (for tax purposes) is regarded as interest income and not as a capital gain. A number of deep discount Treasury bonds are redeemable at par when used to pay federal estate taxes, and are known as *flower bonds.* While the relative safety of U.S. government securities (although subject to interest rate and purchasing power risks) attracts conservative investors, speculators are frequently active in the government securities market because the notes and bonds can be purchased on very low margin—as little as 10 percent—thus giving speculators the advantage of leverage.

Bond Analysis and Ratings

For the individual investor and smaller institutional investor, an initial step in bond analysis (except for U.S. government bonds) is to go to one of the financial services such as Standard & Poor's or Moody's and see what rating they have assigned to the bond. While these financial services are not infallible, their experts are accustomed to judging the relative merits of fixed income securities, and the rating will give you a clear idea of the approximate quality of the bond. It is a useful orientation for looking further into the merits, or lack of them, of the proposed purchase. It may be that when the rating assigned is seen, there may be no further interest in the bond.

In one sense bond evaluation is not very different from stock evaluation. The real basis for evaluation lies in the financial status and earning power of the borrowing corporation or governmental unit. The farsightedness and efficiency of management, the outlook for the industry, the position of the particular firm in the industry, the company's earning power and the soundness of its internal finances as reflected in its balance sheet and income account, all must be carefully considered.

The security behind a bond is, in itself, no guarantee of soundness, since the value of the pledged property is usually dependent on earning power. If the company fails, its fixed assets may prove to be worth very little. A good example is the Seaboard-All Florida Railway's first mortgage 6s, which sold in 1931 at one cent on the dollar, soon after the completion of the road. When you are selecting any security, bonds or stocks, it makes sense to try to choose a company which is likely to expand and prosper rather than to seek to protect yourself in the event of trouble.

Of Risk and Return

Investors are subject to major types of investment risks. These include:

1. Business risk (that is, a decline in earning power), which reduces a company's ability to pay interest or dividends.
2. Market risk (that is, a change in "market psychology"), which causes a security's price to decline irrespective of any truly fundamental change in earning power.
3. Purchasing power risk (a rise in consumer prices), which reduces the buying power of income and principal.
4. Interest rate risk (that is, a rise in interest rates), which depresses the prices of fixed income type securities.
5. Political risk (for example, price-wage controls, tax increases, changes in tariff and subsidy policies).

Common stocks are most vulnerable to (1), (2), and (5). Bonds are most vulnerable to (1), (3), (4), and (5). No securities are free of all risks. Even U.S. government bonds are subject to (3) and (4).

The intelligent investor must learn how to measure risks, estimate rates of return, and decide whether the expected return warrants taking the risk of being wrong. That's what this book is all about.

SUGGESTED READINGS

Brealey, Richard A. *An Introduction to Risk and Return from Common Stocks.* Cambridge, Mass.: M.I.T. Press, 1969.

——— *Security Prices in a Competitive Market: More about Risk and Return from Common Stocks.* Cambridge, Mass.: M.I.T. Press, 1971.

Ibbotson, Roger G., and **Sinquefield, Rex A.** "Stocks, Bonds, Bills, and Inflation: Year by Year Historical Returns (1926–1974)." *Journal of Business,* University of Chicago, January 1976.

——— "Stock, Bonds, Bills, and Inflation: Simulations of the Future (1976–2000)." *Journal of Business,* University of Chicago, July 1976.

Malkiel, Burton G. *A Random Walk down Wall Street.* New York: W. W. Norton & Co., 1973.

The Rating Game. New York: Twentieth Century Fund, 1974.

Smith, Adam [pseud.] *The Money Game.* New York: Random House, 1967.

——— *Supermoney.* New York: Random House, 1972.

2

Buying and Selling Securities

Money doesn't bring happiness, but it calms the nerves.

French Proverb

At a low point in the market two brokers were walking down the street commiserating with each other about market conditions:

One broker to the other: How are you bearing up under all this? Can you sleep nights?

Second broker: Sure, I sleep like a baby.

First broker: What do you mean, you sleep like a baby?

Second broker: I wake up every three hours and cry.[1]

Over the last decade a whole range of problems has confronted a changing financial marketplace. Failure and disappearance of some leading brokerage houses, the paper glut, the antiquated stock certificate, back office problems, the advent of extensive automation, the computer and the role of the specialist, a central marketplace, a composite tape, the rise of institutional trading, the question of institutional membership on exchanges, negotiated commission rates, block positioning, the proposed automated book, rule 394, the third market and the fourth market, members' capital requirements, SIPC (Securities Investors Protection Corporation), box differences, disclosure, fails, give-ups, disintermediation, market governance and structure,

[1] Donald T. Regan, *A View from the Street* (New York: New American Library 1972).

the expansion of NASDAQ (National Association of Securities Dealers Automatic Quotation System)—these are but some of the issues and subjects that have received attention in recent years, and many still remain unresolved.

The investment process encompasses a number of markets and many institutions. There is a money market and a capital market. There are primary markets and secondary markets. There are organized exchanges and over-the-counter markets. There are both borrowers and lenders of short- and long-term funds. There are corporations and individuals with surplus funds who may decide to either invest, lend, or save them. There are a variety of financial intermediaries who facilitate the transfer of funds from those who have surpluses to those who need resources for a diversity of purposes, ranging from productive investment to speculative trading.

Money and Capital Markets

Short-term funds change hands in the money market. It is customary to distinguish between the money and capital markets by saying that the money market is the arena in which claims to funds change hands for from one day up to one year, but not beyond. Money market instruments include promissory notes and bills of exchange, commercial paper, bankers' acceptances, Treasury bills, short-term tax-exempts, dealer paper, and negotiable time certificates of deposit. Institutions participating in the money market include the commercial banks, corporations (large and small), the Federal Reserve, U.S. government securities dealers, and indeed anyone who lends or borrows on short term, including those who borrow on the collateral of securities to speculate. Activities in the money market range from a one-day loan of several millions by one commercial bank with surplus reserve funds to another which is short of reserves—the federal funds market—to an investor borrowing to buy securities on margin. Corporations with temporarily surplus funds may place them in Treasury bills for 91 or 182 days or in time certificates of deposit tailored to their financial time requirements. The money market is the vital arena in which the Federal Reserve influences the reserve positions of commercial banks, and therefore their capacity to lend, by engaging in open-market operations in U.S. government securities.[2]

---

[2] For further information, see Wesley Lindow, *Inside the Money Market* (New York: Random House, 1972); also *Money Market Investments: The Risk and the Return* (New York: Morgan Guaranty Trust Co., latest edition); and *Instruments*

In contrast, the capital market focuses on long-term funds. It is in the capital market that the demand for, and supply of, investment funds are brought together. Savings are converted into investments. The major supply of funds for the capital market is channeled through specialized financial institutions such as insurance companies, pension and retirement funds, and savings institutions. At times dealings between borrowers and lenders may be direct, but often transfers are effected through intermediaries such as investment bankers, stockbrokers, and securities dealers. Instruments in the capital market include, of course, bonds, notes, mortgages, stock, and warrants.

Like the money market, the capital market has many facets. A large corporation borrowing directly from an insurance company is participating in the capital market even though the whole transaction may be arranged by phone. Another corporation borrowing through the facilities of an investment banker who in turn makes use of a selling organization that spans the country is also participating in the capital market. There is a market for corporate bonds, a market for longer term U.S. government issues, a market for state and local bonds—"municipals," a market for corporate equities, and a mortgage market.

Primary and Secondary Markets

There is an active primary or new issues market as well as large secondary securities markets. For mortgages, for example, the new issue market is significant and substantial, while the secondary market is negligible. For equities, on the other hand, the new issues market is relatively limited, but the secondary market is large and active. For bonds there is both a large and active new issues market and a substantial secondary market.

Of total new corporate issues, in recent years 70 to 80 percent consist of bonds. The percentage is even higher if U.S. government and state and municipal issues are included. The new issues market is therefore normally mainly a bond market. Securities in this market can be sold either through investment bankers or by private placements. About a third of all new corporate bond issues have been

---

of the Money Market (Federal Reserve Bank of Richmond, latest edition); *Money Market Investments* (Federal Reserve Bank of Cleveland, latest edition); *Money Market Handbook for the Short-Term Investor* (New York: Brown Brothers, Harriman & Co., latest edition); and *The U.S. Government Securities Market*, Government Bond Division, Harris Trust and Savings Bank (Chicago, latest edition); also Jerome B. Cohen, "Short-Term Investments," *Financial Analyst's Handbook* (Homewood, Ill.: Dow Jones–Irwin, 1975), chap. 15.

placed privately. Many of the largest firms with the best credit ratings have come to favor this quiet, unobserved method of financing. For large companies the method offers a variety of advantages, though investment bankers claim that the interest cost is somewhat higher than in a public offering. A private placement frees a borrower from the uncertainties of market conditions. Market fluctuations are avoided. For example, as IBM's computer program unfolded, it obtained a $500 million long-term credit from Prudential and drew down the funds from time to time as needed, without having to worry about changing conditions in the financial markets. Also, registration with the SEC was not necessary.

Investment bankers are, however, the traditional middlemen in the capital market. For the most part, they buy the new issue from the borrower at an agreed-upon price, assume a market risk, and hope to resell to the investing public at a higher price. In this respect, they differ from the stockbroker, who usually acts as an agent, earns a commission, and takes no risk. In the sale of certain issues, however, the investment bankers may function more as stockbrokers. Instead of buying the issue they may take it on a "best efforts" basis, accepting a commission for what they are able to sell but not buying the issue themselves. This type of arrangement occurs for the most part in cases that are poles apart. The seller may be a small company whose securities are too unseasoned to warrant the investment banker's assuming the risk of purchase and redistribution. Or, on the other hand, the seller may be a very large corporation whose securities are so well known that it wants to pay the investment bankers only for their sales efforts and not for assuming the risks of distribution.

Prices set in the primary market when the new issue appears may thus be negotiated prices, or competitive auction prices, or privately agreed-upon prices. Usually all three take into consideration prevailing prices for comparable or nearly comparable outstanding issues traded in secondary markets. Institutional investment managers are much more involved in prices and purchases in the primary market than are individual investors. While the value analysis of the individual investor is directed toward existing securities and secondary markets, institutional investment managers give substantial attention both to new issue markets and to secondary markets.

Secondary markets for securities—the organized exchanges and the over-the-counter markets—provide the trading forums, the liquidity, the familiarity with issues and companies, and the price and value determinations which encourage public interest in security investment and facilitate new financing. When individuals or institutional investors buy securities, they buy claims to assets or to future income, or to both, and faith in these claims are enhanced or diminished depending on the ease or difficulty of finding a ready market for the claim on short notice, if desired. No doubt many would hesitate to buy securities if they could not count on a ready market if needed. Clearly the development of the now elaborate machinery for trading in existing securities came about in response to a felt need.

The organized exchanges provide physical marketplaces where trading in existing securities occur. They furnish facilities for the maintenance of a free, close, and continuous market for securities traded—free in that the trading price of any security, in the absence of now illegal manipulation, is governed by the forces of supply and demand; close in that the spread between the bid price for a security and the price at which it is offered for sale is normally relatively narrow; and continuous in that successive sales ordinarily are made at relatively small variations in price, thus providing a liquid market. Organized exchanges are auction markets with prices set by thousands of buyers and sellers in numerous little auctions occurring daily on the floor of the exchange. The New York Stock Exchange is, of course, the most important, and accounts for about 80 percent of all trading on organized exchanges. The American Stock Exchange ranks next, with the Midwest and Pacific Coast and PBW (Philadelphia, Baltimore, Washington) exchanges of importance.

The over-the-counter market consists of a loose aggregation of brokers and dealers who make a market principally, though not exclusively, for securities not listed on organized exchanges. The term *over-the-counter market* itself is misleading. There are no counters and there is no market in the sense of a given place where buyers and sellers meet to dispose of wares. The over-the-counter market is rather a complex network of trading rooms all over the country, linked by telephone and electronic communications. The phrase is a carry-over from the past, when shares were literally sold over the counter of private banking houses.

Securities transactions on the over-the-counter market run about 60 percent of the volume on all organized exchanges. Most federal, state, and municipal securities, most bonds, and many bank and insurance company stocks are traded over the counter. There is also an over-the-counter market in exchange-listed securities, the so-called third market. Over-the-counter securities are traded in a negotiated rather than an auction market like the organized exchanges. The price at which a given security can be purchased or sold on the over-the-counter market is determined by bargaining, with the broker-dealer usually acting as a principal in the transaction, although sometimes asked to act as agent.

THE REGISTERED EXCHANGES

The New York Stock Exchange

The New York Stock Exchange is almost as old as the country. Established in 1792, it wasn't until 1863 that its name was changed to New York Stock Exchange. The exchange is now a corporation and has 1,366 members who have bought "seats" (memberships) on the exchange. Only members of the exchange are permitted to trade on its "floor." A seat, or membership, has sold for as high as $625,000 (1929) and for as low as $17,000 (1942). The price of membership since 1950 has ranged from $38,000 to $515,000 (1969). The securities of more than 1,500 major companies are "listed" on the New York Stock Exchange, which means that they have been accepted for trading. Only those securities which have been accepted for listing may be traded on the exchange floor. Trading takes place between the hours of 10 A.M. and 4 P.M., New York time, Monday through Friday.

Located at the corner of Wall and Broad Streets, physically the exchange floor is almost the size of a football field. On the trading floor are 19 posts, at which some 2,000 listed stock issues are traded, and the "Bond Crowd," where 2,300 bond issues are bought and sold. Much more bond trading takes place in the over-the-counter market than on the floor of the New York Stock Exchange.

Automation has taken over at the Big Board but it is in such a state of flux that what is true today may be obsolete tomorrow. A high-speed ticker now provides a "composite" tape carrying reports of trades in New York Stock Exchange listed stocks wherever traded, whether on the floor of the NYSE itself, or on the regional exchanges, or in the third market. There is also a "consolidated quotation system." Your broker, using a desk top electronic machine, can know immediately the state of the market in any listed security by simply punching in the stock symbol. Getting an immediate "quote" on a stock you are interested in takes only a matter of seconds.

If you invest or trade you should learn the stock symbols. "T" stands for American Telephone & Telegraph; "A" for Anaconda Copper; "GE" for General Electric and "GM" for General Motors, but "N" is for Inco. Ltd., "NG" for National Gypsum, "X" for U.S. Steel; "Y" is Allegheny Corp.; and "Z" is F. W. Woolworth & Co. When a broker asks "how's Mickey Mouse?" he's referring to Disney (Walt) Productions (DIS) and if he says "Knockout" he means Coca-Cola Co. (KO).

There are some names derived from symbols that the listed companies themselves abhor—like Slob for Schlumberger (SLB). By logic that has nothing to do with the sound of their ticker symbols, Holiday Inns (HIA) is known as "Hot Beds" and Simmons Co. (SIM), the "world's playground." What the brokers call two AMEX stocks, Fluke Manufacturing Corp. (FKM), and Shaer Shoe Corp. (SHS) you can imagine.

How does a transaction taking place on the floor of the Exchange get onto the ticker tape in seconds or minutes? There is an optical scanner or card reader at each trading post on the floor of the Exchange. The card reader scans optically the details of a transaction marked on a special IBM card by a reporter at the trading post and simultaneously transmits this information electronically—stock symbol, number of shares, and price—to the Exchange's computer center and in turn it is automatically printed on thousands of stock tickers and display devices.

The pneumatic tubes which were used formerly to convey completed transaction information from the trading posts to the ticker room have now gone the way of the horse and buggy and the trolley car. So also have the huge annunciator boards whose flashing or flapping numbers used to summon brokers from the trading posts to their phone and order booths lining the floor in the Exchange. Brokers no longer need to keep their eyes on the annunciator call boards because radio paging is now in effect. Members now carry five-ounce pocket radio receivers which audibly beep and indicate with lights which booth or booths are paging them.

Automated equipment has begun to be used extensively, and in the coming central market system and certificateless society, vast changes are at hand. The NYSE and the AMEX have established a joint subsidiary, the Securities Industry Automation Corporation, and it is now engaged in a variety of experimental programs and techniques. Perhaps, just ahead, is the Consolidated Limit Order Book (CLOB), the electronic "black box," which may some day supersede the specialist.

The Securities Industry Automation Corporation (SIAC) has developed a new automated bond trading system (ABS) and a Common Message Switch. Orders for odd lots (that is, fewer than 100 shares) are routed through the Common Message Switch and executed automatically. This occurs at a price based on the first auction market round-lot trade that follows receipt of the odd-lot order at the trading post. It has also developed the Designated Order Turnaround (DOT) system to speed up the processing of small orders of 100–199 shares DOT maximizes automation in order processing while adhering to auction market pricing.

Under pressure from Congress and the SEC, the securities industry is now moving, or being pushed, toward a computerized automated national market system.

Functions of Members. A member of the New York Stock Exchange may be a general partner or holder of voting stock in one of the brokerage concerns which, by virtue of his or her exchange membership, is known as a member firm or member corporation. There are 508 such member organizations—247 partnerships and 261 corporations. About half the members of the New York Stock Exchange are partners or officers in member organizations doing business with the public—so-called *commission houses.* These members execute customers' orders to buy and sell on the exchange, and their firms receive negotiated commissions on those transactions. Many commission brokerage houses, particularly the larger ones such as Merrill Lynch, Pierce, Fenner & Smith; Bache Halsey Stuart; and Paine, Webber, Jackson & Curtis have more than one member.

About one fourth of all members of the exchange are *specialists,* so-called because they specialize in "making a market" for one or more stocks.

What exactly do the specialists do? How do they help provide liquidity in the central marketplace? Specialists have two jobs. First, they execute limit orders that other members of the exchange may leave with them. These orders are left with the specialists when the current market price is away from the prices of the limit orders, for instance, when a commission broker receives a limit order to buy at 55 a stock selling at 60. By executing these orders on behalf of other exchange members when the market price reaches the price stated on the orders, the specialists make it possible for these members to transact other business elsewhere on the exchange floor. In handling these orders the specialists act as brokers or agents.

The second, more complex role is that of dealers or principals for their own accounts. As dealers, the specialists are expected, insofar as reasonably practical, to maintain continuously fair and orderly markets in the stocks assigned to them. When there is temporary disparity, for example, between supply and demand, they are expected to buy or sell for their own accounts to narrow price changes between transactions and to give depth to the market. By doing this, they keep price continuity more orderly than would otherwise be the case and contribute to the liquidity of the market. They thus usually make it possible for investors' orders to be executed at better prices when temporary disparity exists.

To maintain the market the specialists usually purchase stock at a higher price than anyone else is willing to pay. For example, let's assume that a stock has just sold at 55. The highest price anyone is willing to pay is 54¼ (the best bid), and the lowest price at which anyone is willing to sell is 55¼ (the best offer). The specialists, acting as dealers for their own accounts, may now decide to bid 54¾ for 100 shares, making the quotation 54¾–55¼, which narrows the spread between the bid and offer prices to ½ point. Now, if a prospective seller wishes to sell 100 shares at the price of the best bid, the specialist will purchase the stock at 54¾. By doing this, the specialist not only provides the seller with a better price, but also maintains better price continuity, since the variation from the last sale is only ¼ of a point.

Here on the other hand, is an example of how the specialists may sell stock for their own accounts to maintain a market. Let's assume that with the last sale in a stock at 62¼ the best bid is 62 and the best offer 63. The specialist offers 500 shares at 62½ for their own account, changing the quotation to 62–62½. A buyer enters the market and buys the stock from the specialist. Thus the buyer purchased the stock ½ point cheaper than would have been the case without the specialist's offer.

Many times, when the specialists do not have sufficient stock in their inventories, they will sell "short" to maintain a market. In doing this, they must observe all the rules and regulations governing "short" selling.

Specialists enter limit orders on their "books" under each price category in the sequence in which they are received. For each order the specialists show the number of shares and from whom the orders were received. They represent these orders in the market, frequently competing against other members representing other customers. As they are successful in executing the orders on their books, reports are sent to the members for whom the specialists have acted according to the sequence of listing in their book.

Most of the orders received by brokers on the floor before the opening of the market are left with specialists. Using these orders and also dealing for their own accounts in varying degrees, the specialists arrange the opening price in each stock assigned to them. The opening is expected to be near the previous close unless some startling new development takes place in the interim.

The exchange sets specific requirements for specialists concerning market experience, their dealer function, and the amount of capital they must possess. Specialists are expected to subordinate their own interests in the market to the public's. Specialists, for example, cannot buy in the exchange market at any price for their own account until they have executed all public buy orders held by them at that price.

The same rule also applies to sales by specialists. Specialists on the New York Stock Exchange must now be able to carry 5,000 shares of each stock handled, while on the American Stock Exchange, the specialist must either have a capital of $50,000 or be able to carry 1,000 shares of each stock, whichever is larger.

The specialists' business is concentrated in one or more stocks at one trading post. They "keep the books" in these stocks. They usually have associates or assistants, and one or the other is always at the post during trading hours. Thus the specialists can also act for other brokers who cannot remain at one post until prices specified by their customers' buy and sell orders—either purchases below or sales above prevailing prices—are reached. The specialists must assume full responsibility for all orders turned over to them. Part of the commission the customers pay their own brokers goes to the specialists when their services are used, and much of their earnings come from commissions on orders they execute for other brokers.

Because the specialists keep the books in the stock and thus have advance notice of prospective buy and sell orders at varying prices, and because they can also deal for their own accounts, suspicion has always been raised concerning their objectivity and impartiality and doubts have been expressed about their conflict of interest between making a market and making money for themselves. Their trading practices are carefully supervised but the supervisors, exchange officials or other members, are either their employees or associates.

As one of the basic steps toward a national automated market system, competing market making has started on the NYSE and a computerized book, open to hand scrutiny, has been proposed.

Other members serve as *floor brokers,* assisting busy commission brokers to ensure swift execution of orders. Investors complain if their orders are not handled rapidly and efficiently. Commission brokerage houses are very sensitive to this.

Smaller houses, which have only one member of the firm on the floor of the exchange, need help when orders flow in rapidly or in bunches. They can call upon the floor brokers to take over some of their volume and by this means secure quick execution of orders which might otherwise be delayed. The commission brokerage houses which utilize the services of floor brokers share commissions with them. Floor brokers are still popularly known as "$2 brokers," although the commission they receive for their services has long been above that amount.

There are some 90 members of the New York Stock Exchange, now known as *registered traders,* who use their privilege of being able to engage in transactions on the floor of the exchange, simply to buy and sell for their own accounts. Their transactions must meet certain exchange requirements and must contribute to the liquidity of the markets in the stocks in which they trade. Registered traders may also be called upon to help expedite the handling of blocks of stock bid for or offered on the exchange.

Listing Requirements. To be listed on the New York Stock Exchange, a company is expected to meet certain qualifications and to be willing to keep the investing public informed on the progress of its affairs. In determining eligibility for listing, particular attention is given to such qualifications as: (*a*) whether the company is national or local in scope; (*b*) its relative position and standing in the industry; (*c*) whether it is engaged in an expanding industry, with prospects of at least maintaining its relative position.

While each application for *initial listing* is judged on its own merits, the exchange generally requires the following as a minimum:

a. Demonstrated earning power under competitive condition of $2.5 million annually before taxes, for the most recent year and $2 million for each of the two preceding years.
b. Net tangible assets of $16 million, but greater emphasis will be placed on the aggregate market value of the common stock.
c. A total of $16 million in market value of publicly held common stock.
d. A total of 1 million common shares publicly held.
e. 2,000 holders of 100 shares or more.

As a matter of general policy, the exchange has for many years refused to list nonvoting common stocks, and all listed common stocks have the right to vote.

Of the approximately 1,700,000 publicly and privately held corporations filing reports with the U.S. Treasury, 30,000 have their shares quoted over-the-counter; about 11,000 have sufficiently wide ownership to be considered publicly owned; and 2,900 are listed or traded on stock exchanges. The NYSE currently lists the common stock of 1,500 corporations but these include most of the larger, nationally known companies. They earn about 90 percent of total corporate income.

THE AMERICAN AND REGIONAL STOCK EXCHANGES

AMEX, sometimes called the Little Big Board, is located a few blocks away from the NYSE. Founded in the 1850s, it was known as the New York Curb Exchange until its name was changed in 1953. Its earlier name resulted from the fact it was an outdoor market from its origin until 1921, its members conducting trading along the curb on Broad and Wall Streets. Brokers' clerks sat or leaned out of second-story windows of office buildings lining the street and by the use of hand signals conveyed orders and messages to their brokers on the street down below. The brokers wore picturesque hats of various bright multicolored hues, so they could be distinguished from each other and recognized by their clerks in the second-story windows. One of the most colorful sights of old New York disappeared. Yet even today the hand signals survive, and a visitor to the American Stock Exchange can watch the rather esoteric hand signals between the telephone clerks in tiers around the floor of the exchange and brokers milling around the various trading posts.

Basically procedures on the American Stock Exchange are much like those on the New York Stock Exchange. The listing requirements follow those of the NYSE but are not as stringent. While some stable old-line companies are listed on the AMEX, generally the companies listed are less mature and seasoned than those listed on the NYSE. Indeed, the AMEX has served as a kind of proving ground for newer companies, many of which, as they grow and expand, transfer their listing to the NYSE. Thus, for example, both Du Pont and General Motors were in their earlier days first traded on the AMEX. Starting in 1976, dual listing of shares on both NYSE and AMEX was permitted in yet another move toward a central market system.

Many of the stocks on the AMEX are low priced (the average is about $15 per share versus approximately $55 on the Big Board), and many trade in round lots of 10, 20, and 50 shares, instead of the customary hundred. Unlike the New York Stock Exchange, the AMEX permits trading in some 60 unlisted companies. Specialists are granted the right by the American Stock Exchange to make a market in certain issues, even though the companies have not applied for listing privileges. There is also considerable trading in foreign securities on the AMEX. In fact, AMEX originated the ADR—American Depositary Receipts—by means of which American investors can trade in claims to foreign securities, the shares themselves being held by U.S. banks abroad. Many large commission brokerage houses hold membership on both the AMEX and the NYSE.

The AMEX has been automating as rapidly as the NYSE and in cooperation with it and the Securities Industry Association, AMEX has suggested that the two exchanges merge both for enhanced efficiency and as an economy measure to cut costs. Such a move would be one of the logical steps toward the desired central marketplace for securities. It seems likely that in time they will merge.

The Regional Exchanges. Over the last decade the regional exchanges expanded their proportion of total shares sold on registered exchanges. By 1975 their share of total volume traded was a little more than 11 percent, while their proportion of total value of shares traded reached 12 percent.

The three principal regional exchanges are the Midwest Stock Exchange (MSE), the Pacific Coast Stock Exchange (PCSE), and the Philadelphia-Baltimore-Washington (PBWSE) exchange. Over a third of the member organizations of the MSE are also members of the NYSE, and over 90 percent of the issues traded on the MSE are also traded on either the NYSE or the AMEX.

The Pacific Coast Stock Exchange resulted from a consolidation in 1957 of the San Francisco and Los Angeles Stock Exchanges. It has two divisions, one in San Francisco and one in Los Angeles, each with its own trading floor, interconnected by an extensive communications system. The PCSE has the largest volume of shares traded of all regional exchanges. About one third of the PCSE member firms are members of the NYSE, and over 90 percent of its stocks are those traded on either the NYSE or the AMEX. Because of the time differential, the PCSE provides trading facilities after the close of the NYSE and AMEX.

Generally the larger regional exchanges list some 600 to 900 companies each, while the smaller ones list about 100 companies each. The companies listed are for the most part regional or local concerns, but there is extensive trading in securities listed on the NYSE or the AMEX. Such shares usually enjoy unlisted trading privileges on the regional exchanges. Odd lots are a larger part of total trading volume on regional exchanges than on the NYSE. For dually traded issues, transactions on the regional exchanges are usually based on the prices and quotations of the NYSE or the AMEX. The NYSE, AMEX, MSE, PCSE, and PBWSE account for 99 percent of the dollar volume and 99 percent of the share volume of securities traded on all exchanges.

EXECUTION OF TRANSACTIONS ON THE EXCHANGES

Types of Orders

Most generally used is the *market* order. When a customer places an order "at the market," it means that the commission broker is authorized to execute the order at the best possible price that can be obtained at the time the order reaches the post at which the stock is traded: in brief, at the then prevailing market price or close thereto. Probably about 75 percent to 85 percent of all orders are market orders.

They can be executed very quickly. Market orders are perhaps more common in sales than in purchases, since the seller is usually more anxious to obtain action than the buyer.

When the buyer or seller wishes to specify the price at which the order is to be executed, a *limit order* is placed. The broker is expected to execute it at the limit set or better. If it is a buy order, this means either at the price specified or lower, while if it is a sell order, at the price specified or higher. It may be that the order cannot, at the time given, be executed at the price specified. In that case the customer will have to wait until the market gets around to that price. Naturally the floor member of the commission brokerage house given the order to execute cannot wait at the trading post until the market moves to the specified price. This may take days, or weeks, or may never occur at all. Instead of waiting, the commission broker gives the order to the specialist in the stock. It is immediately entered in the specialist's book. If and when, minutes, or hours, or days, or weeks, or months later, the market price moves to the price specified in the limit order, and it is still in effect, the specialist will execute the order at the price specified and notify the commission broker, who in turn will notify the customer.

How an Order Is Handled

Perhaps routine auction market operations will be clearer if we trace a typical order. Assume that Anne Wilton of New Orleans decides to buy 100 shares of American Telephone & Telegraph Company. She asks the member firm's registered representative to find out for her what AT&T shares are selling for on the exchange. Employing an electronic interrogation device which has instant access to a computer center that receives current market data from the exchange, the representative reports that "Telephone" is quoted at "50 to a quarter." This means that, at the moment, the highest bid to buy AT&T stock is $50 a share, the lowest offer to sell is $50.25 a share. Ms. Wilton thus learns that a round lot—100 shares—will cost her about $5,000 plus commission. She decides to buy. The registered representative writes out an order to buy 100 shares of T "at the market." This is transmitted to the New York office at once and phoned from the firm's New York office to its clerk in a phone booth on the floor of the exchange. The clerk summons the firm's member partner and gives him the order. Each stock listed on the exchange is assigned a specific location at one of the trading posts, and all bids and offers must take place at that location. The floor partner hurries over to Post 15 where T is traded.

About the same time a Minneapolis grain merchant, Edward Hardy, decided he wants to sell his 100 shares of Telephone. He calls his broker, gets a "quote," tells his broker to sell. That order, too, is wired or phoned to the floor. Hardy's broker also hurries to Post 15. Just as he enters, the AT&T "crowd," he hears Ms. Wilton's broker calling out, "How's Telephone?" Someone—usually the specialist—answers, "50 to a quarter."

Ms. Wilton's broker could, without further thought, buy the 100 shares offered at 50¼, and Mr. Hardy's broker could sell his 100 at 50. In that event, and if their customers had been looking over their shoulders, they probably would have said, "Why didn't you try to get a better price for us?" And they would have been right. Ms. Wilton's broker should reason: "I can't buy my 100 shares at 50. Someone has already bid 50, and no one will sell at that price. I could buy at 50¼ because someone has already offered to sell at that price but no one has come forward to buy. Guess I'd better try 50⅛." Mr. Hardy's broker reasons: "I can't sell my shares at 50¼ because someone has already tried and no one will buy them. I could sell at 50 but why don't I try 50⅛?" At that moment he hears Ms. Wilton's broker bid 50⅛ and instantly he shouts: "Sold 100 at 50⅛." They have agreed on a price and the transaction takes place.

The two brokers complete their verbal agreement by noting each other's firm name and reporting the transaction back to their phone clerks so that the respective customers can be notified. At the moment the transaction took place, an exchange reporter noted it on a card and placed the card in the optical card reader at the post. This transmitted the report of the transaction to the exchange's Computer Center and to the ticker. Automatically in a few seconds it appears as T 50⅛ on some 12,000 tickers and display devices all over the United States and Canada. In two or three minutes the buyer in New Orleans and the seller in Minneapolis are notified of the transaction. In a transaction on an organized exchange when you buy, you buy from another person. When you sell, you sell to another person. The exchange itself neither buys, nor sells, or sets prices. It merely provides the marketplace, the physical setting, and the equipment. Prices are determined in "double auction," a number of prospective buyers and a number of prospective sellers bidding in an active market.

Special Types of Orders

Do you know what a W.O.W. order is? It is one of the numerous special types of orders, but you won't need to know about it until you buy your seat on the exchange. There are a few special types of orders, however, that are important.

Stop orders may be used in an effort to protect a paper profit or to try to limit a possible loss. There are stop orders to sell and stop orders to buy. They are essentially conditional market orders. They go into effect if something happens. For example, you bought IBM at 150 and now it is 300. You want to continue to hold it as long as it keeps going up, but you want to protect your gain in case the market turns down. You place a stop order to sell at, say, 290, 10 points below the current market. If the market turns down and goes to 290 or lower your stock will be sold. Though you lose the last 10 points of your stock's climb, you preserve all the rest of the gain.

Or, to take another use, you note that General Motors is selling at 62. You think and hope it's going up farther and then split. You buy 100 shares at 62 but at the same time place a stop order to sell at 60. If your guess is incorrect and GM falls instead of rising, you will be out of it with a 2-point loss, plus commissions.

The stop order to buy is used in a short sale to limit losses. You sell Celanese short at 60. You expect and hope that it will decline to 40. If it does, you will cover at that time and have a 20-point gain. But there is also the possibility that it may go up farther. To cut your possible loss, if it does, you place a stop order to buy at 65. Thus if the stock goes up contrary to your expectation, you will have bought back and covered at 65, and your loss will be held to 5 points.

The investor is not assured of getting the exact price designated by the stop order. If the market takes a sudden drop, the specialist sells the stock at whatever can be obtained; and that might be somewhat below the stop price. If you place a stop-loss order at 50, an accumulation of prior sell orders at this price, or a sharp drop in the market, may prevent the specialist from executing your order until the price is somewhere below 50. There is, however, a hybrid version called the *stop-limit order.* This enables the investor to stipulate the maximum or minimum price acceptable for purchase or sale. If the specialist cannot execute at that price or better, no transaction takes place.

At times the New York Stock Exchange has become worried about stop-loss orders in high-flying glamour stocks, because a downward dip in the market could set off a chain of stop orders and by enlarging sales cause a sharp break in the given stock or stocks. It has, therefore, from time to time, suspended the placement of stop orders in designated stocks to prevent undue market repercussions.

Both stop-limit and stop-loss orders may be day, week, month, or "open" (GTC) orders. A market order is always a day order, good until the close of trading on the day it is written. When you give your broker a limit or stop order, you can specify that it is to be good for only one day—or for a week—or for a month. If the order is not executed during the period designated, it automatically expires. An open or GTC order is one that holds good indefinitely. The order holds until either the broker executes it or the customer cancels it. GTC means "good till canceled."

A discretionary order is one which allows the broker to determine when to buy and when to sell, what to buy, what to sell, in what volume and when. This is a complete discretionary order. It must be given in writing by the customer and approved by a member of the firm. A limited discretionary order permits the broker to determine only the price and timing. Discretionary orders are used by those who are ill, aged, or off on a prolonged vacation. A long and close relationship with a reputable broker is a basic requirement for the use of such orders.

What It Costs to Buy and Sell Stocks

Until 1971–72 the NYSE was able to maintain a fixed rate structure for all transactions regardless of amount. Membership was limited and it was able to require all members to charge fixed rates depending on the price of the stock and the number of shares involved. Pressure on the fixed-fee system came from Congress, from the SEC, and especially from institutional investors. Institutions have pressed either for membership on exchanges or for negotiated commissions. Obviously an order that is 10 times as large as a round lot (100 shares) does not involve 10 times as much overhead—telephoning, bookkeeping, execution, and delivery costs. Yet until 1975, commission charges on a 1,000-share order were 10 times as large as the fees on the 100-share (round-lot) order. As a result of institutional pressures commissions became competitive (negotiated) on transactions of $500,000 and over in 1971 and this was lowered to $300,000 or more in 1972. On May 1, 1975 all fixed commission rates were abolished and commissions became competitive (negotiated).

With the move to competitive rates in 1975 the chief beneficiaries were the institutional investors. Discounts of up to 60 percent off the old fixed rates were granted on large transactions, according to the financial press.

In its first report to Congress on changes in commission rates, the SEC noted that "rates paid by institutions are lower for each order size category, declining about 15 percent for small orders and about 28 percent for the largest orders. . . . In contrast, rates paid by individuals have changed relatively little . . . rates remain relatively stable except on the very largest orders. Rates have increased on small orders by about 4 percent and are down almost 44 percent for orders of 10,000 or more shares.

The small investor was benefited by the rise of the retail discount house. Prior to May Day (May 1, 1975) discounters offered substantial reductions from fixed rates and since then they have made their rates even more attractive.

Settlement

After a transaction has taken place on the floor of the exchange, shares must be delivered from seller or buyer, and funds must pass the other way. The customary standard procedure in the absence of any agreement to the contrary is for delivery of certificates and cash to be made by noon of the fifth business day following the day of the transaction. Thus, transactions on Tuesday require delivery by noon on the following Tuesday, since Saturday and Sunday are not counted as they are not business days. Holidays are not counted either. Technically this is the requirement, but in fact many transactions take much longer to complete.

In addition to *regular way* settlements, there are two other principal forms, *cash contracts* and *seller's option*. A *cash contract* calls for immediate delivery. A transaction for cash made before 2 P.M. on a given day requires delivery before 2:30 P.M. on the same day. If the transaction occurs after 2 P.M., delivery must be made within a half hour. There are a variety of special circumstances which dictate a cash contract, but three are recurrent. They involve expiration of tax years, rights, and conversion privileges. To establish a capital loss on December 30 or 31, a cash transaction is required, because a regular way contract would bring delivery and settlement into the following year. A cash contract is necessary to acquire rights on the last day of the period for which they run. When convertible securities are called for redemption, cash contracts are necessary the last three days the conversion feature is available. The cash contract must be specified at the time the transaction occurs and calls for same day settlement. *Seller's option* is a form of settlement contract which gives the seller, at his or her option, up to 60 days to deliver.

Recent Problems

While the various rules and regulations regarding delivery and clearance are straightforward enough, conforming to the rules has been quite a problem in recent years.

The back office paper glut of 1968–69 was followed by a capital crisis in 1970 and again in 1973–74. More than 160 NYSE member organizations—and an undisclosed but presumably large number of non-NYSE brokerage firms—went out of business. Most of the NYSE firms either merged with or were acquired by other NYSE firms—quite often through arrangements facilitated or initiated by the exchange itself. Some 80 firms dissolved, retired from the securities business or self-liquidated. A number of well-known brokerage houses disappeared.

To minimize the possibility of future bankruptcies, the NYSE raised the capital requirements of member firms. In addition, the government established the Security Investors Protection Corporation (SIPC; pronounced Sipic) to cover certain investors' losses should it again become necessary to liquidate broker-dealer firms. Generally speaking, the corporation will protect customers against losses of up to $50,000 of securities held for them by a broker-dealer, and $20,000 of cash. Where both are involved and the claim is over $50,000, only $50,000 will be paid. The securities industry, through assessments by SIPC on its member firms, is the principal source of SIPC funds. However, SIPC may borrow up to $1 billion from the U.S. Treasury through the SEC if the commission determines that such a loan is necessary for the protection of customers and the maintenance of confidence in U.S. securities markets.[3]

BUYING ON MARGIN AND SELLING SHORT

Pay Cash or Buy on Margin?

Stock can be purchased for cash or on margin. When you buy on margin, you put up only part of the purchase price, and the broker lends you the remainder. What part you put up and what part you can borrow are not matters of negotiation. They are determined by the Federal Reserve System, but the New York Stock Exchange also has its own requirements in addition. The Federal Reserve is involved because it is charged with control and regulation of the volume of credit. Under Regulation T, it controls the initial extension of credit to customers by members of national securities exchanges and by other brokers or dealers. Under Regulation U, the Federal Reserve regulates loans by banks for the purpose of purchasing and carrying

[3] For a brochure entitled "An Explanation of the Securities Investor Protection Act of 1970," write to Securities Investors Protection Corporation, 485 L'Enfant Plaza, S.W., Suite 2150, Washington, D.C. 20024.

stocks registered on national securities exchanges. Most unregistered securities can only be purchased on a cash basis.

Since the Federal Reserve Board first set margin requirements in 1934, the amount of margin which a purchaser of listed securities has been required to deposit has ranged from 4 percent to 100 percent of the purchase price.

The purpose of buying on margin, of course, is to stretch your funds. You can command more shares on margin with a given amount of funds than if you pay cash. If the stock rises in price, your profits are enhanced. On the other hand, if the stock goes down and you cannot put up more margin, assuming that you are long, and you are forced to sell, or are sold out, you can lose more than you would if you had used the same amount of money to buy the stock for cash. With a 50 percent margin you can buy twice as many shares as in a cash transaction. With a 25 percent margin you can buy four times as many. The principle of leverage comes into play. By operating with other people's money, you magnify opportunity for profit or loss. This may be seen in Table 2–1. Keep in mind, however, that if the chance for profit is increased two- or fourfold, the chance for loss also increases.

Table 2–1
Relative Gain or Loss under Different Margin Requirements

Requirement for Margin	*Funds Advanced by Buyer*	*Amount of Credit Needed*	*Number of Shares Purchased at $50 each*	*Per Share Change in Market Value*	*Profit (+) or Loss (−) Involved*
10%	$1,000	$9,000.00	200.00	±$5	±$1,000.00
20	1,000	4,000.00	100.00	± 5	± 500.00
50	1,000	1,000.00	40.00	± 5	± 200.00
75	1,000	333.33	26.67	± 5	± 133.33
100	1,000	0.00	20.00	± 5	± 100.00

Bull or Bear: Long or Short?

Where the expressions first arose we don't know, but a bull market is a rising market; a bear market is a falling market. A "bull" in Wall Street is an optimist, one who expects the market to go up. A "bear" is, of course, just the opposite, a pessimist who expects stock prices to decline. To take advantage of his forecast, a bull buys stock today in the hope of selling it later at a higher price. He goes "*long*." The bear, on the other hand, expecting the market to go down, "*sells short*"; that is, he sells stock today in the hope of buying it back at a lower price, thus profiting from the decline.

Short selling in the securities market basically is selling shares you don't own and borrowing the same number of shares to deliver to the purchaser. When you buy the stock later to return to the lender, you hope to do so at a lower price, thus making a profit. How is it possible to sell something you don't own and buy it back later? In securities markets the short sale is possible as long as you can borrow the shares you have sold and deliver them to the buyer. Almost always you can do this, because your broker can borrow the stock either from some left in "Street names" with him, from some of his other customers, or from some other broker.

Why are these people willing to lend? Because it is usually to their financial advantage. When you sell short and borrow a hundred shares, say of General Motors, to deliver to the purchaser, he, in turn, pays for the stock. You, the short seller, receive payment. If General Motors was selling at 100, you receive $10,000 (less costs). But you can't keep this $10,000.[4] You have to give it to the person or firm that loaned the 100 shares of General Motors. They hold it as collateral for the loan. When you return the shares, you get your funds back. Meanwhile they can use the money, lend it out at short-term and get the prevailing interest, or use it to buy more stock, or for any other purpose.

Since stock involved in a short sale usually lends "flat," no fee attached, no charge, whereas the use of the cash turned over as collateral may bring a return, it is financially advantageous to lend stock, and that is why short sellers can function. The loan can be "called" at any time by either side. The borrower of the stock can ask for his funds back and return the shares, or the lender of the stock can ask for the shares back and return the funds, at any time.

If you are alert, several possible dilemmas may have suggested themselves. What, for example, if the lender of the stock wants his shares back, and you are not ready to close the short sale? Very simple. You borrow 100 shares of General Motors from someone else. Suppose that General Motors rises to 110 and thus the stock is worth $11,000, but the money collateral given was only $10,000. The lender of the shares will call for more money collateral to support the loan. This is called "mark to the market." You, the short seller, will have to provide an additional $1,000, either from your own resources or by borrowing it. Conversely, if the stock price falls to $90 from the original $100—the short seller can and will ask for $1,000 of his cash collateral back. Both sides must "mark to the market."

Another problem may occur to you. Suppose that a dividend is

---

[4] The short seller must also provide the prevailing percentage margin.

declared while the short sale is underway. Who is entitled to the dividend? It would seem as if two parties are, since seemingly two parties "own" the shares—the party to whom you sold the shares and the lender from whom you borrowed the shares you sold. Actually, both parties get the dividend. General Motors pays the dividend to the registered owner, and the short seller pays the dividend to the lender. Usually, this is not an extra cost to the short seller because when the stock goes *ex-dividend,* the market price of the stock drops by an amount approximating the dividend and when the short seller covers later, it will be at a lower price than if the stock had not gone ex-dividend.

In a declining market, extensive short selling might cause a panic drop. Both the SEC and the exchange have been determined that short selling not be used to depress security prices artificially. There are rules to enforce this. No short sale of a stock is permitted except on a rising price. One can sell short at the price of the last sale providing that price was above the next preceding different price. For example, two sales of ZXY occur: the first at 44⅛, the second at 44. You cannot sell short at this point. You must wait for an uptick. The next transaction is at 44. You cannot sell short yet. The next price is 44⅛. Now you can sell short. The next transaction is also at 44⅛. You can sell short. As long as this price lasts, you can sell short, since the next preceding different price was lower. The market uses the terms "plus tick," "minus tick," and "zero plus tick," to indicate subsequent transactions. Dials at each post for each stock indicate the last sale and by + or −, whether a plus tick or minus tick. You can sell short on a plus tick. You cannot sell short on a minus tick. You can sell short on a zero plus tick. The prices 44, 44⅛, 44⅛ in succession provide an example of a zero plus tick.

Short selling is done mainly by professionals. The small investor seldom engages in short selling. The risk is very much greater than in a long transaction. If you buy 100 shares of a stock at 30, the worst that can happen, if the company goes bankrupt, is that you can lose $3,000. But if you sell short at 30 and sit mesmerized and watch the stock go up to 70, 80, 90, 100, and so on, your potential loss is open-ended. It depends on your stubbornness and upon your financial resources. To engage in short selling, resources should and must be very ample and your temperament should include a quick capacity to admit a mistake.

THE OVER-THE-COUNTER MARKET

"The over-the-counter markets are large and important, they are heterogeneous and diffuse, they are still relatively obscure and even mysterious for most investors, and they are also comparatively unregulated." This is the way the *Report of the Special Study of the Securities Markets* characterized the over-the-counter market.

Transactions in securities not taking place on an exchange are referred to as over-the-counter transactions. The over-the-counter market, unlike the exchanges, has no centralized place for trading. There are no listing requirements for issues traded, and all registered broker-dealers are entitled to participate. The broker-dealers vary in size, experience, and function; the securities differ in price, quality, and activity. While the OTC market includes from 30,000 to 40,000 common stocks of public corporations, only about 10,000 to 12,000 issues trade with any regularity within a given year and only 5,000 of these could be described as actively traded.

It is generally agreed that the over-the-counter market is the biggest securities market in the world—but exactly how big nobody knows. In a year's time, the National Quotation Bureau quotes prices on approximately 40,000 securities: 26,000 stocks and 14,000 bonds.

The over-the-counter market encompasses all securities not traded on national securities exchanges. Securities traded over the counter are quite diverse in kind, price, quality, and activity, reflecting the free entry of securities into the over-the-counter market. Most of the trading in government and municipal bonds, bank and insurance company stocks, and common and preferred stocks in some seasoned industrial companies as well as in thousands of newer or smaller industrial companies, takes place in the over-the-counter market. The SEC Special Study estimated that $556 billion out of a total of $1,092 billion in securities outstanding in the United States were not listed on any national securities exchange. There is also an active over-the-counter market in exchange-listed securities.

The issues of corporate stocks traded over the counter vary considerably in asset size, number of shareholders, and shares outstanding. There are substantial numbers of over-the-counter companies that cannot be distinguished from companies with securities listed on exchanges. Many others, however, are small companies, often speculative ventures in the promotional stage which have recently obtained public financing.

Just as there is an unlimited right of entry of securities into the over-the-counter markets, there is also virtually free access of persons into the over-the-counter securities business. There are about 5,000 active broker-dealers registered with the SEC. By comparison, approximately 1,200 member firms participate in trading on the securities exchanges. There is a high concentration of over-the-counter business with a few large firms. Fifty-six broker-dealers, or less than 2 percent of the total number, accounted for half the dollar volume of over-the-counter sales.

Activity in the over-the-counter market breaks down into two general categories—wholesale and retail. The wholesale dealers "make markets" by standing ready to buy or sell securities for their own accounts from or to professionals who act for themselves or for the public. There are about 1,100 broker-dealer firms who "make markets" in OTC securities. The retail firm, on the other hand, is engaged in selling securities to public customers and buying or finding buyers when its customers wish to sell. Sales efforts are extensive and have been greatly facilitated by the development of NASDAQ, described below.

In executing OTC transactions a firm may act either as principal or as agent for a public customer. If the firm owns the securities that the customer wishes to buy, it may sell them from its own account at a "net" price. The confirmation which the customer receives does not disclose the cost of the security to the firm, or its markup or profit.

If the broker-dealer does not own the security at the time of a customer's inquiry, it may buy the security from another broker-dealer (a wholesale dealer), place the security in its own account, and immediately resell it to the customer on a principal basis. Again the difference between the firm's cost (the price paid to the wholesale dealer) and the net price to the customer, known as the "markup," is *not* disclosed to the customer.

Alternatively, the transaction may be consummated on an agency basis. In this event the customer's firm buys the security from the wholesale dealer on behalf of its customer without placing the security in its own account. It charges a commission, which is disclosed to the customer in the confirmation. If the customer's broker-dealer uses the services of another firm to communicate with the wholesale dealer, or to "shop around," this second firm may also charge a fee for this service, in which case it is said to be "interpositioned." Although this fee may be passed on to the customer it is *not* disclosed.

NASDAQ

The over-the-counter market faced a special problem. The old system for obtaining quotations in this negotiated market necessitated a broker-dealer checking with several dealers by telephone in order to develop reasonably accurate bid and asked figures. Even then the broker couldn't be sure he had the correct range unless he checked all market members and this often wasn't practicable. As volume reached record heights, the system which had worked for years reached its limits. It became saturated with more trading activity and more demand for quotes than it could handle effectively. Stockbrokers were having difficulty securing bid and asked prices for their clients. And the clients were becoming disillusioned with the inadequate service.

The National Association of Securities Dealers (NASD) set out to correct the situation. After much study and discussion the NASD signed a contract with the Bunker-Ramo Corporation to build an electronic communication system to tie the OTC segment of the industry into one vast electronic stock market. The result was NASDAQ, the NASD's automated quotation system which became operative in February 1971 and drastically changed and modernized the OTC market.

Self-styled as "The Nation's No. 2 Stock Market," NASDAQ had 19 percent of the 1976 share volume and 11.5 percent of the 1976 dollar volume. NASDAQ is a computerized communications system that collects, stores, and displays up-to-the-second quotations from a nationwide network of OTC dealers making markets in stocks which have been approved for inclusion in the NASDAQ system. NASDAQ companies must also meet the same SEC reporting and disclosure standards as established for exchange listed stocks.

Serving as an electronic link between almost all of the major retail firms and OTC market makers, NASDAQ made trading more efficient because the best market for a security, no matter where it was, could be located instantly. Because each dealer could see competitors' quotations, price spreads (the difference between bid and asked quotations) narrowed. With accurate and timely trading information, and with heightened competition narrowing spreads, the NASDAQ dealer market seemed a significant alternative to the exchange-listed auction market.

Market makers are, in effect, the trading sponsors of OTC securities. They stand ready to buy and sell as individual and institutional orders appear. A market maker's role is similar in many ways to that of a stock exchange specialist. An important difference, however, is that often only one specialist makes a market in an exchange listed stock, while a half-dozen or more market makers may compete in a particular NASDAQ/OTC security.

Thus, with stocks in the NASDAQ system, you can call your broker for a quote, receive it immediately, make your decision to buy or sell then and there, while you are still on the telephone.[5]

---

[5] See "The NASDAQ Revolution: How Over-the-Counter Securities Are Traded," Merrill Lynch, Pierce, Fenner & Smith. For a free copy write to the firm at One Liberty Plaza, New York, N.Y. 10006.

Toward a Central Market

With change creeping at a glacial pace through the securities markets, the consensus of informed opinion seems to be that we are headed for an automated central marketplace, but having agreed on this the experts then part company. Each seems to have his own view of the shape and form, inclusiveness or exclusiveness of a "central marketplace," and the degree of automation which should accompany it. Perhaps the organization choices were best posed by Dr. Donald Farrar, who headed the Institutional Investors Study for the SEC.

Fundamentally, three alternatives have been put forth to date for the organization of the nation's securities markets:

1. *A Single, Central Marketplace from Which Competition Is Excluded by a Variety of Devices.* Supported vigorously by the New York Stock Exchange, this alternative includes the package of prohibitions contained in the Martin report. Its effect would be to return the NYSE to the position it once enjoyed as the exclusive market for securities of major corporations.

2. *A System of Separate but Competing Markets.* Supported by some of the regional exchanges, this proposal includes maintenance of fixed-minimum commissions, institutional membership, and opportunities for the regionals to compete with the NYSE through differences in rules regarding the recapture, use, and distribution of excess commissions. Its effect would be to preserve, if possible, the multiple trading structure in which regional exchanges and third markets (OTC markets in exchange-listed securities) have flourished.

3. *A Single, Central Market System That Eliminates Barriers to Access.* Supported by various reformers, major third-market firms, some of the larger NYSE houses, many institutional investors, leading economists, and a virtually unanimous business press, this alternative embodies the operational provisions advocated by the IIS. Its effect would be to create a marketplace in which competitive forces are accorded the widest latitude.[6]

The Securities Amendments Act of 1975 ordered the SEC to appoint a board to advise the commission on "steps to facilitate the establishment of a national central market system for the trading of securities." Congress directed that the National Market Advisory Board submit a report to it by December 31, 1976. The SEC named a 15-

---

[6] Donald E. Farrar, "The Coming Reform on Wall Street," *Harvard Business Review*, September-October 1972.

member board, with John J. Scanlon, formerly vice president and chief financial officer of AT&T, as chairman.

Congress instructed the SEC to use its authority to "facilitate the establishment of a national market system" by expanding the commission's authority over a number of matters including automated systems providing last sale and quotation information, unjustified competitive restraints, market makers, exchange trading of unlisted securities, off-market trading in listed securities, commission rates, and rules of self-regulatory organizations. The new national market system is to be "fair and orderly," "in the public interest," for the "protection of investors," and "efficient." *Efficient* can have several meanings. "An economically efficient execution of securities transactions" can mean that the cost of transferring securities should be reasonable. Markets may be structured so as to secure an efficient allocation of scarce resources (capital). Or the term *efficient markets* may be used in the way economists use it to mean markets in which prices respond quickly to new information.

No blueprint for a national market system was given in the 1975 Amendments Act. Earlier the Senate Committee had said that no definition was needed because "the general concept is sufficiently clear from the words themselves and it is best to allow maximum flexibility in working out specific details."

There have been a number of reports and a variety of proposals. More are due. Compromise and modern technology are playing a part in the evolving outcome.

SUGGESTED READINGS

Merrill Lynch, Pierce, Fenner & Smith *Proposal for a National Market System.* New York, 1975.

Regan, Donald T. *A View from the Street.* New York: New American Library, 1972.

Securities Industries Association *Report of the National Market Systems Committee.* New York, 1976.

Welles, Chris *Last Days of the Club.* New York: E. B. Dutton & Co., 1975.

3 Obtaining Investment Information

Investigate before you invest.
Better Business Bureau

The *Bawl Street Journal* comes out once a year. In it many a true word is said in jest. "We sincerely hope the market catches up with our predictions before the SEC does," advertised one brokerage house specializing in growth stock recommendations. "Now that logical reasoning is no longer required in this crazy market we have more confidence in our recommendations," announced another large firm. "Let us review your holdings with an aim at increasing our commissions," suggested another jokingly. "If you're looking for laughs come in and see us! Some of our offerings are hilarious," said a new issue house. "Get our research bulletin: Rarely do so many who know so little say so much," advertised another firm. Wall Street poking fun at itself but highlighting a real problem—which of many, many sources of information to rely upon? Where to go for unbiased, accurate information?

For the small, inexperienced investor, the vast outpouring of investment information, advice, alleged facts, and recommendations can be bewildering and confusing. Even the skilled analyst can be misled. For example, one large investment advisory service was sued by an irate investor who had lost a large sum in a land company, whose stock had been recommended by the advisory service. In pretrial discovery and examination it developed that the service had made its recommendation based, in part, on a forecast of earnings. To develop this forecast the securities analyst of the investment advisory service had made a trip to Florida, talked with company officials, including the president and financial vice president. The information they provided turned out to be incorrect, and changes they had made in accounting techniques gave an artificially favorable cast to current and prospective earnings. Instead of the expected and forecasted increase in earnings per share over the next two years, losses developed.

The Individual Investor

No one invests in a vacuum. We act on some type of information, whether it be a tip from a friend, advice from a banker, a broker's recommendation, a newspaper report, or a magazine article. Not knowing which of the many sources of information to rely upon, one investor hit upon a simple expedient which may yield substantial returns in bull markets. He watched the most active list in the daily paper, and whenever a stock, which had not previously been on the list, appeared twice and each time showed an increase in price, he bought, held six months and a day, and then sold, regardless of where the stock was at that time. He was getting his investment advice and suggestions from the market itself, reasoning that whatever was being bought in large volume had many favorable judgments behind it, some carefully considered and reasoned, others possibly less well based, but all, on the whole, serving as an evaluation and recommendation.

Individual investors have a difficult time. They don't usually have the facilities, resources, or time to research a stock in depth before making their investment decision. They have a business life, a family life, a social life, and the time remaining from these pursuits, if any, is likely to be very limited. What they read, what they look into, must be most judiciously selected because it can't, by definition, be very extensive. For the small investor, investment selection may become almost a hit-and-run operation.

Ideally the intelligent investor should ask and obtain answers to at least four basic questions: (1) What is the state of business and the economy? In the light of such conditions is it a favorable time to invest? Where are we in the business cycle? Is the boom likely to top out shortly? Is a recession near at hand? Questions in this area will vary with the stage of the business cycle. (2) What is the state of the market? Are we in the early stages of a bull market? Has the low point of a bear market about been reached? Is the bull market about to top out? Questions to be asked will vary with the state of the market. (3) If answers to the preceding two questions seem favorable, then there must be an investment selection. What industries are likely to grow most rapidly? Are there any special factors which favor a particular industry? (4) Which company or companies within the industry are likely to do best? Which companies are to be avoided because of poor prospects?

While small investors may not be able to devote the time to answer all these questions in depth, they must spend some time, with one or more sources of information, to come to an investment decision. Which source or sources should they choose? Reliance on a broker, on the financial press and on one or more investment services seems minimal.

The Financial Analyst and the Institutional Investor

The financial analyst and the institutional investment manager have both the time and the resources to dig deeper than the individual investor. Increasingly, they also have the capacity. Financial analysts, or securities analysts, organized in a national federation, have introduced a professional qualification examination leading to a C.F.A. designation—Chartered Financial Analyst. A formal training program with three stages of examinations lead to this designation. It requires not only a thorough knowledge of accounting, balance sheet and income statement analysis, of economics and finance, but also competence and maturity in investment management and securities analysis.

Institutions are able to employ skilled economists, financial analysts, and investment managers. They are able to mesh economic forecasts with investment research. They can study SEC filings and SEC Form 10–Ks for detailed financial information about companies in which they have an interest. They can purchase copies of registration statements and read them with understanding. Where published financial information is not clear or adequate, or where questions arise about the financial affairs of a company, or about its management or management policies, the institutional investment manager or the financial analyst can afford the time and expense of calling upon the company at its home office and putting the questions privately before making an investment decision or judgment. Not only is the initial investment commitment a considered one but there is usually continuous review and scrutiny of issues held. When and if conditions develop which are adverse, securities are eliminated from the portfolio on the basis of facts, research, and experienced evaluation. Many small investors tend to put securities away and forget about them. Institutional investors seldom do this. The institutional investor usually has a great advantage over the average individual investor.

Brokerage Houses

Brokerage houses with research departments provide information for both individual and institutional investors. Some large brokerage houses maintain substantial research staffs. They publish market letters or market reviews. They provide individual company analyses and recommendations. They undertake portfolio reviews. They provide industry studies. If you tell them the approximate amount you wish to invest, they will provide a suggested portfolio in line with the investment objective you have indicated.

The largest brokerage house, Merrill Lynch, Pierce, Fenner & Smith, has a huge research department, as might be expected. They have published extensively and readily mail out samples of their reports.

Other large brokerage houses issue similar material. Most firms make available weekly or monthly "market" letters as well as "recommended" lists from time to time covering selected companies in favored industries. Most brokerage houses make their research bulletins and reports available to their clients without charge. They will analyze and evaluate an existing portfolio, provide sample portfolio suggestions for given investment objectives such as growth, capital gains, income, and stability, or they will develop an individually tailored portfolio to meet age, amount, and investment objective requirements. Smaller brokerage houses which do not have research departments of their own sometimes buy their "research" from "wholesale" organizations like Argus Research or Data Digests, or else obtain it from large houses through which they clear.

The Financial Press

The intelligent investor and the professional securities analyst generally browse through, read, or study a significant part of the financial press each week, ranging from the financial section of a large metropolitan daily newspaper, or the *Wall Street Journal* to the *Financial Analysts Journal* (published every two months) or the *Journal of Finance* (published quarterly). The financial section of a newspaper can range from the elaborate and informative pages of the *New York Times* to a mere listing of daily stock quotations.

The *Wall Street Journal* is a daily, published every weekday by Dow Jones & Co. in New York, Chicago, San Francisco, and Los Angeles. It provides full coverage of business and financial news, including special news of companies, corporate profits reports, new issues, bond financing, national and local over-the-counter quotations and NYSE and AMEX stock prices, and CBOE option quotations.

The *Wall Street Journal* each day contains the Dow Jones Industrial stock price average, the most widely quoted and extensively used stock price average, though not the most accurate. The Dow Jones Industrials consist of 30 blue chip stocks. There is also an average of 20 transportation stocks, 15 utility stocks, and a composite average of the 65. The DJI goes back a long way; originally it was published in 1897 based on 12 stocks. In 1916 it was broadened to 20, and in October 1928, it was raised to 30. From time to time over the years, individual stocks have been dropped from the list and replaced by others. There have been some 30 such substitutions since October 1928. The 30 at present are: Allied Chemical, Aluminum Co. of America, American Can, AT&T, American Brands, Bethlehem Steel, Chrysler, Du Pont, Eastman Kodak, General Electric, General Foods, General Motors, Goodyear, International Harvester, International Nickel, International Paper, Johns-Manville, Minnesota Mining & Manufacturing (3M), Owens-Illinois, Procter & Gamble, Sears Roebuck, Standard Oil of California, Exxon (Standard Oil of New Jersey), Esmark (Swift & Co.), Texaco, Union Carbide, United Technology (United Aircraft), United States Steel, Westinghouse, Woolworth. The only names in the above group that appear in the original 12 are American Tobacco (now American Brands) and General Electric.[1]

The first computations were quite simple. The prices of the 12 stocks were added and the result divided by 12. That was the average. Complications developed when some stocks in the average split their shares. Some sort of compensation had to be made to avoid distorting the average. To cite an example given by Dow Jones & Co., take, for example, a three-stock average. One sells for $5, another for $10, a third for $15 a share. The average price is $10. Then the $15 stock is split three for one, automatically reducing the value of each share to $5. The day of the split the $5 stock advances to $6, the $10 stock to $11, and the split stock to $6—an average of $7.67 a share, down sharply from the preceding day's average of $10 a share despite the fact that the market actually advanced. To correct for this distortion, Dow Jones came up with a solution which has been in effect since 1928. They changed the divisor to reflect the split. Instead of dividing by 30, when a stock split they divided by a lessor divisor. Over the

[1] The other ten were American Cotton Oil, American Sugar, Chicago Gas, Distilling and Cattle Feeding, Laclede Gas, National Lead, North American, Tennessee Coal and Iron, U.S. Leather Preferred, and U.S. Rubber. At various times the following were included: Victor Talking Machine, Standard Rope and Twine, Pacific Mail, Central Leather, Amalgamated Copper, Famous Players Lasky, Baldwin Locomotive, Studebaker, Hudson Motors, Nash Kelvinator, and Wright Aeronautical.

years each new split within the 30-stock group dropped the divisor lower. Thus now, when the Dow Jones Industrial average is computed, the total of the 30 stock prices isn't divided by 30 but rather by 1.474.

There is, of course, a tremendous disparity, as a result of the way the average is derived, between DJI points and dollars and cents. This has led to some highly misleading descriptions of the market. The DJI advances 10 points, for example, and immediately there are reports that the market is soaring; the fact is that the stocks in the DJI have moved up an average of 55 cents a share. If the DJI declines 15 points, the market is said to have plunged; again the fact is that the stocks in the DJI have lost an average of 83 cents a share. With a divisor of 1.474, a 1-point change in the DJI equals about 6 cents in the arithmetical average of the stocks in the DJI. A 10-point decline is the equivalent of a dip of 55 cents per share in the dollar value. A 20-point decline represents $1.11 in dollar value.

In the light of the excitement about the DJI finally breaking through 1,000 in 1972–73, it is interesting to note that but for one substitution, the DJI would have broken through the 1000 level in December 1961. In 1939 IBM was removed from inclusion in the DJI 30 and AT&T was substituted. Had IBM remained, the DJI would have reached a December 1961 high of 1017.39 instead of 734.91.

"It's *Catch-22*. Everyone looks at the Dow because it's prominently displayed. It's displayed because everyone looks at it," said one observer.

After the Dow Jones Industrial average, probably the most widely known market barometer is the index prepared by Standard & Poor's Corporation based on 400 industrial stocks. It also has a 40-stock financial group, a 20-stock transportation index, a 40-stock utility index, and a 500-stock composite of the four, as well as other individual industry stock price indexes. Standard & Poor's, in arriving at an index figure, doesn't just add up per share prices and divide. It starts by multiplying the price of each share by the number of shares in that issue; for example, in the case of a stock selling at $10 a share with 10,000 shares outstanding, it would get $100,000. These market value figures are then added, giving the aggregate market value of the issues covered. This aggregate is expressed as a percentage of the average market value during the years 1941–43. Then, finally, this percentage figure is divided by 10. There is no need for a changing divisor. Adjustment for stock splits is made automatically—because each stock enters the index not as a per share price but as a market value figure covering all the shares in the issue. Take the $10 stock with 10,000 shares outstanding and a consequent market value of $100,000. If that is split two for one, the result is 20,000 shares of $5 stock—still worth $100,000. It's the $100,000 not the $10 or the $5 that goes into the index.

The S&P 400 Industrial Stock Price Index is numerically far down the ladder from the DJI. At the time that the latter was about 900, the S&P index was about 90. This was not an accident. When a prior S&P industrial index was discontinued in 1957 and the present new index inaugurated, the old index was at around 370 on a 1935–39 equals 100 base. When the new index was launched on a 1941–43 base, it was made equal to 10 not to 100. This, in effect, divided the index by 10. The new Standard & Poor's index started in 1957 at 47. That was almost precisely the same as the then average price of $45.23 for all common shares listed on the NYSE. The DJI 30 stocks represent about 25 percent of the market value of all NYSE listed stocks. Standard & Poor's index of 500 stocks accounts for about 74 percent of the market value of all listed shares.

In mid-1966 both the American and the New York Stock Exchanges developed and introduced their own stock price indexes. The AMEX average is computed by adding all of the plus net changes and minus net changes above or below previous closing prices. The sum is then divided by the number of issues listed and the result added to or subtracted from the previous close. For example, on a given day, the sum of all price changes was an increase of $170.94. Dividing by 952, the number of common stocks and warrants then listed, produced a result of $0.18, which, added to the closing value of the index on the previous day—$13.15—produced a price level index of $13.33.

Changes in the number of issues used as a divisor will be made when new stocks are listed or existing ones removed; adjustments in the previous day's closing index will be made in the case of stock splits, stock dividends, and cash dividends. Since the AMEX index considers net price changes only, no consideration is given to the importance of the relationship of the net change to its price. This means that a $1 move in a $5 stock receives the same weight as a $1 change in a $100 stock.

The NYSE Common Stock Index is a composite index of all the equity issues listed on the Exchange. In addition the NYSE also publishes four separate indexes as follows:

a. The Finance Index includes 75 issues of closed-end investment companies, savings and loan holding companies, real estate holding and investment companies, and others in commercial and installment finance, banking, insurance, and related fields.

b. The Transportation Index is based on 76 issues representing railroads, airlines, shipping, motor transport, and other operating, leasing, and holding companies in the transportation field.
c. The Utility Index includes 136 issues of operating, holding, and transmission companies in gas, electric, power, and communications.
d. The Industrial Index comprises the nearly 1,000 NYSE-listed stocks not included in the other three subgroup indexes. These, of course, represent a wide variety of industrial corporations in many fields of manufacturing, merchandising, and service.

The Composite Index takes into consideration the total market value of every common stock traded on the exchange. To compute the Common Stock Index, the market value of each common share is multiplied by the number of shares of that issue which are listed. The results are added to obtain total market value. The index is a number that expresses simply the relationship between total current market value and a base market value (as of December 31, 1965) after necessary adjustments have been made.

To establish a close relationship at the outset between the Common Stock Index and the actual average price of all listed common stocks, a figure of 50 as of December 31, 1965, was selected as the base for the index. The actual average price on that date was about $53. The subindexes are also based on 50 as of December 31, 1965. If the index gets too far away from the actual average price of listed stocks, the exchange plans to bring it back in line by changing the base date or splitting the index.

All the indexes are expressed in points. Point changes in the all-stock index are also converted into dollar and cent changes in the average price per share, which many investors may find more meaningful than points and easier to relate, in terms of actual market value, to the particular issue in which they may be interested.

Computers of the Stock Exchange's Market Data System calculate the new indexes throughout the trading day. Each half hour the exchange's international ticker network carries the Common Stock Index, with its net change in points from the previous day's close, and the net change in the average price of NYSE common stocks. The Industrial, Transportation, Utility, and Finance Indexes, with net changes, are reported hourly in points. Final results for the day are printed on the tape after the close of the market.

There are other stock price averages or indexes such as the Value Line Average of 1,600 stocks. It should be noted that in the Value Line Composite, prices are not weighted by the number of outstanding shares as in the case of the NYSE and S&P averages. From the viewpoint of investment analysis, the Standard & Poor's indexes with their 97-category industry breakdown would appear to be the most useful. These indexes are published weekly in the *Outlook*.

To increase the usefulness of these price indexes, Standard & Poor's computes companion series of *per share data* by industry groups, all related to the stock price indexes, including per share earnings, dividends, sales, operating income depreciation taxes, book value, working capital, and capital expenditures, and significant ratios and yields. These data are published in Standard & Poor's *Analysts Handbook* annually, back to 1946. The *Analysts Handbook* is kept current through a monthly supplement, which also contains S&P's official group earnings estimates and indicated dividend rates.

Dow Jones & Co. publishes *Barron's National Business & Financial Weekly* as well as the *Wall Street Journal*.

Each Monday, the *Wall Street Journal's* "Outlook" column on the front page explores specific economic trends and opinions. Other regularly appearing articles deal with monthly changes in industrial production (mid-month), employment and unemployment (around the 4th), retail sales (around the 10th), and consumer prices (around the 8th).[2]

Barron's usually may be viewed as having three categories: leading articles in depth; departments such as The Trade, Up & Down Wall Street, Investment News & Views, Capital Markets, "The Striking Price" (Options), and "Market Laboratory" as well as a substantial statistical section which includes "new highs and lows in stocks," "mutual funds," "short interest," "stock quotations," "over-the-counter market," "bond quotations," and "pulse of trade and industry." The market laboratory section contains a wealth of basic figures on the Dow Jones averages, price-earnings ratios, odd-lot trading, stock yields and bond yields, and the 20 most active stocks of the week.

Forbes is published twice monthly. It features articles on industry and company financial developments and trends. There are regular columns on "The Market Outlook," on "Stock Analysis," "Investment Pointers," "Market Comment," and "Technician's Perspective." The January 1 issue each year is devoted to rating companies within industries, comparing and contrasting profitability and performance. The August 15 issue each year contains the *Forbes* evaluation and rating of comparative mutual fund performance. It is one of the better tools available for mutual fund evaluation.

---

[2] See "How to Become Your Own Economist; Facts That Count Are Easy to Get and Understand," *Wall Street Journal* (March 21, 1977), p. 36.

Billed as the "world's most expensive weekly newspaper," the *Wall Street Transcript,* is published every Monday and costs $10 a copy. This is clearly for professional analysts and money managers. It reproduces complete texts of top-management speeches and interviews at meetings of 35 security analysts societies. The *Transcript is* hundreds of information sources in a single publication. In a year of issues some 2,000 company analyses, 300 industry surveys, and 500 management reports are reproduced. Features include a "Technical Corner," which reproduces technical analysis of leading brokerage houses and financial services; "Executive's Corner" covering speeches of company officials at company annual stockholders' meetings, or at financial analyst society meetings; "New Issue Corner," which presents summaries of new issue prospectuses; "Connoisseur's Corner," which each week has a long article on valuation of art or antiques, or wines.

The *Media General Financial Weekly,* published in Richmond, Virginia, covers the financial waterfront each week. In addition to a series of feature articles and columns, it provides financial and statistical facts on 3,400 common stocks, including 720 OTC issues; indicator charts on every NYSE and AMEX common stock plus 720 OTC issues. It has "Stocks in the Spotlight," the 40 leading and lagging issues in 6 major price categories and 40 leading issues in 6-volume categories. There are two pages of charts showing the performance of all 60 major industrial groups, compared with Media General's Composite Market Index. There are long series of fundamental and technical indicators, shown in both charts and figures. This too is a publication primarily for the security analyst and the professional money manager.

The *Money Manager* is a weekly, edited exclusively for the investment professional. It is a source of financial intelligence on the Money Market, the Government, Municipal and Corporate Bond Markets, the Stock Market, the Mortgage Market, Foreign Finance and developments in the economy.

The *Financial World,* published weekly, and the *Magazine of Wall Street,* published biweekly, both feature articles on the trend of the market, industry evaluations, and individual company analyses. The *Financial World* has a monthly supplement in which common stocks are rated. Comparable data on preferred stocks and mutual funds are published quarterly. The publisher of the *Magazine of Wall Street* issued weekly a separate "Investment and Business Forecast." This is in the nature of an investment advisory report.

The *Financial Analysts Journal* is published every two months by the Financial Analysts Federation, an association devoted to the advancement of investment management and security analysis. Each issue features 7 to 12 articles on varying phases of investment analysis and portfolio management. For example, topics covered have included: "Valuing Quality Growth Stocks," "The Trouble with Earnings," "The Efficient Market Model," "Stock Prices and the Money Supply," "Profile of the Financial Analyst," "Financial Forecasting by Corporations," "Minimax Portfolio Policies," "The Third and Fourth Markets," "How Willing Is Management to Disclose," and "How Good Is Institutional Research." In addition each issue reports current developments in "Securities Law and Regulation," "Accounting for Financial Analysis," and "Corporate Information and Disclosure."

The *Institutional Investor* is a monthly journal published for professional money managers. It also features articles on investment analysis and portfolio management but there is more emphasis on money manager personalities, and the articles are often grouped about a theme such as "Wall Street's Search for Leadership." Its more learned and academic counterpart is the *Journal of Portfolio Management.*

The *Journal of Finance* is published quarterly by the American Finance Association. It is much more academically and theoretically oriented than the *Financial Analysts Journal.* In recent years it has attempted to cover not only all phases of finance—banking, investments, international finance, real estate finance, corporate finance—but monetary and economic theory as well.

Even more mathematical and theoretically oriented is the *Journal of Financial and Quantitative Analysis,* published quarterly. Other publications of possible interest include the *Chronicle, Finance, Financial Executive, Financial Management, Investment Dealer Digest, Journal of Commerce, Money, Trusts and Estates,* and *Wall Street Letter.*

Investment Advisory Services

A wealth of information is available in the publications of the investment advisory services. The major services are:

Moody's Investor Services, (owned by Dun & Bradstreet)
99 Church Street
New York, N.Y. 10007

Standard & Poor's Corporation (owned by McGraw-Hill)
345 Hudson Street
New York, N.Y. 10014

The Value Line Investment Survey (owned by Arnold Bernhard & Co.)
5 East 44th Street
New York, N.Y. 10017

A comprehensive and copious flow of bulletins and reports emerges daily, weekly, and monthly from these services. It is possible to subscribe to part or all of the publications. The annual cost of any of the services is a properly deducted expense from investors' income under the personal income tax regulations. A well-stocked college or university library will have one or more of these services, and the larger public libraries also make them available.

A basic part of both the Moody's and the Standard & Poor's services are the reference volumes: Moody's *Manuals* and Standard & Poor's *Corporation Records*. Moody's *Manuals* are big thick volumes published each year and issued for various fields—industrials, OTC industrials, public utilities, transportation, municipal and government, and banks and finance. Each volume contains reports on thousands of corporations (or governmental bodies), giving the financial history and full investment data for a period of years. Standard & Poor's *Corporation Records* are continuous and alphabetical regardless of field. The volumes are kept up to date by current supplements. Standard & Poor's six-volume *Corporation Records* are augmented by a daily bulletin, while the six Moody's *Manuals* are kept up to date by a semiweekly report. Most large brokerage offices will have one or the other of these basic services.

Standard & Poor's issues a weekly magazine, the *Outlook,* while Moody's issues a weekly *Stock Survey*. Both review market conditions and recommend investment choices in common stock. The *Outlook* generally contains an overall market forecast and policy recommendation, a list of the ten best performing groups of the week, and ten poorest performing groups, an occasional "Stock for Action" recommendation, stocks in the limelight, on-the-spot reports on individual companies, a report on business, and special articles, such as "Stocks with Tax Exemption on Dividends," "Portfolio for New Investors," "Low-Priced Speculations," and "Buys among Institutional Favorites." A master list of recommended issues is maintained, classified into: "Group 1—Foundation Stocks for Long-Term Gain"; "Group 2—Stocks with Promising Growth Prospects"; "Group 3—Cyclical/Speculative Stocks"; and "Group 4—Liberal Income with Inflation Protection." The annual forecast of the *Outlook* features ten stocks for action in the year ahead, industries best situated for the year ahead, speculative stocks for aggressive investors, candidates for dividends increases, and stocks to outrun inflation.

The Standard & Poor's *Stock Guide* is a pocket-size condensed handbook, issued monthly, containing a thumbnail sketch of essential facts about some 5,000 common and preferred stocks, listed and unlisted. Most of the 5,000 stocks are rated for earnings and dividend stability and growth.

Each month the *Stock Guide* also contains a list of "stocks for potential price appreciation" and another list of "stocks for good income return." There is one feature article such as "Cyclical Buys Offering Sound Values," and "Electronics-Electrical Prospects Brighter." At the back of the *Guide* each month are to be found "quality ratings of utility preferred stocks" and a section on the performance of 400 mutual funds.

Both Moody's and Standard & Poor's publish compendiums on individual companies. Moody's *Handbook of Common Stocks,* first published in 1964, is issued quarterly. It covers over 1,000 companies. For each one it has a chart, showing the years 1953 to date, the industry group stock price trend, and the company's stock price performance. Basic financial statistics for the past decade are given. The written analysis covers the company's financial background, recent financial developments, and prospects. The Standard & Poor's compendium is called *Standard N.Y.S.E. Stock Reports.* It covers about 1,850 stocks. Full financial facts are given for each company. A chart shows the market performance of the stock, the average performance of stocks in its industry, and the performance of the stock market as a whole, in addition to showing the trading volume of the stock. Each report carries a Standard & Poor's opinion of the investment merits of each stock.

Both Standard & Poor's and Moody's publish weekly and monthly bond guides. Standard & Poor's issue a weekly *Bond Outlook,* Moody's a weekly *Bond Survey.* Each issue discusses new offerings in the corporate and municipal markets, opportunities in convertibles, changes in bond ratings, new issue ratings, bonds called for payment. Both services issue one-page summaries of individual bond situations.

The extensive nature of the many services provided for investors and for security analysts may be seen from the following list of publication services provided by Standard & Poor's.[3]

---

[3] A booklet describing these services entitled "Standard & Poor's Services and Publications Cover Every Financial Information Need" may be obtained by writing to Standard & Poor's at 345 Hudson Street, New York, N.Y. 10014. Moody's comparable services are described in a booklet entitled "How Moody's Can Help You." A copy may be obtained by writing to Moody's Investor Service, 99 Church Street, New York, N.Y. 10007.

Analysts Handbook
Bond Guide
Called Bond Record
Compmark Data Services
Convertible Bond Reports
Corporation Records
Daily Stock Price Records
Dividend Record
Outlook
Poor's Register of Corporations, Directors, and Executives
Registered Bond Interest Record
The Review of Securities Regulation
Earnings Forecaster
Fixed Income Investor
Industry Surveys
International Stock Report
Investment Advisory Survey
Municipal Bond Selector
Opportunities in Convertible Bonds
Security Dealers Directory
Statistical Service
Stock Guide
Stock Reports
Stock Summary
Transportation Service
Trendline Charts

Of particular interest are the *Analysts Handbook* and the *Earnings Forecaster*. The *Analysts Handbook* provides composite corporate per share data on a true comparison basis. It maintains the best possible continuity since 1946 for 95 industries and the S&P 400 Industrial Index, making possible a great variety of significant per share comparisons. It is available annually with monthly updatings. The *Earnings Forecaster* provides weekly new and revised earnings estimates on the 1,800 companies prepared by S&P and other leading investment organizations and brokerage firms. Continuously updated, this 40–52 page summary offers at-a-glance check of the various estimates against one another. For each company, listings include identification of source of estimates, per share earnings for the past full year, and where possible, for the next year.

The *Value Line Investment Survey* covers 1,640 stocks in 75 industries. It is essentially a reference and current valuation service. Each stock in the list is reviewed in detail once every three months. Interim reports are provided in weekly supplements on any new developments between the time of the regular quarterly reports. Each week the new edition of the *Value Line Investment Survey* covers four to six industries on a rotating basis. Each industry report contains full-page reports on individual stocks. About 125 stocks are covered every week in the order of their industries. After all 1,640 stocks have been covered in 13 weeks, the cycle starts over again.

Each week there are three or four parts to the survey. Part I is the

"Weekly Summary of Advices and Index." It provides an average of estimated yields for the ensuing 12 months; the estimated average price-earnings ratio for the period 6 months past and 6 months future; the average appreciation potentiality of all 1,640 stocks in an hypothesized economic environment three to five years ahead; a rank of industrial groups according to probable market performance over the next 12 months; a rank for each stock's safety (total risk); and the beta based on 5 years of weekly price fluctuations. Part II is the "Selection & Opinion" section. It covers topics such as "Business and the Stock Market," "Recommended Stock," "Inflation and Common Stocks," and presents computer screens for stock selection. Part III, "Reports and Ratings," provides the industry and company analyses described above.

Value Line has developed statistical techniques designed, in each stock report, to answer five questions:

1. How safe a stock is it in relation to 1,640 others?
2. How well can it be expected to perform in the market during the next 12 months compared to other stocks?
3. How attractive is it over a three- to five-year pull?
4. How much will this stock yield over the next 12 months?
5. How suitable is the stock for the individual investor in the light of his or her investment objectives?

In addition to the Investment Survey, *Value Line* also has a Special Situation Report and a Convertible Survey on Convertible bonds, preferred and warrants.

Investment Counseling Services

For the well-to-do investors who want to avoid the burdensome and often time-consuming chore of digging up facts for themselves, following industry and company trends, and judging the state of the economy and of the market, there is an easy and relatively inexpensive "out." They can use an investment counselor, or the investment counseling department of a bank, or of one of the large investment services. Under the Investment Advisers Act of 1940, independent (nonbank) investment counseling firms must be registered with the SEC. Busy professional people, active business executives who have little or no time to do the digging involved in managing their own investments, or widows or widowers who have no knowledge whatsoever of finance and investments, make up the clientele, in general, of the professional money managers.

The usual annual fee charged by an investment counselor is 0.5 percent of the value of the portfolio being managed. For a $200,000 portfolio this means an annual fee of $1,000. Most of the larger investment counseling firms will not take accounts with portfolios of less than $100,000. The largest firms in the business—Scudder, Stevens & Clark; Loomis-Sayles; Lionel D. Edie; Calvin Bullock; Stein, Row & Farnham; Van Strum & Towne; Eaton & Howard, Inverness Counsel —maintain professional staffs of security analysts and portfolio managers to assist clients. They do the investment research and make recommendations to customers. The counselors prefer to have discretionary accounts in which they have the legal powers to manage the client's funds. In almost all cases, of course, the client is informed of portfolio changes, proposed or accomplished. Many clients prefer to retain final authority for passing upon a proposed change. In some cases the investment counselors have custody of the client's securities, since this makes for more expeditious purchasing and selling; a number of clients prefer to retain possession of their own securities and turn them over to the investment counselor only to effect a transaction.

Some of the large investment counselors have their own mutual funds which they manage. Others advise corporate pension funds or college or university endowment funds. The mutual funds are for the investors whose assets are nowhere near the $100,000 minimum level. It has been estimated that the investment counselors' average client has a portfolio of about $250,000. Since investment counselors publish no records of performance, selecting a firm is usually an act of faith based on someone's recommendation or on the firm's general reputation.

Banks provide investment advisory services, sometimes on a formal, fee basis, sometimes on an informal customer-relations complimentary basis. A wealthy individual who wants investment help from the bank can usually obtain it without formally turning funds over to the bank's trust department. An investment officer in the trust department, or in the investment advisory department, if the bank has one, will serve as an investment counselor to those with portfolios of $100,000 and over. The investment officer ascertains the client's investment objectives and attempts to tailor his or her recommendations to meet the objectives. Again the account may be discretionary or nondiscretionary, custodial or the customer may retain possession of the securities. While the portfolio is reviewed regularly, the customer usually receives a quarterly report from the bank on his or her portfolio. The investment officer makes recommendations and in the case of the discretionary account arranges portfolio changes. For wealthier investors who wish to be free from money-management problems and are comfortable in conservative investment hands, this is a handy arrangement. In the discretionary account the owners do not surrender title to their own securities. The bank acts only as their agent. This is in contrast to the more formal trust arrangement.

Bank administered trusts may be either living trusts *(inter vivos)* set up during an individual's lifetime or testamentary trusts set up at death by will or other prior arrangement. There are individual trusts or common trust funds. The common trust fund, akin to a mutual fund, is gaining in popularity and is designed to appeal to smaller investors, those with from $5,000 to $75,000 to invest, but some accounts go up to $100,000 and more. You set up a trust, name the bank as trustee, and the bank, in turn, mixes or pools your funds with other small individual trust accounts for investment in a common portfolio of securities. In a common trust fund, investments are spread far more widely than would be possible in an individual trust. Also, the cost is lower.

Banks offer several types of common trust funds. If you set up the trust without specifying the type of investment you want, the bank is required by law to put you into what is called a legal investments fund. This is a conservative type, about 65 percent bonds and 35 percent stock. But if you give the bank discretion, you may be placed in one of four types of funds: the balanced fund, about 60 percent common stock, 40 percent bonds; the 100 percent common stock fund; the tax-exempt bond fund (a rapidly growing type); or finally a taxable corporate bond and preferred stock fund for income. When you establish the trust, you can name the type of fund you want. Thus banks have increasingly developed flexibility in serving investors.

Recently there has been a trend toward accommodating the small investor, both on the part of banks and of financial services. Citibank (of New York) will accept investment advisory accounts with a $10,000 value minimum. The cost of its advice is 1 percent a year on the market value of the investment, with a $250 minimum charge. The Marine Midland banks will give investment advice on accounts as low as $8,000. The fee is 0.75 a year with a $160 minimum charge. Danforth Associates, of Wellesley Hills, Massachusetts, takes clients with as little as $5,000, charging a fee of 2 percent a year on portfolios up to $25,000 in value and 0.25 percent on additional amounts over that, with a $100-a-year minimum fee.[4]

---

[4] W. Scott Bauman, "The Investment Management Organization," *Financial Analyst's Handbook*, vol. 1 (Homewood, Ill.: Dow Jones-Irwin, 1975), chap. 41.

Business Conditions and Corporate Profits

If the investor's starting point is an examination of business trends, including a forecast of the outlook for business, the economy, and corporate profits, it is not difficult to find material. Indeed, the real problem may be choosing from among the multiplicity of sources. A number of the leading banks publish monthly reports or surveys dealing with the business outlook and other topics. The First National City Bank of New York publishes a *Monthly Economic Letter.* The leading article is always on "General Business Conditions." The *Morgan Guaranty Survey* is published monthly by the Morgan Guaranty Trust Company of New York. The first article always covers "Business and Financial Conditions." The Bank of New York issues *General Business Indicators* which is a statistical tabulation of selected economic indicators. It provides the bank's forecast of prospective gross national product, disposable personal income, index of industrial production, corporate profits, and earnings of the Dow Jones Industrials, over the coming year. The Chase Manhattan Bank publishes *Business in Brief,* issued bimonthly by its Economic Research Division. The first article usually covers an analysis of the business outlook.

The 12 Federal Reserve Banks publish monthly bulletins devoted to banking, economic, and financial topics. The Federal Reserve Bank of New York, for example, publishes a *Monthly Review,* which always includes an article on "The Business Situation." The Federal Reserve Bank of Philadelphia publishes the *Business Review,* monthly. The Federal Reserve Banks of Chicago and St. Louis also issue excellent monthly reviews. In addition to its monthly review, the Federal Reserve Bank of St. Louis issues a number of other publications, monthly, including *National Economic Trends, Monetary Trends, Federal Budget Trends,* and so forth. The Board of Governors of the Federal Reserve System in Washington, D.C., publishes the *Federal Reserve Bulletin,* monthly. It contains a "National Summary of Business Conditions." This can be obtained as a separate release, monthly, as can "Money Stock Measures," a statistical release covering trends in M_1, M_2, and M_3. The Federal Reserve also publishes a *Chart Book on Business, Economic, and Financial Statistics,* monthly, as well as an annual *Historical Chart Book.*

The library of the Federal Reserve Bank of Philadelphia has issued an excellent index, *Federal Reserve Bank Reviews Selected Subjects 1950–1970.* This is kept current by a quarterly index, *The Fed in Print,* which may be obtained free of charge from the Federal Reserve Bank of Philadelphia.

The federal government provides a number of useful sources of information on developing business trends. The *Survey of Current Business* is published monthly by the U.S. Department of Commerce. It has two principal parts. The first deals with basic business trends and starts with an article on "The Business Situation" which reviews recent developments, pointing out underlying strengths or weaknesses. The second section is an elaborate compilation of basic statistical series on all phases of the economy. There is also a weekly supplement in which the indexes of business activity, prices, production, and so forth, appearing in the *Survey of Current Business* are kept up to date. The President's Council of Economic Advisors publishes the monthly *Economic Indicators* and the *Annual Economic Review,* which deal with the state of the economy and the outlook.

For economic forecasting purposes, perhaps the most useful publication of the government is *Business Conditions Digest,* issued monthly by the Bureau of the Census of the U.S. Department of Commerce. This report brings together many of the available economic indicators in convenient form for analysis and interpretation. The presentation and classification of the series follow the business indicator approach of the National Bureau of Economic Research (NBER). The classification of series and business cycle turning dates are those designated by NBER, which, in recent years, has been the leader in this field of investigation. About 90 principal indicators and over 300 components are included in the report. Among others there are the NBER leading indicators, the NBER roughly coincident indicators, the NBER lagging indicators, and series for international comparisons. The movements of the series are shown against the background of the expansions and contractions of the general business cycle so that "leads" and "lags" can be readily detected and cyclical developments spotted.

A private source provides data on the NBER indicators weekly. This is the Statistical Indicator Associates of North Egremont, Massachusetts, directed by Leonard H. Lempert. These weekly reports include both current statistics and interpretive text and forecasts. *Business Week,* in its "Business Outlook" section reviews the indicators from time to time and regularly provides an analytic review of changing business and economic developments. Published by McGraw-Hill, and written in a lively and interesting style, *Business Week,* provides coverage of major developments in many areas of business and finance. Two other journals which provide somewhat similar coverage are *Nation's Business* and *Dun's Review. Fortune* magazine has a section each month entitled "Business Roundup." This is a monthly report on the economic outlook. The Conference Board issues a monthly *Record,* a weekly *Desk Sheet of Business Indicators,* and a chart service, *Road Maps of Industry.*

The federal government's influence in shaping the American economy is inescapably a factor in investment decisions. As a result, a number of private services have been established with Washington as their base of reporting. These include, among others, "Research from Washington," a subsidiary of Smith, Barney, & Co.; "Washington Service," prepared by the Government Research Corporation, a subsidiary of E. F. Hutton & Co.; and "Washington Economist" by Bradley, Woods, & Co.

On corporate profits, overall trends can be seen in the *Quarterly Financial Report for Manufacturing Corporations,* published jointly by the Federal Trade Commission and the Securities and Exchange Commission. The purpose of this survey is to produce, each calendar quarter, an income statement and balance sheet for all manufacturing corporations, classified by both industry and asset size. Profitability is reported in two ways—"profits per dollar of sales" and "annual rate of profit on stockholders' equity at end of period." The quarterly summaries may be used to measure efficiency and appraise costs by comparing a company's operating results with the average performance of companies of similar size or in the same line of business.

Each year, in the April issue of its *Monthly Economic Letter,* the Citibank (of New York) publishes the results of its survey of the profits performance of almost 4,000 U.S. corporations, not only in manufacturing lines but also in trade, transportation, utilities, services, real estate, and banking. Profits are reported, for the two prior years, on two bases, as "percent return on net worth" and as "percent margin on sales." The detailed industry classification and breakdown permits an investor or a securities analyst to compare a given company with the reported industry average.

The outlook for corporate profits is usually tied to a forecast of business conditions. While securities analysts may occasionally undertake their own forecasts, individual investors usually are not equipped, nor do they have the time, to make independent forecasts on their own. They must rely on one or more of the estimates of the business outlook described previously. There are, of course, many sources in addition to those mentioned. Competent investors will absorb as much material as their time and energies permit. The wider their reading, the better equipped they will be to assess the outlook.

The Securities Markets

The competent investor must constantly make a judgment as to the trend and level of the market as a whole to provide the appropriate environmental setting for selection and timing of portfolio additions or deletions.

On an elementary level, one can keep abreast of the market by reading the financial section of a daily newspaper such as the *New York Times* or the *Wall Street Journal.* On a weekly basis, review of *Barron's,* Standard & Poor's, the *Outlook,* and the Sunday financial section of the *New York Times,* will provide basic data on stock market action and trends. Looking daily at the *Times* market summary story and tabulation page and at the *Wall Street Journal* "Abreast of the Market" "Heard on the Street" columns and Dow Jones index page, and weekly at *Barron's* "Study of Price Movement—Market Laboratory" page, and at the *Outlook's* "Forecast and Policy" page and at its "Indexes of the Security Markets" page, will build a continuing awareness of price trends.

On an intermediate level, fundamental and technical analysis may help to provide a perspective of where the market is and where it is likely to go. Fundamental market analysis involves the use of composite stock yields, composite price/earnings ratios, and the yield spread between stocks and bonds as market indicators. For example, the level of the market may be judged by yields on the Dow Jones Industrials. At major bull market peaks in the past, the DJI and yields on its 30 stocks were as follows:

Date	*DJI*	*Yield*
September 3, 1929	381.17	3.33%
March 10, 1937	194.40	3.76
May 29, 1946	212.50	3.23
January 4, 1960	679.06	3.07
December 13, 1961	734.91	3.03
February 9, 1966	995.15	2.92
December 3, 1968	985.21	3.22
January 11, 1973	1,051.70	3.07

It would appear that when the DJI yields approach the 3 percent level, at least in the past, major bull markets have tended to peak. The record at bear market lows is not as clear:

Date	*DJI*	*Yield*
July 8, 1932	41.22	10.40%
April 28, 1942	92.92	7.58
June 13, 1949	161.60	6.84
April 3, 1958	440.50	4.89
October 25, 1960	566.05	3.78
June 26, 1962	535.76	4.32
May 26, 1970	631.14	4.62
December 6, 1974	577.60	6.52

Figure 3–1
Dow Jones Price/Earnings Ratio

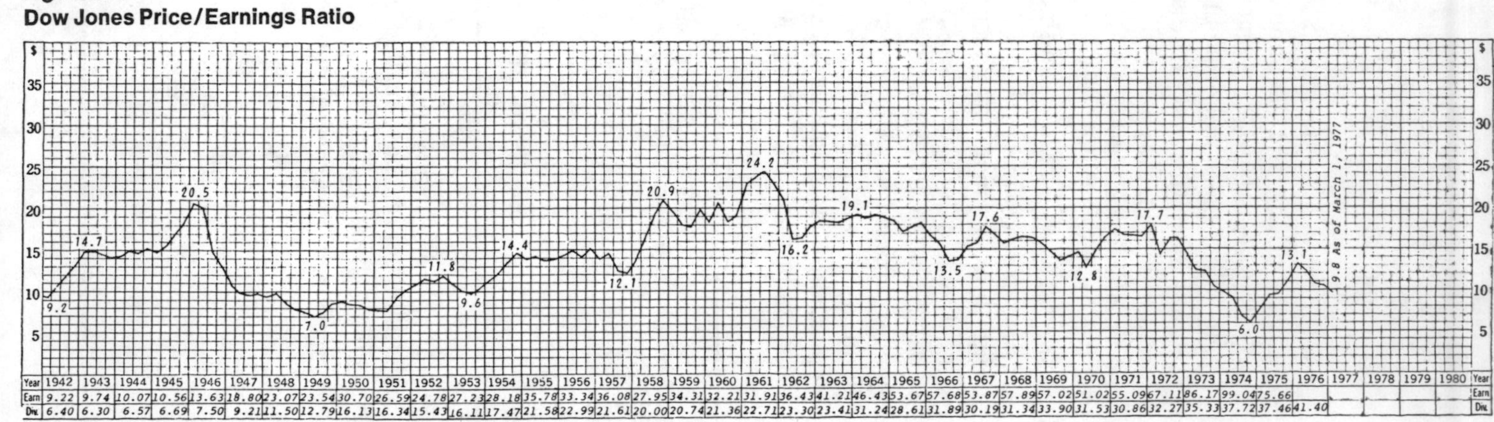

Source: M. C. Horsey & Co., "The Stock Picture," Salisbury, Maryland, 1977.

The price/earnings ratio on the DJI has often, in the past, been used to judge the level of the market. At previous bull market highs, for example, the record was as follows:

Date	*DJI*	*Earnings*	*P/E Ratio*
September 3, 1929	381.17	$19.94	19.1
March 10, 1937	194.40	11.12	17.5
May 29, 1946	212.50	10.24	20.8
January 4, 1960	679.06	33.82	20.1
December 13, 1961	734.91	31.91	23.0
February 9, 1966	995.15	53.67	18.5
December 3, 1968	985.21	57.89	17.0
January 11, 1973	1,051.70	62.80	16.7

In the past, at least, one could say that when the DJI–P/E went into or above the 17–19 average, bull markets tended to top out, but again the record at bear market lows is not consistent, the P/E ratio at selected lows ranging from 7 to 16 approximately. See Figure 3–2 and Table 3–1.

Figure 3–2
Corporate Profits and Stock Prices

Source: The Bank of New York.

Table 3–1
Selected Financial Indicators

	Index of Prices, 500 Stocks 1941-43=10	Dow-Jones Industrial Averages				# Federal Funds Rate	U.S. Treas.		Bond Buyer 20 Mun #	Moody's Corporate Bonds		#Yield on S&P 500
		Price Range	Earns.	Divs.	*P-E Ratio		#3 Mo Bills New Issues	#Long Term Bonds		Aaa#	Baa# ϕ	
		------------Per Share------------				--------------------------Percent--------------------------						
1977												
April	99.13P					4.68P	4.54	7.13P	5.[illegible]4P	8.05P	9.09P	
March	100.57					4.69	4.61	7.20	5.89	8.10	9.12	4.37
Feb.	100.96	1000-919		$10.46		4.68	4.66	7.15	5.89	8.04	9.12	4.21
Jan.	103.81					4.61	4.60	6.68	5.87	7.96	9.08	3.99
1976												
Dec.	104.66					4.65	4.35	6.39	5.94	7.98	9.12	3.93
Nov.	101.19	1005-924	$24.25	12.13	10-10	4.95	4.81	6.62	6.29	8.25	9.23	4.04
Oct.	101.89					5.03	4.93	6.65	6.30	8.32	9.29	3.85
Sept.	105.45					5.25	5.08	6.70	6.51	8.38	9.40	3.71
Aug.	103.29	1015-960	23.50	9.85	11-10	5.29	5.15	6.79	6.61	8.45	9.64	3.74
July	104.20					5.31	5.28	6.85	6.79	8.56	9.82	3.64
June	101.77					5.48	5.44	6.92	6.87	8.62	9.89	3.75
May	101.16	1011-958	25.85	10.19	11-11	5.29	5.19	6.99	6.87	8.58	9.86	3.76
April	101.93					4.82	4.88	6.73	6.60	8.40	9.94	3.66
March	101.08					4.84	5.05	6.87	6.92	8.52	10.12	3.65
Feb.	100.64	1009-859	23.12	9.23	12-10	4.77	4.85	6.92	6.94	8.55	10.24	3.67
Jan.	96.86					4.87	4.96	6.94	7.02	8.60	10.41	3.80
1975												
Dec.	88.70					5.20	5.50	7.17	7.31	8.79	10.56	4.14
Nov.	90.07	861-784	23.34	9.63	11-10	5.22	5.47	7.21	7.43	8.78	10.56	4.07
Oct.	88.57					5.82	6.08	7.29	7.39	8.86	10.62	4.22
Sept.	84.67					6.24	6.38	7.29	7.44	8.95	10.61	4.39
Aug.	85.71	882-792	18.37	9.05	12-10	6.14	6.46	7.06	7.17	8.95	10.59	4.36
July	92.49					6.10	6.16	6.89	7.07	8.84	10.55	4.02
June	92.40					5.55	5.19	6.86	6.95	8.77	10.62	4.02
May	90.10	879-743	17.04	8.97	11-7	5.22	5.31	6.99	6.97	8.90	10.69	4.08
April	84.72					5.49	5.69	7.03	6.95	8.95	10.58	4.34
March	83.78					5.54	5.54	6.73	6.74	8.67	10.48	4.42
Feb.	80.10	787-632	16.94	9.81	8-7	6.24	5.58	6.61	6.39	8.62	10.65	4.61
Jan.	72.56					7.13	6.49	6.68	6.82	8.83	10.81	5.07
1977E			$109.25									
1976	102.01	1015-859	96.72	$41.40	10-9	5.05	5.00	6.78	6.64	8.43	9.75	3.77
1975	86.16	882-632	75.66	37.46	12-8	5.82	5.82	6.98	7.05	8.83	10.61	4.31
1974	82.85	892-578	99.04	37.72	9-6	10.50	7.87	6.98	6.17	8.57	9.50	4.47
1973	107.43	1052-788	86.17	35.33	12-9	8.74	7.04	6.30	5.19	7.44	8.24	3.06
1972	109.20	1036-889	67.11	32.27	15-13	4.44	4.07	5.63	5.26	7.21	8.16	2.84
1971	98.29	951-798	55.09	30.86	17-14	4.67	4.35	5.74	5.48	7.39	8.56	3.14
1970	83.22	842-631	51.02	31.53	17-12	7.17	6.46	6.59	6.35	8.04	9.11	3.83
1969	97.84	969-770	57.02	33.90	17-14	8.22	6.68	6.10	5.77	7.03	7.81	3.24
1968	98.69	985-825	57.89	31.34	17-14	5.66	5.34	5.25	4.46	6.18	6.94	3.07
1967	91.93	943-786	53.87	30.19	18-15	4.22	4.32	4.85	4.44	5.51	6.23	3.20
1966	85.26	995-744	57.68	31.89	17-13	5.11	4.88	4.66	3.77	5.13	5.67	3.40
1965	88.17	969-841	53.67	28.61	18-16	4.07	3.95	4.21	3.54	4.49	4.87	3.00
1964	81.37	892-766	46.43	31.24	19-16	3.50	3.55	4.15	3.12	4.40	4.83	3.01
1963	69.86	767-647	41.21	23.41	19-16	3.18	3.16	4.00	3.26	4.26	4.86	3.17
1962	62.38	726-536	36.43	23.30	20-15	2.68	2.78	3.95	3.05	4.33	5.02	3.37
1961	66.27	735-610	31.91	22.71	23-19	1.96	2.38	3.90	3.42	4.35	5.08	2.98
1960	55.85	685-566	32.21	21.36	21-18	3.22	2.93	4.01	3.38	4.41	5.19	3.47
1959	57.38	679-574	34.31	20.74	20-17	3.30	3.41	4.07	3.77	4.38	5.05	3.23
1958	46.24	584-437	27.95	20.00	21-16	1.57	1.84	3.43	3.38	3.79	4.73	3.97
1957	44.38	521-420	36.08	21.61	14-12	3.11	3.27	3.47	2.97	3.89	4.71	4.55
1956	46.62	521-462	33.34	22.99	16-14	2.73	2.66	3.08	3.21	3.36	3.88	4.09
1955	40.49	488-388	35.78	21.58	14-11	1.78	1.75	2.84	2.56	3.06	3.53	4.08
1954	29.69	404-280	28.18	17.47	14-10	-	0.95	2.55	2.38	2.90	3.51	4.95
1953	24.73	294-256	27.23	16.11	11-9	-	1.93	2.94	2.54	3.20	3.74	5.80
1952	24.50	292-256	24.78	15.43	12-10	-	1.77	2.68	2.38	2.96	3.52	5.80
1951	22.34	276-239	26.59	16.34	10-9	-	1.55	2.57	2.11	2.86	3.41	6.13
1950	18.40	235-197	30.70	16.13	8-6	-	1.22	2.32	1.66	2.62	3.24	6.57
1949	15.23	201-162	23.54	12.79	9-7	-	1.10	2.31	2.07	2.66	3.42	6.59
1948	15.53	193-165	23.07	11.50	8-7	-	1.04	2.44	2.19	2.82	3.47	5.54
1947	15.17	187-163	18.80	9.21	10-9	-	0.59	2.25	2.35	2.61	3.24	4.93
1946	17.08	213-163	13.63	7.50	16-12	-	0.38	2.19	1.89	2.53	3.05	3.85
1945	15.16	196-151	10.56	6.69	19-14	-	0.38	2.37	1.42	2.62	3.29	4.17
1944	12.47	153-134	10.07	6.57	15-13	-	0.38	2.48	1.62	2.72	3.61	4.86
1943	11.50	146-119	9.74	6.30	15-12	-	0.37	2.47	1.77	2.73	3.91	4.93
1942	8.67	120-93	9.22	6.40	13-10	-	0.33	2.46	2.17	2.83	4.28	7.24
1941	9.82	134-106	11.64	7.59	12-9	-	0.10	1.95	2.24	2.77	4.33	6.82
1940	11.02	153-112	10.92	7.06	14-10	-	0.01	2.21	2.14	2.84	4.75	5.59
Source:	S&P Corp.	---------Dow Jones and Co.---------				F.R.B.	F.R.B.	F.R.B.	B.B	--Moody's--		S&P Corp.

***** - Based upon High & Low Prices.
# - Average for the period.
d - Deficit.

Source: The Bank of New York, May 1977.

This is a rudimentary approach, of course. Whether stock prices respond to or anticipate changes in earnings, in inflationary expectations, in the money supply, in consumer outlook and sentiment, in investment in capital goods, or to a combination of all or of several of those or other factors, or to none at all, is a matter of continuing debate and dispute among financial economists. For example, in a pioneering study Beryl Sprinkel found that broad changes in the money supply preceded broad changes in the direction of stock prices. He was quite specific and formulated an investment rule that, "a bear market in stock prices was predicted 15 months after each peak in monetary growth and that a bull market was predicted two months after each monetary growth trough was reached."[5]

Other observers have stressed the relationship between the trend of corporate profits and the trend of stock prices. By looking at both fundamental indicators and at the host of technical indicators, one is able to gain relative bearings in the market and thus make more intelligent judgments as to approximate values.

Industry Analysis

Generally, after examining the state of business and corporate profits and the condition of the market, investors make industry-to-industry comparisons to select those industries whose growth and profitability outlook is most favorable.

To secure data for industry studies and comparisons, the investor may either research an industry in depth, using a variety of sources, or if they have less time available and wish compact and concise information, they may turn to one of the investment services. Standard & Poor's issues an excellent series of *Industry Surveys*, covering 45 industries. In each case a *Basic Analysis* is issued, usually annually, followed by supplementary sections entitled "Current Analysis and Outlook," issued at varying intervals, usually quarterly, during the year. The *Basic Analysis* contains a wealth of data, which would require an extensive expenditure of time by individual investors if they were to attempt to gather it themselves. In the report on the container industry, for example, the *Basic Analysis* includes:

---

[5] Beryl W. Sprinkel, *Money and Stock Prices* (Homewood, Ill.: Richard D. Irwin, 1964) see also his subsequent *Money and Markets* (Homewood, Ill.: Richard D. Irwin, 1971).

The Outlook.
Paper.
Packaging.
Metal containers.
Glass containers.
Plastic packaging.
Closures.
Ecology.
Financial.
Composite industry data.
Company analysis.
Market action.
Statistical data.

Where the industry is more homogeneous, as in the case of automobiles, the content of the *Basic Analysis* will reflect more internal operational data. Thus the automobile industry survey contains:

The Outlook.
Sales and production.
Technology.
Auto parts.
Market action.
Imports-exports.
Financial.
Composite industry data.
Comparative company analysis.
Statistical data.

In most of the industry surveys, data are provided for forecasting purposes. For example, as shown in Figure 3–3 in the electronics-

Figure 3–3
Electrical Appliance Sales versus Disposable Income

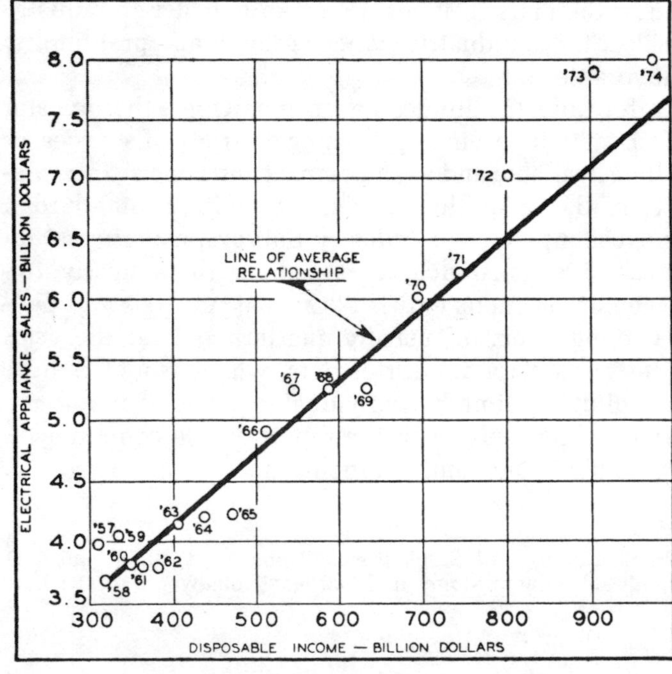

Figure 3–3 (continued)

Year	*Electric Appli-ance Sales*	*Total Retail Sales*	*Dispos-able Income*
1974	8.01	537.8	979.7
1973	7.90	503.3	903.7
1972	7.03	448.4	802.5
1971	6.22	408.9	746.4
1970	6.07	375.5	691.7
1969	5.69	357.9	634.4
1968	5.41	341.9	591.0
1967	5.25	313.8	546.3
1966	4.91	304.0	511.9
1965	4.22	284.1	473.2

Source: Department of Commerce and Standard & Poor's *Basic Analysis.*

electrical equipment *Basic Analysis,* a line of average relationship, or least squares line, has been fitted to show the relationship between electrical appliance sales production and disposable personal income, a component of gross national product. Using a GNP and DPI estimate for the ensuing five years, a forecast can be obtained for electrical appliance sales, and this in turn can be brought down to profitability to determine an earnings-per-share estimate for the forecast period.

The "Current Analysis and Outlook" updates the figures in the basic survey, provides a short-run forecast, gives brief analyses of representative companies in the industry, and provides updated data on the comparative statistical position of leading common stocks in the industry.

Forbes publishes an "Annual Report on American Industry" at the beginning of each calendar year. It covers each of the major industries and within the industry makes comparisons of companies based on two yardsticks of performance: growth (five-year compounded rate for both sales and earnings) and profitability (five-year average for return on equity, and on total capital). See Figure 3–4 for an example covering the electronics industry. Each industry reviewed is analyzed for both past and prospective performance.

For the investor who wishes to do an industry study in depth, a variety of sources are available. Various trade journals covering different industries include *Chemical Week; Drug and Cosmetic Industry; Modern Plastics; Computer Age; Pulp, Paper and Board Quarterly, Coal Mining; Mining Journal; Electrical World; Electrical Week; Electronics; Food Industries; The Timberman; Iron Age; Paper Trade Journal; Oil and Gas Journal; Petroleum Times; Ward's Auto World;*

Figure 3–4
Electronics & Electrical Equipment: Yardsticks of Management Performance

	PROFITABILITY								GROWTH			
	Return on Equity				Return on Total Capital				Sales		Earnings/Share	
Company	5-Year Average	5-Year Rank	Latest 12 Months	Debt/ Equity Ratio	Latest 12 Months	5-Year Rank	5-Year Average	Net Profit Margin	5-Year Average	5-Year Rank	5-Year Average	5-Year Rank
ELECTRONIC EQUIPMENT												
Natl Semiconductor	30.5%	1	20.0%	0.1	15.8%	1	24.2%	4.8%	51.3%	1	123.6%	1
Schlumberger	23.6	2	26.6	0.1	24.1	2	20.4	15.7	20.1	3	27.5	2
Avnet	20.5	3	21.8	0.2	16.3	5	13.8	5.6	14.9	5	14.0	8
Hewlett-Packard	18.3	4	16.0	0.0	15.4	3	18.0	8.1	21.5	2	23.3	4
Teledyne	18.2	5	30.9	0.7	16.5	11	10.6	7.6	10.2	13	26.8	3
Texas Instruments	16.6	6	15.4	0.1	14.3	4	14.6	5.6	13.0	7	19.6	5
Raytheon	15.5	7	17.4	0.2	14.9	6	13.3	3.4	9.4	15	11.7	10
Fairchild Camera	14.4	8	4.7	0.3	4.5	10	10.6	2.1	9.0	17	D-P	
RCA	14.1	9	13.3	0.9	8.5	15	8.6	3.0	7.1	20	8.9	13
Motorola	13.0	10	12.1	0.2	10.9	9	11.5	5.1	11.0	10	16.0	7
Perkin-Elmer	13.0	11	12.0	0.0	12.0	7	13.2	6.0	10.1	14	12.0	9
Tektronix	12.8	12	15.1	0.2	13.8	8	12.7	8.6	13.3	6	9.3	12
General Tel & Elec	12.6	13	13.8	1.2	6.5	19	6.1	6.6	11.4	9	4.7	15
Lear Siegler	12.1	14	17.9	0.5	11.1	14	8.6	3.9	4.6	21	0.8	18
North Amer Philips	12.0	15	14.0	0.3	8.2	13	8.7	3.2	16.8	4	11.4	11
Corning Glass Works	11.8	16	14.4	0.3	11.4	12	10.0	7.8	12.0	8	4.6	16
American Tel & Tel	10.3	17	10.9	0.9	6.1	18	6.4	11.4	10.9	11	5.5	14
Honeywell	9.4	18	9.8	0.4	6.7	17	6.7	3.8	10.4	12	4.4	17
Harris Corp	8.5	19	14.9	0.3	11.9	16	7.0	5.5	7.5	19	–0.6	20
Varian Associates	5.6	20	6.9	0.2	6.1	20	5.0	2.8	9.1	16	18.5	6
General Instrument	5.0	21	2.2	0.9	3.0	21	4.6	1.2	8.8	18	0.6	19
Bunker-Ramo	def	22	def	0.5	def	22	2.2	def	4.2	22	P-D	21
Ampex	def	23	10.4	1.5	5.7	23	def	2.6	–0.4	23	P-D	21
Medians	**12.8**		**14.0**	**0.3**	**11.1**		**10.0**	**5.1**	**10.4**		**10.4**	
ELECTRICAL EQUIPMENT												
Reliance Electric	21.7%	1	25.9%	0.5	14.9%	6	13.8%	6.2%	14.4%	5	12.6%	5
W W Grainger	20.9	2	18.1	0.0	17.8	3	18.3	6.7	18.9	2	18.2	2
AMP	20.8	3	17.2	0.2	14.3	2	18.8	8.9	16.2	4	13.7	4
Square D	20.5	4	20.6	0.2	17.3	1	18.8	8.3	13.1	7	5.7	10
Emerson Electric	19.1	5	18.9	0.2	17.4	4	17.4	7.8	14.4	6	10.0	9
UV Industries	19.1	5	21.6	0.7	11.8	11	9.3	7.2	19.7	1	22.6	1
General Electric	17.9	7	17.7	0.3	14.5	5	14.5	5.1	8.0	11	10.7	6
Fischbach & Moore	17.6	8	14.0	0.5	10.2	7	13.2	1.7	18.5	3	10.6	7
Eltra	13.4	9	13.3	0.2	11.0	8	11.6	5.0	10.6	8	10.1	8
Cutler-Hammer	12.9	10	13.4	0.4	10.3	9	10.2	4.0	9.2	9	15.2	3
McGraw-Edison	10.3	11	14.5	0.2	12.9	10	9.5	5.5	7.4	12	–0.7	12
Westinghouse Elec	8.2	12	11.3	0.3	8.6	12	6.6	3.5	8.9	10	–0.3	11
Medians	**18.5**		**17.5**	**0.3**	**13.6**		**13.5**	**5.9**	**13.8**		**10.7**	
Industry Medians	**13.4**		**14.5**	**0.3**	**11.8**		**10.6**	**5.5**	**10.9**		**10.7**	
All-Industry Medians	**12.7**		**12.9**	**0.4**	**9.8**		**9.1**	**4.6**	**11.8**		**9.4**	

P-D = Profit to deficit. D-P = Deficit to profit; not ranked. def = Deficit.
Source: *Forbes*, January 1, 1977, p. 123.

Airline Management & Marketing; Airline Newsletter; Brewers Digest; Textile World; Automotive News; Ocean Oil Weekly Report; Metals; and so on. The *Business Periodicals Index* and the *Science and Technology Index* list articles in all trade journals. In addition, each industry has one or more trade associations with specialized libraries and books, bulletins and monographs on industry developments.

The deeper investors dig into a given industry, the more likely they are to find a superabundance of information, rather than a paucity. Selecting, organizing, and analyzing the information may become a major task. The economy and usefulness of the financial services will become apparent in the course of the process.

Company Analysis

After industry analysis comes company selection within the chosen industry or industries. The most obvious source of information about a company is its own annual reports, including balance sheets and income accounts.[6] Frequently these are not as informative as they might be, and the analyst may wish to look at various reports filed with regulatory agencies.

In addition, the various investment services publish individual company reports. Standard & Poor's covers both listed and unlisted companies. An example of both sides of an S&P individual company report is shown in Figure 3–5. These reports provide, in capsule form, much of the relevant information the investor seeks. They provide data on sales, operating revenues, common share earnings, recent developments, fundamental position, dividend data, prospects, finances, capitalization, and pertinent balance sheet and income account statistics for the prior ten years. In addition, the investment service recommendation is given. The individual company reports are dated and are revised every three or four months or more often as developments require.

Extensive sources of company data and information are to be found in the registration statements, prospectuses, proxy statements, and other reports resulting from SEC, ICC, FPC, FCC, CAB, NYSE "full disclosure" philosophy. SEC filings, for example, contain much essential information that may be generally omitted from voluntary reports.

The registration statement is the basic disclosure document in connection with a public distribution of securities registered under the Securities Act. It is made up of two parts. The prospectus, the first section, is the only part which is generally distributed to the public. Part II of the registration statement contains information of a more technical nature dealing with such matters as marketing arrangements, the expenses of the distribution, relationships between the registrant and certain experts, sales of securities to special parties, recent sales of unregistered securities, a list of subsidiaries, and treatment of proceeds from stock being registered.

The Exchange Act has four types of disclosure requirements relating to registration, periodic reporting, proxy solicitation, and insider trading. Listed and OTC-registered companies are required to file cer-

---

[6] For those who are little acquainted with balance sheet, income account, and financial ratio analysis, the following are recommended: "How to Read a Financial Report," Merrill Lynch, Pierce, Fenner & Smith, New York, current; "Understanding Financial Statements," New York Stock Exchange, latest edition.

Figure 3–5
Individual Company Report

T[1]
Options on CBOE

American Tel. & Tel.

182

Stock—	Price May 18'77	*P-E Ratio	Dividend	Yield
COMMON	65	10	[2]$4.20	[2]6.5%
$4 CONV. PREFERRED	68		4.00	5.9

SUMMARY: AT&T is dominant in communications, not only through its telephone subsidiaries but also through Western Electric and Bell Telephone Laboratories. The Justice Department filed an antitrust suit in 1974 charging AT&T with monopolizing the market for telecommunications services and equipment, and seeking the break up of the company. The quality of the company's earnings is high owing to the use of conservative accounting; nevertheless, continuing rate relief will be needed to maintain long-term share earnings progress.

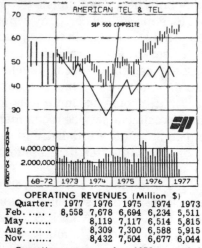

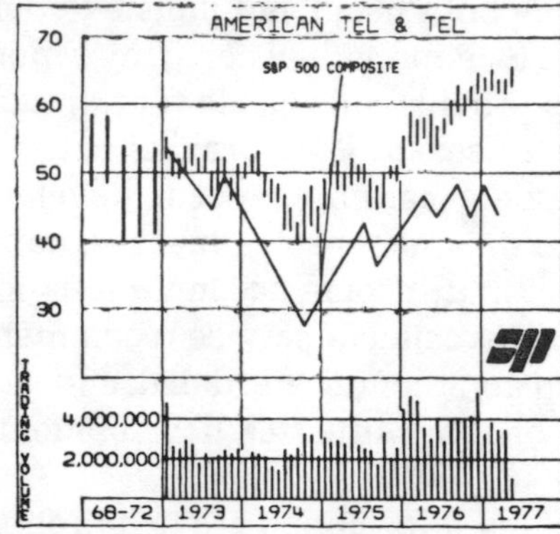

OPERATING REVENUES (Million $)

Quarter:	1977	1976	1975	1974	1973
Feb.	8,558	7,678	6,694	6,234	5,511
May		8,119	7,117	6,514	5,815
Aug.		8,309	7,300	6,588	5,915
Nov.		8,432	7,504	6,677	6,044

Operating revenues for 1976 exceeded those of the year before by 13%, reflecting rate increases and gains of 7.9% for toll call volume and 3.9% for phones in service. The operating ratio declined to 82.1%, from 82.3%, and the gain in operating income was extended to 15%. After 9.9% larger other income and only 4.6% greater interest deductions, net income moved ahead 22%. Earnings equaled $6.05 a share ($0.53 subject to possible refund) on 4.8% more shares, compared with $5.13 ($0.20). Western Electric accounted for $0.37 of share earnings versus $0.19, and interest charged to construction (ICC) $0.36 against $0.42.

For the three months ended March 31, 1977, revenues rose about 11%, year to year. Net income was up 26%. and share earnings amounted to $1.70. against $1.39.

COMMON SHARE EARNINGS ($)

Quarter:	1977	1976	1975	1974	1973
Feb.	1.55	1.33	[3]1.13	[3]1.26	1.16
May		1.51	[3]1.32	[3]1.39	1.28
Aug.		1.60	[3]1.33	[3]1.31	1.28
Nov.		1.61	1.30	[3]1.32	1.27

PROSPECTS

Despite rising costs, including wages, share earnings for 1977 are projected at about $6.55, up from 1976's $6.05, aided by moderate economic growth, rate increases, and anticipated better comparisons for Western Electric. The dividend was raised to $1.05 quarterly, from $0.95, with the April 1, 1977 payment.

Long-term prospects point to continued growth in operations, reflecting expanding telephone usage, new services and instrument additions. Productivity should continue to benefit from the introduction of new technology. Electronic switching systems (ESS) provide faster call processing, increased reliability and reduced maintenance. By 1981 25%-30% of phones are to be ESS served and by the mid-1980s 50%, compared with 19% at the beginning of 1977.

RECENT DEVELOPMENTS

State-level rate increases granted in 1977 through late April amounted to $166 million, with pending requests totaling about $1.5 billion. Carry-over rate increases from previous years to be booked in 1977 were estimated at $512 million.

The FCC in February, 1977 concluded that AT&T's interstate phone rates are reasonable, and also decided not to take action on the question of AT&T's divesting itself of Western Electric. However, the FCC did say that telephone company procurement processes needed greater autonomy from Western Electric.

DIVIDEND DATA

A dividend reinvestment plan is available. Payments in the past 12 months:

Amt of Divd $	Date Decl	Ex divd Date	Stock of Record	Payment Date
0.95...	May 19	May 24	May 28	Jul. 1'76
0.95...	Aug. 18	Aug. 25	Aug. 31	Oct. 1'76
0.95...	Nov. 17	Nov. 23	Nov. 30	Jan. 3'77
1.05...	Feb. 16	Feb. 22	Feb. 28	Apr. 1'77

[1]Listed N.Y.S.E.; com. also listed Boston, Midwest, Pacific & Philadelphia S.Es. & traded Cincinnati S.E.; pfd. also listed Philadelphia S.E. [2]Indicated rate. [3]Restated to reflect revised depr. rates. *Based on latest 12 mos. earns.

STANDARD N.Y.S.E. STOCK REPORTS STANDARD & POOR'S CORP.

Published at Ephrata, Pa. Editorial & Executive Offices, 345 Hudson St., New York, N.Y. 10014

Vol. 44, No. 100 Tuesday, May 24, 1977 Sec. 6

Figure 3–5 (continued)

[1]INCOME STATISTICS (Million $) AND PER SHARE ($) DATA

Year Ended Dec. 31	Revenues Local	Revenues Toll	[3]Gross	% of Gr. Revs. Depr. & Maint.	% of Gr. Revs. Oper. Taxes	[2]Oper. Ratio	[7]Fxd. Chgs. & Pfd. Divs. Tms. Earns.	[8]Net Inc.	Common Share ($) Data [4][9]Earns.	Divs Paid	Price Range	Earns Ratios HI LO
1977--	----	----	----	--	--	--	-			2.00	65⅛ 61[illegible]	
1976--	15,609.0	16,065.5	32,815.6	33.9	18.0	82.1	2.41	3,829.2	6.05	3.70	64¾-50⅞	11 8
1975--	14,027.8	13,925.2	28,957.2	34.6	17.5	82.3	2.18	3,147.7	5.13	3.40	52 -44¾	10- 9
1974--	12,812.8	12,460.9	26,174.4	34.6	18.2	82.1	2.31	3,169.9	5.27	3.16	53 -39⅝	10- 8
1973--	11,418.5	11,278.5	23,527.3	34.7	18.5	82.2	2.47	2,946.7	4.98	2.80	55 45⅜	11 9
1972--	10,362.9	9,771.4	20,904.1	35.1	18.2	82.9	2.50	2,532.1	4.34	2.65	53½ 41⅛	12 9
1971--	9,135.5	8,632.8	18,442.1	35.5	18.0	83.4	2.66	2,202.0	3.92	2.60	53⅛ 40¾	14 10
1970--	8,456.0	7,874.1	16,954.9	34.8	19.3	83.4	3.25	2,192.2	3.99	2.60	53⅛ 40⅜	14 10
1969--	7,774.4	7,297.8	15,683.8	33.5	22.3	83.6	4.70	2,198.7	4.00	2.40	58⅛ -48⅛	15-12
1968--	7,184.1	6,341.2	14,100.0	32.7	23.4	83.3	5.34	2,051.8	3.75	2.40	58⅜ -48	16 13
1967--	6,737.7	5,737.9	13,009.2	32.5	22.1	82.2	5.95	2,049.4	3.79	2.20	62¾ 49¼	17 13

[1]PERTINENT BALANCE SHEET STATISTICS (Million $)

Dec. 31	Gross Prop.	Capital Expend.	%Depr. of Gross Prop.	[6]%Earn. on Net Prop.	[5]Long Term Debt	% Long Term Debt of Net Prop.	% Long Term Debt of Gross Rev.	% Long Term Debt of Invest. Cap	Total Invest. Cap	[6][7]%Earn on Inv. Cap.	Net Inc. per Tel.	($) Book Val. Com. Sh.
1976--	94,167	9,747	19.4	7.8	32,525	42.8	99.1	41.3	78,684	8.0	31.11	69.81
1975--	87,621	9,329	19.6	7.3	31,793	45.1	109.8	43.5	73,172	7.5	26.57	64.46
1974--	81,146	10,074	20.0	7.2	32,308	49.8	123.4	46.4	69,575	7.6	27.69	59.74
1973--	74,005	9,322	20.9	7.1	28,371	48.4	120.6	45.2	62,748	7.6	26.71	55.08
1972--	67,082	8,306	21.6	6.8	26,020	49.5	124.5	45.7	56,969	7.2	24.05	50.95
1971--	60,568	7,564	22.1	6.5	22,828	48.4	123.8	44.7	51,112	7.0	21.96	47.36
1970--	54,813	7,159	22.4	6.6	20,454	48.1	120.6	44.2	46,286	7.0	22.70	45.53
1969--	49,244	5,731	22.8	6.8	15,868	41.7	101.2	38.9	40,792	7.1	23.72	43.96
1968--	44,975	4,742	22.7	6.8	13,430	38.8	95.2	36.0	37,366	7.0	23.31	42.24
1967--	41,476	4,310	22.1	7.2	11,901	36.8	91.5	34.1	34,905	7.3	24.46	40.63

[1]Data for 1973 & thereafter as originally reported; data for each yr. prior to 1973 as taken from subsequent yr.'s Annual Report. [2]After depr. & taxes. [3]Aft. deduct. uncollectible revs. [4]Based on avge. shs. [5]Incl. interim debt to be refinanced prior to 1975. [6]Based on bk. value, may differ from return on rate base. [7]Fixed chgs. only prior to 1971; aft. 1969 reflects change in FPC method of accounting for allowance for funds used during construction. [8]Bef. spec. cr. of $0.08 a sh. in 1973. [9]As restated to reflect 1975 elimination of provisions for certain contingencies sh. earns. were $5.28.

Fundamental Position

A holding company, American Telephone & Telegraph, through its telephone subsidiaries comprising the Bell System, controlled 123.1 million phones at year-end 1976, about 80% of the U. S. total. Noncontrolling interests are held in other telephone operating companies. The parent directly operates long-distance lines connecting regional units and independent systems.

Of 1976 revenues, toll accounted for 51% and local 49%. Telephones in service rose 3.9% in 1976, versus 3.5% in 1975 and 3.7% in 1974; toll calls were up 7.9% in 1976, 5.2% in 1975 and 7.5% in 1974.

Equipment is purchased largely from 100%-owned Western Electric Co., an important contributor to earnings. Research is done for AT&T and Western Electric on a non-profit basis by Bell Telephone Laboratories.

Auxiliary services of AT&T include private line telephone services, and transmission of data and radio and TV programs. Overseas service to over 235 countries is provided through cable, radio, and satellite circuits.

Rapid depreciation is used for tax purposes with normalization. Savings from investment tax credits are amortized.

In November, 1974 the Justice Department filed an antitrust suit charging AT&T with monopolizing the market for telecommunications services and equipment through the use of illegal methods against competitors, mainly in the area of business services. The suit sought divestiture of Western Electric and its division into two or more companies, and the divestiture of AT&T's Long Lines Department or the sale of some or all of the 23 local telephone companies served by Long Lines. Legal proceedings may continue for many years.

Dividends paid in each year since 1885, averaged 61% of earnings in 1972-76.

Employees: 929,000. Stockholders: 2,903,-000.

Finances

Capital spending for 1977 is estimated at $11.2-$11.4 billion. New money financing in 1977 is estimated at about $2.8 billion, of which $1.9 billion is to be raised through the sale of debt and the balance through the sale of common stock via dividend reinvestment and employee purchase plans.

At 1976 year-end common equity per share was $55.08 and the 1976 return thereon 10.8%. For 1976 the Federal income tax rate equaled 40.8%, and construction credits 6% of common earnings.

CAPITALIZATION

LONG TERM DEBT: $32,034,229,000.

MINORITY INTEREST: $904,092,000.

$4 CUM. CONV. PREFERRED STOCK: 24,-627,000 shs. ($1 par; $50 stated value); red. at $50; conv. into approx. 1.05 com.

$77.50 PREFERRED STOCK: 625,000 shs. ($1 par; $1,000 stated value). Privately held.

$3.74 CUM. PREFERRED STOCK: 10,000,000 shs. ($1 par; $50 stated value).

$3.64 CUM. PREFERRED STOCK: 10,000,-000 shs. ($1 par; $50 stated value).

COMMON STOCK: 610,258,709 shs. ($16 2/3 par).

Incorporated in N.Y. in 1885. **Office**—195 Broadway, NYC 10007. **Tel**—(212) 393-9800. **Chrmn & Chief Exec Officer**—J. D. deButts. **Pres**—C. L. Brown. **Secy**—F. A. Hutson, Jr. **VP-Treas**—W. G. Burns. **Dirs**—W. M. Batten, C. L. Brown, E. W. Carter, W. S. Cashel, Jr., C. B. Cleary, A. K. Davis, J. D. deButts, W. M. Ellinghaus, P. E. Haas, E. B. Hanify, W. A. Hewitt, J. A. Holland, B. K. Johnson, D. S. MacNaughton, W. J. McGill, J. I. Miller, W. B. Murphy, E. B. Speer, R. Warner, Jr. **Transfer Offices**—Company's offices: 180 Fulton St., NYC; New England Tel. & Tel. Co., Boston; Illinois Bell Telephone Co., Chicago; Pacific Tel. & Tel., San Francisco. **Registrars**—Bankers Trust Co., NYC; First National Bank, Boston; First National Bank, Chicago; Wells Fargo Bank, San Francisco.

N.J.DeV

Source: Standard & Poor's *Standard N.Y.S.E. Stock Reports,* June 11, 1976.

tain periodic reports. The most important of these reports are Forms 8–K, 10–K, and 10–Q, of which 10–K is the most useful.

Form 10–K is an annual report which is due 90 days after the end of each fiscal year. The SEC's Regulation S–X governs the form and content of most of the financial statements, including 10–K, required to be filed with the commission. The Form 10–K report contains certified financial statements, including a balance sheet, a profit and loss statement for the fiscal year covered by the report, an analysis of surplus and supporting schedules. A new and tougher set of disclosure requirements were stipulated for all 10–K filings on or after December 31, 1970. The SEC ordered companies to break down both sales and earnings for each major line of business. Under the new rules, however, a company with sales greater than $50 million does not have to carry an individual breakdown unless a product line contributes 10 percent or more to total volume or pretax profits. For smaller companies, the disclosure point is 15 percent. While companies must break out such product line data on their annual 10–K reports to the SEC, they need not disclose it in the annual report to the shareholder, though more companies are now beginning to do so. Also according to this new ruling on 10–K content, companies are required to reveal the dollar amount spent on R&D in the preceding year. Again it need not be revealed to the stockholders unless it is "material." Also where it is "material and applicable" additional information must be disclosed on the 10–K, such as dollar amount of order backlogs; availability of essential raw materials; competitive conditions in the industry; and financial statements of unconsolidated majority-owned subsidiaries.

In 1973, the SEC ruled that companies must disclose in the 10–K, any leasing and rental commitments and their dollar impact on both present and future earnings. They must also explain any differences between the effective tax rates that they report to shareholders and the statutory corporate income tax rate. They must also spell out in the footnotes to the 10–K statements any compensating balance arrangements they have with banks and other lenders.

But not all that is now found in a 10–K finds its way into the company's annual report to its shareholders. Thus the careful investor must work with the 10–K and not with the annual report.

Because of microfiche, the 10–K enjoys widening circulation. Under a contract with the SEC, Disclosure of Bethesda, Maryland, microfilms all the basic reporting documents a corporation must submit to the commission. Depending on the company, this can run to 11 documents a year or more; counting the 10–K, the stockholder's annual, proxies, quarterly reports (the official version is the 10–Q), any registration statements or prospectuses, and the 8 K form. Large public libraries, larger financial houses, and leading business school libraries subscribe to and make available all or part of the Disclosure microfiche service. It is a useful tool for the intelligent investor.

Forms, publications, and reports may be consulted at the commission's main and regional offces.[7] All officially filed forms may be consulted and photocopied. In similar fashion, official filings of certain types of companies may be consulted at the offices of the Interstate Commerce Commission (railroads and trucking companies). Federal Communications Commission (telephone and broadcasting companies), Federal Power Commission (electric and gas utilities), Comptroller of the Currency, and Federal Deposit Insurance Corporation (commercial banks). A vast array of data on individual companies can be found in official filings with governmental agencies. Increasingly these data are being made available to the public in accordance with the SEC's "full disclosure" concept. They are, of course, of great value to the competent investor.

SUGGESTED READINGS

Baker Library Mini-List No. 3 *Basic Investment Sources.* Compiled by Lorna M. Daniells, Reference Dept. Revised July 1976. Harvard Business School.

Merrill Lynch, Pierce, Fenner, and Smith *How To Read a Financial Report.* Latest edition. A free copy can be obtained by writing to this firm at One Liberty Plaza, New York, N.Y. 10006.

Woy, James *Investment Methods: A Bibliographic Guide.* Ann Arbor, Michigan: R. R. Bowker Co., 1973.

---

[7] Regional offices (and branches of regional offices) are maintained in New York City, Boston, Atlanta (Miami), Chicago (Cleveland, Detroit, St. Paul, St. Louis), Fort Worth (Houston), Denver (Salt Lake City), San Francisco (Los Angeles), Seattle, and Arlington, Virginia.

Part Two
Security Analysis

No one can argue with the old adage: buy cheap and sell dear. But everyone seems to argue over the meaning of *cheap* and *dear* when discussing stocks and bonds. Each trading day, many people want to buy the same securities others want to sell. Clearly, there are some significant differences of opinion about the meaning of security *values*.

Part Two of this book offers methods of evaluating stocks and bonds. It begins with a chapter on financial statements, stressing the need for a skeptical attitude toward income statements and balance sheets. Frequently, the appearance of profitability and high net worth are quite different from the reality.

Common stock evaluation, the next topic, is shown to revolve around a two-part question: What is the potential growth of earnings and dividends of a company whose stock is being analyzed? What is a reasonable price to pay for that potential? Chapter 5 deals with the growth potential of all corporations combined, and with various methods of determining the appropriate price to pay for growth—both in terms of stocks in the aggregate and in terms of individual stocks. Chapter 6 considers some of the problems and techniques involved in estimating the growth potential of individual companies and industries.

The approach we recommend proceeds always from the general to the specific, and from the retrospective to the prospective. First, one must understand total economic activity and overall market values. Next, the role of different industries within the economy and the marketplace should be examined. Finally, attention should focus on the position of a company within its industry. In each of these steps, we believe in emphasizing an understanding of the factors responsible for the historical record. By considering possible *changes* in these factors, one finds a basis for estimating future developments.

While common stock evaluation tends to focus on corporate growth prospects, bond evaluation is more defensive. Bond investors are usually much more concerned with the possibility of loss than with the opportunity for gain. Consequently, the methods of appraising bonds are different from the methods of appraising stocks as will be described in chapter 7.

Some investors think they can "have their cake and eat it too." They are particularly attracted to convertible securities, options, and so-called special situations. Chapter 8 highlights the pitfalls which may be in the path of investors who believe that rewards can be gained in such securities without offsetting risks.

Although specific analytical procedures are presented in the chapters of Part Two, including a checklist of financial ratios in chapter 9, it would be a serious error for the reader to come away with the impression that the process of security analysis is somewhat analogous to baking a cake. One cannot simply mix together a number of statistical ingredients in accordance with a fixed formula and produce an acceptable result. An effective analyst must combine a firm grasp of technical skills with a large element of imagination, creativity, and intuition. Without a spark of ingenuity, all the *number crunching* in the world will be of little help.

4

Deficiencies of Financial Statements

We can easily represent things as we wish them to be.

Aesop

A company's financial statements provide valuable information about the level and trend of its earning power and debt repayment ability. But financial statements leave much to be desired.

Many years ago, investors had to guard against the possibility that corporate financial statements might be fraudulent. Today, however, regulations of the Securities and Exchange Commission (SEC), the American Institute of Certified Public Accountants (AICPA), and the Financial Accounting Standards Board (FASB) have all but eliminated this problem except in the case of small, closely owned corporations. Nevertheless, investors cannot accept at face value the figures designated by a company as net income or net worth.

A company's financial statements may be given a *clean opinion* by its independent auditors, certifying that:

a. Nothing precluded the application of reasonable auditing procedures.

b. The accounts are a fair and adequate representation of the company's financial position and of the results of its operations, conforming to *generally accepted accounting principles* (GAAP).

c. No substantive uncertainties exist which were not provided for in the accounts.

Unfortunately, the comfort investors can derive from such a clean opinion is diluted by the fact that *generally accepted accounting principles* are neither unambiguous nor uniformly interpreted and applied. The purpose of this chapter, therefore, is to alert investors to the need for some healthy skepticism when they read a company's reports to its shareholders.

THE INCOME STATEMENT

For purposes of investment analysis, it is convenient to think of the income statement in the following format:

	Sales		xxx
Minus:	Cost of Goods Sold	xxx	
	Selling and Administrative Expenses	xxx	
	Depreciation and Depletion*	+xxx	
			−xxx
Equals:	Net Operating Income		xxx
Plus:	Nonoperating Income		+xxx
			xxx
Minus:	Nonoperating Expenses	xxx	
	Interest on Loans	+xxx	
			−xxx
Equals:	Net Income before Taxes		xxx
Minus:	Federal and State Income Taxes		−xxx
Equals:	Net Income		xxx
Minus:	Dividends on Preferred Stock		−xxx
Equals:	Net Income on Common Stock Equity		xxx
Minus:	Dividends on Common Stock		−xxx
Equals:	Net Income Transferred to Surplus or Retained Earnings		xxx

* In many income statements, depreciation is not shown separately in the body of the report, but is allocated to Cost of Goods Sold ("product costs") and Other Expenses ("period costs"). In such reports, depreciation will be given either in a footnote or in the Statement of Changes in Financial Position.

Problems of interpretation are involved in almost every item of this sample income statement. Let us examine the more important ones.

When Is a Sale a Sale?

A noted authority on accounting theory has stated that revenue should be recognized only when it is *captured, measurable,* and *earned.* Revenue is said to be *captured* when a company is reasonably certain that it will be paid by its customers. It is *measurable* if the medium of payment can be valued without serious difficulty. And it is *earned* when no significant activities remain to be performed for the customer. These innocent-sounding phrases can create problems, however, as has been illustrated dramatically in the case of land development companies, which sell parcels of land to buyers who pay in periodic installments over a period of many years, or in the case of producers of expensive equipment, who often *lease* their products to customers rather than sell them outright. After how many payments can it be assumed that a customer has a sufficient stake to be likely to continue his payments? What allowance should be made for future costs in connection with service contracts and warranties?

Many products have a very long production period—ships, planes, buildings, process-control systems, and so on. Some companies are conservative and refrain from recording revenues on their income statement until an order has been completed and delivered. Other companies, however, record revenues on a *percentage of completion* basis. That is, as each critical phase of the production process is completed, a percentage of the final value of the product is recorded as a sale. But how are these critical phases to be determined objectively?

Accounting guidelines have been issued on minimally acceptable answers to these and other questions, but some companies choose a more conservative accounting policy than suggested by the guidelines while others follow only the minimally acceptable standards. Investors may be annoyed at the lack of uniformity, but it is a fact of life. Those who recognize this fact of life should be on notice to make at least qualitative, if not quantitative, adjustments to net income when evaluating, say, two companies, one of which follows very conservative practices in recording revenues and one of which typically opts for the most liberal treatment available under GAAP.

Cost of Goods Sold

Accountants calculate cost of goods sold in an indirect manner. At the beginning of an accounting period, the value of the firm's inventories on hand is ascertained. The sum of this value plus the value of goods subsequently acquired for sale equals the cost of all goods *available* for sale during the period. By subtracting from this sum the value of inventories on hand at the *end* of the period, a determination is made of the cost of what was actually sold. For wholesale and retail firms, this is simply the value of merchandise which they bought from others. For manufacturing firms, cost of goods sold includes not only merchandise—that is, raw material—costs, but also wage and other costs directly associated with the manufacturing process (for example, depreciation of owned plants and rents on leased plants).

Inventory Accounting. If prices were unchanging, the method of determining cost of goods sold would involve no problems. It would merely be a matter of counting the *number of units* in inventory at the start of the period, adding the number purchased or produced during the period, and subtracting the number on hand at the end of the period. But the fact is that prices do change. And this means that the number of units is only one variable in determining cost. To illustrate, suppose that a retailing firm begins the year with no inventory, and during the year buys three lots of 1,000 units of an item at successive prices of $15, $16, and $17 per unit. Its purchases, then, will be:

1,000 units at $15 =	$15,000
1,000 units at $16 =	16,000
1,000 units at $17 =	17,000
Total purchases	$48,000

Assume now that during this same year the firm sold 2,500 of the 3,000 units purchased. This being the case, it will end the year with 500 units of inventory. A key question is how to value these 500 units. The traditional rule is "lower of cost or market," which usually means cost in a period of rising prices. But what is the "cost" of the 500 units on the shelves?

On the one hand, the firm can assume that units were sold in the same order as they were purchased. This is the so-called first-in-first-out method of inventory accounting, referred to in brief as Fifo. Using Fifo accounting, final inventory will have a unit cost equal to the most recent price—$17—and will be worth $8,500. On the other hand, it can be argued that when prices are trending up (or down), Fifo does not properly match current costs with current selling prices. Those holding this view prefer so-called Lifo (last-in-first-out) accounting, whereby the most recent purchase costs are charged against sales before earlier costs. Under this method, the unit cost of the final inventory in our example would be the earliest price—$15—and the total inventory value would be $7,500.

Thus, both accepted accounting procedures produce different inventory "costs"—$8,500 and $7,500. When final inventory is subtracted from the $48,000 of purchases, cost of goods sold becomes either $39,500 or $40,500. But the value of *sales* during the period was what it was, regardless of the method of inventory accounting. Therefore, the *gross profit* on these sales will be highest under Fifo accounting (sales minus $39,500), and lowest under Lifo accounting (sales minus $40,500). This occurs during a period of rising prices. During a period of falling prices, Fifo would produce the lowest profits and Lifo the highest.

In other words, Fifo accounting causes reported profits to move in the direction of price changes as compared with Lifo accounting. Stated another way, Fifo accounting incorporates inventory profits and losses while Lifo accounting does not.

During the highly inflationary environment of recent years, many companies switched from Fifo to Lifo in order to avoid having to pay income taxes on inventory profits. Unfortunately, the tax savings achieved by switches to Lifo accounting had an offsetting cost to investors in terms of their ability to understand the financial statements produced. In the first place, Lifo makes the inventory figures shown on the balance sheet almost meaningless during a period of inflation. In our example, if inventory remained stable at 500 units for many years, it would always be carried on the balance sheet at $7,500, even though its market price might have risen to $25 or $30 per unit.

Second, Lifo provides management with a tool for manipulating its earnings reports. If, during an inflationary period, the results of operations are not as good as management would like to present to the shareholders, an improvement can be made simply by not replacing inventory, thereby allowing the level of (low-cost) inventory to run down. Since the current selling prices are much higher than the original carrying cost of inventories which are not replaced, inventory profits are realized at the sole discretion of management. Investors should be suspicious, therefore, if the value of Lifo inventory shown on a company's balance sheet declines during a period of rising prices. They should wonder whether management had a good business reason for letting inventory run down, or whether an attempt is being made to put a better face on earnings than is really warranted.

Pension Costs. A company's financial obligations under its pension plans can be divided into two major segments. One part, the *past service liability,* stems from the fact that when a company adopts a pension plan it has a large number of old hands among its employees. Thus, if a worker with, say, 25 years of service is 50 years old when the plan is adopted, the company will have to begin paying him a pension in 15 years. But the amount of his pension will be based on as much as 40 years of service. Therefore, the company starts right out with a *past service liability* to which is added the *current service liability* for service rendered after the adoption of the plan. Past service liabilities are also incurred when benefits under an existing plan are improved.

There are various legal, tax, and personnel relations reasons for putting money aside in advance to provide for these liabilities, usually with a commercial bank or life insurance company. This is known as *funding*. But the rate at which pension liabilities are funded, and reflected in current net income, is a matter of managerial discretion within rather broad guidelines. Given this range of discretion, some companies have manipulated their pension charges in such a way as artificially to smooth reported earnings by increasing charges in good years and reducing them in poor years.

Depreciation

When a company acquires a plant or machinery, or other fixed asset, it obviously expects to use the asset for many years. Consequently, it would not be appropriate to charge the full cost of the asset against the income of the year in which it was acquired. Instead, the asset is recorded on the balance sheet at cost (which is what is meant by *capitalizing an expense*), and each year thereafter, for the duration of the asset's estimated life, a portion of the cost is charged against income. At the same time, the balance sheet value of the asset is lowered by the amount of the depreciation charge.

One problem created for investors in this context results from the fact that management has considerable leeway in the rate at which it depreciates assets. There are many acceptable accounting techniques, and the Internal Revenue Service sanctions several of them. For example, under *straight-line* depreciation the charge-off occurs in equal annual installments. But under other methods, a greater proportion of an asset's cost is charged off in the earlier years of its life, the specific proportion varying with the method. Thus, different companies may depreciate similar assets at very different rates, with resulting differences in reported earnings.

Expensing versus Capitalizing. Another aspect of intercompany differences in depreciation policies concerns *intermediate-term expenses*. Some items purchased by a company are so obviously short lived that they are almost invariably charged against income during the year in which they are acquired. Examples of such items are pencils, pads, drill bits, light bulbs, and so forth. Other items are so obviously long lived that they are capitalized (set up on the balance sheet as assets) and charged off gradually—for example, buildings, lathes, and office furniture. But many companies incur expenses which cannot be clearly labeled as short or long term in nature. Some of these companies follow a policy of *expensing* such items immediately, while others capitalize them and charge them off over several years.

Examples of intermediate-term expenses are numerous. Automobile companies, for example, spend huge sums for dies when they make basic style changes in their cars. These dies are usually used on a few years' models thereafter, but it is not too long before a major restyling is underway again. Should these dies be expensed or capitalized? Oil companies are constantly exploring for new wells. Should the drilling expenses of each year be attributed to that year's operations, or should such expenses be considered in the nature of long-term capital outlays? Should a distinction be made between expenses incurred in actually bringing in wells versus drilling dry holes? Similar questions may be raised with regard to the initial marketing expenses of introducing a new product, to interest charges paid during the construction phase of a new plant, and to the costs of producing a motion picture which, if successful, will be rerun periodically or sold to television. Should these costs be charged to income as incurred or spread over a period of several years?

There are no right or wrong answers to these questions. They are largely matters of managerial discretion. Although the FASB has been moving in the direction of requiring expensing in the year incurred, management has sufficient discretion to create a problem for investors who try to compare the level and trends of profitability among companies. A clue is present that important expense items are being capitalized, rather than charged against income as incurred, if there are unusual increases in the item labeled *deferred charges* in the *other assets* section of the balance sheet. A deferred charge is a corporate outlay which has not yet been charged against net income.

Price-Level Accounting. In addition to posing an analytical problem because of differences in accounting treatment, depreciation also causes a problem because of one outstanding similarity of treatment. Regardless of the rate of depreciation, accepted accounting practice and tax regulations allow only the original cost of an asset to be written off during its useful life. The reason this is significant to investors is that there is a second function of depreciation. The first function, as we have seen, is to allocate the cost of capital assets over their useful lives. But a second, indirect, function is to provide a fund for the replacement of the assets after they have worn out, either physically or technologically. Of course, depreciation per se does not provide a company with cash. It is an expense. Cash is generated primarily by making sales. But by deducting depreciation from sales revenues in computing net income, the company withholds cash which might otherwise be paid out in the form of higher wages, dividends, and taxes.

The function of depreciation as an (indirect) source of funds for asset replacement creates problems for investors during inflationary periods. For having charged off the original cost of assets, companies find that their recorded "profit" is not adequate to replace worn out facilities and they have to cut dividend payments to provide the replacement funds.

To overcome the apparent exaggeration of reported profits under *original cost accounting* during periods of inflation, there has been advocated a new system of accounting. The essence of the new system is (*a*) to record tangible assets on the balance sheet at current rather than historical values and (*b*) to charge income with cost of goods sold and depreciation on the basis of current replacement values of inventories, plant, and equipment. However, serious controversies surround such proposals and the problem of how best to determine profits during inflation remains unresolved.

Extraordinary Items

One of the main reasons for studying corporate income statements in investment analysis is to estimate and forecast the *normal* earning power of the companies being studied, as to both level and trend. To the extent that reported net income reflects revenues and charges attributable to transactions which are not part of a company's everyday operations, normal earning power may be obscured. Therefore, it has been customary for investors to disregard items which are labeled *extraordinary* or *nonrecurring*. However, four observations suggest that it is not necessarily wise to ignore these items:

1. With the trend toward corporate diversification, it is quite difficult to distinguish between a company's ordinary versus extraordinary activities.

2. Accounting principles give management a good deal of discretion in deciding which items are extraordinary, although the range of discretion has been steadily narrowing. Being only human, there is a tendency for management to treat unusual *expense* items as extraordinary more readily than unusual *income* items.

3. There are so many varieties of unusual items that one may occur one year, another a second year, and another a third year. While their timing and magnitude cannot be predicted, they are likely to occur and reoccur.

4. It is quite common for a new management, either after a merger or takeover of a company, or after the board of directors ousts the existing management, to make huge *extraordinary* write-offs of unproductive assets or unsuccessful projects.

Having made these observations, many knowledgeable investors do not simply ignore extraordinary items. These investors agree that straightforward inclusion of such items may be a distorting factor because they may be very large in one year and very small in the next. But they agree that inclusion of the extraordinary items on some sort of smoothed basis, such as a three-year or five-year moving average, may present a more realistic picture of the results of corporate activities than would be presented by pretending that they never occurred.

Income Tax Questions

A simple test can be very rewarding in investment analysis, and indeed is now required in annual reports. It is to compare reported net income with the reported income tax. Since most publicly owned corporations are subject to a 48 percent tax on regular income, their reported net income and income tax should be roughly equal in amount. If they are not, an explanation will be given in a footnote to the income statement and the footnote should be read carefully. Among the reasons for a lack of equivalence between net income and income taxes, the following are particularly important.

1. A significant portion of the company's income may not have been taxable at regular income rates; for example, capital gains, earnings from foreign operations, dividends from affiliates, and so on. It is important for investors to be aware of the magnitude of these low-taxed earnings in order to be able to judge the probable impact of proposed changes in the tax law—for example, proposals to tax unrepatriated foreign earnings more heavily.

2. The company may have been the beneficiary of a significant tax credit. Two types of credits may be noted here.

a. The tax law provides that when a company operates at a net loss it can, in effect, merge the losses with earlier or later years of profits in order to determine its tax liability on profits. This means that a company may report substantial profits in some years yet pay little or no income tax. Investors, however, should not permit the incidence of tax credits to distort their views of earnings trends.

b. The Congress has legislated an *investment credit,* whereby companies making specified types of plant and equipment expenditures may credit a percentage of such outlays against their income tax. Companies have an option of reporting such credits to stockholders in full during the year taken (known as *flow-through* accounting), or of spreading them over the lifetime of the capital assets whose purchase generated the credits. Clearly, problems of interfirm and interperiod comparability can arise from investment credits. In the first quarter of 1975, for example, Ford Motor Company reduced its reported loss from $106 million to $11 million by switching its accounting for investment credit from a spreading basis to flow-through.

Income Manipulation—A Summary

As has been shown throughout this discussion, the accounting rules governing the reporting of net income permit a great deal of managerial discretion. While honest managers may have honest differences in the accounting treatment they accord similar types of transactions, investors must be wary of managers whose motives are less pure, and who are quite willing to puff up current reported earnings even though such puffery ultimately will result in diminished future earnings. Generally, such managers will engage in one or more of the following practices:

1. Recognize sales as having occurred long before final delivery has been made to the customer's satisfaction, and paid for.
2. Select inventory valuation methods which minimize cost of goods sold.
3. Accrue pension expenses at the lowest possible rates.
4. Charge depreciation and amortization at the lowest permitted rates.
5. Capitalize all manner of *intermediate-term* expenses.
6. Classify numerous outlays as extraordinary expenses.
7. Flow through to earnings all available income tax benefits.

Calculation of Earnings per Share

Whatever dollar figures the investor ultimately accepts as indicative of a company's earnings, it is customary to express those figures in *per share* terms. Similarly, dividend and stock price information is expressed in per share terms.

To illustrate, suppose that in 1975 Company A had 1 million shares of common stock outstanding and had net income available to common (that is, net income minus preferred dividends) of $2 million. In 1976 Company A decided to expand its business by acquiring another company. To consummate the deal, Company A issued 250,000 shares of its stock in exchange for the other company's stock. Thus, Company A now had 1¼ million shares of stock outstanding.

Suppose that the acquisition raised 1976 earnings on common stock to $2½ million from the $2 million earned in 1975. From the point of view of the individual stockholder, earnings did not rise at all. The 25 percent increase of total dollar earnings was accompanied by a 25 percent increase in capital stock *held by others.* From the point of view of individual investors, progress means higher earnings on each ownership interest so that the individual can look forward to higher dividend payments or to a higher market value on the stock.

In our example the dividend potential of the individual shareholding did not increase at all. This can be shown by dividing each year's net income (after deducting any preferred stock dividend obligations) by the number of shares outstanding *that year.* Thus 1975's earnings of $2 million, divided by the 1 million shares outstanding in 1975, produces earnings per share of $2. And 1976's earnings of $2½ million, divided by that year's 1¼ million shares outstanding, also produces per share earnings of $2. No progress is indicated for the individual investor.

Stock Splits and Stock Dividends. In the above example, the 25 percent increase in outstanding shares reflected new capital invested in the business. Many times, however, the number of shares rises because of stock splits and stock dividends. (There is a technical difference between the terms *stock split* and *stock dividend,* but for purposes of this discussion the difference is not important.)

The principal reason for stock splits of, say, 20 percent or more is to broaden the market for a company's stock. Most small investors have an aversion to very high-priced stocks, notwithstanding their apparent willingness to buy a few shares of IBM or Du Pont at prices above $100 a share. Thus, a two-for-one split of, say, an $80 stock cuts its price to $40, other things being equal, and makes it more attractive to a wider group of investors.

The reasoning behind small stock dividends is not as clear. The public seems to like them, according to various surveys which have been taken. Some of this attitude is probably due to the fact that stock prices seem to respond favorably when stock dividends are declared.

On the other hand, there is considerable statistical evidence to suggest that the favorable price response is not due to the stock dividend per se, but rather to the fact that the cash dividend per share is usually maintained on the greater number of shares, so that the stock dividend really means an effective increase in the cash dividend.

Whatever the reason, let's assume that Company A, in our example, split its stock two for one in 1977, at a time when earnings had risen to $5 million. That is, total dollar earnings had doubled without any additional capital being raised. But since there were 2½ million shares outstanding, instead of 1¼ million, earnings per share remained at $2. Thus, no progress is indicated in the per share data when, in fact, there was great progress. The dividend potential of each individual investor's holdings had doubled. He had twice as many shares, and earnings on each share remained constant.

In order to make the series of per share earnings meaningful, we must go back and adjust all the *presplit* data. What we want to do is put the presplit data at the level they would have been had the stock always been split. Thus, in 1975, when earnings were $2 million on 1 million shares, per share earnings on a split basis were $2 million divided by 2 million shares, or $1 per share instead of $2. And in 1976, $2½ million of earnings should be divided by 2½ million shares instead of 1¼ million, for per share earnings of $1 instead of $2. Accordingly, per share earnings for 1975, 1976, and 1977, on an adjusted basis, would be $1, $1, and $2, respectively. No progress would be shown from 1975 to 1976, as before, but a doubling would be shown from 1976 to 1977.

A simpler method of adjusting presplit per share data is to apply the following formula: Divide presplit per share data by 100 percent plus the percentage stock dividend or split. Thus, with a two-for-one stock split, divide presplit data by 100 percent + 100 percent. Dividing by 200 percent is the same as dividing by ²⁄₁, which is the same as multiplying by ½. So $2 presplit, times ½, equals $1 adjusted.

Likewise, with a 20 percent stock dividend we would divide presplit data by 100 percent + 20 percent. Dividing by 120 percent is the same as dividing by ⁶⁄₅, which is the same as multiplying by ⅚. Conversion to fractions, however, is inconvenient for small stock dividends. Therefore, with a 2 percent stock dividend we would divide presplit data by 100 percent + 2 percent, or 1.02. It should be noted that while we have been discussing *earnings* per share, the same comments apply to price per share, sales per share, and dividends per share.

THE BALANCE SHEET

Prior to the depression of the 1930s, the balance sheet—the statement of a company's assets and liabilities—was the financial statement on which investors focused their attention. During the depression, however, it became apparent that the book values at which a company's assets were carried were quite meaningless unless the operations of the company were generating a commensurate level of earnings from those assets. Gradually, the focus of attention shifted to the income statement and, like most such shifts of attention, it carried too far. For it is not an exaggeration to state that most investors in the 1950s and 1960s were so concerned with earnings per share, and the growth thereof, that they forgot about the necessity of a sound financial structure to support the growth. And it is the balance sheet to which one must turn when evaluating financial structure.

The principal items to be found in a balance sheet are shown below, followed by a discussion of some key problem areas.

Assets

Current Assets:
- Cash and short-term marketable securities
- Accounts receivable
- Inventories
- Prepaid expenses

Plant and Equipment (net of depreciation)

Other Assets:
- Investments in affiliates and in nonconsolidated subsidiaries
- Other securities held for long-term investment
- Intangibles:
  - Patents
  - Goodwill
- Deferred charges

Liabilities and Capital

Current Liabilities:
- Trade accounts payable
- Taxes payable within one year
- Bank loans payable within one year
- Portion of long-term debt due in one year
- Other short-term accruals

Other Liabilities:
- Deferred taxes
- Reserve items
- Minority interest in consolidated subsidiaries

Capital:
- Long-term debt (due in over one year)
- Preferred stock (par or stated value)
- Common Equity:
  - Par or stated value of common stock (net of Treasury stock)
  - Paid-in surplus
  - Retained earnings

Some Questions about Assets

The *Current Asset* section of the balance sheet is supposed to provide evidence regarding a company's liquid resources. Unfortunately, it is too often the case that only the cash and short-term obligations (such as Treasury bills, commercial paper, and certificates of deposit at commercial banks) are liquid. For example, in the discussion of sales it was noted that considerable discretion exists regarding the timing of revenue recognition. Therefore, the same doubts to which the sales figures are subject also apply to receivables. When are the receivables due to be paid? Have adequate allowances been established for returns or other customer credits? Has adequate allowance been made for bad debts? For example, in 1975 Beckman Instruments lowered its allowance for doubtful accounts from 1.9 percent to 0.9 percent, in the face of a bad economic environment. Was this change justified?

Furthermore, we have described earlier how the same physical volume of inventories can be carried on the balance sheet at a variety of values. Under Lifo accounting, the balance sheet value of inventories typically is vastly understated. With Fifo accounting, the balance sheet value of inventories reflects current prices. But the amount that actually could be realized from the forced sale of Fifo-valued inventories usually is considerably less. The exact opposite, of course, is true of the value of plant and equipment. Due to inflation, the value shown on the balance sheet, which represents the original cost of the assets reduced by annual depreciation charges, typically is much lower than the current value of the assets. But how much lower is not known by the investor. Under SEC prodding, companies are beginning to show estimates of replacement value in footnotes to their financial statements, but different methods of estimation will produce different results.

Another asset whose value is very difficult to determine is *goodwill.* This asset usually arises in the course of mergers or of acquisitions by one company of the assets of another company. The two principal methods of accounting for such transactions are *purchase of assets* and *pooling of interests.* Great controversy has surrounded choices between the two methods. For purposes of this discussion, however, let it merely be noted that with purchases, as opposed to poolings, if the acquiring company pays more for the acquired assets than the existing book value of those assets, the excess usually is shown on the acquirer's balance sheet as an intangible asset called *goodwill* or *cost of acquired assets in excess of book value.* This intangible asset is subsequently written off (*amortized*) over a period of years via charges against earnings.

Until the goodwill is fully written off, investors have to decide how much, if any, value to ascribe to it. Many investors assign a value of zero to goodwill, as well as to patents, deferred charges, and all other intangibles in appraising a company's financial structure. At the other end of the spectrum, not only may goodwill be taken into account at its balance sheet value, but a strong effort may be made to determine if its true current market value is substantially higher. That is, just as the balance sheet values of plant and equipment may be totally unrepresentative of inflated current market values, so may this be true of the balance sheet values of intangibles.

Liabilities

Turning from the asset to the liability side of the balance sheet, several questions need to be explored. Among them are:

1. When is debt a *current* liability and when should it be considered a *long-term debt*?
2. Are *deferred taxes* debt, or equity, or neither?
3. Does the balance sheet reflect all of a firm's liabilities?

Current versus Long-Term Debt. When a company issues bonds or notes having a maturity in excess of one year, there is generally no question that the obligation would be considered a long-term debt, with any repayment of principal required within one year considered a current liability. However, it has become quite common for companies to enter into so-called revolving credit agreements with commercial banks. Under such an arrangement, a company is given a line of credit for, say, three or four years, which may be drawn down in whole or part at any time at the company's option. Each draw-down is repayable in installments over the life of the agreement. But the company may repay in advance at any time without penalty, and may borrow again and again *at its option* for the life of the agreement. Moreover, the company may have an option to convert the line into a true long-term loan. Under current accounting rules, considerable leeway is permitted in the treatment of such borrowing as either current or long term. As will be seen in a later chapter dealing with bond analysis, the treatment which is chosen can have a significant impact on credit evaluation.

Deferred Taxes. A company may report lower earnings to the Internal Revenue Service than to its stockholders. When this occurs, the company is required under GAAP to set up a so-called *deferred tax liability* in its balance sheet and to charge this amount against stockholder-reported earnings. But the fact is that in many cases these deferred taxes may never have to be paid, or may be payable so far in the future that their *present value* is negligible. As a result of this ambiguity—that is, whether the deferred tax is really going to have to be paid and, if so, when—there may be times when it should be considered as true long-term debt, other times when it should be considered simply as an *other* liability, and still other times when its payment is so unlikely that it really should be added to stockholders' equity.

Off-Balance Sheet Liabilities. One of the most difficult tasks of balance sheet analysis is to determine the nature and extent of liabilities which are not shown on the face of the balance sheet. Probably the most significant of these obligations is the long-term lease. The following questions have arisen regarding leases:

1. Is a long-term lease, in general, analogous to other long-term debt?
2. Are some kinds of leases more analogous to long-term debt than others?
3. If leases are analogous to debt, what mathematical procedures should be used to determine what the debt equivalent of a lease is?
4. When debt equivalents are determined, should they be shown in the body of the balance sheet or in footnotes?

Those who answer question (1) affirmatively argue that long-term leases, just like ordinary long-term debt, create an obligation for future payments which cannot be canceled, a default on which may result in bankruptcy or the loss of essential operating properties. The opposing argument is that in actual bankruptcy cases, the courts have limited the lessee's liability to, at most, a few years' rental payments.

As for question (2), some leases provide for a rental amount which returns to the lessor the full amount invested after only a few years, followed by a sharply reduced rental amount thereafter or an option which enables the lessee to take title to the property for a relatively low price. Other leases provide for a much more even stream of rental payments over a longer period of time, with no option to buy. And there are hybrids in between. Some analysts argue that the first type of lease is really a disguised debt-financed purchase and, therefore, should be treated as debt. Others acknowledge the difference in form but ask, "So what?"

The method of determining the debt equivalent amount of a lease is fairly simple in concept, but in practice involves a number of rather subjective judgments. Finally, even after these judgments have been made, it has been difficult for the accounting profession to decide whether these amounts should be shown in footnotes or directly on the liability side of the balance sheet, together with an offsetting fixed asset representing the value of the property acquired through the lease.

The SEC and the FASB have been steadily moving in the direction of showing, in the body of balance sheets, auditors' estimates of the debt-equivalent amounts of specific types of long-term leases. But while this may create a certain degree of uniformity among companies, many subjective, and arbitrary, judgments remain.

There are many other types of *off-balance sheet* liabilities which the investor should be alert for, such as the following:

1. It is fairly common for a large corporation to guarantee payment of the debt of one or more affiliated companies or suppliers because the affiliates may have difficulty raising debt capital without the guarantee. Outright guarantees usually are reported in footnotes to the balance sheet. Questions which arise are: Should investors consider these guarantees to be debt equivalents? If yes, should the debt equivalent be the full amount of the guarantees or an amount reduced in proportion to the probability that the guarantor will never have to make good on the guarantees because the debtors will pay their debts as they come due?
2. While outright guarantees are supposed to be footnoted, there are many disguised guarantees which may be hidden. Typical are so-called take-or-pay contracts whereby a company agrees to purchase the output of a supplier at a price sufficient to service the supplier's debt. Such contracts may require payments to be made even when the supplier is unable to produce the output contracted for. Also common are *working capital maintenance* agreements, whereby a corporation agrees to put sufficient funds into another corporation such that the latter's working capital never falls below a specified amount. The potential liability under such an agreement can be open-ended, yet not show up in the balance sheet. Mention should also be made of companies which *factor* their receivables (that is, sell the receivables at a discount), giving the factor "recourse" (that is, the right to demand payment from the seller of the receivables) if the receivables turn bad.

CASH VERSUS ACCRUAL ACCOUNTING

The many problems involved in understanding both income statements and balance sheets should cause investors to turn their attention increasingly to a financial statement commonly referred to as *sources and uses of funds*, or *funds flow*. More technically, it is known as the Statement of Changes in Financial Position.

To the unsophisticated observer who has not studied accounting, net income represents the difference between what a business *takes in* during a period and what it *pays out*. If it takes in more than it pays out, it has *earned a profit;* if it pays out more than it takes in, it has *suffered a loss*. Most individuals think of their own personal transactions in these terms, and many businesses and nonbusiness organizations, in fact, keep their books on this basis, known as *cash accounting*. Net income for a period is equal to the increase in the cash balance for that period; net loss is equal to the cash reduction.

Most modern accounting is done on an accrual basis, rather than a cash basis. Accrual accounting seeks to match the recording of expenses and income on a basis which represents the economic process rather than the timing of receipts and disbursements of cash. Thus, for example, a current outlay of cash for machinery is reflected by the recording of an asset on the balance sheet rather than a current charge against income, and the charge is recorded gradually over the future useful life of the machinery. On the other hand, pension costs are charged against current income (and recorded as liabilities on the balance sheet) even though the actual cash outlays to pay pension benefits will not occur until many years in the future.

While accrual accounting surely makes more economic sense than cash accounting, it can permit positive net income to be recorded year after year in the face of a progressive depletion of liquid resources which ultimately may result in bankruptcy. The sources and uses of funds statement focuses on changes in liquid resources. It is, in many respects, wider in scope than either the income statement or the balance sheet and, indeed, integrates the two statements, as will be shown.

Noncash Income. There are a number of items which are recorded as revenue or other income on the income statement, but which do not necessarily generate cash. For example, when a company sells goods or services it credits income. But its customers may not pay all the bills during the accounting period. As a result, accounts receivable rise, rather than cash, to the extent of the uncollected income. As another illustration, a company's income statement may include the earnings of a foreign subsidiary. But until these earnings are repatriated to the United States, they do not generate cash for the parent's use.

Noncash Expenses. As has been noted earlier, depreciation is a charge against income which does not represent a current cash outlay, but rather represents a gradual apportionment of an earlier lump-sum cash outlay for the purchase of capital assets. Amortization and depletion are similar noncash charges. Likewise, a deferred tax charge against income reflects income tax which may have to be paid at a future date, but does not reflect a current cash outlay. The same is true of any other *reserves* which may be established by charges against current income. Finally, cost of goods sold and other operating expenses may be accompanied by a buildup of accounts payable. To that extent, these costs are not cash outlays. Notc that this is the opposite of the case where sales do not reflect *cash income* to the extent of a buildup of *accounts receivable*.

Cash Items Not Recorded in Income Statement. While many income statement items do not reflect cash inflow or cash outgo, many receipts or outlays of cash do not appear in the income statement. Among the cash receipts not recorded as income are: proceeds from new debt or stock issues; proceeds from the sale of capital assets (only the net gain or loss over book value is recorded in the income statement); and payments received from customers in advance of delivery (for example, when a fire insurance company receives a premium covering the next three years; generally, only one third of the premium is recorded as income and two thirds is recorded on the balance sheet as a deferred credit). Among the cash outlays not recorded as expenses are: capital expenditures; stockpiling of inventory; repayment of debt or repurchase of stock; dividends paid on stock; and items referred to earlier as *intermediate-term expenses* which may be *capitalized* and gradually amortized rather than expensed as incurred (examples of such deferred charges, cited earlier, were tool and die expenses of an auto company and various outlays of oil drilling companies).

Sources and Uses Format. It should be clear from these illustrations that a company's flow of cash is very difficult to trace from its published income statements and balance sheets.

Because the cash flow network is so varied and complex, there is no uniform format used by accountants to present it. However, three basic types of format can be discerned. (When one is considering these formats, it is helpful to bear in mind with regard to noncash balance sheet items that decreases in assets and increases in liabilities generally reflect cash inflows, while increases in assets and decreases in liabilities reflect cash outflows.)

The first type of format might be called Reconciliation of Cash. Here, the effort is to show how the cash balance at the start of the period changed to the cash balance at the end of the period. For example:

	Starting Cash Balance		$ 2,000,000
Plus:	Reported Net Income	$10,000,000	
	Noncash Charges (depreciation, deferred taxes, etc.)	2,000,000	12,000,000
Plus:	Increase in Accounts Payable	1,000,000	
Less:	Increase in Accounts Receivable	750,000	250,000
Less:	Capital Expenditures	5,000,000	
	Inventory Accumulation	1,000,000	
	Common Stock Dividends	5,000,000	(11,000,000)
Equals:	Ending Cash Balance		$ 3,250,000

The second type of format might be referred to as Reconciliation of Working Capital. Here, the focus is on changes in total working capital (current assets minus current liabilities) and the components of working capital. For example:

	Reported Net Income			$10,000,000
Plus:	Noncash Charges (components would be shown)			2,000,000
Equals:	Working Capital Provided by Operations			$12,000,000
Less:	Capital Expenditures	$5,000,000		
	Common Stock Dividends	5,000,000		(10,000,000)
Equals:	Increase in Working Capital			$ 2,000,000
	Consisting of:			
	Increase in Cash		$1,250,000	
	Increase in Inventory		1,000,000	
	Increase in Accounts Receivable		750,000	
	Increase in Accounts Payable		(1,000,000)	
			$2,000,000	

The third type of format is less common but, from the viewpoint of the investor, probably most meaningful. It might be called Reconciliation of Cash Available for Growth and Providers of Capital. It focuses on the generation of funds available for dividends, capital expenditures, and debt reduction. For example:

	Reported Net Income		$10,000,000
Plus:	Noncash Charges (components would be shown)		2,000,000
Less:	Increase in Working Capital (components would be shown)		(2,000,000)
Equals:	Cash Available for Growth and Providers of Capital		$10,000,000
	Used for: Capital Expenditures	$ 5,000,000	
	Common Stock Dividends	5,000,000	
		$10,000,000	

Whichever of these formats is chosen, it is certain that investors who pay attention to the Statement of Changes in Financial Position will have a far deeper understanding of a company's operations than those who focus only on the Income Statement and Balance Sheet. Indeed, the best way to be sure you really understand a company's financial statements is to:

1. Be sure you can trace through the integration of Income Statement and Balance Sheet through the Statement of Changes in Financial Position.
2. Be sure you read and understand all of the footnotes to the various statements.
3. Be sure you review the auditor's opinion and are alert for unusual wording, unusual length, and references to changes in accounting policies.

SUGGESTED READINGS

Briloff, Abraham J. *Unaccountable Accounting.* New York: Harper & Row Publishers, 1972.

——— *More Debits than Credits.* New York: Harper & Row Publishers, 1976.

Nickerson, Clarence B. *Accounting Handbook for Non-Accountants.* Boston: Cahners Books, 1976.

Spiro, Herbert T. *Finance for the Nonfinancial Manager.* New York: Wiley-Interscience, 1977.

5

Common Stock Valuation I: Basic Concepts

The greatest of all gifts is the power to estimate things at their true worth.
La Rochefoucauld

Investors need standards for judging whether stock prices are high or low. To develop standards, it must be assumed that investors as a whole are essentially rational over the long run (although their actions occasionally seem to border on the insane), and that rational individuals attempt to measure the economic, or *going-concern* values of the corporations whose stocks they buy and sell. Since there are millions of investors, there will exist vastly different ideas about the value of any given stock at any given time, and purchases and sales of stock will be made in accordance with this multitude of ideas. Therefore, over an extended period of time, prices will fluctuate in a wide range, *but they will tend to fluctuate around some concensus of value.*

The normal tendency of the marketplace, it is assumed, is to drive prices to extremes. When optimism is dominant, conceptions of value are liberalized, and prices rise steadily. Ultimately, it is recognized that the optimism was excessive, and prices react downward. As prices fall, caution turns to fear, and the price decline snowballs until it is finally recognized that the pessimism was overdone. At this point a price reversal occurs once again. Successful common stock investors, therefore, will try to avoid becoming overly optimistic or overly pessimistic. They will attempt to determine the approximate level around which the price tides will swell and ebb.

The Sources of Common Stock Value

Readers who ponder the problem for a while will realize that a common stock has value for only three possible reasons. First, the ownership of common stock confers a claim to a corporation's net income. This claim bears fruit when the corporation's board of directors declares dividends. Second, if the corporation enjoys growing success, earnings and dividends will rise, and the price of its stock may rise also. The third source of common stock value is that if a corporation is liquidated (or sold), the common stock owner has a pro rata claim to any asset value that may remain after all creditors and preferred stockholders have been paid. This claim on assets, however, is not usually an important source of value because corporations are not often liquidated.

Many people believe that dividends are distinctly subordinate to earnings as a determinant of stock values. The evidence offered in support of this belief is the activity of thousands, perhaps millions, of investors whose dominant objective in buying common stock is to sell it to someone else at a higher price rather than to collect dividends.

It is, of course, true that many individual stockholders do not intend to hold their stocks for dividends, hoping instead to sell the stocks to others at capital gains. But to conclude from this observation that "dividends don't count" would be quite mistaken. In the first place, it is a frequent occurrence for the price of a stock to change substantially when a dividend increase or dividend reduction is announced. One likely explanation for this is that since reported earnings do not necessarily represent *true* earnings (see chapter 4), investors look to dividends for an indication of what management really thinks earnings are, or are going to be.

On a more theoretical plane, the significance of dividends has sometimes been illustrated by hypothesizing the existence of a corporation which has written into its bylaws a perpetual prohibition of dividend payments or of return of capital to stockholders via sale of assets or by any other means. With these bylaws, no rational investor should be willing to purchase the corporation's stock, no matter how high its earnings or how low the asking price. (We exclude from consideration purchasing the stock in order to become an operating officer and thus receive a salary, or purchasing the stock in the hope of changing the bylaws.) Of course, people sometimes become irrational or follow the "greater fool theory," whereby each buyer assumes that he or she will be able to sell at a higher price to a "greater fool." For example, in the tulip mania in Europe a few centuries ago, people bought and sold tulip bulbs at fantastic prices without the vaguest intention of actually planting the bulbs to get flowers. But such bubbles must inevitably burst. Our hypothetical corporation's stock might trade for a while, but people must eventually recognize that they are buying and selling a mere piece of paper, without any *value* in the absence of an ability to pay dividends or liquidate. Thus, while much of a stock's value to an investor undoubtedly lies in the prospect of price appreciation, prices cannot be divorced from dividend prospects any more than they can be divorced from prospective earning power.

The Concept of Present Value of Future Dividends

Those who recognize the significance of dividends as a determinant of stock values can understand the reasoning behind a widely accepted tenet of investment theory. The tenet is that a common stock is "worth" the *present value* of all future dividends.

The concept of present value is really quite simple and can be prosaically illustrated. Assume that Mr. A wants to borrow money from Mr. B, repayable at a future date. Mr. B is willing to make the loan, but feels that, considering the risks involved, he is entitled to a 10 percent annual rate of return. This being the case, how much money will B advance to A on A's IOU for $10 payable one year hence? The answer is $9.09, because the $10 paid next year provides 91 cents interest, which is 10 percent of a $9.09 loan. Thus, $9.09 is the *present value* of $10 payable one year hence at a *discount rate* of 10 percent.

Likewise, if A offers a $10 IOU payable *two* years hence, how much will B be willing to lend? Answer: $8.26. Ten percent of $8.26 is 83 cents (first year's interest); $8.26 plus $0.83 = $9.09. Ten percent of $9.09 is 91 cents (second year's interest); $9.09 plus $0.91 = $10. The present value of $10 payable two years hence is $8.26 at a discount rate of 10 percent. (The reader will recognize that the concept of present value is the reverse of compounding.)

Returning to the matter of future dividends on common stock, suppose we estimate that dividends on Standard & Poor's Stock Price Index will grow at a rate of 7 percent per annum far into the future. Suppose we estimate that *the market*—not any individual investor but all investors as a group—will always demand a 10 percent rate of return in order to undertake the risks of common stock investment. Recognizing that these assumptions are made purely for illustrative purposes, what is the value of the S&P Index today?

There is a simple formula for approximating the present value of long-term dividend growth, at a given discount rate. The formula is:

$$\text{Present value} = \frac{\text{Current dividend rate}}{\text{Discount rate minus growth rate}}$$

Under our illustrative assumptions, this works out as:

$$\frac{\text{Current dividend rate}}{0.10 \text{ minus } 0.07}$$

Thus, the formula and the illustrative assumptions tell us that the appropriate current dividend "yield" of the S&P Index is 3 percent. (Note that if one assumes a growth rate equal to, or greater than, the discount rate, a nonsense negative number results.) To derive the value of the index, under these assumptions, we would divide the current dividend rate by 0.03. For example, early in March 1977, the indicated dividend rate on the S&P Industrials Index was about 4.25. Dividing by 0.03 produces a "value" of about 142. Since the actual level of the Index was about 112 at the time, we can say that, under our illustrative growth and discount rate assumptions, stocks were priced quite low in relation to their "fair value". Let us now examine these critical assumptions more closely.

ESTIMATING THE VALUE OF *THE MARKET*

Dividend Growth Prospects for Stocks in Aggregate

The question of future dividend growth can be broken into three parts. First, what rate of growth of total economic activity, as measured by gross national product (GNP), can be expected in the years ahead; second, will earnings per share of common stock keep pace with GNP; and third, will dividend growth keep pace with earnings growth? It should be emphasized at the outset that our main purpose is to provide a framework for thinking about these problems rather than to argue that our specific answers are correct.

GNP Growth. The growth of gross national product can be conveniently divided into four variables for analytical purposes: the growth of the employed labor force, the trend of average hours worked per week, the trend of output per hour worked ("productivity"), and the rate of change in the price level. By combining forecasts of the first three of these variables, a forecast of growth of so-called *real* GNP is derived—that is, growth of physical output of goods and services excluding the effects of price changes.

The three determinants of real GNP have had a stable enough history during the past century to enable us to make some long-term estimates with a fair degree of confidence. Without outlining their views in detail, it can be said that the estimates of most economists fall within the following ranges: approximately 1.5–2 percent per annum growth in the employed labor force; stability or up to a 0.5 percent per annum decline in hours worked per week; and 2–3 percent per annum growth of output per hour worked. These elements combine to produce a 3–5 percent range of real GNP growth possibilities, with about 3.5–4 percent being the most common forecast. To put this range in historical perspective, consider these past growth rates of real GNP: 1900–76: 3.25 percent; 1900–29: 3.75 percent; 1947–76: 3.75 percent.

To the 3.5–4 percent physical growth rate, we must add an allowance for inflation. Here the "experts" have developed a much wider range of views than with regard to real GNP. Two contrasting quotations will illustrate this diversity. The first is typical of those who equate the rate of inflation with speedups and slowdowns in the nation's utilization of its physical and human resources, and who forsee a return to a relatively low rate of inflation because they expect significant underutilization of resources to be characteristic of the years ahead. It is taken from the November 14, 1975 *Economic Comment* of the investment banking firm, White Weld & Co.

> The major worldwide recession that is now ending has left more unemployed men and idle machines in the United States and in other countries than have been seen since the 1930s. This economic slack is unlikely to be dissipated any time soon. Businessmen and consumers throughout the industrialized world are likely to remain cautious and more concerned with rebuilding liquidity than with embarking on spending sprees. More important, massive governmental monetary and fiscal stimulus seems unlikely since voters now appear to want less government involvement in their economies than earlier, and seem more willing to accept higher unemployment as a trade-off for lower inflation.
>
> History suggests that in this environment, inflation should not be a major problem in the years ahead, and a consumer price inflation rate of 2 percent to 3 percent in the United States seems likely. Other major industrial countries with greater commitments to maintaining full employment will probably have somewhat higher inflation rates, but still well below recent levels.

The second quotation reflects a view that modern inflation is essentially different from historical inflation, having its roots in the changed sociopolitical environment known as the *welfare state*. The authors, Albert T. Sommers and Lucie R. Blau, presented this view in a booklet entitled, *The Widening Cycle* (published by The Conference Board in August, 1975). While the particular quotation cited here does not specify an inflation rate, most proponents of this view believe that the nation will be lucky if inflation can be held to a 5 percent rate, and believe that a 6–8 percent range is more likely.

> Starting shortly after the middle Sixties, the United States (along with much of the rest of the world) has experienced an inexorable uptrend in prices. This new inflation does not appear to be fundamentally cyclical; rather, it looks like a new strain, highly resistant to conventional anti-inflationary policy, and flagrantly in violation of the theoretical explanations of price behavior that were part of the consensus of 1965. The inflation has proceeded with and without high unemployment, before and after devaluation, before, during and after a frantic experiment with direct controls. And it seems to draw in its wake a suspiciously persistent stream of inflationary accidents that augment the general rate of inflation and seem to imbed themselves irremovably in the price structure.

If we take these two statements as representative of the alternative future paths of inflation, the growth rate of "current dollar" GNP can be projected on the low side at about 6 percent (3 to 4 percent real growth plus 2 to 3 percent inflation), and on the high side at over 10 percent (3 to 4 percent real growth plus 7 percent or higher inflation).

Earnings per Share Relative to GNP. Turning to the question whether earnings per share will keep pace with GNP, a look at the past is in order. Figure 5–1 shows the ratio of earnings on the Standard & Poor's Industrials to GNP for the post–World War II period. For comparison purposes, the average ratio for 1923–29 is also shown. The chart indicates clearly that over the past several decades, earnings per share have *not* kept pace with GNP. There has been a steady deterioration of profit margins, by this and other measures, with earnings per share growing about 1.5 percent per annum *slower* than the growth rate of current dollar GNP. In our view, there are few persuasive reasons for believing that the historical erosion of profit margins will be reversed, particularly in view of the increasingly "politicized" economy which has evolved in recent years.

Dividends Relative to Earnings. Except during periods of recession, when dividend payout ratios rose sharply because managements tried to maintain payments to stockholders even in the face of declining earnings, dividends on the S&P Industrials averaged about 55 per-

Figure 5–1
Ratio of After-Tax Earnings (S&P Industrials) to Current Dollar GNP

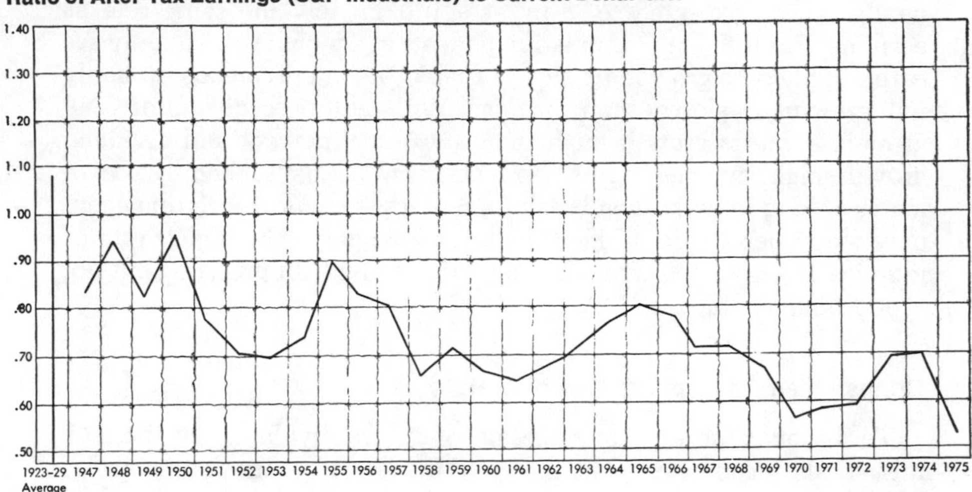

cent of reported earnings for several decades—*until 1970.* A sharp reduction in payout ratios then occurred, to less than 40 percent in 1974. Even in 1975, when earnings declined sharply while dividends were maintained, the payout ratio was less than the long-term 55 percent central tendency.

Part of the reduction in payout ratios reflected temporary federal controls on corporate dividend payments. But much more important was the fact that *generally accepted accounting principles* tend to overstate reported earnings during periods of strong inflation such as were witnessed during the early 1970s. As discussed in chapter 4, original cost-based depreciation does not reflect the inflated replacement cost of fixed assets, and Fifo accounting understates cost of goods sold without making provision for the inflated replacement costs of inventory. Given the need to finance these high replacement costs, management reduced dividend payout ratios to supplement the use of borrowed funds.

Looking to the future, it seems appropriate to argue that if the optimists on inflation are correct, the pressure on managements to retain more earnings will abate and dividends will once again grow in line with earnings. On the other hand, if the pessimists are correct, further reductions in payout ratios would not be surprising. In summary, if the rate of inflation returns to a fairly low level and current-dollar GNP grows at a 6 percent rate, earnings can be expected to continue the historic pattern of growth at a slower rate—about 5 percent—and dividends can be expected to grow at approximately the same rate as earnings. But if the rate of inflation persists at a high level, not only are earnings likely to grow more slowly than GNP, but dividends probably will grow more slowly than earnings. With a 10 percent rate of GNP growth, earnings growth might be only 8 or 9 percent and dividend growth might average only some 7 percent. We have, then, two estimates of long-term dividend growth: 5 percent in a low-inflation economy and 7 percent in a higher inflation economy. The higher rate of inflation is associated with a higher rate of dividend growth—but not *proportionately* higher.

Choosing an Appropriate Discount Rate

To discount the estimated stream of future dividends on the S&P Industrials, we must have some idea of the rate of return that investors will demand in order to take the risks of common stock investment. Bear in mind that we are speaking of investors in aggregate, not any single investor, and that we are considering all stocks in aggregate, not any specific stock.

We cannot go out and ask millions of investors what their yield demands are. Even if it were physically possible to do so (for example, using a sampling technique), it is doubtful that we would get very reliable answers. But there are at least three independent items of indirect evidence which seem pertinent:

1. The annual return on stockholders' equity in American industry has typically been about 11 percent–13 percent. But *stockholders* should not expect this whole rate to be passed on to them. The marketability and diversification potential inherent in share ownership justifies a somewhat lower rate of return than that earned by corporations directly.

2. During the past 20 years, the rate of return on the *safest* kinds of long-term, fixed-income securities, U.S. government bonds and *triple-A* corporate bonds, has been about 5–6 percent in periods of low inflation and about 8–9 percent in periods of greater inflation. Clearly, the added risk of owning common stocks justifies a higher rate of return than can be earned on high-quality bonds.

3. During the past half century, the compound rate of return (including dividends and price appreciation) on broad, market-value-weighted, indexes of common stocks, such as the S&P Industrials, was about 9 percent.

These three items of evidence are suggestive of appropriate discount rates to be applied to estimated dividend growth. The first bit of evidence suggests a discount rate below 12 percent. The second item of evidence suggests a discount rate greater than 6 percent during low-inflation periods and greater than 9 percent during higher inflation. The third piece of evidence suggests a discount rate not too different from the historical 9 percent. All three criteria would be met reasonably well by applying a discount rate of 8 percent during periods of low inflation and 11 percent during periods of higher inflation.

Estimated Value of the S&P Industrials

It will be recalled that the formula for calculating the present value of long-term dividend growth, at a constant discount rate, is:

$$\frac{\text{Current dividend rate}}{\text{Discount rate minus growth rate}}$$

Our analysis has indicated that reasonable estimates for the denominator of this formula are as follows:

		Low Inflation	*Higher Inflation*
	Discount rate	8%	11%
Minus:	Growth rate	5	7
Equals:	Fair value current yield	3	4

Using these estimates, the value of the S&P Industrials Index at a time of fairly low-inflation expectations would be the then-current dividend rate divided by 3 percent; and at a time of fairly high-inflation expectations, the divisor would be 4 percent. Actually, since our dividend growth rate estimates refer to *trends,* the dividend rates which should be used in the numerator of the formula should be trend levels rather than actual current dividends, since the latter may be cyclically high or low.

Figure 5–2 is a reproduction of a chart utilizing these concepts. It superimposes a *value range* on the monthly movements of the S&P Industrials Index since 1959. The value range is derived as follows: (1) Define dividend trend amount each year as the average dividend of that year plus the immediately preceding and succeeding years (except for retrospective calculations, this procedure requires an estimate of dividends for the current and succeeding years). (2) Center the dividend trend amount on June 30 and divide by 3 percent and 3.5 percent

Figure 5–2
Standard & Poor's Industrials: Actual Prices* versus Estimated Values†

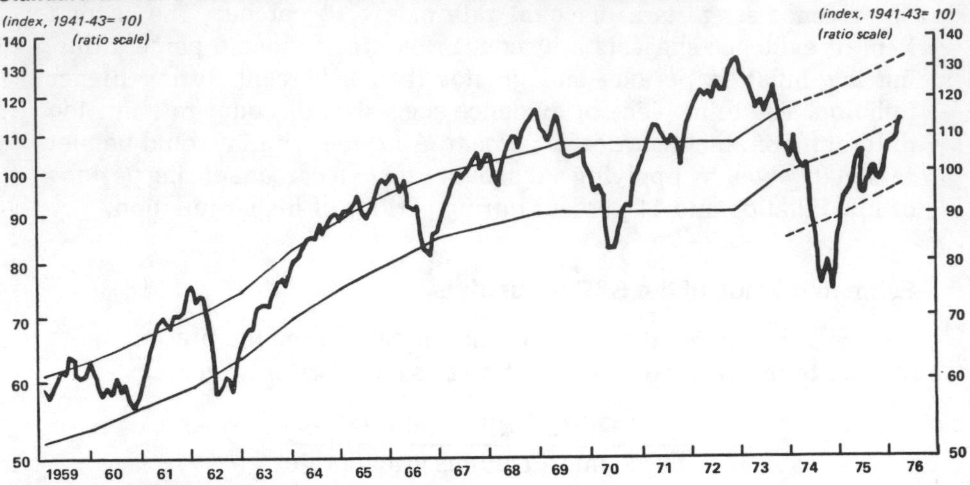

* Monthly average of daily close.
† See text for derivation of values.
Source: Prudential Insurance Company of America and Loeb, Rhoades & Co.

to derive upper and lower points, respectively, of the range of stock *values* for periods of low- or moderate-inflation expectations. For periods of high-inflation expectations such as 1974–75, derive a lower value range by dividing dividends by 4 percent. (3) Connect the June 30 values with freehand curves. The chart is drawn on *semilogarithmic* graph paper, which is scaled to make equal vertical distances represent equal percentage changes.

It will be observed that the chart has been most useful in putting the swings of the market into broad perspective. The areas above and below the *band of value* have been opportune selling and buying zones. For example, the chart suggested quite clearly in 1972, and during the early months of 1973, that the stock market was seriously overpriced. Similarly, in late 1974, the chart strongly suggested that the stock market decline had carried too far.

Recapitulation

It will be helpful to pause at this point for a brief review of the discussion thus far. A widely accepted investment theory is that the value of a common stock is equivalent to the *present value* of all future dividends. To calculate the value of a stock on the basis of this theory, it is necessary to estimate the growth rate of the stock's dividend stream and to discount the estimated dividends at a rate which is felt to be appropriate.

It has been shown that the present-value theory can be applied with practical results to an appraisal of a general index of common stock prices such as Standard & Poor's Industrials. Specifically, reasons have been given why dividends on a broad cross section of common stocks can be expected to exhibit a long-term growth rate of about 5 percent under conditions of low inflation and 7 percent at higher rates of inflation. In addition, a case has been made for discounting an aggregate dividend series at a rate of about 8 percent when inflation expectations are low and 11 percent when inflation is expected to be more rapid. Finally, it has been shown that these assumptions produce a *fair value dividend yield* of between 3 percent and 4 percent.

No one can be so presumptuous as to claim that a set of economic assumptions will remain valid forever. Thus, it is not claimed that a 3 or 4 percent dividend yield will be an effective basis for evaluating the Standard & Poor's Industrial Stock Price Index for all time to come. However, a chart has been presented which illustrates the usefulness of the assumptions herein described, and it is hoped that the assumptions will continue to be useful in appraising the level of stock prices in general. In any event, an analytical framework has been presented which can provide the basis for any revisions that seem called for due to changed circumstances.

ESTIMATING THE VALUE OF INDIVIDUAL STOCKS

Since the concept of the present value of future dividends has proven to be useful in estimating the value of common stock prices in aggregate, it is reasonable to try to apply the concept to the evaluation of individual common stocks. Unfortunately, there are several reasons why this often is not feasible.

First, it is much more difficult to project the growth rate of an individual company than it is to project total corporate growth. Second, it is much more difficult to select an appropriate discount rate for an individual company's estimated dividend stream than it is to select a rate for all corporations combined. Finally, the discounting approach has been framed in terms of dividends rather than earnings, making it difficult to deal with companies which do not pay cash dividends.

Extraordinary Growth. Theoretically, a corporation cannot grow indefinitely at a faster rate than companies generally, because it would ultimately swallow up the entire economy. But there are many companies which have managed for a decade or longer to outperform the average company by a wide margin. International Business Machines Corporation is probably the foremost example of such a company With occasional interruptions, its earnings and dividends have grown at a rate of 10 percent–20 percent per annum for many years. If we try to derive a value for IBM by discounting its annual dividend growth potential during the next 25 years or more, we know that an ultimate slowdown in its growth rate must be assumed. But the specific pattern of this projected slowdown will have a great impact on the calculated value.

Uncertainty. An estimate of the growth potential of a company should be considered in light of the probability of its being accurate. Clearly, one is likely to feel more confident of an estimate of the future growth of stocks in the aggregate than of a single company's growth. An estimate of the future behavior of a broad aggregate contains a built-in protection against error—the protection of diversification. An estimate of the future behavior of a single component of the aggregate does not have this hedge and is less likely to be correct, particularly if the estimate is that the component will grow more or less rapidly than the aggregate. Furthermore, the projected growth of a company whose past earnings have fluctuated violently usually contains a greater element of uncertainty than the projected growth of a company with a history of stability.

Present-value theory adjusts for uncertainty via the discount rate. The more uncertain the growth projection, the higher the discount rate should be. But the appropriate relationship between uncertainty and discount rate is not at all apparent. Thus there are grave difficulties posed by the need to select different discount rates for different stocks —and even to select different discount rates for different time periods in the growth cycle of any individual stock. In the case of IBM, for example, we might be more certain about an above-average growth rate projected for, say, the next five years than for an above-average growth rate projected for, say, the ten years thereafter. This means that we might select two, three, or even more different discount rates in evaluating IBM stock by the method of discounting future dividends.

Nondividend Payers. Many rapidly growing companies, especially young ones, plow all of their earnings back into the business, paying no cash dividends to their common stockholders. Ultimately, of course, a dividend-paying policy may be instituted. But if the company's stock is to be valued by discounting its future dividends, a rather precise estimate must be made of when the policy will commence—quite a difficult task when there is no history of management's attitude toward dividends.

A More Pragmatic Approach—The Price/Earnings Ratio

Since the concept of present value of future dividends is so hard to apply to the valuation of individual stocks, most investors utilize a different approach. They measure a stock's price/earnings ratio (price divided by earnings per share), and apply various rules of thumb to judge whether the ratio (usually referred to simply as P/E) is too high, too low, or just about "right." The basis for these rules of thumb range from pure intuition to elaborate statistical analysis.

Price/Earnings Ratio of the Market. Most investors began their attempt to select an appropriate P/E for an individual stock with a judgment regarding the appropriate price/earnings ratio for the market as a whole—that is, for one of the popular stock indexes. Figure 5–3 traces the price-earnings ratio of Standard & Poor's Composite Stock Price Index (Industrials, Finance, Utility, and Transportation stocks) since 1950. Note the steady rise from 10 to 20 between the early 1950s and 1961. From 1962 through 1972, the P/E had a steady central tendency of about 17. Thereafter, it dropped back to the lower levels of the 1950s.

The central tendency of about 17 for the market's price-earnings ratio during the decade 1962–72 relates directly to an earlier finding. As illustrated in Figure 5–2, the *fair value* of the market can be derived, during periods of modest inflationary expectations, by dividing

Figure 5–3
P/E Ratio of Standard & Poor's 500 Stocks, 1950–1975

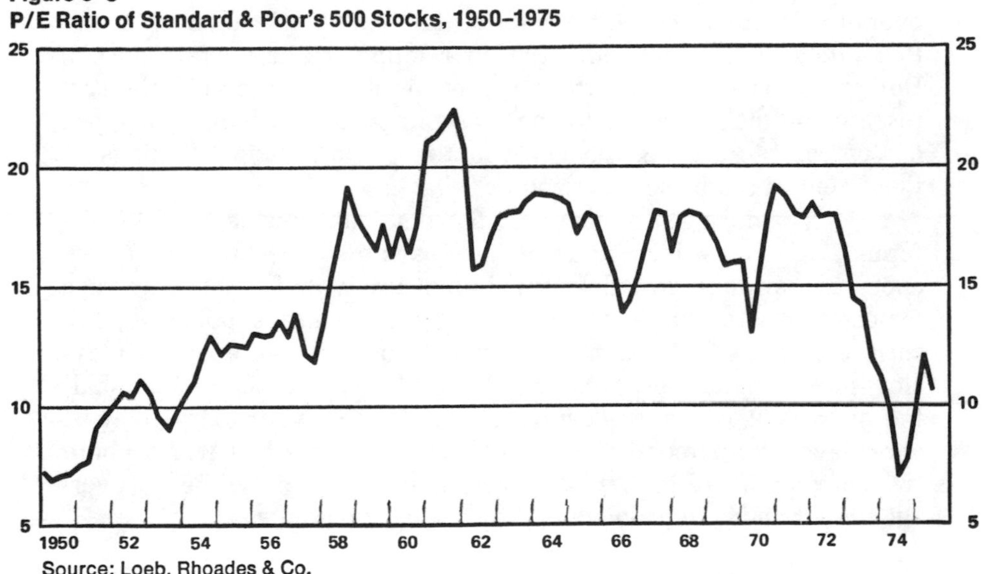

Source: Loeb, Rhoades & Co.

the trend amount of dividends by 3–3.5 percent. It also has been indicated that companies in the S&P Index typically distributed about 55 cents of dividends, on average, for every dollar earned. Given this information, a simple algebraic transformation can be made. Letting *D* equal dividends and E equal earnings:

$$\frac{D}{0.03} = \frac{0.55E}{0.03} = 18E$$

$$\frac{D}{0.035} = \frac{0.55E}{0.035} = 16E$$

In other words, a 3–3.5 percent yield on the trend amount of dividends is equivalent to 16–18 (averaging 17) times the trend amount of earnings (the *trend amount* being one which is neither a cyclical peak nor a cyclical trough).

Similarly, the sharp decline in the market's price/earnings ratio during 1973–75 also relates directly to our earlier discussion. With the dividend payout ratio dropping to about 40 percent in reflection of inflation's impact on reported earnings, and with the *fair value dividend yield* rising to 4 percent, the algebraic transformation works out as follows:

$$\frac{D}{0.04} = \frac{0.40E}{0.04} = 10E$$

That is, a 4 percent yield is equivalent to only ten times earnings if the dividend payout ratio drops to 40 percent because of inflation.

P/E Ratio of the Industry. Given a judgment about the level of the overall market's price-earnings ratio, the next step is to consider the P/E ratios of different industries in relation to the overall market. During the past 15 years, there has been an outpouring of scholarly research on differences in the price/earnings ratios of different types of companies at any given point in time. The principal findings of these studies can be summarized as follows:

1. Except during bear markets, the dominant reason for P/E differences among various industrial groups is the expectation of differences in earnings growth rates. Industries with far-above-average expected growth, such as office equipment or medical supplies, tend to carry P/E ratios 1.5 to 2.0 times that of the overall market, while very-slow-growth industries, such as railroads, carry P/E ratios of one-half the average P/E. As a general rule of thumb, every extra (that is, above-average) percentage point of expected growth is worth about two extra points of P/E, while every percentage point of below-average growth tends to penalize P/E by about two points.

2. Both in bull and bear markets, but especially in bear markets, factors other than earnings growth differences influence the price-earnings ratios of different groups of stocks. The most important additional explanatory factor is *stability* of sales and earnings around their trend paths. Industries which are relatively immune to fluctuations in the overall business cycle tend to carry P/E ratios 2 or 3 points higher than industries with equal expected growth rates but which are likely to be more vulnerable to cyclical fluctuations.

Table 5–1 offers some perspective on the P/E ratios of groups of companies, classified by industry. The data are shown both in absolute terms and as a percentage of the P/E of the S&P Industrials on the corresponding dates. They are compiled in such a way as to minimize the impact of abnormal earnings (see the footnote to the table for a description of the methodology). The dates chosen for the illustration occurred during both bull and bear phases of the stock market.

P/E Ratio of the Company. The investor's final step is to make a judgment as to whether the particular stock under study usually will sell at an equivalent, a higher, or a lower P/E than that of other companies in its industry group. Clearly, the most important considerations, flowing from the previous discussion of industry P/E differences, are whether the particular company is likely to experience faster or slower earnings growth than its competitors, and whether its growth path will be more or less erratic from year to year. Research studies reveal that additional factors influencing company price-earnings ratios are:

1. Management and product *image*. Companies with the admittedly nebulous, and perhaps ephemeral, characteristic of being *quality* firms tend to sell at P/Es 2 or 3 points higher than companies not so endowed.
2. *Dividend payout* and *debt* policies. Particularly in bear markets, there is often a premium of 1 or 2 P/E points for an above-average dividend payout ratio, or below-average debt-to-equity ratio, given equal earnings growth expectations. In this connection, we would repeat the emphasis given in chapter 4 to the fact that increases in *reported earnings* do not necessarily imply increases in *cash available for dividends* (or for capital expansion, as opposed to capital replacement). Earnings which are truly available to benefit shareholders are worth a higher P/E multiple than earnings which are merely the result of arbitrary accounting policies.

Deviations of the Stock's P/E around Its Typical Level. Thus far, we have been discussing differences among P/E ratios *at a point in*

Table 5–1
Industry Group Price/Earnings Ratios, 1970–1975

	1/2/70* S&P Industrials P/E 16.3x		9/1/72* S&P Industrials P/E 20.8x		10/1/74† S&P Industrials P/E 7.2x		12/31/75† S&P Industrials P/E 12.2x	
	Average	Relative	Average	Relative	Average	Relative	Average	Relative
Aerospace	9.9x	0.61	14.6x	0.70	4.07x	0.57	5.84x	0.48
Airlines	16.1	0.99	19.3	0.93	5.92	0.82	12.46	1.02
Aluminum	12.5	0.77	26.9	1.30	5.29	0.74	10.06	0.83
Automobiles	9.0	0.55	11.2	0.54	7.00	0.97	16.45	1.35
Automobile parts	10.4	0.64	13.3	0.64	6.85	0.95	12.73	1.05
Banks, N.Y. and other	11.5	0.71	13.3	0.64	5.13	0.71	5.99	0.49
Beverages	23.1	1.42	29.9	1.44	7.78	1.08	12.06	0.99
Chemicals	13.2	0.81	18.0	0.86	6.67	0.93	15.18	1.25
Coal	31.1	1.91	18.2	0.88	5.73	0.80	7.89	0.65
Construction supplies	16.4	1.01	15.5	0.75	5.33	0.74	9.91	0.81
Containers	14.6	0.90	13.2	0.64	4.38	0.61	6.20	0.51
Copper	9.7	0.60	12.8	0.62	3.45	0.48	19.04	1.56
Cosmetics	29.8	1.83	31.7	1.53	9.10	1.27	16.38	1.35
Drugs	34.4	2.11	34.9	1.68	15.84	2.20	18.26	1.50
Electric equipment	19.8	1.21	22.6	1.09	7.52	1.05	12.52	1.03
Foods	16.1	0.99	14.8	0.71	6.77	0.94	10.23	0.84
Forest products	19.1	1.17	17.8	0.86	4.87	0.68	12.77	1.05
Home furnishings	14.7	0.90	17.6	0.84	4.34	0.60	11.74	0.96
Hotel and motel	36.3	2.23	36.7	1.76	5.50	0.76	10.63	0.87
Machinery	11.6	0.71	17.4	0.84	7.53	1.05	8.75	0.72
Metal fabricating	13.9	0.85	16.5	0.79	4.54	0.63	8.91	0.73
Office equipment	33.3	2.04	32.4	1.56	8.41	1.17	14.49	1.19
Oils	12.2	0.75	16.7	0.80	5.38	0.75	8.28	0.68
Paper	13.9	0.85	20.5	0.98	5.66	0.79	9.65	0.79
Publishing	21.8	1.34	19.5	0.94	4.23	0.59	7.24	0.59
Railroads	8.9	0.55	10.3	0.49	5.42	0.75	8.83	0.73
Railway equipment	12.6	0.77	15.8	0.76	6.03	0.84	6.33	0.52
Real estate	24.0	1.47	20.3	0.97	2.75	0.38	0.68	0.06
Restaurant	29.2	1.79	25.6	1.23	9.10	1.27	17.45	1.43
Retail trade	14.8	0.91	14.6	0.70	8.89	1.24	10.24	0.84
Rubber	11.4	0.70	9.8	0.47	4.77	0.66	8.89	0.73
Shoes	12.8	0.79	15.1	0.73	5.21	0.72	10.39	0.85
Soap	16.4	1.01	27.2	1.31	9.65	1.34	13.90	1.14
Steel	12.0	0.74	14.8	0.71	3.97	0.55	5.14	0.42
Textiles	10.8	0.66	11.6	0.56	3.99	0.55	11.54	0.95
Tobacco	12.3	0.75	13.8	0.66	7.68	1.07	9.78	0.80
Utilities								
Electric power	12.3	0.75	10.9	0.52	5.98	0.83	8.16	0.67
Gas	11.3	0.69	11.8	0.57	6.24	0.87	7.22	0.59
Telephone	15.7	0.96	14.7	0.55	6.36	0.88	9.14	0.75
Vending	18.6	1.14	21.4	1.03	5.96	0.83	8.25	0.68

* For each company, and for the S&P Industrials, price was divided by earnings per share of the latest four quarters reported as of the date shown. The dates chosen for this particular illustration were selected so that the earnings used in the calculations were not recession-level earnings. Aggregation of the company data into industry groupings was done in two steps, the objective being to minimize the influence of companies with abnormal P/E ratios: (1) An average was computed only for those companies in the industry whose P/E was greater than zero (thus eliminating companies with deficit earnings) and less than 100 (thus eliminating companies with only nominal earnings). (2) Each remaining company's P/E was compared with the preliminary industry average calculated in (1). Those companies whose P/E was more than double the preliminary average were also eliminated, and a final average was computed. Each industry average P/E was divided by the S&P P/E to derive the relative P/E.

† The P/E ratios presented here are also based on latest-12-month earnings. However, a less detailed procedure was followed to eliminate distortion. Data exclude stocks with P/Es that are negative or abnormally high (75 times or more). The average multiple for the particular industry is the arithmetic average of the P/E ratios of stocks comprising the respective group; the relative multiple is obtained by dividing the industry group multiple by the multiple of the S&P.

Source: First Boston Corporation.

time. But what about changes in a stock's relative price/earnings ratio (that is, the stock's P/E in relation to the P/E of the market and the industry) *over time*?

Obviously, the relative P/E of a stock should be expected to change if the investment community's appraisal of its basic growth potential, or stability, or *quality* changes. But what if these basic appraisals do not change? What causes short-term P/E fluctuations? At least a partial answer seems to be that P/Es move up and down in response to acceleration and deceleration of earnings. That is, the basic earnings growth rate (or *velocity*, to use a physical analogy) is usually the prime determinant of the normal P/E of a stock. But shorter term movements of earnings around the basic trend (acceleration and deceleration) seem to cause shorter term movements of the stock's P/E around its own norm.

Conclusion. A variety of techniques are available to determine common stock values. Our own preferences were described in this chapter. The reader will doubtless encounter others elsewhere. Perhaps the best advice is to try several techniques and attempt to reconcile any differences in resulting valuations. In any case, since almost all valuation methods put heavy emphasis on estimates of future growth in earnings and dividends, we turn next to this subject.

SUGGESTED READINGS

Brealey, Richard A. *Security Prices in a Competitive Market*. Cambridge, Mass.: M.I.T. Press, 1971.

Cagan, Phillip *Common Stock Values and Inflation—The Historical Record of Many Countries*. New York: National Bureau of Economic Research, 1974.

Lorie, James H., and **Hamilton, Mary T.** *The Stock Market: Theories and Evidence*. Homewood, Ill.: Richard D. Irwin, 1973, chaps. 6–9.

6

Common Stock Valuation II: Analysis of Corporate Growth

Observe always that everything is the result of a change.

Marcus Aurelius

Experience indicates clearly that a forecast of the future must begin with an examination of the past. As applied to investments, this lesson suggests that we must first become familiar with the historical record of sales and earnings growth of companies and industries in which we are interested. We try to learn *why* the past record was what it was. As we begin to understand the conditions that created the past trends, we question whether these conditions are likely to persist in the future. If the answer is yes, the past trends can simply be projected forward at the same rate. But if we expect certain past conditions to be altered in form, or disappear entirely, we must try to estimate the impact of the changes and make allowance for them in our forecasts.

This chapter will illustrate how the past can be used as a guide to the future. We will observe the impact of changing economic conditions on sales, prices, and costs—the determinants of profits. We will also consider the subject of management's response to change.

SALES GROWTH

The Industrial Life Cycle

It often has been observed that industries, like people, go through a few fairly well-defined stages of development. In the early part of their lives they grow at a very rapid rate. After a time the growth rate slows down; they continue to expand, but at a more moderate pace. Finally, they stop growing and either live a relatively stable existence for a long time—or die. The *industrial life cycle,* visualized from an investment perspective, is pictured in Figure 6–1.

Figure 6–1
The Industrial Life Cycle

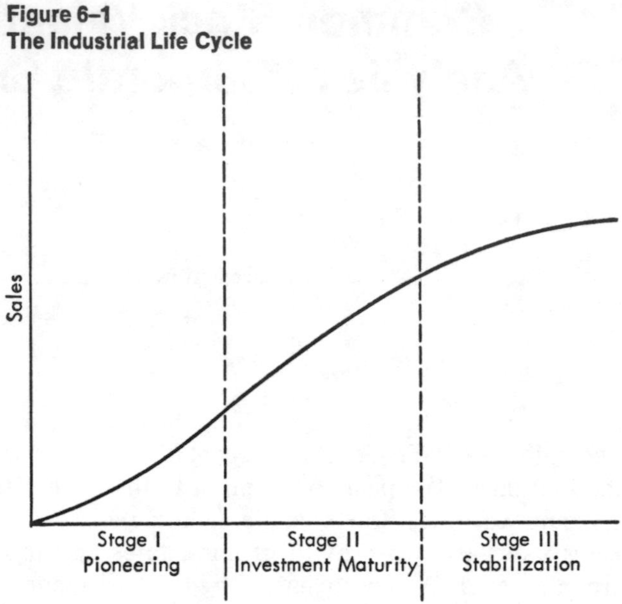

Illustration. The life cycle framework provides an interesting basis for an initial review of an industry's sales history. Take the aluminum industry, for example.

The history of the American aluminum industry is a long one. Aluminum production was begun in 1888 by the Pittsburgh Reduction Company, a predecessor of the Aluminum Company of America. As shown in Table 6–1, the industry's growth rate in its formative years was in excess of 20 percent per annum, and a 15 percent growth rate was maintained from 1910 to 1920. As its markets became increasingly saturated, the growth rate slowed markedly in the 20s, but evidence of the continued vitality of the industry was the 6 percent growth rate achieved during the years of the Great Depression. World War II gave rise to major new aluminum-consuming industries such as mass-produced aircraft, and the industry's growth rate accelerated. Since 1960, a slowing has taken place once again, but a rate well in excess of

Table 6–1
Life Cycle of Aluminum

Period	Growth Rate (percent)
1900–1910	21
1910–1920	15
1920–1930	5
1930–1940	6
1940–1950	13
1950–1960	11
1960–1970	7
1970–1976	5

Source: Underlying data on U.S. primary aluminum production from the Aluminum Assn.

aggregate real economic growth has been maintained. Thus, one might categorize the aluminum industry as having been in its pioneering phase until about 1920, and in an extended investment maturity phase since then. A question emerging from this view is whether the stabilization phase was approaching as the decade of the 1970s unfolded. A closer examination of aluminum sales in recent years is needed in order to attempt an answer to this question.

Relative Growth in Recent Years

The top panel of Figure 6–2 shows the ratio of annual aluminum dollar sales to gross national product since 1953. The bottom panel presents the same comparisons in unit terms. (The underlying data for the charts were derived from a variety of governmental, trade association, and investment service sources.) Sole reliance on *dollar* sales data is inadvisable because, as is well known, the prices of different products do not change uniformly. Differences in price movement exist both in timing and in magnitude.

Analysis of the Data. Note that Figure 6–2 is in ratio form. That is, industry sales are divided by GNP and the resulting ratios are plotted on a graph. The *absolute* amounts of the ratios are not significant; the *trends* and *changes* in the ratios are.

We must ask ourselves if a ratio line is rising or falling. Has the numerator of the ratio (the industry) grown more or less rapidly than the denominator (GNP) over the whole length of the period? And what has been the behavior of the line during years of general economic recession? To facilitate this comparison, it is convenient to shade in the years of recession, as indicated on the chart for the years 1954, 1958,

Figure 6–2
Sales of Aluminum Relative to GNP

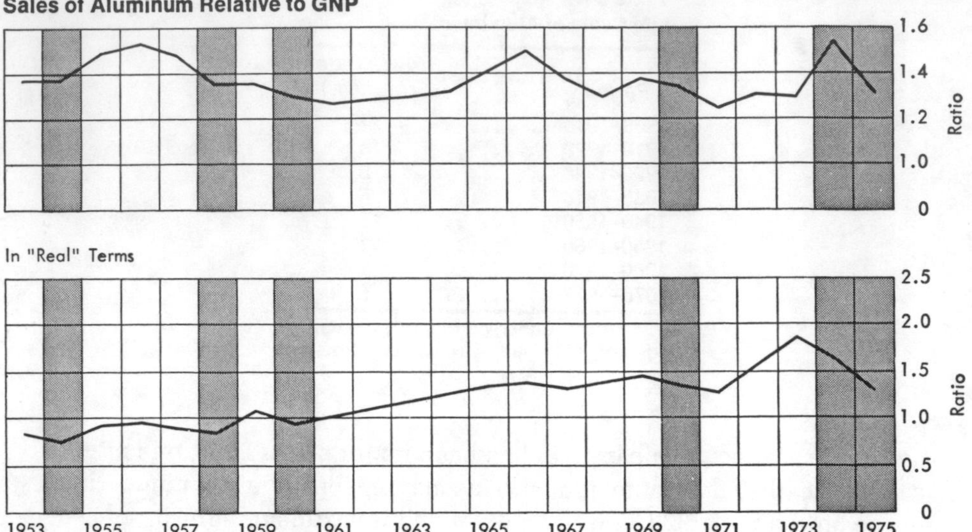

Recession years indicated by shading.

1960, 1970, and 1974–75. (See Chapter 10 for a detailed chronology of modern business cycles.)

When these questions are applied to the chart at hand, some interesting observations emerge. Taking the bottom panel of the chart first, one can see that over most of the period the ratio line rose fairly sharply, meaning that unit sales of aluminum rose much more rapidly than total economic output. The relative growth, however, did not proceed steadily from year to year. In each recession year, aluminum was more vulnerable than the overall economy (the ratio line declined).

When *dollar* sales are examined relative to gross national product (the top panel), the impact of the business cycle becomes more pronounced and the long-term trend of relative growth also takes on a different configuration. The growth in dollar sales was no greater over the full period than GNP—note that the ratio line fluctuated cyclically around a fairly horizontal trend. The weaker showing of the industry when examined in dollar terms as opposed to unit terms suggests the possibility of underlying weakness in the price structure. This aspect of an industry's history will be considered next.

Prices

There are two price factors which should be distinguished because they may have different implications for the future. One is the natural long-term price decline of growth products; the other is the erratic price movement of industries whose productive capacity periodically spurts far ahead of immediate sales potential.

Think of an industry which has grown rapidly in sales volume for a period of 10 or 20 years, and then think of what has happened to its selling prices relative to the general price level. Almost invariably, the selling price of a growing product has shown a long-term downtrend—either in absolute terms or at least relative to other prices. Aluminum is an example; nylon, the miracle drugs, television, semiconductors, and air transport are others.

Where the basic demand for a product is strong, managements try to tap and expand the market by reducing cost and improving quality. Productivity gains are used, in part, to lower selling prices. On the other hand, in nongrowth industries, like steel and railroad passenger transport, selling prices tend to be raised whenever possible, instead of lowered to broaden markets. When prices do get cut in nongrowth industries, it usually takes the form of price warfare rather than secular price reduction. Price warfare refers to intraindustry price cutting in an attempt to capture a larger share of a relatively fixed market. But long-term price reduction is designed to enlarge the total demand for a product or service.

Frequently, however, situations are encountered where an industry exhibits the price characteristics of a stagnant market and yet demand for the industry's product is, in fact, growing at an above-average rate. Typically, the cause of this peculiar behavior is excess capacity. Although demand for the product is rising, productive capacity may be rising much more rapidly. As a result, the companies in the industry engage in extremely vigorous price competition in order to build up their sales relative to capacity. Then, when a better sales/capacity balance is achieved, they attempt to restore their previous prices. Perhaps as good an example as any of this pattern has been the aluminum industry.

Overcapacity of primary aluminum ingot plagued the industry from 1957 to 1963, and had a depressing impact on price. By the second half of the 1960s, however, the industry once again was operating at capacity, and sometimes above. A firm price structure accompanied the return to high utilization of capacity.

With the recession of 1970–71, demand for aluminum dropped both in the United States and in Europe, which also experienced a recession. Meanwhile, a rash of new aluminum smelters had been opened, many in nations new to the industry and built with government subsidies. Aluminum prices declined sharply in the face of the renewed overcapacity.

This experience caused the industry to curtail expansion of capacity. In the United States, for example, primary aluminum capacity rose only 5 percent in the three years, 1971–74. But production rose 25 percent and the utilization rate rose from 84 percent to 100 percent. As a result, prices soared. From a realized price level of 24 cents a pound in 1971, the price of aluminum rose to 34 cents in 1974 and to 40 cents in 1975—the latter increase coming in the face of the worst worldwide economic recession of the postwar years.

The unprecedented strength of aluminum prices during a severe economic recession caused many analysts to proclaim that a new era had arrived for the metal, and, indeed, for many other raw materials whose prices showed similar strength. Their argument was that the costs of building new capacity had risen to such high levels (for example, from about 20 cents per pound of aluminum in 1971 to about 35 cents in 1975) that without high selling prices no new capacity would be built. But while this argument perhaps had *long-run* merit, the fact was that by late 1975, with production slowing markedly in lagged response to the recession, price-cutting reappeared in the industry. Although the renewed price weakness may, in retrospect, be viewed as a temporary aberration (by the summer of 1976, the price had risen to another new high), the long history of aluminum prices just recited suggests two conclusions regarding the years ahead. First, aluminum prices are more likely than not to decline in the long run relative to other prices, in line with the industry's expansion of markets. Second, this long-term trend is likely to be punctuated by periodic episodes of overexpansion and cyclical price reductions—perhaps from a higher level of price than earlier, but substantial nevertheless.

Market Analysis

Thus far, our examination of an industry's sales history has been in aggregate terms. For a more in-depth understanding, study of the individual markets for the industry's output is extremely helpful.

An industry can grow at an above-average rate in three ways: (1) by supplying a stable share of rapidly growing markets; (2) by supplying a growing share of markets having only average growth; and (3) most dynamically, by supplying a growing share of rapidly growing markets.

There are many ways to delineate an industry's markets—for example, by geographic area, by age or income bracket of individual consumers of its products, by the various "life styles" of consumers, or most commonly, by consuming industry. The various trade associations are important sources of information on markets. For example, Table 6–2 summarizes the Aluminum Association's estimates of the

Table 6–2
Estimated Distribution and Growth of U.S. Aluminum Shipments, by Market

	Percent of Total Shipments			*Growth Rate*
Market	*1960–1965*	*1966–1970*	*1971–1974*	*(percent)*
Construction	25	22	25	7
Transportation	21	19	18	7
Packaging	7	11	15	15
Electrical	12	13	13	10
Consumer durables	11	10	9	6
Machinery and equipment	7	7	7	6
Exports	8	8	6	5
Other	9	10	7	7
	100	100	100	7

Source: The Aluminum Association.

end-user markets for its industry since 1960. It will be noted that the most rapid growth areas for aluminum have been packaging (cans and foil) and electrical (wire and cable). These two markets now account for about 30 percent of the aluminum industry's total shipments. Shipments to each other identified major market—construction, transportation, consumer durables, and industrial machinery—have grown at a rate of at least 6 percent, and as high as 8 percent, well in excess of *real GNP* growth; and export growth also has been above average. Strong growth in various "other" markets reflects the increasing substitution of aluminum for copper, steel, and other metals.

Having determined the major markets which have accounted for aluminum's *past* growth, we next ask: (1) What are the growth prospects of these markets themselves? (2) What is the likelihood that the penetration of these markets by aluminum will rise? A detailed discussion of these questions is beyond the scope of this chapter. If we can rely on the opinions of professional economists, it would appear that the construction and transportation markets are likely to grow at about the same rate as GNP. As for growth of electric generating and transmission facilities, this long seemed certain to be well above average, but the "energy crisis" and resulting soaring costs of electricity have caused consumers to cut back their use of electricity. Therefore, average rather than above-average growth seems the safest prediction for this demand sector as well as for construction and transportation.

A continuation of the postwar trend toward convenience foods makes packaging a likely above-average growth market, while growth of the consumer durables and industrial machinery markets is generally expected to be about average or slightly above average. Finally, the potential growth of foreign markets of aluminum is quite high. The Aluminum Association estimates per capita consumption in the United states at over 60 pounds, compared with 40 pounds in West Germany, over 30 in Japan, 25 in Great Britain and France, and only 5 or 10 in underdeveloped countries. However, as was noted earlier, there has been considerable expansion of overseas smelting capacity in recent years, so the actual export market for U.S. companies may not be as great as these comparative consumption data suggest.

The subject of per capita consumption of aluminum turns us from the question of the growth prospects of aluminum's markets to the second question; namely, the intensity of aluminum's use in those markets. In residential construction, for example, the quantity of aluminum used to build a house has more than tripled during the past 15 years while the amount of aluminum used in the average American passenger car, as well as in packaging and electrical uses, has also grown markedly.

Yet further market penetrations by aluminum cannot be taken for granted. While aluminum's light weight and corrosion resistance are obvious advantages over other metals, its competition is not inherently limited to other metals. Since World War II, plastic technology has progressed by leaps and bounds. Plastics are being used for pipes, walls, auto parts, containers, and countless other products formerly made of metals. In the packaging field, aluminum has benefited mightily from the inventiveness of housewives and package designers in finding uses for aluminum foil and thin sheet. But plastic and paper producers have not lacked for inventiveness themselves. Goods are being packaged in plastic film, squeeze bottles, rigid containers, and semi-rigid coated paper containers. In addition, the steel industry itself has counterattacked with such products as "thin tin" and vapor-coated aluminum steel for canneries. And the glass industry has countered with less expensive bottles. In short, steel, copper, aluminum, wood, and glass are not clearly defined materials with clearly defined markets. They must face the competition of substitute materials and of refined versions of the old stand-bys. Moreover, if the predictions of permanently high aluminum prices prove correct, the metal may find itself priced out of markets it otherwise could capture.

Analysis of markets leads to a reasonable basis for estimating the growth in physical volume of aluminum sales during the next five to ten years. The sum total of the markets which use aluminum seems likely to grow at a rate slightly above that of aggregate economic activity. Within these markets, the penetration of aluminum should grow, but one's confidence in this judgment must be tempered by a recognition of the dramatic changes that are taking place in the materials field. Assuming that "real" gross national product grows at a 3.5 percent–4 percent per annum rate, as suggested in Chapter 5, a 6–7 percent growth rate of unit sales volume of the major aluminum companies can be used as a working hypothesis. But we also have noted that aluminum prices are likely to decline relative to the overall price level. Adding price and volume gains produces total dollar sales gains for the major aluminum companies which is modestly higher than total GNP growth—perhaps 8 percent in a low-inflation environment and 12 percent if inflation is more severe (versus GNP growth of 6 percent or 10 percent, depending on the rate of inflation).

Market Share of Competing Companies

Once an estimate is made of industry sales growth, investors can turn to a study of the sales growth of the company in which they are interested, compared with the sales pattern of its principal competitors. For example, sales data for the leading North American aluminum companies—Aluminum Company of America, Reynolds Metals, Kaiser Aluminum, and Alcan Aluminum—can be gathered readily from their annual reports or from the manuals of the investments services. But while the data thus gathered will be reliable, they may not be appropriate for comparative growth analysis.

The problem that frequently arises is that mergers or acquisitions introduce discontinuities into sales totals for a company. When two companies merge, the sales of the surviving company will be larger than they were before the merger. But this sales increase does not necessarily represent "growth" in a meaningful sense. "Growth" means doing more with the same resources; increasing the output per unit of input. To the shareholder, sales growth means increasing sales (output) per unit of capital (input).

It is advisable to convert total dollar sales into per share form for intercompany sales comparisons (and also, for that matter, in examining the sales trend over time for an individual company in isolation).

Only if complete "pro forma" data are available, or if there were no mergers or acquisitions, is the use of total dollar sales advisable. Table 6–3 presents per share sales data for the four major aluminum companies. The data are fully adjusted for all stock splits and stock dividends.

Table 6–3
Sales per Share—Four Major Aluminum Companies

Year	*Alcan Aluminum Ltd.*	*Aluminum Co. of America*	*Kaiser Aluminum & Chemical*	*Reynolds Metals*
1955	$13.78	$27.64	$22.50	$ 25.03
1960	16.71	26.94	27.08	25.75
1965	26.63	36.27	36.96	44.50
1970	41.52	47.19	46.27	61.14
1971	43.43	44.60	47.48	63.34
1974	69.99	82.10	90.57	115.23
1975	63.63	68.60	82.11	97.36

Generally speaking, there is little point in gathering physical volume data when comparing different companies in a homogeneous type of industry such as aluminum. This is because their price movements usually will be quite similar. Of course, where the *product mix* varies considerably from company to company, even though they are in the same "industry" it would be quite informative to have comparative volume data. But companies that handle a broad product line usually do not publish volume data.

Table 6–4 relates per share sales of Alcoa to the sales of the other three companies. The table reveals that Alcoa's sales per share declined markedly relative to the sales of the three other aluminum producers until 1971, and since then have stabilized. To some extent

Table 6–4
Ratios: Alcoa's Sales per Share to Competition

Year	*Alcoa/Alcan*	*Alcoa/Kaiser*	*Alcoa/Reynolds*
1955	2.0	1.2	1.1
1960	1.6	1.0	1.0
1965	1.4	1.0	0.8
1970	1.1	1.0	0.8
1971	1.0	0.9	0.7
1974	1.2	0.9	0.7
1975	1.1	0.8	0.7

the decline was merely a reflection of the fact that Alcoa was a giant when the others were just being born. In this light, a decline in Alcoa's market share was inevitable. But there are some who attribute the decline to a lack of competitive vigor on the company's part—a lack which these same observers believe has now been rectified. If they are correct, there would appear to be a fairly good chance that the earlier erosion of Alcoa's market share has ended and that investors can assume for the company the same growth rate of dollar sales that is assumed for the entire aluminum industry.

EARNINGS GROWTH

As noted earlier, sales growth does not assure earnings growth of the same magnitude. To best understand the forces influencing earnings growth, it is helpful to divide the past record into several key component parts. In the discussion which follows, illustrating how this is done, we shall make the simplifying assumption that financial data can be used directly as reported by a company, without making allowance for the many accounting problems described in Chapter 4.

The Sources of Earnings Growth

Net income per share of common stock is equal to the rate of return on stockholders' equity multiplied by the per share value of stockholders' equity. This can be shown algebraically, as follows:

$$\frac{\text{Net income}}{\text{per share}} = \frac{\text{Net income}}{\text{Stockholders' equity}} \times \frac{\text{Stockholders' equity}}{\text{Number of common shares}}$$

Note that stockholders' equity appears in the denominator of one fraction and in the numerator of the other, thus canceling out and leaving Net income/Number of common shares, or net income per share. Stockholders' equity, frequently referred to as *book value,* equals the balance sheet value of common stock plus surplus items, which is the same as total assets minus liabilities and preferred stock.

It follows from this relationship that *growth* of net income per share can stem from either an increase in stockholders' equity per share, or from an increase in return on stockholders' equity, or from some combination of the two. (Actually, a sufficient increase in one can offset a reduction in the other.)

Growth of stockholders' equity per share has two principal sources: (1) sale of new stock (either directly for cash or in a merger via an exchange of shares) at a price higher than the existing book value per share; and (2) the plowback of earnings into the business—that is, paying out only a portion of net income in cash dividends to common stockholders and retaining and reinvesting the balance. Of these two sources, the second is far and away the most important for most companies.

The contribution of earnings retention to growth of net income per share can be illustrated by a numerical example. Assume that a company is earning an average 12 percent on stockholders' equity—that is, $1.20 of net income per common share for every $10 of stockholders' equity per share. And assume, further, that the company has a typical dividend payout ratio of about 50 percent—that is, it pays dividends of $0.50 per share for every $1 of available earnings. Its "retention rate," then, is also 50 percent—$0.50 plowed back into the business out of every $1 earned, or $0.60 plowed back from $1.20 earned.

Now, if the company continues to earn 12 percent on its old capital and, in addition, is able to put the new, plowed-back funds to work at a 12 percent return, its earnings per share will grow by 6 percent. This may be shown as follows (all data in per share terms):

Earnings on beginning stockholders' equity

$$12\% \times \$10.00 = \$1.20$$

Earnings on plowback

$$12\% \times \$\ 0.60 = \underline{\ 0.072}$$

$$\text{New level of earnings} \qquad \$1.272$$

Growth rate of earnings

$$1.272/1.20 = 6\%$$

It should be noted that the percent growth rate is equal to the rate of return on stockholders' equity (12 percent) multiplied by the retention rate (50 percent). That is, 50 percent × 12 percent = 6 percent. This rule is of great significance in investment analysis.

Alcoa Data. Table 6–5 shows the rates of return on equity and the retention rates of Aluminum Company of America from 1965 to 1975. It will be noted that the company's rate of return has been substandard more often than not in comparison with the typical 11 percent to 13 percent return on equity of industrial corporations. As for earnings retention versus dividends, Alcoa appears to have a long-run "target" dividend payout ratio of about 40 percent, with a 60 percent retention rate. (The low retention rates in 1971 and 1975 reflect sharp declines in earnings rather than increased dividends.)

Table 6–5
Return on Equity and Retention Rates of Alcoa

Year	Rate of Return on Average Stockholders' Equity	Retention Rate
1965	8.9%	59%
1966	11.7	67
1967	11.0	63
1968	10.1	62
1969	11.0	68
1970	9.7	65
1971	4.4	26
1972	8.1	61
1973	7.8	58
1974	12.1	74
1975	4.2	27

Based purely on this historical record, one might conclude that Alcoa's most probable future rate of return on stockholders' equity is about 10 percent. Multiplying this rate of return by the company's typical retention rate (60 percent), the earnings growth potential would appear to be about 6 percent (10% × 60%). This would imply earnings growth at a considerably lower rate than the sales growth estimates made in the preceding section (8 percent to 12 percent, depending on future inflation). Before accepting this lower figure, however, an examination of the components of return on equity is in order.

Analysis of Return on Equity

Return on common stock equity can be viewed as the product of the *profit margin* on every dollar of sales multiplied by the *equity turnover,* or number of dollars of sales per dollar of stockholders' equity. This can be expressed algebraically as follows:

$$\underset{\text{(Profit margin)}}{\frac{\text{Net income}}{\text{Sales}}} \times \underset{\text{(Equity turnover)}}{\frac{\text{Sales}}{\text{Stockholders' equity}}} = \underset{\text{(Rate of return on equity)}}{\frac{\text{Net income}}{\text{Stockholders' equity}}}$$

To illustrate the significance of this equation, assume that a company's return on equity declined from 15 percent to 12 percent between the years 1965 and 1975. This might have occurred in one of several ways, as shown.

In Case A, the problem was a reduced profit margin, and the analyst who knows this can proceed to find out why. For example, was the price structure of the industry upset? Were the operating expenses of the company out of control? Were there heavy, but temporary, start-up

	Year	Profit Margin (percent)	×	Equity Turnover	=	Rate of Return on Equity (percent)
Case A	1965	 5		3		15
	1975	 4		3		12
Case B	1965	 5		3		15
	1975	 5		2.4		12
Case C	1965	 5		3		15
	1975	.... 4.8		2.5		12
Case D	1965	 5		3		15
	1975	 3		4		12
Case E	1965	 5		3		15
	1975	 6		2		12

expenses attributable to the launching of a new plant or of a new product? How does the trend of this company's profit margin compare with that of its competitors?

In Case B, the profit margin was maintained, but turnover declined. Why? Was the problem a declining sales trend due to the inroads of competing products? Or were sales being maintained, but with overly large capital investment?

In Case C, both ratios deteriorated, so joint problems must be explored, while in Cases D and E, one of the ratios actually rose but was accompanied by a more than offsetting decline in the other. With regard to Case D, it might be noted that a decline in the profit margin on sales need not necessarily be undesirable. If turnover can be improved sufficiently, it may pay to follow a deliberate policy of trimming profit margins to expand sales and improve the ultimate return on equity. Indeed, this is the principle underlying, for example, mass-retailing operations such as food chains or discount department stores. Of course, in Case D the rise in turnover was not adequate to offset the profit margin decline.

Alcoa Data. Turning to Alcoa again, Table 6–6 indicates that except for a few years, the company's profit margin typically has ranged between 6 percent and 8 percent while turnover has oscillated around a 1.4 level (1974's turnover of 1.9 was most unusual). Multiplying the 6–8 percent margin range by an equity turnover of about 1.4 produces a return on equity of about 8 percent under relatively poor conditions and 11 percent under more favorable conditions. This would suggest that our earlier estimate of about 10 percent as Alcoa's "most probable" rate of return was reasonable and, if so, that long-term earnings per share growth in excess of 6 percent per annum is not likely. In order for earnings growth to be significantly higher, Alcoa would have

Table 6–6
Profit Margins and Equity Turnover of Alcoa

Year	Net Income/Sales	Sales/Average Stockholders' Equity
1965	6.3	1.4
1966	7.5	1.6
1967	7.7	1.4
1968	7.6	1.3
1969	7.8	1.4
1970	7.3	1.3
1971	3.7	1.2
1972	5.7	1.4
1973	4.7	1.7
1974	6.3	1.9
1975	2.7	1.5

to achieve, in the future, a much higher level of profit margin or equity turnover than it has achieved in the past—or, alternatively, the company would have to cut its dividend payments to a much lower proportion of earnings than its shareholders have been accustomed to.

The possibilities of higher profit margins, or higher equity turnover, or greater earnings retention can be appraised by investors who have the time for further study. For example, a firm's net profit margin reflects not only its basic operating efficiency but also its *nonoperating* income and expense, and its income tax rate. These factors can be examined separately. Moreover, the major components of operating costs can be studied—labor, materials, selling and administrative expenses, depreciation—to see how much room might exist for future cost-savings. In addition, it should be recognized that equity turnover reflects not only the degree of utilization of a company's assets but also its method of *financing* those assets—debt versus equity. Since a company's asset utilization and its financial policies are two quite different factors, they can and should be examined separately, with asset utilization further subdivided into turnover of receivables, turnover of inventories, and turnover of fixed assets.

Space does not permit us to illustrate such a detailed analysis. The reader may be interested, however, in Figure 6–3, which is a schematic diagram of the entire network of factors underlying return on equity. The application of this schematic to the problem of forecasting Alcoa's earnings—as well as those of another well-known company, Texas Instruments—may be found in Chapter 7 of the Third Edition of our book, *Investment Analysis and Portfolio Management* (Homewood, Ill., Richard D. Irwin, 1977).

Figure 6–3
Components of Return on Equity

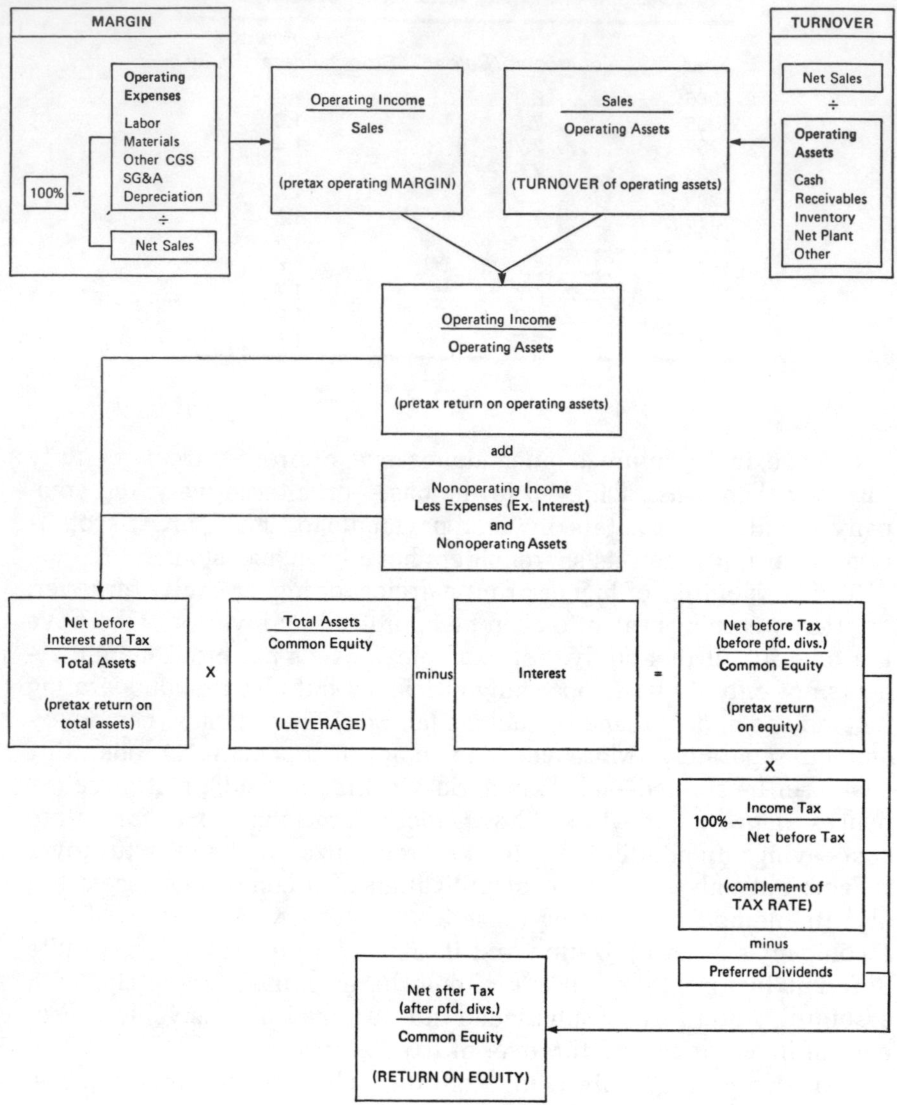

MANAGEMENT: THE QUALITATIVE FACTOR

Ever hear of Midvale Steel & Ordinance, Central Leather, International Mercantile Marine, Chile Copper, Magnolia Petroleum, Ohio Cities Gas, Atlantic Gulf & West Indies, American Cotton Oil, United

Verde Extension Mining? They were among the top 100 industrial companies in 1917. Of the top 100 in 1917, only 43 were among the top 100 fifty years later. Twenty-eight of 1917's leading companies had disappeared entirely.

One obvious reason why so many companies "fall from grace" is that the growth of the industries of which they are members slows down relative to the growth of other industries. This is a natural accompanyment of a healthy and growing competitive economy. But *inter*industry competition is far from a complete explanation, although it is an important factor. *Intra*industry competition is also crucial.

Why do some companies in the same industry have better growth records than others? Sometimes it is because they possess an unduplicatable characteristic such as a unique geographic location or a patented production process. More often, however, it is because they are *better managed*. For example, the difference between the dynamic S. S. Kresge and the now bankrupt W. T. Grant may be attributed to differences in the caliber of their management.

Clearly, an outside investor is at a great disadvantage in trying to assess the caliber of a company's managers. The outsider usually does not have an opportunity to observe management in its day-to-day work. But the astute investor must search for clues wherever they can be found. In this section, we will try to suggest briefly what some of those clues might be.

Management's *Grand Design*

One thing the investor should try to ascertain is whether the senior officers of the company, by their actions, exhibit a strong drive to make their company grow. Without the presence of such ambition among the key personnel, "competence" usually will not suffice.

In business, at least, it is a fairly valid generalization that a firm must either grow or lose its market share. A firm whose essential philosophy is to preserve the status quo soon becomes unable to attract or retain capable young personnel, for whom the death or retirement of existing officers is the only route to promotion. Preservation of the status quo tends to be an unattainable goal because the firm's products become displaced by the newer and better products of expansion-minded competitors. A policy of nonexpansion incurs grave risks of loss of markets through technological obsolescence and consumer withdrawal.

It is true, of course, that growth-oriented managers may pose another risk for investors in their enterprises. For they may seek growth at the expense of *profit*. This risk, however, appears less serious than the risks posed by managers of opposite temperament. Whether the managerial drive is share of the market, power, prestige, public approval, or "the mere love of the game," it usually gets reflected on the bottom line.

Conception of the Market. History suggests that if managers are to bring their desires for growth to fruition, they should have a rather broad conception of their company's "natural" product line. Few successful companies have continued to produce the same type of product throughout their lifetime. Successful companies are usually market oriented rather than product oriented, and the type of product demanded by the *relevant market* tends to undergo radical changes as time passes. Unless a company's product mix is restructured to meet the market's changing demands, growth is impeded, if not prevented.

Consider the contrast between IBM and Underwood prior to the Olivetti takeover of Underwood. Here is a classic example of the difference between a well-conceived and an ill-conceived product line. For almost 50 years, until World War II, Underwood was the premier business machine company in the nation. During this period, the word *business machine* was virtually synonymous with *standard manual typewriter,* and Underwood was the typewriter king.

But a new business machine technology was developed during and after the war. For one thing, manual typewriters were increasingly displaced by electric typewriters. When Underwood failed completely to make the shift, IBM virtually took over the market. Furthermore, typewriters became only a small segment of a much broader office equipment market, which included electric calculators, punched card equipment, electronic computers, and duplicating devices. Underwood waited to move into electronic computers—long after its competitors—and was hopelessly outclassed. IBM, on the other hand, maintained a consistent technological lead in punched card equipment and computers, and more recently has moved into the duplicating machine field.

Significantly, IBM itself might not have made the move into electronic computers if the elder Mr. Watson had not turned the company's leadership over to his son. This points up all the more strongly the dangers of a management resting on its laurels, continuing to do that which it has always done best but overlooking newer aspects of the relevant market.

Plan of Action. But a broad conception of the market is not a sufficient precondition for rapid growth. The investor should read speeches made by management at annual meetings, letters to shareholders, and similar communications to determine whether management has specific objectives, and specific plans and timetables for achieving those objectives. "We're keeping a watchful eye on things" is not very convincing evidence that management is doing its job.

Research and Development. Nowhere, perhaps, is the innovative spirit of a company's managers more discernible than in the conduct of its research and development activities. For the investor, the problem is not so much to determine whether or not a firm is engaged in research. Almost every modern firm is as a matter of survival. What the investor really has to do is distinguish between the sheer *volume* of research and the *quality* of research.

A clue to the quality of research lies in the actual record of product and process developments and improvements. In examining the record, the investor should recognize that a steady stream of new ideas, each of which makes only a modest contribution to the company's total activities, is probably more symptomatic of high-quality research than a single "blockbuster" invention that transforms the entire character of the company.

In probing the quality of a company's research effort, the investor also must make sure that research is a continuing program. If a company expects to make continuing profits from innovation, it must continually innovate. Otherwise, its profit potential will be exhausted when the market for a particular product becomes exhausted. Too often research is treated as a variable, rather than a fixed, cost. Thus, when business is good, research outlays are expanded, only to be cut back when hard times hit. Such programs are likely to fail, if only because capable research personnel will not stay with the company.

Organization

In most modern large enterprises, the "one-person show" has given way to some form of decentralized operation. On paper, a decentralized organization typically has the following characteristics: Each major product line, or each major geographic area, of a company is headed by a different vice president and is run as if it were a separate company. That is, the vice president of the "division" supervises a number of functional officers—production, marketing, finance, research, and so forth—and this team makes the decisions for that division. These decisions, however, are made within a broad framework of corporate policy established by the highest echelon of management—the chairman, president, and one or more executive vice presidents—acting in concert with both the divisional vice presidents and a group of vice presidents in the "corporate home office" who have *functional* rather than divisional responsibilities. For example, there will usually be a vice president–marketing at the corporate level, and a number of lower echelon marketing managers at the divisional level. The marketing managers are responsible to their respective divisional vice presidents, but the decisions of the latter are made within an overall corporate sales policy framework which is strongly influenced by the vice president–marketing. In addition, at the corporate home office level there usually will be a group of vice presidents and "staff" personnel whose authority and responsibilities cut across divisional lines—for example, in the financial and legal areas.

Thus, most large firms nowadays are decentralized, *at least on paper.* What investors must be concerned with, however, is whether the paper surface is truly reflective of the underlying substance. All too frequently it is not. What occurs in some cases is that the divisional vice presidents' authority is severely limited by the "home office" superstructure, with corporate people interfering with, instead of supporting, divisional activities. When this condition is present, there is a grave danger that the vitality of the entire organization will eventually be sapped—if it is not already—and investors must be alert to sense this.

To be sure, decentralization is not entirely free from criticism. For example, in the 1960s U.S. Steel Corporation found it necessary to reorganize drastically because its decentralization had gotten completely out of hand. Multiple layers of supervisory personnel had evolved, and too many independent production divisions and overlapping sales, accounting, and engineering offices were operating with inadequate policy guidelines.

Illustration. Thus, it is possible for decentralization to run rampant and for top management to lose control. One of the best illustrations of a company which has practiced decentralization without a loss of top management control is General Motors.

Each of GM's 29 divisions is headed by a general manager who functions relatively independently in running his operation. He has authority, for example, whether to add or reduce products in his line, how to formulate marketing strategy, where to buy his components and supplies, including going outside the company itself if he can get a better product or a better price. Each division general manager reports to a group vice president who in turn reports to top management. Policy making, however, is really the prerogative of two top committees, the executive committee and the finance committee. The operating side of GM is controlled by the five-member executive committee.

It is the executive committee that makes final decisions on proposed innovations and decides how much control will be exercised over the operating divisions. The 12-man finance committee wields the most power, however, with control over major expenditures. It sounds cumbersome, but for General Motors it has worked well over the years. Executive succession has been smooth and there have been no major organization crises. Find out if the company *you* are considering for investment can say the same.

Executive Development. A Washington regulatory official paid AT&T a backhanded compliment when he said: "If the entire Bell top management were snapped off the earth, the system would continue operating without a detectable tremor." In more positive fashion, the head of the American Management Institute has said: "If I were allowed only one question by which to evaluate an executive, this one would suffice: *Has he developed an adequate replacement for his own job?*" Perhaps this question can serve as a useful guideline to investors seeking to appraise the quality of a company's management team.

Frequently, a company's compensation system can serve as evidence of its policies regarding executive development. The investor should be wary of an organization whose proxy statements (which list management compensation figures) reveal that the chief executive earns several times as much as the three or four closest subordinates, or whose junior officials have impressive titles but unimpressive material rewards.

What Kind of Directors Does the Company Have? In carrying out its functions of review, appraisal, and appeal, a board of directors can be independent and objective or a mere rubber stamp. It can be a truly valuable and useful corporate asset, or a mere public relations showpiece. An investor is not usually privy to the inner workings of a company's board and must judge it on the basis of indirect evidence.

Foremost among the pieces of evidence is whether or not a majority of the board members are drawn from outside the management. Although it is acknowledged that some companies have done very well with "inside" boards, it would seem that they have done well in spite of the system rather than because of it. For an inside board—even if composed of full-time directors—tends to be too parochial in perspective and too much under the thumb of the chief executive. On the other hand, outside board members can provide the operating managers with new insights based upon their diversified experience and knowledge. So, study the background of your company's board by reading their biographies in one of the major *Who's Who*-type publications. As with every other aspect of this discussion of management, you won't find out everything you want to know; but you can add tile after tile to a mosaic which may suggest whether or not you're looking at a *well-managed* company.

SUGGESTED READINGS

Butler, William F.; Kavesh, Robert A.; and **Platt, Roberts,** eds. *Methods and Techniques of Business Forecasting.* Englewood Cliffs, N.J.: Prentice-Hall, 1974.

Chambers, John C. *An Executive's Guide to Forecasting.* New York: John Wiley & Sons, 1974.

Drucker, Peter F. *Management: Tasks, Responsibilities, Practices.* New York: Harper & Row, 1974.

Levine, Sumner, ed. *Financial Analysts Handbook.* Vol. 2. Homewood, Ill.: Dow Jones-Irwin, 1975.

Levitt, Theodore *Marketing for Business Growth.* New York: McGraw-Hill Book Co., 1974.

7

Bonds and Preferred Stocks

It's better to be safe than sorry.
Proverb

Except in the case of convertibles, which will be discussed in the next chapter, investors in bonds and preferred stocks sacrifice most of the benefits that may ensue from a company's future growth. In exchange for this sacrifice, bondholders get a promise by the company to pay a fixed amount of interest on specified dates, and to repay the principal at a specified time. Investors in preferred stocks do not get a promise, but they do get a claim on income and assets ahead of the common stock.

Since bond or preferred stock investors forego the benefits of growth, they must try to assure themselves that the issuers will be able to fulfill their obligations. They must be more concerned with an issuer's probable earnings under adverse circumstances than under favorable circumstances. They must pay more attention than common stock investors to balance sheets, to off-balance sheet obligations, and to realization values of assets as opposed to book values. Finally, they must give more weight to the possibility of a bear market for fixed income securities than a bull market—not because a bear market is more likely, but because risks should be more emphasized than opportunities in this area of investment. (A bear market in bonds occurs when the level of interest rates rises sharply. If you buy a 7 percent coupon bond at par, and two years later newly issued bonds of the same quality carry a higher coupon, no one will pay you par for your bonds. The price you can get will decline until the yield is competitive with new issues. At a later point, yield calculations are discussed more precisely.)

In view of these cautions, we advise investors to take the following approach to bond and preferred stock evaluation:

1. Establish standards of quality which will not be compromised readily.
2. Determine whether the outlook for interest rates militates against the purchase of fixed-income securities generally. That is, determine whether an extended uptrend of interest rates is in prospect.
3. If the time is ripe, compile a list of securities meeting the quality standards, and choose the most attractive securities on the list. Frequently this means the highest yielding securities on the list, but not necessarily, as will be shown.

QUALITY ANALYSIS

The Rating Agencies

One way of judging the quality of a bond is to examine the unbiased opinions of informed and experienced professionals. Bond rating agencies, such as Moody's, and Standard & Poor's, provide the investment community with an up-to-date record of their opinions on the quality of most large, publicly held corporate and governmental bond issues. These rating organizations are not in the business of selling bonds. Moreover, their ratings are made by committees rather than by single individuals. Thus, there is a minimal possibility that ulterior motives will cause one bond to be more highly rated than another. Indeed, agency ratings are held in such high regard that official regulatory commissions utilize them in evaluating the safety of the securities held by banks and insurance companies. The ratings and descriptions of the rated bonds are made available in a variety of publications which are sold on a subscription basis. For example, the indexes at the front of Moody's *Manuals* indicate Moody's ratings of the bonds of the indexed corporations or governments.

Bond ratings are designed essentially to rank issues in order of the probability of default—that is, inability to meet interest or sinking-fund payments or repayment of principal. Only issues of the federal government carry no risk of default, because Congress has the power to issue money to pay its debts. Thus, *triple-A* bonds (*Aaa* using Moody's designation, *AAA* using S&P's) are those judged to have a negligible risk of default and therefore to be of highest quality. *Double-A* bonds are of high quality also but are judged not to be quite as free of default risk as triple-A. Bonds rated A and BBB (*Baa* is Moody's designation) are generally referred to as medium-quality obligations, with the BBB possessing a higher risk of default than the A. Bonds not falling within the first four rating categories are believed to contain a considerable "speculative" element.

Rating Statistics. Some 4,000 corporate bond issues are rated by the agencies. Of these, about 60 percent are the bonds of utility companies, 25 percent are industrial issues, 12 percent are finance company issues, and the balance are bonds of transportation companies (railroads, airlines, and shipping).

Table 7–1 shows the distribution of ratings on outstanding corporate

Table 7–1
Rating Distribution of Agency-Rated Corporate Bonds* (percent of par value outstanding, December 31, 1975)

	Total Corporate	*Utilities*	*Industrial*	*Finance*	*Transportation*
AAA	23%	26%	21%	19%	7%
AA	26	25	26	33	10
A	33	32	34	34	27
BBB	13	16	10	5	18
BB	2	1	3	1	8
B	1	—	2	1	8
CCC and lower	2	—	4	7	22
	100%	100%	100%	100%	100%

* Convertible bonds are not included in the data.
Source: Salomon Brothers.

bonds in terms of par value. The table indicates that about 15 percent of utility and finance company bonds are of BBB quality or lower. Of industrial bonds, about 20 percent of the par value (and a much larger percentage by number, not shown in the table) are BBB or lower. Lower quality bonds were about 50 percent in the transportation sector.

Of the bonds rated by several agencies, perhaps half are rated identically. Where differences exist, they usually are not in excess of one rating category. That is, a bond rated, say, Aa by Moody's is most unlikely to be rated BBB by Standard & Poor's. While cynics may suspect collusion from the fact that such similarity exists, a more reasonable conclusion is that bond quality evaluation has become a rather precise art. This will become clearer as we examine the factors that the rating agencies take into consideration.

Statistics on ratings of state and local government bonds are not available in as fine detail as corporate bond data. From what is available, however, it appears that about two thirds of the value of rated bonds of such governments are in the top three rating categories, but that this percentage has been declining rather steadily in recent years. In terms of number of issues, moreover, a considerably smaller portion is in these categories. Furthermore, there are a vast number of relatively small issues (around $1 million to $5 million in value) that are unrated, even though publicly held.

Inadequacies of Ratings. Although agency ratings should be held in high regard, investors in fixed-income securities should go beyond mere examination of ratings in evaluating the quality of various issues. Agency ratings should be used primarily as a tool for quickly eliminating obviously unsuitable issues from consideration. For example, the investor may say: "Any issues rated lower than BBB/Baa (less than 10 percent of the par value of all rated corporate bonds) are probably too risky for me. Maybe a few *would* be suitable, but the effort involved in ferreting them out is very great, and I'll always have doubts. It's just not worth it to me."

But having said this much, the investor is still left with an enormous range of issues from which to choose. And four ratings categories is not a very detailed classification system for 90 percent of all rated bonds. Every AAA bond is not necessarily of equal quality; and it may well be that a given investor may think that a particular A bond is really as good as many AA issues. For example, a corporation's unsecured debentures will almost automatically be rated one category lower than its mortgage bonds. Yet the quality of the debentures may be so high that for practical purposes they can be considered as good as the mortgage bonds. Moreover, even the rating agencies often differ in evaluation by one rating category.

Determinants of Ratings. While the rating agencies, as well as other astute bond analysts, take "everything" into account when evaluating the quality of an issue, it is clear that some factors are more important than others. For corporate bonds and preferred stocks, these factors are:

1. The level and trend of *fixed charge coverage,* which is the relationship between earnings and interest charges (or, in some cases, between earnings and total debt service requirements, including both interest and sinking funds).

2. The level of long-term debt in relation to equity, with debt measured both by the amount shown on the balance sheet and the amount represented by off-balance sheet obligations.

3. The debtor's liquidity position, current and prospective.

4. The size and economic significance of the company and of the industry in which it operates.

5. The standing of the specific debt issue in the hierarchy of priorities in bankruptcy (for example, secured versus unsecured, senior versus subordinate) as well as the overall *protective provisions* of the issue.

Fixed Charge Coverage

The concept involved in fixed charge coverage (also referred to as *times charges earned*) is quite simple to grasp, for it is analogous to a measure used by banks and finance companies in judging applications for consumer credit. The lending officer considering the application will examine the relationship between the applicant's normal monthly or annual income and the size of the required monthly debt payments. The higher the income relative to debt service liabilities, the safer it is to extend credit, other things remaining equal. It is precisely the same with a bond.

Charges. In corporate bond analysis, the amount of charges to be covered usually is equal to the item *interest on loans,* which appears on the income statement. Typically, the bulk of this item equals the par value of outstanding funded debt times the coupon rate, although it also includes interest on short-term bank loans. In addition, the interest component of rentals under long-term leases should be included as a fixed charge.

If a corporation has more than one class of bonds outstanding—say first-mortgage bonds and debentures—the pertinent figure is usually the sum of the annual interest charges on *all* of the debt. This is because all the bonds are legally enforceable claims; a default on any one of them can put the company into bankruptcy, thus jeopardizing the holders of the other issues as well. Therefore, we do not usually speak of coverage of mortgage bond charges and coverage of debenture charges, but rather coverage of total debt charges. However, there may be some justification for evaluating senior mortgage bonds separately. Senior mortgage bondholders generally receive better treatment in reorganization than other bondholders. For example, in the event of bankruptcy the courts may allow a well-secured issue to continue to receive interest payments even though payments on other issues are suspended.

Sinking-fund requirements—that is, amortization of principal—usually are not included in the definition of fixed charges when analyzing corporate bonds, although they are included in appraising consumer credit and municipal revenue bonds (often they also are included in railroad bond analysis). There are two main reasons for the omission: (1) Although sinking-fund default is an act of bankruptcy, creditors usually are willing to waive payments for a year or two if the company is temporarily embarrassed. (2) Sinking-fund payments are presumed to be covered by depreciation charges.

Earnings Available. A convenient working definition of the amount of earnings available for the payment of bond charges is: net income before taxes, before interest, and before the interest component of rents under long-term leases. The use of pretax earnings is suggested in preference to after-tax earnings even though many analysts and investment services use the latter. Since interest is a tax-deductible expense, it is logical to compare it with net *before* taxes. Earnings are taken before deduction of interest, since we want to know how much is available for payment of interest. If it is felt desirable to include sinking-fund requirements in fixed charges, earnings available for payment should be defined as *predepreciation* pretax earnings. Moreover, if the *total* amount of rentals is included in fixed charges, rather than just the interest component of these rentals, earnings available should be defined as pretax earnings before interest and before rent.

Coverage Ratio. After calculating (*a*) earnings available for payment of bond charges, and (*b*) the amount of bond charges, the earnings coverage ratio is calculated by dividing (*a*) by (*b*).

In earnings coverage analysis of preferred stocks, preferred dividend requirements are added to interest charges, if any, in calculating charges to be covered, and this sum is divided into total *available earnings*. Preferred dividends are *not* added back to derive available earnings, because they were not deducted to derive net income. In other words, earnings available for preferred dividends are the same earnings that are available for bond charges. Moreover, since preferred dividends are not tax deductible like interest, in order to equate them with interest charges they ought to be doubled since the corporate tax rate is about 50 percent.

To illustrate the coverage calculations, assume that a company's net income before taxes amounts to $33 million. And assume that its balance sheet shows:

5% First-mortgage bonds	$20,000,000
6¼% Debentures	16,000,000
7½% Preferred stock	20,000,000

Total charges to be covered, adjusted for the preferred stock tax factor, are as follows:

Preferred dividends	7.5% × $20,000,000 =	$1,500,000
Times: Adjustment factor		×2
Equals: Adjusted preferred dividends		$3,000,000
Plus: Interest on bonds:	5% × $20,000,000 =	1,000,000
	6.25% × $16,000,000 =	1,000,000
Equals: Total charges, adjusted		$5,000,000

Earnings available for payment of the $5 million of adjusted total charges equal net income before taxes ($33 million), plus bond interest ($2 million), or $35 million. The coverage ratio of the preferred stock, therefore, is $^{35}/_{5}$, or 7. On the other hand, the coverage of the bonds is $^{35}/_{2}$, or 17½. Note that where a company has both bonds and preferred stock in its capital structure, the coverage of the preferred always will be lower than the coverage of the bonds. Thus it is entirely possible that the bonds will be of acceptable quality whereas the preferred stock will not.

Standards. The next logical question is whether 7 times charges or 17½ times charges should be considered high or low, good or bad. It is impossible to be dogmatic in answering this question. Different investors have different safety standards. However, we would suggest the guidelines shown in Table 7–2.

Table 7–2
Standards for Grading Coverage Ratios of Fixed-Income Securities

Typical Coverage Ratio	*Characteristic of Company*	*Relative Quality of Issue*
6 and over	Cyclical	Very high
4 and over	Stable	Very high
3–6	Cyclical	Medium to high
2–4	Stable	Medium to high
Under 3	Cyclical	Low
Under 2	Stable	Low

Note that a distinction is made between companies whose earnings are very vulnerable to the business cycle (for example, steel), and companies which are more stable (for example, utilities). A better coverage is demanded of the more cyclical companies. Note also that these suggested standards are formed in terms of the *typical level* of fixed charge coverage. In addition, investors should be concerned with the *trend* of coverage. A lower than ideal level may be tolerated if the trend is clearly upward.

Capital Structure

Another quality measure which almost all bond analysts stress is the proportion of total capitalization represented by debt versus equity. The individual bond or preferred stock owner would be best off if the certificate were the only senior security outstanding, because earnings coverage then would be at a maximum (assuming that the corporation could raise elsewhere the funds necessary to operate a prosperous business). Thus, to the bondholder or preferred stockholder, the greater the junior capital as a percent of total capitalization the better. An analysis of the corporation's capital structure is, therefore, a sort of *asset coverage* measure which supplements the earnings coverage measure previously discussed.

Illustration. Assume that the following information was derived from a company's year-end balance sheet and that there were no significant off-balance sheet liabilities (in million dollars):

Long-term debt (excluding due in 1 year)	$ 500
Preferred stock ($100 par)	150
Common stock (20,000,000 shares no par)	20
Capital surplus	50
Retained earnings	780
Total Long-Term Capital	$1,500

The capital structure can be stated as:

Long-term debt	33%	(500/1,500)
Preferred stock	10	(150/1,500)
Common stock and surplus	57	(850/1,500)
Total	100%	

Standards. Again the question arises: Are these ratios high or low? Again, one cannot be dogmatic. Some guidelines may be offered, however (see Table 7–3).

Table 7–3
Maximum Percent of Senior Capital for Security Quality Classifications

Company Characteristic	*Quality*		
	Very High	*Medium to High*	*Low*
Cyclical	30	40	60
Stable	50	60	70
Public utility*	50–60	60–75	75

* Separate standards are given for public utility companies as distinct from stable companies generally, and are given as a *range,* because the subject of optimal leverage is even more controversial for public utility companies than for corporations in aggregate.

Liquidity

Some companies may appear to have satisfactory earnings and capital yet be "cash poor." That is, their earnings look satisfactory relative to obligations and they do not seem to be overly leveraged, yet bondholders or preferred stockholders may not be sure that enough cash will be on hand to pay their claims as they come due. This condition may have several causes. For example:

1. The company may be "pushing sales" (and thereby increasing reported earnings) by extending unusually long credit terms to its customers, thus tying up its resources in receivables which are not very liquid.
2. The company may be tying up resources in excessive inventories in order to be able to respond promptly to all incoming orders.
3. The company may be relying heavily on trade payables and short-term bank borrowings to provide its working capital needs, rather than building up its long-term capital base, and in a period of general economic difficulty may find that its vendors and bankers are reluctant to continue being as liberal in extending credit.

The appraisal of a company's liquidity position should encompass the type of sources and uses of funds analysis described in Chapter 4. Such an analysis will highlight the past and probable future sources of cash available to the enterprise, and the probable uses of cash for both mandatory and discretionary corporate purposes. Since this type of analysis is complex, however, various financial ratios have been used as a substitute for the more rigorous analytical effort. The principal ratios in common use are:

1. Receivables Collection Period. This ratio measures the number of days it takes, on average, to collect accounts and notes receivable. To do the calculation, first determine the average daily selling rate (usually taken as annual sales divided by 360, or quarterly sales divided by 90). Then determine the average amount of accounts receivable outstanding during the year, or the quarter, being measured (usually taken as one half of beginning and ending receivables). Finally, divide average receivables by average daily sales. For example, suppose annual sales of a company are \$180 million, receivables at the start of the year are \$24 million, and receivables at year-end are \$36 million. The receivables collection period would be 60 days:

$$\frac{24 + 36}{2} \div \frac{180}{360} = 30 \div 0.5 = 60 \text{ days}$$

If the investor in this case determined that the typical *terms of trade* in the industry were 2/10:net/30, and that competing companies have a collection period of, say, 45 days or less, it would be clear that some sleuthing is needed to find out why this particular company has a 60-day collection period. The reason could be, as noted above, that the company is "pushing sales" by extending unusual credit terms; or the company might be doing a poor collection job; or the company might have a number of customers who are in financial difficulty.

2. Number of Days to Sell Inventory. Analogous to the prior ratio described, this ratio is derived by dividing average daily cost of goods sold into the average of beginning and ending inventory. The resulting figure should be compared with similar calculations for other firms in the same industry, both in the current period and in prior periods, to judge whether the company in question is operating with especially sparse or especially heavy, and possibly obsolete, inventory.

3. Number of Days' Bills Outstanding. Here, the average daily cost of goods sold is divided into average accounts payable. The resulting number is compared with that of other firms in the same industry, and is also tracked over time in comparison with the receivables collection period. Though days receivable and days payable can be quite different magnitudes, generally speaking one would expect to find a fairly *constant relationship* between the two. If they begin to depart from their customary relationship, further investigation is called for.

4. Working Capital Ratios. Whereas the prior three ratios dissect working capital (current assets minus current liabilities) into its major components—accounts receivable, inventory, and accounts payable—analysts like to take an overall view of a company's ability to meet current liabilities. The most common measures, in this regard, are:

a. Current Ratio. Current assets divided by current liabilities.
b. Quick Asset, or Acid-Test, Ratio. Current assets exclusive of inventory, divided by current liabilities.
c. Cash Ratio. Bank deposits plus liquid securities owned, divided by current liabilities.

It is even more difficult to generalize about what constitutes a high- or low-working capital ratio than it is to generalize about earnings coverage or capitalization ratios. Although a current ratio of at least 2 to 1 often is set as a standard (1 to 1 for the acid test), liquidity requirements are very much a function of the nature of a company's business. For example, a telephone company can operate with a very low current ratio because there is a relatively short time lag between the provision of services to subscribers, the billing, and the receipt of payment. On the other hand, a machinery company faces a long time span between the acquisition of raw materials, the construction and shipment of machines, and the receipt of payment. This is particularly true if the machine is leased rather than sold. Consequently, the only feasible procedure is to compare the working capital ratios of the company under analysis with the ratios of other similarly situated companies, although there is an obvious element of circular reasoning in an approach where everyone looks at what someone else is doing.

Economic Significance

Bond analysts place heavy emphasis on the size and trade position of the issuing company and on the nature of the industry. They are inclined to look most favorably upon companies which are in industries that are considered "indispensable." Similarly, large corporations which represent a substantial share of their industries' output are believed to involve less risk to creditors than smaller corporations with less entrenched trade positions. This aspect of bond quality analysis is indirectly reflected in the fact that the average size of outstanding AAA bonds in the marketplace is about $80 million, the average AA bond amounts to about $45 million, As are some $30 million, and BBBs are $25 million. While size of issue and size of issuer are not necessarily perfectly correlated, there is a close enough relationship to infer that bond quality ratings and size of issuer go hand in hand.

Protective Provisions of the Issue

The rights of bond and preferred stock owners are spelled out in detailed legal instruments—bond indentures and preferred stock contracts. The specifics of these instruments are important ingredients of quality estimates although, as will be stressed below, continuance of the issuer's earning power is more significant than the contractual provisions of the issue.

With regard to contractual provisions, there is, first, the question of collateral. A corporate *mortgage bond* provides that in the event of bankruptcy the bondholders have first claim on the value of specified corporate assets. Where a bond is not secured by a mortgage, it is referred to as a *debenture.* Unless they are explicitly *subordinated* by the terms of the indenture (as is common, for example, with convertibles), debentures are like accounts payable. They are general liabilities of the corporation which have a claim on the value of corporate assets, in the event of bankruptcy, that precedes the claim of preferred and common stock owners (and of subordinated creditors) but comes after the claim of mortgage bondholders, corporate employees (for unpaid wages), the government (for unpaid taxes), and other claims to which the bankruptcy statutes give priority. The claim of preferred stockholders may be exercised after the general creditors have been satisfied and before the common stockholders receive anything.

Various clauses may be inserted into the indenture of a bond to protect its priority position vis-à-vis other creditors. For example, an *equal-and-ratable-security* clause specifies that if a lien *subsequently* is placed on corporate assets, the bond in question will have an equal and pro rata share in the lien. *Open-end* mortgage clauses provide that additional bonds may be issued with an equivalent lien, but only if the additional debt does not cause the total to exceed a specified percentage of the mortgaged assets. Other limitations on the issuance of additional debt may be that earnings have to bear a minimum relationship to the amount of debt or to the amount of interest charges, and that working capital has to be maintained at some minimum level. *After-acquired-property* clauses state that if property is acquired after the issuance of a first-mortgage bond, it automatically will fall under the lien of that mortgage unless waived by the existing mortgage bond owners. In the case of preferred stock contracts, it usually is provided that subsequent issues of stock with a priority over the preferred are not permitted unless approved by the holders of a certain percentage of the preferred stock outstanding.

Collateral De-emphasized. The collateral provisions of bonds used to be very heavily stressed by investors. They are much less emphasized today. Not that they are ignored—indeed, the rating agencies usually grade a corporation's debentures one notch lower than the same corporation's first-mortgage bonds, and subordinated debentures generally are rated lower than senior debentures. But collateral and priorities are less emphasized than in earlier days.

The reasons for the de-emphasis of collateral are quite clear. Property value is a function of the earnings which the property can produce. Most property which serves as bond collateral is in the form of specialized plant and equipment—for example, a steel mill. When the economics of the issuing company deteriorate to the point of bankruptcy, the likelihood is that its property is incapable of earning a decent rate of return and is therefore not worth very much.

In some cases, the property may be convertible into some other use, or may be made more profitable by more efficient managers. Such property can have an intrinsic worth sufficient to meet the claims of secured creditors. But in bankruptcy cases involving truly valuable property, the courts have been extremely reluctant to allow secured creditors to exercise their lien and sell the property to meet their claims. Typically, reorganization proceedings are ordered, the end result of which is to liquidate existing claims by issuing new securities to the claimants. The trouble is that the more valuable the property, the more strenuously the junior claimants will fight to keep from being left out of the reorganized company.

The Preferred Stock's Priority. While investors often have given too much weight to the collateral features of bond contracts, they often have paid too *little* heed to the nature of preferred stock contracts. Preferred stock is classified legally as equity, but investors traditionally have looked upon preferreds as almost the same thing as bonds. The reasoning has been as follows.

The major legal difference between a bond and a preferred stock lies in the nature of the holder's claim. Bondholders get a legally enforceable claim while preferred stockholders do not. Legally, they get only a priority above common stockholders. Failure to pay bond interest is an act of bankruptcy; failure to pay a preferred stock dividend is not. But practically speaking, when a corporation is operating profitably, the claims of both bond and preferred stock owners usually will be met. And when a corporation is in serious trouble, it isn't too much comfort that you're a bondholder rather than a preferred stockholder; you're in trouble either way. This very practical observation has led many investors to believe that a preferred stock is, by its nature, just about as good as a bond.

The conclusion that preferred stocks are inherently as investment worthy as bonds is faulty, however. It omits consideration of the great number of corporations which are neither so consistently profitable that there is no question of omitting interest or preferred dividend payments, nor in such dreadfully poor condition that the bankruptcy courts loom ahead. Such corporations will make every possible effort to meet their bond obligations as they come due but often will not be nearly as diligent in paying preferred stock dividends. Numerous instances can be cited of companies whose earnings were high enough to pay preferred dividends but whose directors chose to keep the money in the business to build up future earning power. True, the inclusion of a cumulative dividend feature in most preferred stock issues acts as a deterrent to the promiscuous passing of dividends. (An unpaid dividend on a cumulative preferred stock is carried as an "arrearage" which must be cleared before common stock dividends can be paid.) Nevertheless, when management thinks it is to the company's long-term advantage to pass preferred dividends, it will do so. Unfortunately for the preferred stockholders, even if management is right about the long-term merits of its action, passing a dividend invariably depresses the market price of the preferred stock considerably.

Sinking Funds. About 80 percent of industrial bonds, 20 percent of utility bonds and some preferred stocks require an annual *sinking-fund* payment by the corporation in order gradually to retire the issue. The specific bonds or preferred stock certificates to be retired at any given time may be selected at random and "called" at a specified price, or they may be bought in the open market if a sufficient supply is available at below the call price. In rare cases nowadays, are the annual sinking-fund payments left in an escrow account (earning interest) for eventual retirement of the entire issue at once.

Sinking funds are disadvantageous to investors in one significant respect. After they have gone to all the trouble of evaluating and purchasing a security at what they consider to be an attractive rate of return, the investors may find the security snatched away from them by a sinking-fund call. And at that time interest rates may be considerably lower than when they purchased the issue, so that reinvestment in an equally attractive issue may not be possible. But there are several advantages of sinking funds to investors, and these are generally considered to outweigh the disadvantage:

1. Sinking funds for bonds, like amortization provisions in home mortgages, give the lender greater assurance that the principal amount of the debt will be repaid by the maturity date. Chances of the borrower being embarrassed are much greater when a huge principal balance suddenly comes due. If the original proceeds of the issue had been used to acquire plant and equipment, as is likely, sinking fund payments as the property depreciates help maintain a healthy balance between fixed assets and long-term liabilities.

2. With preferred stocks, a sinking fund compensates for the fact that such securities have no maturity dates as bonds do. This can be particularly important in a period of persistently rising interest rates and resulting declining prices of fixed-income investments. The owner of a preferred stock which has no sinking fund is doomed to a capital loss, whereas the owner of an issue which has a sinking fund knows that eventually the par value will be returned.

3. If the company's earnings hold steady, the retirement of a portion of its bonds or preferred stock leaves the remaining investors better protected.

4. If the price of the bonds or preferreds falls below par, the company will use the sinking fund to buy up securities in the open market rather than call them at par, or par plus a premium. This provides some price support for the issue, although it by no means constitutes a floor.

Of course, the other side of the coin must also be recognized, namely that call price tends to set a ceiling on market price. Since an investor who pays more than the call price will suffer a loss if his holding is called, he is reluctant to pay the high price.

Analysis of Municipal Bonds

Since the focus of this book is on corporate securities, we will not dwell at length on the techniques employed in analyzing the bonds of states, municipalities, and other local subdivisions, all of which are classified under the broad heading, "municipals." Nevertheless, some discussion is in order in view of their important role in the securities markets.

There are two general types of municipal bonds—general obligations (also known as G.O.s or full-faith-and-credit bonds), and revenue bonds (or assessment bonds). The former are backed by the total taxing power of the issuer, while the latter are backed only by specific revenues, usually those derived from the facilities which are constructed with the proceeds of the bonds, such as turnpikes, dormitories, and sewers. With municipal bonds, even more than with corporates, the bondholder's security lies in the *income* potential of the community or facility rather than in *asset* values. For courts certainly will not allow vital public facilities to be seized by creditors.

In the analysis of general obligations, three ratios are perhaps most widely used. They are:

1. Principal amount of tax-dependent debt as a percent of the assessed valuation of taxable real estate. This measure is used because property taxes are the key revenue-raising devices of most local governments, and property values are a good indirect measure of the wealth and income of a community. In comparing the level of this ratio among different communities, allowance must be made for differences in assessment methods. For example, one community may assess property at, say, 70 percent of estimated market value, while another may assess at full value. Another complication stems from the existence of overlapping debt, which occurs when the same piece of property is taxed by different governmental units.

After allowance is made for these analytical problems, a ratio of 8 percent of debt to property values for smaller governments, and 10 percent for larger ones, traditionally has been considered a practical maximum in order for their bonds to be rated high quality.

2. Debt per capita. Small cities with good credit ratings generally do not have more than $250–$350 principal amount of debt per resi-

dent. For larger cities, the figure may run to $500 or more before their bonds get accorded less than highest ratings.

3. Debt service (annual interest and debt retirement obligations) as a percent of the community's budgeted operating expenses. If debt service begins to approach 20 percent of the budget, a clear warning signal usually can be inferred. (Note that most municipal bonds are issued in so-called serial maturity form. Under this procedure, a portion of the issue actually matures each year, so the holder knows precisely when the bonds will be retired as opposed to the holder of a sinking-fund bond. Different maturity dates of the serial issue usually carry different interest rates.)

In addition to these ratios, municipal bond analysts also place heavy emphasis on the amount of debt maturing within five years (when it exceeds 25 percent of total debt, caution is advisable), on the prospective capital expenditures of the governmental unit, on the unit's ability to avoid persistent deficit financing, and, in recent years, on broader "sociological" trends.

Revenue bonds are very much like the bonds of business corporations. Their quality depends largely on the "profitability" of the facilities whose revenues are pledged to support the bonds. Therefore, the key ratio in revenue bond analysis is earnings coverage. Since civic facilities are not profit-making operations in the business sense—fees are usually designed to meet only operating expenses and debt service, with a small addition for contingencies—coverage ratios are not expected to be as substantial as for corporate bonds. Ratios of 1½ to 2 times charges are common for good quality obligations.

SELECTION AMONG QUALIFYING ISSUES

We have been describing the methods by which a fixed income investor can establish quality standards to use in compiling a list of "eligible" bonds or preferred stocks. We turn, now, to the problem of determining proper prices of issues on the list, so that they can be ranked in order of attractiveness for purchase or sale at any given time.

Yield Mathematics Simplified

When a bond is priced at par, it is customary to refer to its coupon rate as its yield. At prices above or below par, however, yield and coupon rate are not synonymous.

Yield to Maturity. When a bond is selling at a premium (above par) or discount (below par), yield is sometimes defined as *current yield.*

This is simply the coupon rate expressed in dollars, divided by the price. Thus, an 8 percent coupon bond selling at 90 (that is, $900 per $1,000 bond) has a current yield of 80/900, or 8.89 percent. This is the same type of calculation used in determining the yield on a common stock—dividend divided by price—and is applicable to preferred stocks as well.

For most purposes, however, current yield is an inadequate measure of a bond's rate of return. It fails to reflect the fact that unless the issuer defaults, the holder will receive the par value at maturity. In addition to annual coupon payments, therefore, allowance must be made for the ultimate appreciation in value of bonds purchased at a discount or the ultimate depreciation of bonds purchased at a premium. Even if the individual investor has no intention of holding the bond to maturity, it ultimately will be sold to a party who does so intend. And more important than the personal predilections of investors is the need for a common denominator in expressing the yields on different bonds of varying maturity. Obviously, a discount of, say, $100 per $1,000 bond is worth more if the bond will mature in 5 years than if it will mature in 20 (assuming that it will, in fact, be paid off at maturity). For these reasons, the concept of *yield to maturity* is the accepted common denominator in the financial community.

A simple analogy should make the yield-to-maturity concept clear. Assume that you are examining an 8 percent coupon bond, with ten years remaining to maturity, selling at a price of 90. The yield to maturity in this situation is equivalent to the rate of interest, compounded semiannually, which a savings bank would have to guarantee to enable you to deposit $900 today, withdraw $40 every half year (bond interest usually is paid semiannually), and have $1,000 in your passbook ten years hence.

Tables are published which can be used to determine yield to maturity, and these are available at any financial library or brokerage office. In the absence of tables, a simple approximation formula can be applied.

Yield Tables. Table 7–4 is excerpted from a book of bond yield tables. It is a relatively simple matter to find one's way through such a book, despite its forbidding appearance. In the upper right- or left-hand corner of each page a percentage figure appears—in our example 8 percent. This represents the coupon rate of the bond under study. Having turned to the appropriate page, move to the column which corresponds to the number of years (and months) remaining to maturity, as indicated by the column heading—ten years in our example. Then scan the price column to locate the price of the bond under con-

Table 7–4
Excerpt from Bond Yield Table **8%**

	Years to Maturity			*Years to Maturity*	
Price	*10*	*20*	*Price*	*10*	*20*
90	9.58	9.09	100	8.00	8.00
91	9.41	8.98	101	7.85	7.90
92	9.24	8.86	102	7.71	7.80
93	9.08	8.75	103	7.57	7.70
94	8.92	8.64	104	7.43	7.61
95	8.76	8.53	105	7.29	7.51
96	8.60	8.42	106	7.15	7.42
97	8.45	8.31	107	7.01	7.33
98	8.30	8.21	108	6.88	7.24
99	8.15	8.10			

sideration. The yield to maturity will be found at the intersection of the price row and the maturity column—9.58 percent in our example. (While Table 7–4 shows yields in the body of the table, with price shown in the first and fourth columns, many such tables show prices in the body, with yield shown in the initial columns. The underlying principles of interpreting the tables are the same, however.)

Yield Formula. When yield tables are not handy, an approximation formula can produce fairly satisfactory results. The formula is:

$$\frac{\text{Annual coupon interest} + (\text{Discount/Number years to maturity})}{(\text{Current price} + \text{Par value})/2}$$

or

$$\frac{\text{Annual coupon interest} - (\text{Premium/Number years to maturity})}{(\text{Current price} + \text{Par value})/2}$$

Applying this formula to our example would produce this result

$$\frac{80 + 100/10}{(900 + 1{,}000)/2} = \frac{80 + 10}{950} = \frac{90}{950} = 9.47\%.$$

Our approximation would thus be 0.11 percent away from the correct yield. Now suppose that the same bond were selling for 108 instead of 90. Applying the formula, we would get:

$$\frac{80 - 80/10}{(1{,}080 + 1{,}000)/2} = \frac{80 - 8}{1{,}040} = \frac{72}{1{,}040} = 6.92\%.$$

Turning back to Table 7–4, you will note that a price of 108 produces a yield of exactly 6.88 percent. Our estimate is off by only 0.04 percent, or 4 *basis points* (a basis point is equal to onc hundredth of 1 percent).

Maturity and Risk. A comparison of the 10- and 20-year maturity columns of Table 7–4 brings out another very significant fact to bond investors. Note that a 10 point price rise from 90 to 100 is associated with a 158 basis point yield decline (from 9.58 percent to 8 percent) for a 10-year maturity bond, but with only a 109 basis point yield decline for a 20-year bond. Similarly, a yield increase of 55 basis points (from 6.88 percent to 7.43 percent) produces a price decline of 4 points (from 108 to 104) on a 10-year bond; but a yield increase of 56 basis points (from 7.24 percent to 7.80 percent) drops price 6 points (from 108 to 102) on a 20-year bond. It is usually the case that fluctuations in the general level of interest rates cause long-term bonds to fluctuate more in price than shorter term bonds. When interest rates rise, long-term bonds fall more sharply in price than shorter term bonds; when interest rates fall, long terms rise faster in price.

The Coupon Factor. In the previous paragraph, we assumed that the coupon rates of the various issues were identical (8 percent), and that only the maturities were different. What if the maturities were the same but the *coupons* were different? Suppose, for example, that two different bonds of equal quality both have 25-year maturities and are priced to yield about 7.5 percent, but that one has a 4 percent coupon (selling at 550) and one has a 9 percent coupon (selling at 1,200). What is likely to happen to the price of each bond if the general level of interest rates either rises sharply or falls sharply?

The answer is that the lowest coupon bond will have the greatest price change and the highest coupon bond will have the least, other factors remaining equal. For example, if the yield on the two bonds cited above rose from 7.5 percent to 9 percent, the 4 percent coupon bond would drop about 27 percent in price from 550 to 400, while the 9 percent coupon bond would drop about 17 percent from 1,200 to par (1,000). The reason for the greater volatility of the low coupon bond is that a large portion of its yield to maturity represents capital gain which will not be realized until a distant date, while the yield of the high coupon bond will be realized much earlier in the form of large semiannual interest payments. Therefore, to obtain a yield improvement, a large proportionate increase in capital gain component (that is, a larger proportionate price decline) is required from the low coupon bond than from the high coupon bond. Similarly, a *yield decline* is associated with a larger proportionate *price improvement* on the low coupon bond.

Thus, we have seen that bond price responses to changes in yield levels tend to vary *directly with maturity and inversely with coupon.*

Another important consideration in trying to determine the appropriate price of a bond is its callability feature.

Taking Account of the Call Privilege. Some bonds are fully callable at their issuer's option (usually with 30 days' notice). Others are not callable for any purpose other than sinking-fund requirements. Between these extremes, some bonds are callable for other than refunding purposes. That is, they cannot be called with the intent of replacing them with new bonds at lower yields, but they may be called to be retired or replaced with stock, or in a debt consolidation move, or because of a merger, or for some similar reason. Still other issues are nonrefundable for a specified number of years, but are refundable thereafter.

When a bond is callable for refunding purposes, the yield-to-maturity calculation may not be an appropriate measure of the issue's expected rate of return. For if there is a significant chance that interest rates will fall to a level which makes refunding attractive to the issuers, they may exercise their call privileges. If they do, the investors will be faced with the necessity of reinvesting their money—presumably at lower interest rates if they do not reduce quality. In addition to reinvesting at lower rates, they will incur the expense and bother of making a new search for an acceptable issue. An offset against this expense will be the "call premium" which the issuers are required to pay in order to exercise their call privileges. The end result of all these factors may be a realized yield that is substantially different from the originally calculated yield to maturity.

Bond investors typically take call features into account by calculating the "yield to first call date." This calculation is usually made on high coupon bonds selling at a premium during a period of low interest rates. In terms of the yield formula described above, instead of amortizing the premium over the number of years remaining to maturity, the number of years to the earliest date at which the bonds may be called for refunding is used in the numerator. In the denominator, the call price is substituted for the par value.

Tax Factors. In comparing the yield of a tax-exempt security with the yield of a fully taxable issue, allowance should be made for the investor's tax bracket. For example, if an individual in the 50 percent tax bracket buys a 5 percent coupon tax-exempt issue *at par,* the same after-tax return as a 10 percent coupon taxable bond *bought at par* is received. The formula for calculating *taxable equivalent yields* is: tax-exempt yield divided by 100 percent minus the tax rate.

Stress is placed on purchase at par value in the preceding paragraph, because yield to maturity of a bond purchased at a discount or premium includes not only regular income but also a capital gain or loss component. Gains and losses are taxed differently from regular income. Suppose that the same 5 percent municipal bond is purchased by the same 50 percent bracket individual, but at a discount to yield 6 percent to maturity. As a crude rule of thumb, the following calculation can be made:

	Pretax Yield (percent)	*Tax Rate (percent)*	*After-Tax Yield (percent)*
Coupon income	5.00	0	5.00
Capital gain	1.00	25*	0.75
Total	6.00		5.75

* The regular rate on one half the gain.

If a 5 percent coupon *taxable* bond were available at a discount to yield 9 percent to maturity, we can assume (again, very crudely) that 5 percent of the 9 percent total yield is taxed at regular rates, and 4 percent is taxed at capital gains rates. The calculation for the same individual would be:

	Pretax Yield (percent)	*Tax Rate (percent)*	*After-Tax Yield (percent)*
Coupon income	5.00	50	2.50
Capital gain	4.00	25	3.00
Total	9.00		5.50

Thus, one might have thought that a taxable bond must sell at twice the yield of a tax-exempt bond to equalize the after-tax returns to a 50 percent bracket investor. In this case, however, it is shown that the taxable bond's yield to maturity (9 percent) is nowhere near twice that of the tax-exempt issue (6 percent). Yet, when the differences between coupon and capital gains, and the related taxes, are considered, the taxable bond's net yield to the 50 percent bracket investor is only 0.25 percent lower than the tax-exempt issue.

Yield Changes

Having considered the measurement of bond yields and the factors influencing the relationship of bond price changes to yield changes, we turn next to the characteristics of yield changes themselves over time. Bond investors have to be concerned with three types of yield changes: (1) changes in the *level* of yields; (2) changes in the *yield curve,* which refers to the relationships among yields on short-maturity, intermediate-maturity, and long-maturity bonds; and (3) changes in *yield spreads,* which refers to the yield relationships among bonds of different quality, different coupon, different call features, or different tax status.

Yield Levels. Figure 7–1 portrays the movement of yields on corporate bonds of highest quality since 1900. Three features of the data stand out:

Figure 7–1
Yields of Prime Long Corporate Bonds since 1900

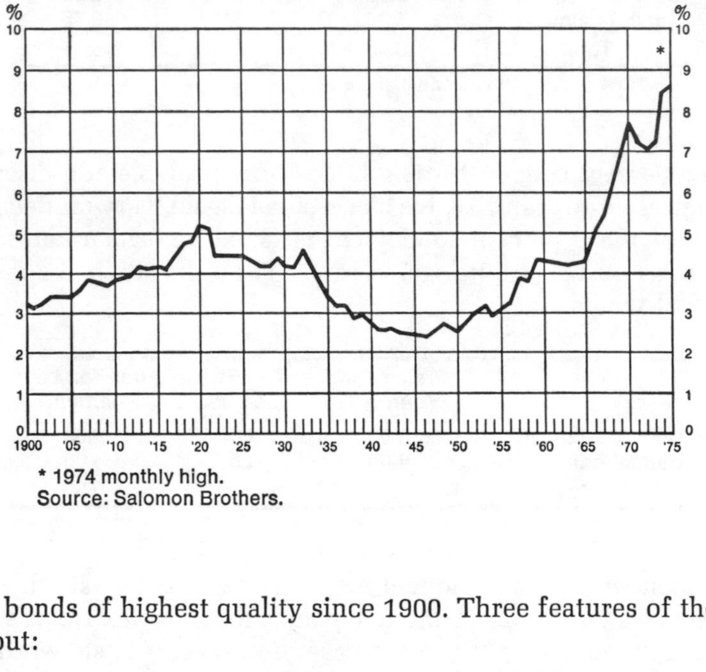

* 1974 monthly high.
Source: Salomon Brothers.

1. There was no overall trend in bond yields during this period, taken as a whole.
2. Although there was no overall trend, bond yields have moved in *long cycles.* Thus they rose from 1900 to 1920, declined from 1920 to 1946, and climbed steadily back to the level of the 1920s from 1946 to 1965. Thereafter, they moved sharply higher, to levels not seen since the Civil War.
3. Superimposed on the long cycles have been cycles of shorter duration.

The nature of interest rate cycles will be discussed in more detail in chapter 10, along with methods by which economists attempt to *forecast* interest rate movements. For the moment, suffice it to say that bond investors must be acutely conscious of the current stage of the interest rate cycle at the time a bond purchase or sale is being contemplated.

Yield Curves. If it is a general expectation among fixed income investors that the overall level of interest rates is likely to rise, they will tend to avoid buying long-term bonds. This is because such bonds will fall substantially in price if the investors are correct and the level of rates does, in fact, rise. Investors will prefer to keep funds in shorter term securities, awaiting a more opportune time for switching into long terms. On the other hand, if investors expect a substantial decline in rates, long-term bonds will appear to be very attractive investments from two points of view: (1) they can provide a high level of income for many years; (2) they will rise in price if rates fall, and can be sold at a profit if a holder so chooses.

Thus, a general expectation of rising interest rates will cause lenders (bond investors) to prefer shorter maturity to longer maturity issues, and a general expectation of falling interest rates will lead to a greater relative desire for longer maturity than for shorter maturity issues. On the borrowing side of the market, however, the relative desires tend to be the opposite. A general expectation of rising interest rates will encourage borrowers to rush their offerings of long-term bonds to market in order to minimize the rise in their cost of capital. An expectation of falling rates, on the other hand, will encourage them to delay their bond offerings and to do as much financing as possible in the short-term market.

In sum, expectations regarding future interest rate levels give rise to differing supply and demand pressures in the various maturity sectors of the bond market. These pressures are reflected in differences in the yield movements of bonds of different maturity. If borrowers prefer to sell long-term bonds at the very time lenders prefer to invest in shorter maturity issues, as is the case when interest rates are expected to rise, longer maturity issues will tend to carry higher yields than shorter maturity issues. The *term structure of interest rates,* or *yield curve,* will be *upward sloping.* Likewise, if borrowers prefer to sell short-maturity issues at the time lenders prefer to invest in longs, as is the case when interest rates are expected to fall, longer maturity issues will tend to yield less than shorter maturity issues. The yield curve will be *downward sloping.* This is illustrated in Figure 7–2.

Thus, investors can infer from the shape of the yield curve whether "the market" expects the general level of interest rates to rise or fall in the future. This knowledge can be useful if the investor is trying to pit his or her own interest rate forecasts against those of the market. A study of yield curves is also important for another reason. Although

Figure 7–2
Yield Curve Determination

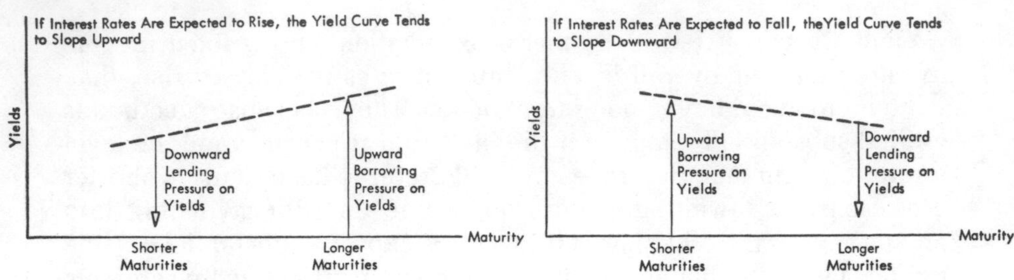

a yield curve is represented as a fairly smooth, continuous curve, attempting to portray the average relationship between yield and maturity, in fact there is a scatter of individual observations above and below the yield curve. Figure 7–3, for example, is a recent yield curve of government securities. Note the number of individual issues above and below the curve—that is, yielding more or less than their maturity suggests they should. These issues can be investigated further to see if their above-average or below-average yields can be explained by some specific characteristics of the issues (for example, callability), or, if not, whether they represent extraordinarily good or poor values.

Yield Spreads. A yield curve expresses the relationship, at a point in time, between yield and one vital characteristic of bonds—maturity. Also of great interest to investors are the relationships between yield and other characteristics of bonds, such as quality, coupon, and call features. These relationships are referred to as yield *spreads*. For example, one would naturally expect the yield of Baa bonds to be higher than the yield of Aaa bonds; lower quality gives rise to a *risk premium* in yield. But the magnitude of the difference—the yield spread between Baas and Aaas—is variable. One factor explaining yield spreads among issues of different quality, other characteristics held equal, is investors' expectations regarding economic prosperity. If a recession is expected, a Baa bond will appear to be riskier than that same bond at a time when continuous prosperity is expected. The riskier the bond appears to be, the higher will its yield tend to be relative to very high grade bonds, such as Aaas or U.S. government bonds.

Of course, yield spreads are not determined solely by investors' preferences. Borrowers' activities also are vital. Thus, a major new financing program by the U.S. Treasury may cause the spread between yields on corporate bonds and yields on Treasury bonds to narrow.

Figure 7–3
Yields of Treasury Securities, July 31, 1975 (based on closing bid quotations)

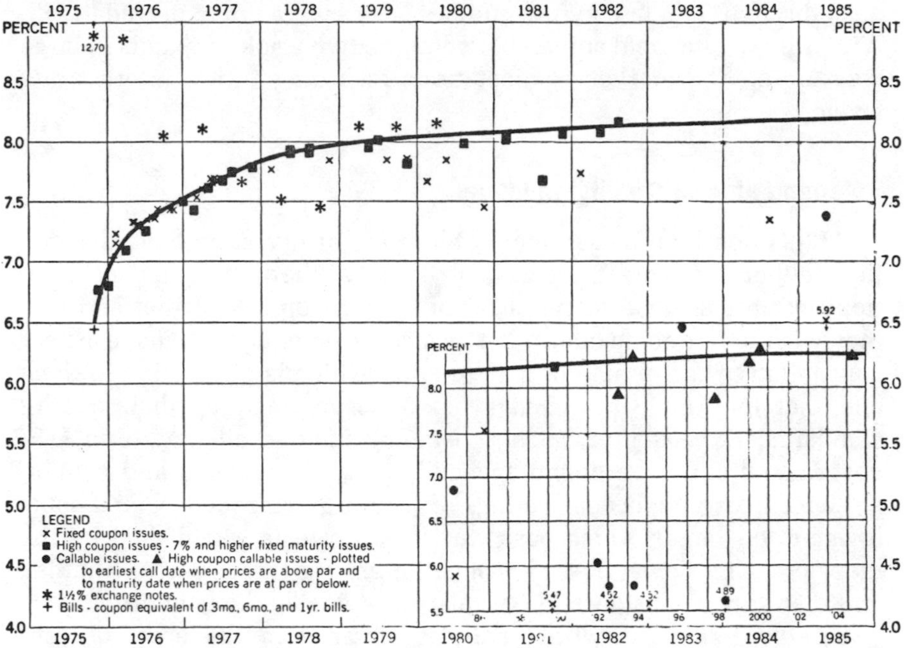

LEGEND
× Fixed coupon issues.
■ High coupon issues - 7% and higher fixed maturity issues.
● Callable issues. ▲ High coupon callable issues - plotted to earliest call date when prices are above par and to maturity date when prices are at par or below.
✱ 1½% exchange notes.
+ Bills - coupon equivalent of 3mo., 6mo., and 1yr. bills.

Note: The curve is fitted by eye. Market yields on coupon issues due in less than three months are excluded.
Source: *Treasury Bulletin,* August 1975.

The corporate yields will still be higher than the Treasury yields because of the quality difference, but the yield spread may be narrower than usual because the large increase in offerings of Treasury bonds causes their yields to be forced upward.

Changes in expectations also cause changes in the yield relationships among bonds of equal quality but carrying different call provisions. Thus, if interest rates are expected to fall, callable bonds become relatively less attractive to investors than bonds with nonrefunding features. Other things being equal, therefore, yields on callable bonds will be higher in relation to yields on nonrefundable bonds than would be the case if interest rates were expected to rise. Similarly, assume two bonds of equality quality, equal maturity, and similar call provisions, but with different coupons—for example, an 8 percent coupon Aa callable bond, selling at par, versus a 4 percent coupon Aa callable bond, selling at a deep discount. Which bond is more likely to be called if interest rates fall sharply? Obviously, the 8 percent coupon bond is more likely to be called. Therefore, if rates are expected to fall, the high coupon bond is less attractive relative to the low coupon, deep discount bond, than it would be if rates were not expected to fall. Accordingly, the yield spread between the two issues depends in large measure on the market's expectations regarding future interest rate levels.

Selecting among Qualifying Issues

At this point, let us assume that a group of investors have decided that neither the interest rate outlook nor any other portfolio considerations militate against the purchase of fixed-income securities and that they wish to buy some bonds. Let us also assume that they have a clear conception of the minimum bond quality which is acceptable to them and that they have compiled a list of issues meeting their quality standards. For example, such a list may include all long-term U.S. government and government agency bonds, all corporate and municipal bonds carrying agency ratings of "triple A" through A, and some lower rated bonds which pass various ratio tests established by the investors. They must now choose from among the issues on the list, and therefore a consideration of relative yields *finally* is in order.

Safety First. The word *finally* is stressed in the previous sentence because we believe strongly that for most nonprofessional investors the proper order of investigation is to consider the quality of a bond or preferred stock before considering its yield. For most investors, if quality is inadequate, yield is irrelevant. Too many bond buyers reverse the order, looking first at yield and then deciding whether sufficient extra yield is being offered to compensate for extra risk. While it is easily possible to exaggerate the need for high quality, the primary objective of bond and preferred stock investment is, after all, a *steady flow of income.* Consequently, a cavalier attitude toward quality can be disastrous.

If one's philosophy is "safety first," then selection even from a list of qualifying issues should not be dictated solely by the determination of which issue has the highest relative yield. While high yield is undoubtedly a plus factor, one should ask the question, even among qualifying issues: Is the yield *enough* higher relative to other qualifying issues to justify any extra credit risk that may be present? Even though one is prepared to assume the risks inherent in, say, "A" quality, if the yield on such issues at a partciular time is not substantially higher than, say, Aa yields, one might be better off buying the higher quality issues.

Consider Table 7–5 where the average spreads among long-term bonds of different quality are shown for a long time period. Note that from 1962 to 1965, there was only a 0.25 percent yield advantage obtainable by purchasing Aa utility bonds in preference to U.S. government bonds, and almost no yield advantage obtainable from A versus Aa utilities. Clearly, this was a period when investors might have been

Table 7–5
Yield Spreads on Long-Term Bonds of Different Quality

		*Utilities**		*Municipals*		*New Aa Utilities versus U.S. Govern-ments*	*New A versus New Aa Utilities*	*New Aa–A versus New Aaa Municipals*
Year	*U.S. Govern-ments*	*New Aa*	*New A*	*New Aaa*	*New Aa and A*			
1962	4.06%	4.36%	4.43%	3.00%	3.20%	0.30%	0.07%	0.20%
1963	4.08	4.33	4.37	3.00	3.20	0.25	0.04	0.20
1964	4.21	4.46	4.53	3.05	3.30	0.25	0.07	0.25
1965	4.26	4.57	4.65	3.10	3.25	0.31	0.08	0.15
1966	4.72	5.45	5.59	3.65	3.85	0.73	0.14	0.20
1967	4.94	5.87	6.02	3.75	3.90	0.93	0.15	0.15
1968	5.40	6.61	6.77	4.20	4.40	1.21	0.16	0.20
1969	6.28	7.75	7.99	5.45	5.65	1.47	0.24	0.20
1970	6.82	8.83	9.18	6.10	6.30	2.01	0.35	0.20
1971	6.12	7.74	7.99	5.25	5.40	1.62	0.25	0.15
1972	5.95	7.45	7.58	4.95	5.05	1.50	0.13	0.10
1973	7.00	7.74	7.93	5.00	5.10	0.74	0.19	0.10
1974	8.01	9.27	9.79	5.70	5.80	1.26	0.52	0.10
1975	8.25	9.51	10.33	6.29	6.42	1.26	0.82	0.13

* With deferred call features.
Source: Salomon Brothers. *An Analytical Record of Yields and Yield Spreads.* October 1971, and December 1975.

well advised to sacrifice some yield and buy highest quality issues. On the other hand, from 1969 to 1971, and again in 1974–75, when the *level* of interest rates soared to unprecedented heights, yield spreads widened dramatically, and investors who were willing to move down the quality spectrum (provided they did not violate their minmium quality standards) were well rewarded for doing so. Note also that in the tax-exempt ("municipals") market, quality spreads remained fairly constant throughout the period shown, with little incentive offered to investors for reducing the quality of their portfolios.

Active Bond Portfolio Management. Our discussion of the "safety first doctrine" should not be taken to imply that, once having determined which category of bonds represents the best trade-off between risk and reward, the investor should simply buy a representative sample of that category of bonds and put them in a vault until they mature.

Not at all. There are many opportunities, within the confines of the safety first doctrine, to "swap" one bond for another—that is, to sell bonds which appear to be overpriced and buy others which appear to be underpriced, and later even to reverse the transaction if a more normal relative pricing structure reappears.

There are three basic types of active bond management, which may be referred to for convenience of exposition as (1) arbitrage, (2) security analysis, and (3) interest rate forecasting. Arbitrage refers to swapping among issues which are essentially identical in quality, maturity, and coupon, but whose yields differ because of temporary supply/demand conditions. Obviously, the lower yielding issues should be sold and the higher yielding issues purchased. Security analysis refers to swapping among issues which are *dissimilar* in some important characteristic, basing the swaps upon one's judgment as to what kind of yield spreads *should* exist among such issues in comparison with the *actual* yield spreads at a given moment of time. Finally, interest rate forecasting refers to the effort to predict major and minor interest rate cycles and to alter the maturity or coupon structure of one's portfolio in conformity with the forecast. One would purchase longer-maturity, lower-coupon issues when interest rates are expected to fall, and shorter-maturity, higher-coupon issues when rates are expected to rise. It should be understood, of course, that while the rewards of acting on accurate interest rate forecasts can be great, the penalties of acting on inaccurate forecasts can be equally great. Therefore, those who "bet the bank" on the basis of a forecast should be prepared to accept the consequences if the forecast is wrong.

SUGGESTED READINGS

Darst, David *The Complete Bond Book.* New York: McGraw-Hill Book Co., 1975.

First Boston Corporation *Handbook of Securities of the United States Government.* New York, issued biennially.

Homer, Sidney, and **Leibowitz, Martin L.** *Inside the Yield Book: New Tools for Bond Market Strategy.* Englewood Cliffs, N.J.: Prentice-Hall, 1972.

Merrill Lynch, Pierce, Fenner & Smith *The Bond Book.* New York, latest edition.

Reilly, James F. *Too Good for the Rich Alone.* Englewood Cliffs, N.J.: Prentice-Hall, 1975.

Sherwood, Hugh C. *How Corporate and Municipal Debt Is Rated.* New York: John Wiley & Sons, 1976.

8

Convertibles, Options, and Special Situations

One cannot eat one's cake and have it too.
T. H. Huxley

The investment counterpart of Huxley's famous expression is that substantial opportunities for capital gains can be achieved only at the risk of substantial losses. In this chapter, we shall discuss some investment media which are used in an attempt to refute the notion that large gains involve large risks of loss. We also shall discuss some investment vehicles which are quite the opposite in nature—"go for broke" investments, in which the investors accept the possibility of losing 100 percent of the principal in exchange for the chance of multiplying the principal severalfold.

CONVERTIBLE SECURITIES

The term *convertible security* usually implies a preferred stock or a debenture which may be exchanged for common stock at the owner's discretion on specified terms.

Many investors see in convertbile securities "the best of all possible worlds." As debentures or preferreds, they offer stable income as opposed to the variable income of common stocks. This stable income appears to make them relatively less vulnerable to price decline during a stock market downturn. At the same time, the conversion privilege appears to offer most of the prospects for capital gain which are offered by common stocks. As we soon show, however, the actual case is not so certain.

Analytical Procedures

The following hypothetical example can be used to illustrate the method of evaluating a convertible security. A 6 percent coupon debenture, with 20 years remaining to maturity, is convertible at any time into common stock "at 50". Since each bond has a par value of $1,000, "convertible at 50" means the bond can be converted into 20 shares of stock ($1,000/$50 = 20). The bond is currently selling at 90 (that is, $900 for a $1,000 bond), and the stock into which it is convertible currently is selling at $42 per share.

Bond Value. The first phase of the analysis is to evaluate the issue as if it were a *straight* (that is, nonconvertible) bond. As indicated in the earlier discussion of bond and preferred stock analysis, this involves a determination of quality of the issue, a decision as to whether the quality is satisfactory, and a judgment as to whether the time is propitious for buying fixed-income securities in general. Suppose it is concluded that the issue is of medium quality, that this estimate is confirmed by the rating agencies (assume Moody's rates it Baa), and that the investor's standards permit the purchase of securities of such quality. Suppose it also is concluded that interest rates may rise a bit, but not substantially enough to militate against the purchase of fixed income securities.

Next, a calculation is made of the price the debenture would carry in the absence of a conversion feature—that is, its bond value. Since it is of Baa quality, the yield at which *straight* Baa issues currently are selling is determined. Suppose Moody's weekly *Bond Survey* shows that such issues currently yield 7.5 percent. The question, then, is: At what price must a 6 percent coupon, 20-year issue, sell to yield 7.5 percent to maturity? The answer can be obtained readily from a set of bond tables, or by the approximation method described in the previous chapter. In either case, it can be determined that the debenture would have to fall in price from $900 to about $830 to yield 7.5 percent. But some allowance also must be made for the fact that a moderate rise in interest rates is believed to be possible. Suppose it is thought that Baa issues can rise 0.5 percent to an 8 percent yield basis. If this were to occur, the debenture could decline in price to about $780.

The conclusion of the first phase of the analysis, therefore, is that purchase of the convertible debenture would entail a price risk of about $120 per $900 invested ($900 purchase price less $780 minimum price), or about 13 percent. The second phase of the analysis is designed to determine how much an investor stands to gain from the conversion privilege.

Stock Value. The first concept to be understood is that of the *conversion parity price* of the common stock. The debenture is convertible into 20 shares of common stock. By paying $900 for the bond, therefore, the investor can be viewed as in effect buying the company's stock at $45 per share (900/20 = 45). This price is the conversion parity price of the stock. (It should be noted that some issues provide for a gradually increasing conversion price during the life of the issue. That is, the longer the investor waits to convert, the fewer shares of common will be received upon conversion.)

The conversion parity price, then, is different for different investors, depending on the price paid for the convertible security. Conversion parity price is equal to the purchase price of the convertible security divided by the number of common shares into which it is convertible. This price is highly significant analytically. For, as will be demonstrated, once the actual market price of the stock rises to the investor's conversion parity price, any further rise is certain to increase the value of his convertible security at least as rapidly percentagewise.

The minimum price of a convertible security, regardless of the level of interest rates or any other considerations, is equal to the current price of the common stock multiplied by the number of shares into which it can be converted. In our example, the current price of the stock is $42 and the debenture is convertible into 20 shares of common. Therefore, the minimum price of the debenture is $42 × 20, or $840. Any lower price would have to be temporary, because it would give rise to *arbitrage* transactions which would restore the balance. For example, if the debenture sold at, say, $800 when the stock's price was $42, a guaranteed profit could be made as follows. Buy the debenture for $800. Simultaneously sell short 20 shares of common for $840. Then convert the debenture into 20 shares with which to cover the short sale, and make a $40 profit, less brokerage commissions and transfer taxes. The existence of the profit guarantee would cause enough such transactions to drive the debenture price up to almost $840.

If the logic presented above is understood, the significance of the *conversion parity price* of the common should begin coming into focus. If the stock in our example rose from its present price of $42 to its conversion parity price of $45, the minimum price of the debenture would be 20 × $45, or $900, which is the purchase price. Every additional $1 rise in the stock would increase the debenture's price by at least $20. The actual price of the debenture might well rise more than proportionately if buyers became enthusiastic enough. Indeed, in strong markets, convertible issues often sell at high and rising premiums over conversion value.

Thus, the conversion parity price can be viewed as a break-even point. Once the common stock attains that value, the investor is assured of at least getting his money back; and any further rise in the price of the common guarantees him at least a proportionate profit. In our example, the $45 conversion parity price is only $3, or 7 percent, away from the current $42 price of the common.

Having considered the relationship of the conversion parity price to the current price of the common stock, the next step of the analysis is to consider the *potential price* of the common stock. To make such a determination, of course, the investor would have to apply the evaluation techniques which were discussed in earlier chapters. Suppose the investor decides that the stock is worth $65.

If the stock were to go to $65, the convertible debenture would be worth at least 20 × $65, or $1,300. Thus, there exists a potential gain, based on the debenture's conversion feature, of $400 per $900 invested, or 44 percent.

Summary. All of these facts now can be brought together in a simple summary statement. The convertible security under analysis offers a potential gain of 44 percent at a maximum risk of 13 percent. If a mistake has been made regarding the value of the stock, and its price declines sharply, the bond value of the security should prevent the loss from exceeding 13 percent. (It should be recognized, however, that the stock's decline may be due to circumstances which also have the effect of lowering the bond's quality from Baa, to, say Ba. In that case, the maximum loss would be a function of yields on straight bonds of this lower quality.) But the investor does not have to be completely right about the stock to earn a profit. A price advance of only 7 percent, to $45, will mean breaking even, because the minimum price of the convertible would then be 20 × $45, equal to the $900 purchase price. A further advance in the price of the stock will produce a profit. Furthermore, while waiting for the capital gain the investor will be earning a current yield on the bond of 60/900, or almost 6.75 percent. This may well be above the dividend yield on the stock.

Thus, our example represents an ideal convertible situation—significant profit potential with small loss possibility and high probability of at least breaking even.

It is useful to state formally the characteristics of an attractive convertible. Ideally, six tests must be passed:

1. The issue must meet the investor's minimum quality standards.
2. The long-range outlook for interest rates should be fairly stable or down.
3. The minimum value of the issue as a straight bond or preferred stock must not be too far below the current selling price (not more than, say, 15 percent below), taking into account any expected rise in the level of interest rates.
4. The current price of the common stock must not be too far below conversion parity (say a maximum of 20 percent).
5. The potential price of the common stock must be well above conversion parity (say 25 percent or more).
6. The *current* yield on the bond or preferred stock should compare favorably with the dividend yield on the common stock.

Cautions. As might be expected, most convertibles fall short of the ideal by at least one of the tests. Frequently, the convertible is selling at such a high price (low yield) that if the underlying stock fell sharply, the convertible might drop 40 percent or more before its yield was competitive with nonconvertible bonds. Another situation which occurs frequently is that the convertible is selling at an attractive yield level but the common stock has to rise so far in price before reaching conversion parity that the convertible does not have a reasonable chance of appreciation.

Finally, mention must be made of the possible drawback presented by a convertible's call price. Consider, for example, a 7 percent, 19-year debenture, issued one year ago, convertible at $25 and selling at $1,200. The common stock is selling at $28 and is expected to rise to $60.

The bond is yielding about 5.5 percent to maturity at its current price. To yield 8 percent, it would have to sell at about $880, so its risk as a bond is about 25 percent ($320 on a price of $1,200). While this risk is higher than our ideal criterion, the conversion parity price of the common stock is $30, or only 7 percent above the present price of $28. Moreover, the potential price of the stock is double the conversion parity level. Therefore, despite the 25 percent downside bond risk, this convertible debenture would appear to be an attractive investment for high current income and large potential appreciation. However, suppose that the issue is callable at 107 (one year's interest is a common call premium). If the bond were called, what would happen?

With the stock selling at $28, the bond has a conversion value of 40 times $28, or $1,120. Thus, as long as the stock's price stays at $28, a bondholder would be better off converting into stock (or selling to someone else who will convert) than turning the bond in for $1,070.

Those investors who bought the bond at par at original issue, one year earlier, would have a 12 percent profit. But those who bought at $1,200 would have a loss of $80, or 7 percent. And if the call announcement depressed the price of the stock because of the imminent addition to the number of outstanding shares, the loss would be greater.

The moral of this example is that even when a convertible security meets most or all of our rules, if it is selling above call price there is a risk present. The risk is that the security will be called before the stock's price rises to conversion parity (once it reaches conversion parity, the investor will at least break even). Therefore, the investor has also to consider the situation from the corporation's point of view as well.

In this particular example, it seems unlikely that the company would call the bonds for the purpose of forcing conversion. For a call at this time might easily boomerang. Suppose that the call announcement depressed the price of the stock to $26. At this price, the debenture would have a conversion value of only $1,040. People would not convert but would turn the bonds in for $1,070 in cash. But this is not what the company wanted. It wanted more common stock in the business, and instead would be faced with a huge depletion of cash and capital. Thus, a call for the purpose of forcing conversion is unlikely, given the set of facts in this case, and purchase of the debenture is probably a wise move.

On the other hand, suppose the company has found a merger partner. And suppose this partner has ample equity capital and can borrow at 6.5 percent. In this situation, a 7 percent *convertible* debenture has less place in the merged company's capital structure than, say, a 6.5 percent straight debenture. A call might well be at hand, and purchase of the debenture would be quite risky.

Sources of Information. Several investment service organizations publish data on convertible securities in tabular or graphic forms which are convenient for quick screening preliminary to an in-depth analysis. Among these are the weeklies of Goldman Sachs; Value Line; Kalb, Voorhis & Co.; R.H.M. Associates; and the convertible bond section of Standard & Poor's *Bond Reports*. A sample of the latter tabular service is reproduced as Figure 8–1.

WARRANTS

Warrants are issued by corporations in conjunction with senior security financing (as "sweeteners"), or as part of *units* of new common stock plus warrants, or independently as compensation to underwriters and others. They became truly "respectable" securities in April

Figure 8–1
Sample of Standard & Poor's *Convertible Bond Report*

XVI

STANDARD & POOR'S CORPORATION

CONVERTIBLE BONDS Issue, Rate, Interest Dates and Maturity	S & P Quality Rating	Bond Form	Outstdg. Mil.-$	Conv. Expires	Shares per $1,000 Bond	Price per Share	Div. Income per Bond	1976 RANGE Hi	1976 RANGE Lo	Curr Bid Sale(s) Ask(A)	Curr. Return	Yield to Mat	Stock Value of Bond	Conv. Parity	STOCK DATA Curr. Price	STOCK DATA P/E Ratio	Earnings Per Share Yr. End	1975	1976	Last 12 Mos	1975 Dil-u't'n
◆Wilshire Oil,Tex ....6s mS 1995	....	R	4.74	1995	150.60	6.64	18.07	111	92⅛	s105½	5.69	5.52	101⅝	7	•6¾	8	Dc	0.78	E0.80	[9]0.85	0.72
•Witco Chemical ....4½ s jD15 1993	BBB	R	15.0	1993	20.00	50.00	28.00	75	61	s71⅜	6.30	7.50	53¼	35¾	•26⅝	6	Dc	2.46	E4.25	[9]4.17	2.28
•Wometco Enterpr5½ s Ms15 1994	BB	R	13.1	1994	64.64	15.47	31.03	95½	77½	s86½	6.36	6.84	73½	13⅜	•11⅜	7	Dc	1.35	E1.70	[9]1.63	1.26
◆Work Wear ....4¾ s mS 1985	B	R	2.09	1985	70.18	14.25	42.11	90	60	s73½	6.46	9.23	71	10½	◆10⅛	5	Dc	1.37	....	[9]2.02	1.31
◆Wyle Laboratories.....5¼ s fA 1988	B	R	14.2	1988	43.96	22.75	12.31	65	52¼	s64½	8.14	10.6	24¾	14⅝	◆5⅝	6	Ja	0.62	....	[7]0.97	0.62
•[1]Wyly Corp ....7¼ s Ms15 1995	CC	R	39.2	1995	22.22	45.00	....	53½	9½	s9⅝	75.3	75.3	2¾	4⅜	•1¼	d	Dc	d6.27	....	[9]d8.78	n/r
◆Wyoming Bancorp...7¼ s mS 1996	....	R	4.10	1996	83.33	12.00	46.66	101	100	100	7.25	7.25	89⅝	12	◆10¾	7	Dc	□1.44	....	[9]1.52	n/r
•Xerox Corp ....6s mN 1995	A	R	155	1995	10.87	92.00	13.04	106½	88½	s98⅞	6.07	6.10	64	91	•58⅞	13	Dc	3.07	E4.60	[9]4.30	n/r
•Zapata Corp...............4¾ s Fa 1988	B	R	14.9	1988	39.25	25.48	11.78	73	57⅞	s65¾	7.22	9.88	48⅝	16¾	•12⅜	4	Sp	4.39	P△3.47	3.47	3.26
•Zapata Corp 'B'..........4¾ s Fa 1988	B	R	14.7	1988	39.25	25.48	11.78	72¾	57⅛	65	7.31	10.0	48⅝	16½	•12⅜	4	Sp	4.39	P△3.47	3.47	3.26
•Zapata Corp 'C' ....4¾ s fA 1988	B	R	35.8	1988	39.25	25.48	11.78	73	57½	s64½	7.36	9.96	48⅝	16⅜	•12⅜	4	Sp	4.39	P△3.47	3.47	3.26
•Zayre Corp ....5¾ s jD15 1994	B	R	18.0	1994	25.00	40.00	....	60	46	s60	9.58	10.8	18⅛	24	•7¼	5	Ja	0.98	....	[10]1.33	0.98
•Zurn Indus...............5¾ s mN 1994	BB	R	17.8	1994	35.09	28.50	16.84	81¼	64½	s75	7.67	8.49	44¾	21⅜	•12¾	8	Mr	1.28	E1.60	[9]1.53	1.22

Uniform Footnote Explanations—See Page XVI. Other: [1]9-15-76 int not paid,exch offer.

EXPLANATION OF COLUMN HEADINGS AND FOOTNOTES

MARKET: Unlisted except where symbols • or ◆ are used:
• –New York Stock Exchange ◆–American Stock Exchange

ISSUE TITLE: Name of Bond at time of offering; otherwise issue footnoted with name change of obligor. Minor changes with old title indicated in brackets, i.e. Gen Tel (Corp) & Elec.
#Prin & int payable in U.S. funds. §Int. and/or prin. in default.

FORM OF BOND: Letters are used to indicate form of bond: C–Coupon only; CR–Coupon or Registered, interchangeable; R–Registered only.

CONVERSION EXPIRES: Footnote keyed to bottom of page when conversion price changes during life of the privilege; also noted on conversion price.
◎Indicates a change in next 12 months. a–No fractional shs. issued upon conversion; settlements in cash.

DIVIDEND INCOME PER BOND: If $1,000 Bond were converted, the annual amount of dividends expected to be paid by the company on the stock based on most recent indication of annual rate of payment.
t–Less tax at origin. g–in Canadian funds less 15% or 10% non–residence tax.

STOCK VALUE OF BOND: Price at which bond must sell to equal price of stock i.e., number of shares received on conversion times price of the stock.

CONVERSION PARITY: Price at which stock must sell to equal bond price, i.e., price of bond divided by number of shares received on conversion.

P–E RATIO: (Price–Earnings Ratio) Represents market valuation of any $1 of per share earnings i.e., the price of the stock divided by estimated or latest 12 months per share earnings.

EARNINGS, in general, are per share as reported by company. **FOR YEAR INDICATED:** Fiscal years ending prior to March 31 are shown under preceding year. Net operating earnings are shown for **banks**; net earnings before appropriation to general reserve for **savings & loan associations**; net investment income for **insurance companies**; **railroads'** earnings are as reported to ICC. **Foreign** issues traded **ADR** are dollars per share, converted at prevailing exchange rate. Specific footnotes used:

△Excl extra–ord income	■–Partial Year	j–Currency at origin
▲Incl extra–ord income	‡–New Year Earns	P–Preliminary
□Excl extra–ord charges	b–Before depletion	p–Pro forma
■Incl extra–ord charges	d–Deficit	R–Fully diluted
*Excl tax credits	E–S&P Estimate	n/r–Not reported
		ƒ–1974 dilution

LAST 12 Mos. indicates earnings through period indicated by superior number preceding figure: [1]for Jan. for Feb., etc. Figure without superior number indicates fiscal year end.

DILUTION: Earnings on a fully diluted basis, as reported in accordance with Accounting Principles Board opinions.

Source: Standard & Poor's *Convertible Securities Reports*. October 13, 1975.

1970, when they were issued as part of a major financing program by AT&T and were accepted for trading on the New York Stock Exchange after a ban of many years. (The American Stock Exchange did not have such a ban, and has many warrant issues listed.)

Warrants give their holders an option to purchase the corporation's securities, usually its common stock, at a stated price. While so-called rights offerings of new stock to existing owners are a form of warrant, the exercise period is only a month or two. "Rights," therefore, are not included in this discussion. Most warrants may be exercised over a period of many years, sometimes at a price which increases the longer the investor waits to exercise. Occasionally, a warrant may be a perpetual option. The holder of a warrant has no voting rights and receives no dividend income. Care must be taken to assure that the warrant has antidilution provisions which cause the exercise price to be reduced and the number of shares under the warrant to be increased in line with any stock dividends or stock splits. (The same type of dilution protection should be present in convertible securities.)

Warrants may provide for the purchase of one share per warrant or more than one share; frequently, fractional share purchases are involved. Whereas short-term "rights" options carry an exercise price below the prevailing market price, the typical warrant carries an exercise price well above the prevailing market price at the time the warrant is issued. To begin to understand the speculative attraction of warrants, assume that a new warrant is issued which gives the holder a ten-year option to buy one share of stock for $30. This price will be referred to as (*EP*), the exercise price. Assume that at the time the warrant is issued, the market price of the stock (*MP*) is $20. Assume also that a particular investor believes there is a good probability that the stock's price will rise to $40 within the next several years.

Minimum Values. If the stock is bought for $20 and it rises to $40, the investor will have earned 100 percent plus any dividends received. Suppose, instead, that the warrant could have been bought for $5. If the stock reaches $40, the minimum value of the warrant will be $10 (MP of $40 less EP of $30). It cannot be less than $10 because, if it were, arbitrageurs would buy the warrant and sell the stock short for a guaranteed profit, in a manner exactly analogous to that discussed earlier in connection with convertible securities. Obviously, if the warrant goes to just $10, the investor will have a 100 percent profit, no more than could have been achieved with the stock, and indeed less because of the absence of dividends on the warrant. But if, when the stock is $40, investors expect it to rise further, the warrant will sell at some premium over minimum value. Suppose that the premium is $5—

that is, the warrant sells for $15. In that case, investors, who bought at $5, will have tripled their investment instead of doubling it.

Now consider another investor who comes along when the stock is $40 and the warrant is $15. This one thinks the stock will keep rising to at least $50. Purchase of the stock would bring a 25 percent profit (plus dividends), whereas the warrant would be expected to rise *at least* to $20 ($50 minus $30), and probably more, for a profit of more than one third. So this investor buys the warrant for $15. But suppose that the analysis of the stock was incorrect and it *falls* 30 percent to $28 instead of rising to $50. The warrant has no minimum value (*MP* is below *EP*), but merely a speculative value reflecting the possibility that the stock will rise again. Suppose that the warrant price declines to $8. Our second investor will have lost almost 50 percent on the warrant but would have lost 30 percent on the stock.

Finally, suppose that a third investor buys the warrant for $8, but by this time it has only a few years left before expiration. And suppose the stock never does rise above $30. At the expiration of the warrant, it will be worth zero, and the investor will have lost his entire principal—a vastly different result than if he had bought the stock instead. Clearly, there is a lot of speculative leverage in warrants. For example, in the last two weeks of 1971, AT&T common stock rose 12 percent from 41 to 46, while AT&T warrants rose 50 percent from 6 to 9. On the other hand, during the 1973–74 stock market collapse, many investors in warrants were virtually wiped out while the owners of the underlying common were not nearly as badly hurt. The toboggan slide of warrant prices in 1973–74 included:

Avco	$18.00 to $0.56
Carrier	$13.00 to $0.75
AT&T	$12.00 to $0.25
Loew's	$39.00 to $2.25
United Brands	$56.00 to $0.43

Guidelines. One expert on the subject[1] has suggested that an investor should ask several questions before purchasing any warrant, including the following:

1. Is the underlying common stock attractive? Don't ask which warrants are attractive now. Examine the outlook for the underlying common stock first and then study the warrant related to that common.

---

[1] Daniel Turov, in his article "Warrants and Options," *Financial Analyst's Handbook, Vol. I* (Homewood, Ill.: Dow-Jones-Irwin, 1975), pp. 473–74.

2. When does the warrant expire? Do not buy unless the warrant has three or four years to run. If you must buy a short-term warrant be sure the premium, if any, is very low. (It will be recalled that the premium is defined as the difference between the actual price of the warrant and its minimum value, which, in turn, is the difference between the market price of the underlying stock and the exercise price.)
3. Is the premium sufficiently low so that if the stock advances the warrant will increase by a greater percentage amount? That is, is the leverage factor favorable?
4. Is the premium reasonable in terms of the normal trading pattern for this particular warrant? Trace the history of the relationship between the price of the warrant and the price of the underlying stock.
5. Is the warrant protected against dilution and against call? Is there provision for the adjustment of the exercise price in case of stock splits, stock dividends, or issuance of additional stock below the exercise price? Be aware that some warrants do not protect against dilution and also can be called by the issuer at will and at nominal prices. Ask your broker to assure you that you have protection against both dilution and call.

PUTS AND CALLS

Whereas warrants are options written by corporations on their own stock, puts and calls are options written by security dealers and by other investors on any stock they care to write an option on, as long as they can find an investor willing to buy the option. A put gives the holder the right to sell 100 shares of the specified stock to the writer of the option (via a registered stockbroker) at a specified price. A call gives the holder the right to buy 100 shares at a specified price. Unlike warrants, the time period of put and call options is relatively short. Therefore, calls are attractive to investors who think a near-term rise in price is in store for a stock, but who prefer not to invest the sum required to buy the stock itself. Likewise, puts are attractive to investors who anticipate a near-term price decline, but who prefer not to sell short.

Until 1973, puts and calls were not a very active business in comparison with direct trading in common stocks. However, in that year the Chicago Board of Trade developed a regular auction market in call options in contrast to the traditional over-the-counter negotiated market. The success of the Board of Trade's venture made the call option a widely used trading vehicle. As a result, the New York and American Stock Exchanges are entering the market for options, and markets are developing for puts as well as calls.

Call options that are traded on the exchange have certain common characteristics that make it possible for investors to trade in options in a more flexible and convenient manner than is possible in the prior over-the-counter market for puts and calls. The striking price or exercise price, the price per share at which the option buyer may purchase a call, is now standardized.

In contrast to the older put and call market where it was possible to buy or write an option with practically any striking price or expiration date, the striking prices of listed options always end in $5 or $0, unless a stock dividend or other capital change occurs after trading in the options has begun. If AT&T is selling at $64 a share at the time options for a new expiration month are being listed for trading, the new AT&T option will have a striking or exercise price of $65 per share. If the stock price closes above $67.50 for two consecutive days, the exchange will add $70 contracts for each expiration date beyond 60 days.

In addition to the standardized exercise price, listed options have standardized expiration dates—the third Friday of either January, April, July, October; or February, May, August, November. This standardization of both exercise prices and expiration dates made possible the development of a secondary market. Each listed option with a common expiration date and striking price is interchangeable with any similar listed option. In contrast the old conventional option is a direct contract between a particular writer, or his brokerage firm, and a particular buyer. One conventional option contract is not interchangeable with another. Moreover, because of the direct tie between buyer and writer, it is frequently difficult for the owner of a conventional option to sell or exchange the option privilege for a price in excess of the intrinsic or exercise value of the option. And more importantly, it is impossible for an option writer (old style) to terminate his obligation except through direct negotiation with the buyer of the specific contract he wrote. With listed options, however, the writer's obligation is to the Options Clearing Corporation, and not to the buyer. The buyer and writer in a listed option transaction have no direct connection. Each has a contract only with the Options Clearing Corporation which is the issuer of listed options. Either the option buyer or the writer can close out their positions by closing purchases or closing sales.

This standardization allows the option to trade in much the same manner as common stocks are traded and it has resulted in a high degree of liquidity which has made the old traditional options market almost obsolete. Open trading and continuous price reporting of options transactions show both buyer and writer where they stand at any given moment. The liquidity allows both parties to close out, or offset, their original transactions at a time of their own choosing.

The standardization and price reporting of listed options may be seen in Figure 8–2.

Who Buys and Who Sells Options and Why?

The most basic reason for buying a call option is in anticipation of an increase in the price of the underlying stock. If the stock goes up, the call will go up and may be sold at a profit, before the cessation of trading in that series, in the secondary market. Or the call may be exercised with the holder of the call acquiring the underlying stock.

The excitement of buying options comes from their leverage effect. Through the use of options the buyers aim to make $1,000 do the work of $10,000. To achieve this leverage the buyers take a risk. They face the possibility of losing the entire amount of the premium they pay for the option against that of participating in the potential capital gain from the stock, without buying the stock itself.

The call buyers hope the stock will rise and their option price will rise with it. If the stock goes down, they stand to lose their whole premium, but that might be fewer *dollars* (although a far larger *percentage*) than they would have lost by owning the stock outright and they would have tied up less capital. If the stock goes up, their percentage return on investment can be considerably higher than if they had bought the stock outright.

For example, on February 15, XYZ common stock is selling for $40 a share and an October 40 call can be purchased for $500 (100 shares at $5 per share). On April 15, XYZ is selling at $46 a share and the October 40 call is trading at $750. The call buyer is now able to sell the option at the higher premium and take the profit. The option is not exercised but sold. And the leverage is as follows:

	Call	*Stock*
Bought February 15	$500	$4,000
Sold April 15	750	4,600
Profit (before transaction costs)	250	600
Percent return on investment (not annualized)	50%	15%

Figure 8–2
How Options Trades Are Reported

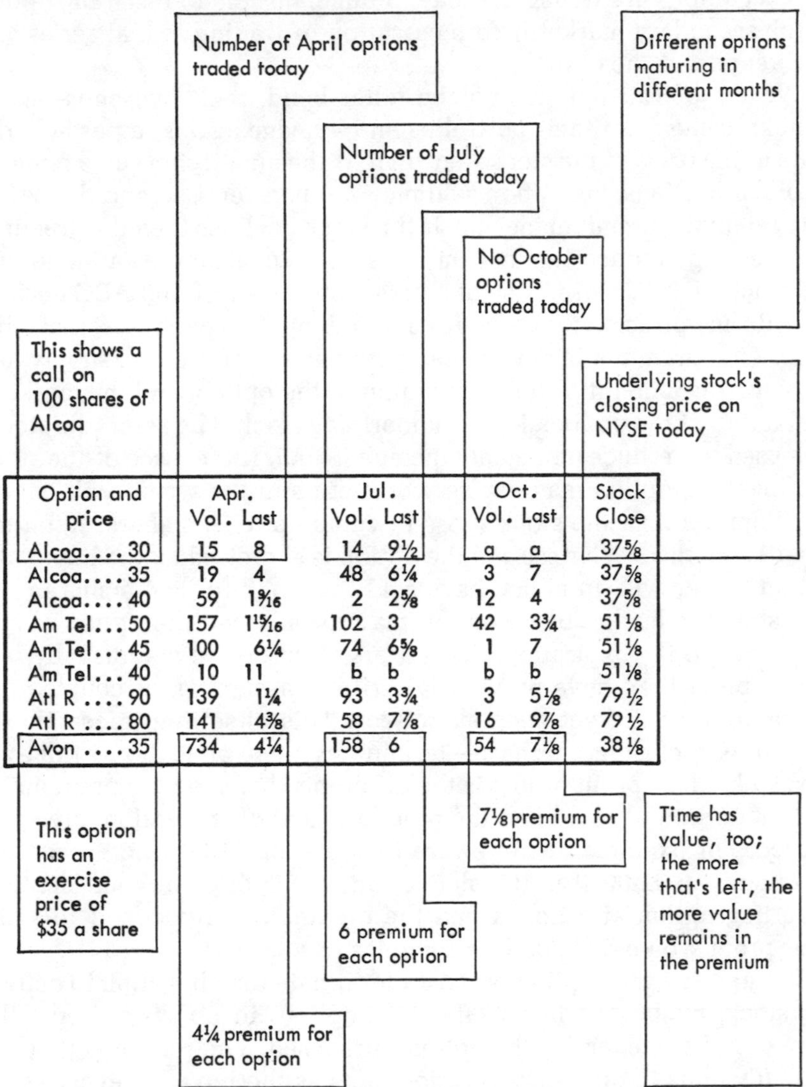
Number of April options traded today
Different options maturing in different months
Number of July options traded today
No October options traded today
This shows a call on 100 shares of Alcoa
Underlying stock's closing price on NYSE today
This option has an exercise price of $35 a share
7⅛ premium for each option
Time has value, too; the more that's left, the more value remains in the premium
6 premium for each option
4¼ premium for each option

Option and price	Apr. Vol.	Apr. Last	Jul. Vol.	Jul. Last	Oct. Vol.	Oct. Last	Stock Close
Alcoa.... 30	15	8	14	9½	a	a	37⅝
Alcoa.... 35	19	4	48	6¼	3	7	37⅝
Alcoa.... 40	59	1⁹⁄₁₆	2	2⅝	12	4	37⅝
Am Tel... 50	157	1¹⁵⁄₁₆	102	3	42	3¾	51⅛
Am Tel... 45	100	6¼	74	6⅝	1	7	51⅛
Am Tel... 40	10	11	b	b	b	b	51⅛
Atl R 90	139	1¼	93	3¾	3	5⅛	79½
Atl R 80	141	4⅜	58	7⅞	16	9⅞	79½
Avon 35	734	4¼	158	6	54	7⅛	38⅛

This is how trading in options is reported in the financial pages of newspapers. Look under Chicago Board Options Exchange and American Exchange Options. The explanation of each item is contained in the box surrounding it.

Source: From *Merrill Lynch Guide to Writing Options,* Merrill Lynch, Pierce, Fenner & Smith, New York, N.Y.

The option buyer risks losing the whole investment rather quickly if expectations are wrong. He may, though, be able to resell the option in the secondary market before cessation of trading in that series and recover part of the cost.

Writers of call options, on the other hand, seek two ends—additional income from their portfolios and a hedge against a possible decline in the price of the stock they own. If the underlying stock remains stable or declines, the option sold may not be exercised and the writer may retain the premium income. If the stock declines then the premium income helps reduce the loss on the stock. For example, assume that the stock of ABC Corp. is selling at 50. An owner of 100 ABC decides to write an option on the stock for a premium of $4 per share, receiving $400. That premium is determined by a variety of factors: supply and demand, the amount of time remaining in the option, and the market's evaluation of the outlook for the underlying stock. The asset (the stock) was used to produce immediate income ($400). If the price of the stock declines, the option may expire worthless and the writer will have a premium to offset the stock's loss in value up to $4 a share. If, on the other hand, the stock rises and the option is exercised by the buyer, the option writer will, in effect, have sold the stock for $54 a share.

Just as the buyers of an option may usually sell the option at any time prior to the expiration, the writers of an option may usually *buy in* an option they have previously written (assuming, of course, that the option has not yet been exercised). This offsetting transaction—known as a closing purchase—terminates their obligation to deliver the stock. Their profit or loss is the difference between the premium of the option initially sold and the premium cost of the option later purchased. For example, if they were to write an ABC option when the premium was $400 (for 100 shares) and later buy back an identical offsetting option at a time when the premium had declined to $200, their profit would be $200 less commissions.

The ability of the option writer to terminate the obligation to deliver the stock, by *buying in* an offsetting option, in no way affects the buyer's right to exercise the option purchased. The reason is that the OCC (Options Clearing Corporation) acts as the buyer to every seller and seller to every buyer. There is no continuing relationship between original buyer and seller. This feature helps to assure the financial integrity of all options bought and sold on the registered exchanges.

The point should, however, be indelibly recorded in the mind of every option writer that, unless an offsetting option has been purchased, the writer can be called on to deliver stock (at the exercise price) at any time prior to the option's expiration. The decision whether to exercise and when to exercise is entirely up to the buyer (holder) of the option, (who must pay the standard brokerage commission for 100 shares of stock when he exercises). Indeed, although it is not customary, there are circumstances under which options are exercised *early;* that is, days, weeks, and even months prior to expiration. For instance, a situation in which the option premium happened to be less than the tangible value of the option (the market price of the stock minus the option's exercise price) would make the purchase of the option attractive to an arbitrageur. Such a trader would make a *short* sale of the underlying stock and cover the short position by buying and exercising the option, thereby realizing a *locked-in* profit.

Early exercise could also result from an option holder's desire to acquire rights to a cash dividend. Unless an exercise notice is given prior to an ex-dividend date for an ordinary cash dividend, the option *writer* retains all such dividends.

Finally, an option may be exercised early if the option holder wishes to acquire the stock at the earliest possbile date. For example, an investor anticipating a cash flow at a future date may have bought the option simply to establish a maximum purchase cost for the stock. Then, when he has cash at hand, he exercises the option, without regard to its remaining time value. Still another investor might exercise early to establish a longer holding period for tax purposes. Thus, it bears repeating: The writer of an option should clearly understand that he or she may be called upon to deliver the stock at the exercise price at any time during the life of the option.

Covered or Naked? *Covered* writing is the most common strategy. It involves writing calls against a long position in the underlying common stock in one's portfolio. The covered writer owns the underlying stock or convertible security such as warrants, convertible bonds, convertible preferreds or a listed option of the same class. He or she is willing to forego possible appreciation in the underlying issue in return for payment of the premium.

The *uncovered* call writer also hopes to realize income from the writing of an option, but without the security of the underlying stock. The uncovered writer is, however, required to maintain margin with his or her broker. As in the case of the covered writer the maximum profit is the premium (less transaction costs). Large risks, however, are involved. These stem from the possibility of a sharp rise in the market price of the underlying stock above the exercise price, leading to the exercise of the option. An uncovered (naked) option sale is not unlike a short sale of the underlying stock. An uncovered writer stands to lose the amount by which the current market price of the underlying stock exceeds the exercise price (which theoretically can be without limit) less the amount of the premium (plus transactions costs).

Uncovered options should be written only by individuals who fully understand the substantial risks and are willing and financially able to assume them. It should be remembered, of course, that an uncovered writer, like the covered writer, may usually cancel the obligation at any time, prior to being assigned an exercise notice, by executing a closing purchase transaction. The profit or loss will depend, of course, on the difference between the cost of such closing transaction and the net proceeds from the original writing transaction. An uncovered writer may also, during the life of the option, buy the underlying stock, thereby becoming a covered writer.

Premiums. Some of the most important factors influencing option premiums are as follows:

1. Puts are usually cheaper than calls because there is less buyer demand for them (investors are more often bulls than bears). Likewise, calls are more expensive in bull than in bear markets; and puts are more expensive in bear than in bull markets.

2. Options on active, highly volatile, stocks usually cost more than on inactive or stable stocks because there is more opportunity for the buyers of such options to make a profit sometime during the option period. For a similar reason, long option periods cost more than shorter term options.

3. The higher the price of the stock, the lower the percentage premium on the option, other things being equal.

4. Option prices seem responsive to changes in interest rates; they have been higher in recent years of very high interest rates than, say, a decade ago.

HEDGING

Convertibles and options are of investment interest not only in their own right, but also as part of so-called hedge transactions. In a hedge, the underlying common stock is bought or sold short, and an *opposite* position is taken via convertibles or options on the stock. The purpose of this opposing position is to limit the dollar loss if the position in the stock turns out to be an error. Some examples will make this clearer.

A *convertible hedge* refers to a transaction in which a bearish investor buys a convertible and simultaneously sells short the common stock into which it may be converted. If the stock declines in price, as anticipated, the price of the convertible declines less than proportionately (he hopes). He then sells the convertible at a loss, buys common at the depressed price, and covers his short sale at a greater profit than the loss on the convertible. If he is wrong about the market, and a rise in the stock's price confronts him with a potential loss on the covering of the short sale, he has two alternatives. If the price of the convertible has risen, he can sell it at a profit which offsets the short-sale loss in whole or in part. Indeed, the price rise of the convertible may exceed that of the stock, resulting in a net profit. At the very worst, if the price of the convertible has not risen, he can exercise his conversion privilege and use the shares received to cover the short sale. His maximum loss will be the difference between the cost of the convertible and the proceeds of the short sale, namely the *premium* which he paid over conversion value. Thus, the main purpose of a convertible hedge is the profit from a declining stock market at a predeterminable risk.

Alternatively, a bearish investor can hedge a short-sale by purchasing a six-months' call. If the stock goes down, as he anticipates, he will not exercise the call. He will have a profit on his short sale, reduced by the amount of the call premium. If the stock goes up, he will lose on his short sale, but his loss is limited to the amount of the call premium since the loss on the short sale will be offset by the profit on the call.

Similarly, if the investor is bullish rather than bearish, he can buy the stock and also buy a put. If the stock rises, he will not exercise the put. He will have a profit on his long position in the stock, reduced by the amount of the put premium. If the stock goes down, he will lose on his long position, but his loss is limited to the amount of the put premium since the loss on the long position will be offset by the profit on the put.

SPECIAL SITUATIONS

Special situations afford the opportunity for capital gains because of some special development either within the company or in the external environment affecting the company. The development, if it occurs, will ensure the gain regardless of the general trend of the market. Narrowly defined, the true special situation has a mathematically predictable gain, like buying a $10 bill for only $7.50. More broadly and more usually, a special situation may work out to a calculable gain if certain developments come to pass. It also includes calculation of downside risk if the developments anticipated do not materialize.

True Special Situations

In the more limited sense of the term, special situations may arise from:

Liquidations. (In a complete liquidation the company disposes of its assets and distributes the proceeds to its shareholders.)

Residual Stubs. (These are certificates of participation or liquidation certificates, or certificates of beneficial interest, representing a residual interest in a company. They usually arise out of liquidations.)

Tenders. (An offer by a corporation to buy back its own shares. Or an offer by an outsider, interested in acquiring control, to buy up shares, usually at a price above the market.)

Spin-Offs. (A corporate divestiture of a division or a subsidiary by distributing shares in the new corporate entity to existing shareholders of the divesting company.)

Appraisals. (Court determination of the fair value of a dissenting shareholder's stock which the dissenter refuses to exchange in a merger or acquisition.)

Oversubscriptions. (These arise in rights offerings when shareholders who have exercised their rights are additionally offered an opportunity to buy remaining unsubscribed shares.)

Mergers and Acquisitions. (A merger usually involves an exchange of shares and a pooling of interests.)

Hedges and Arbitrages. (Out of mergers and acquisitions frequently arises the opportunity to profit by arbitrage and to minimize losses by hedging.)

Reorganizations. (When a company undergoes reorganization certain of its securities bought at panic prices may subsequently emerge from the reorganization at higher values.)

Recapitalizations. (Administrative changes in the capital structure of a corporation may involve a realignment of relationships among the company's securities with attendant profit possibilities.)

True special situations have three distinguishing characteristics:

1. Some unique development is occurring which makes this particular security attractive apart from general industry, economic, or security market conditions.
2. This development is usually noncontinuing in nature. If not seized upon when it appears, the specific opportunity may be lost. The security may continue to be a worthwhile purchase but not as a "special situation."
3. The situation is usually amenable to measurement of expected gains and calculation of probable risks.

Some Examples. Two simple illustrations cited by *Business Week* are as follows:

1. Liquidation
   Hidden Value Corporation was preparing to sell all its assets.

The sales price per share would yield	$10.00
On liquidation, it could claim a tax refund of	4.40
Making a total sure value of	$14.40
But the stock was then selling for	11.00
So the buyer could count on a net profit of	$ 3.40

2. Merger
   Attractive Company was about to merger with High-Powered Company.

Shareholders of Attractive were due to get one share of High-Powered common worth	$26.00
Plus 4/50 of a share of High-Powered preferred (selling at $44 a share)	3.50
Making a total sum value of	$29.50
Attractive Co. stock was selling for	25.75
So the buyer could make a profit of	$ 3.75

Not all mergers, of course, present special situation possibilities. There must exist a chance to purchase shares of the company to be acquired at a discount from their ultimate exchange value in terms of the acquiring company's stock to be received. Even where the desired discount is to be found, it may quickly be narrowed or wiped out by market action. Thus, as in all investments, timing is an important factor in the merger-acquisition special situation. Moreover, this type of special situation is not devoid of risk, because (1) the merger may never be completed; and (2) the merger may be completed only after such a long delay that the profit represents an unsatisfactory return for the length of time the money was tied up.

Reorganizations. Reorganizations are also traditional special situations. In the case of a company facing reorganization, the old securities will be greatly depressed in value. Through careful financial analysis, workout values can be approximated for some classes of securities. Two trading procedures can then be utilized. Either the selected depressed securities can be purchased and held and in due course exchanged for new securities issued under the plan of reorganization, or a hedge operation can be undertaken. This is accomplished by buying the old securities and then subsequently selling on a *when, as, and if issued* basis, the new securities to be received in exchange. This is predicated, of course, on the assumption that the market value of the new securities to be received in the exchange will be greater than the cost of the old securities purchased at very depressed prices. This occurs often in reorganizations but not inevitably or invariably, and thus careful financial evaluation of pro forma balance sheets and income accounts in reorganization plans is essential. It is not an area for amateurs.

The Broader Special Situation

In contrast to the precise calculations involved in traditional special situations, the broader sense of the concept, as used by many investment advisory services and stock brokerage houses, includes the following:

Hidden earnings.
Court orders and litigation.
New technological developments.
Changing government regulations or tax rulings.
New management.
Comeback situations.
New markets.

Several investment advisory firms have special situation services. This is true of *Forbes,* and Value Line. In the view of Arnold Bernhard "a special situation refers to some security in which an extraordinary, nonrecurring corporate development is taking place—a development which can reasonably be expected to enhance the value of the security in question irrespective of the trend of the market as a whole."

The broader special situation concept is illustrated by:

a. Polaroid's introduction of the camera capable of developing prints in seconds after the picture is snapped, sent the stock soaring from 10 to a high of 149½, adjusted for numerous stock splits.

b. Xerox Corporation's stock was selling around $5 a share (adjusted for subsequent stock splits), and its sales were at the $30 million mark, when the company introduced the 914 Copier. This new machine was the first offered commercially, and it revolutionized and expanded the market. Within a little more than five years, sales had expanded by 13 times, and the stock price appreciated over 50 times. On an adjusted basis the stock rose from 1⅞ to 171⅞.

c. Burroughs was a stodgy maker of adding machines and electromechanical accounting equipment until it transformed itself into a highly successful producer of electronic data processing and electronic accounting machines. Earnings rose almost 700 percent in five years, and the stock rose from 5¾ to 126⅜.

d. St. Joe Minerals was misunderstood. The Street thought of it as a lead and zinc company, which it was. But there was also, as *Forbes* Special Situation Service pointed out, a big new commitment to energy. In early 1974, SJO bought Massey Coal for $56 million of SJO stock. Massey's operating income in 1973 was $9 million, in 1974 it was over $43 million. *Forbes* recommended SJO on October 18, 1974 at 35 (17½ adjusted for a 2-for-1 stock split). The stock doubled in less than a year. Mapco, another energy play, recommended by *Forbes,* went from 17½ on July 19, 1974 to 50½ in 1975. Followers of the *Forbes* Service had a 70 percent gain in the first six months.

SUGGESTED READINGS

Fried, Sidney *Fortune Building in the 70's with Common Stock Warrants and Low Priced Stock.* New York: RHM Associates, 1975.

Gastineau, Gary L. *The Stock Options Manual.* New York: McGraw-Hill Book Co., 1975.

The Merrill Lynch Guide to Writing Options For a free copy write to Merrill Lynch, Pierce, Fenner & Smith, One Liberty Plaza, New York, New York 10006.

Noddings, Thomas C. *Guide to Convertible Securities.* Homewood, Ill.: Dow Jones–Irwin, 1973.

Option Writing Strategies A free copy may be obtained from the Chicago Board Options Exchange. LaSalle at Jackson, Chicago, Illinois 60604.

Rosen, Lawrence R. *How to Trade Put and Call Options.* Homewood, Ill.: Dow Jones–Irwin, 1974.

Schiller, Maurece, and **Benis, Martin** "Special Situations," *Financial Analyst's Handbook,* vol. 1. Homewood, Ill.: Dow Jones-Irwin, 1975, chap. 16.

The Versatile Option New York: American Stock Exchange, 1975. A free copy may be obtained by writing to the American Stock Exchange, at 86 Trinity Place, New York, N.Y. 10006.

9

Summary of Widely Used Financial Ratios

That intelligent investors make use of a large number of financial ratios will be evident by now. It may be convenient for the reader to have the most common ratios brought together in one section which can serve as a checklist when attempting a comprehensive analysis of a company's financial statements.

We present the checklist with some trepidation, however, because we fear the reader may take it as a suggestion that investments can be appraised mechanistically. Such an impression would be a serious error, not taking into account either the quality of a company's management, the validity of its accounting procedures, or the fact that the past record is useful mainly as a basis for focusing upon those critical variables which may *change* in the future.

Having sounded this word of caution, we proceed with the summary of financial ratios. An attempt has been made to group the ratios in a sequence which might be followed by an investor. That is, an investor normally would begin with an examination of a company's historical rates of growth of sales and earnings, both in absolute terms and in relation to the growth rates of other companies and of the economy. Next would come an effort to understand the key sources of past earnings growth: profit margin on sales, utilization of assets, and financial policies. The growth analysis would be followed by an appraisal of the company's financial strength, particularly its ability to service its debts and to generate the funds needed to carry out its operating programs. Finally, the prices of its securities would be examined in various perspectives in preparation for a decision to buy or sell.

HISTORICAL GROWTH RATES

To gain an overview of the historical development of a company, it is helpful to calculate the growth rates of its sales, earnings, book value, and stock price over an extended period of time. Preferably, the beginning and ending years of the time period should be at approximately the same stage of the general business cycle or of the particular industry's own cycle, if different from the general cycle. These growth rates should be compared with those of other companies in the same industry, and with the growth rates of broad economic aggregates such as gross national product and total corporate profits.

Since mergers and acquisitions can seriously distort trends in the *dollar totals* of a company's sales and earnings, it is desirable to express these amounts in *per share* terms. This will require adjustment for stock splits and stock dividends, and will take into account the existence of *common stock equivalents.* Per share calculation procedures were described in chapter 4.

Growth rates of the following items should be of particular interest:

1. Sales
   (Note: If data are available, sales growth should be calculated for each major product line, and unit growth should be distinguished from price growth.)
2. Operating Income, equal to
   Sales minus:
   Cost of Goods Sold
   Selling, General, and Administrative Expenses
   Depreciation, Amortization, and Depletion
   (Note: Some analysts define operating income as being *before* depreciation.)
3. Net Available for Common, equal to
   Net Income minus Preferred Dividends
   (Note: Net income usually is taken before extraordinary items; this is the familiar *earnings per share* amount.)
4. Cash Flow, equal to
   Net Available for Common plus Depreciation and Deferred Tax Charge
   (Note: While *Cash Flow* is a misnomer for this figure, it can be very useful analytically.)
5. Dividends on Common Stock
6. Stockholders' Equity (also known as Book Value), equal to
   Tangible Assets minus Liabilities and Preferred Stock Liquidation Value

(Note: Preferred stock is, technically, equity, but it is excluded from equity in the ratios described in this chapter.)

7. Average Price of Common Stock, equal to
   Mean of Annual High and Low Price

DETERMINANTS OF EARNINGS GROWTH

There are many ways to gain insight into the sources of a company's earnings growth. The approach followed in this book is based upon widely utilized methods developed by the Du Pont Corporation. This approach focuses on *profit margins* and *turnover of operating assets.* The interaction of margin and turnover produces a rate of *return on operating assets.* Depending on the degree of *leverage* introduced into a company's capital structure, the *return on equity* will be greater than the return on assets. Finally, given the return on equity, a company's earnings growth (aside from mergers and acquisitions) will depend on whether it pays out most of its earnings as dividends to stockholders or whether it reinvests most of its earnings in additional assets.

All of the ratios listed in this section should be studied both *temporally* and *cross-sectionally*. Temporal analysis refers to a study of the ratios over a period of time. Cross-sectional analysis refers to a comparison of the ratios for different companies at the same point in time.

Profit Margin Analysis. This involves not only measuring the margins, but also examining each major component of costs to determine why the margin is high or low, rising or falling. The most significant ratios are:

1. Operating Margin, equal to
   Operating Income as a percentage of Sales
2. Pretax Margin, equal to
   Net Income Before Taxes as a percentage of Sales
3. Net Profit Margin, equal to
   Net Available for Common as a percentage of Sales
4. Expense ratios, which express each of the following expenses as a percentage of Sales
   a. Labor costs. (Note: This ratio often is supplemented by a study of sales per employee and wages per employee.)
   b. Other costs of goods sold (mainly materials and direct overhead).
   c. Selling, general, and administrative expense. (Note: Research and development outlays often are separately analyzed.)

d. Depreciation, amortization, and depletion. (Note: This item often is expressed as a percentage of average gross plant.)

5. Tax Rate, equal to
   Income taxes as a percentage of net income before taxes.

Turnover Analysis. This involves an examination of the intensity of utilization of each major class of asset, as well as of total operating assets. In addition, various *capital turnover* ratios are common. The key ratios are:

1. Asset Turnover, equal to Sales divided by each of the following:
   a. Cash
   b. Accounts Receivable
   c. Inventory
   d. Current Assets ($a + b + c$)
   e. Working Capital (d − Current Liabilities)
   f. Gross Plant
   g. Net Plant
   h. Total Operating Assets ($d + g$)
2. Capital Turnover, equal to
   Sales divided by the sum of Long-Term Debt, Preferred Stock, and Stockholders' Equity
3. Equity Turnover, equal to
   Sales divided by Stockholders' Equity

Rate of Return. The rate of return measures the relationship of earnings to either assets or capital. There are several rate of return measures upon which analysts focus attention, as follows:

1. Return on Operating Assets, equal to
   Operating Income as a percentage of Operating Assets
   Note: This ratio is the product of the Operating Margin multiplied by the Turnover of Operating Assets; that is,

$$\frac{\text{Operating Income}}{\text{Sales}} \times \frac{\text{Sales}}{\text{Operating Assets}}$$

2. Return on Total Assets, equal to
   Earnings before Interest and Taxes (known as EBIT) as a percentage of Total Assets
   (Note: This ratio adds to the return on operating assets a company's net nonoperating income, before interest and taxes, and its nonoperating assets.)
3. Pretax Return on Total Capital, equal to
   EBIT as a percentage of the sum of Long-Term Debt, Preferred Stock, and Stockholders' Equity

[Note: The *after-tax* return on total capital would use as the earnings amount the sum of (*a*) net available for common, (*b*) preferred dividends, and (*c*) (Interest × [1.0 − Tax rate]).]

4. Return on Stockholders' Equity, equal to
   Net Available for Common as a percentage of Stockholders' Equity
   (Note: The difference between pretax return on total capital and return on equity reflects the tax rate and the degree of financial leverage.)

Financial Policy. This impacts earnings growth in two ways. One major feature of financial policy is *leverage*, or the degree to which a company uses borrowed funds as opposed to equity. Leverage enables the return on assets (if higher than the interest rate on borrowed funds) to be translated into an even higher rate of return on stockholders' equity. Similarly, growth of return on assets becomes magnified into a higher growth of return on equity. Of course, leverage also poses significant risks, because it has a reverse impact on stockholders' well-being if return on assets is low or declining.

A second major feature of financial policy is a company's dividend policy. Given a positive rate of return on equity, every dollar of earnings retained in the business, rather than paid out as dividends to common stockholders, will generate incremental earnings per share in succeeding years. Indeed, as was demonstrated in Chapter 6, a company's *internal growth rate* (the growth potential of earnings per share exclusive of additional issuance of common stock) is equal to the product of its rate of return on equity multiplied by its earnings retention rate.

The key measures of a company's leverage policy are as follows:

1. Total Leverage, equal to
   Total Assets divided by Stockholders' Equity
   (Note: This measure is referred to as total leverage because it reflects the portion of assets financed by all funds other than common equity—that is, short-term debt [notes and accounts payable], long-term debt, and preferred stock.)
2. Debt-to-Capital, equal to
   Long-Term Debt plus Preferred Stock as a percentage of Total Capital
   (Note: This ratio considers only long-term leverage. Preferred stock is considered a form of borrowed capital. Definitions of terms will be elaborated below.)

3. Debt-to-Equity, equal to
   Long-Term Debt plus Preferred Stock as a percentage of Stockholders' Equity
   (Note: This concept is identical to debt-to-capital, but expresses the relationship a bit differently.)
4. Debt to Tangible Assets, equal to
   Total Liabilities plus Preferred Stock as a percentage of Total Assets excluding Intangibles
   (Note: This measure is related to total leverage, and permits a division of debt into long-term and short-term portions, with each portion expressed as a percentage of tangible assets.)

In all of the leverage measures, the following definitions are generally applicable:

a. Long-term debt should include the capitalized value of long-term lease obligations as well as many of the other off-balance sheet liabilities discussed in Chapter 4.
b. Preferred stock should be taken at the liquidation value stated in the contract, if different from par.
c. Minority interests generally should be treated as "other liabilities."
d. Intangibles should be deducted from assets and stockholders' equity, unless the analyst believes they have realizable value.
e. Deferred tax liabilities may be treated as either long-term debt, "other liabilities," or stockholders' equity, depending on the investor's views regarding the likelihood that they will have to be paid.

The key measures of a company's dividend policy are:

1. Payout Ratio, equal to
   Common Dividends as a percentage of Net Available for Common
   (Note: As a supplement, dividends may be expressed as a percentage of "cash flow.")
2. Retention Rate, equal to
   100 percent minus the Payout Ratio

MEASURES OF FINANCIAL STRENGTH

Generally, the ratios enumerated below are measures of credit quality and, therefore, are of greatest interest to bond and preferred stock investors. But they are by no means insignificant for common stock investors. For if a company's credit-worthiness deteriorates, there are negative implications for owners as well as for creditors. The key ratios on which analysts focus have to do with fixed charge coverage, leverage, and liquidity. Since leverage already has been covered above, only the coverage and liquidity ratios will be itemized here.

Coverage Ratios. Coverage ratios are designed to measure the relationship between a company's earnings and its obligations to pay interest, preferred stock dividends, and any sinking-fund obligations. The principal ratios are:

1. Fixed charge coverage, equal to
   Earnings before Interest and Taxes (EBIT) divided by Interest
   (Note: Interest should include relevant long-term lease obligations.)
2. Coverage of Interest and Sinking Funds, equal to
   Earnings before Interest, Taxes, *and Depreciation* divided by Interest plus Sinking Fund Requirements
   (Note: The assumption is that depreciation bears a relationship to sinking-fund requirements.)
3. Coverage of Interest and Preferred Dividends, equal to
   EBIT divided by Interest plus [Preferred Dividends ÷ (1.0 − Tax rate)]
   (Note: The preferred dividend [not tax-deductible] is adjusted upward to make it comparable to interest [tax-deductible].)
4. Alternative Fixed Charge Coverage, equal to EBIT as a percentage of the Principal Amount of Long-Term Debt or Debt plus Preferred Stock.
   (Note: This alternative measure is used to compare companies whose debt was issued at different times and, as a result, bears very different coupon rates of interest. The concept is that since the debt probably will be refunded from time to time, the coupon rates may be less relevant than the principal amounts.)

Liquidity Measures. These measures are needed because a company may be generating a lot of "bookkeeping earnings," but may be "cash poor." The most widely used ratios are:

1. Current Ratio, equal to
   Current Assets divided by Current Liabilities
2. Acid Test (or Quick Asset) Ratio, equal to
   Sum of Cash (and equivalents) plus Accounts Receivable divided by Current Liabilities
3. Cash Ratio
   Cash (and equivalents) divided by Current Liabilities

4. Working Capital-to-Sales, equal to
   (Current Assets minus Current Liabilities) as a percentage of Sales
5. Cash Flow-to-Debt, equal to
   Cash Flow as a percentage of Principal Amount of Debt
6. Receivables Collection Period, equal to
   Average Receivables divided by Average Daily Sales
7. Days to Sell Inventory, equal to
   Average Inventory divided by Average Daily Cost of Goods Sold
8. Internal Funding of Capital Expenditures, equal to
   Capital Expenditures as a percentage of the sum of Retained Earnings plus Depreciation

MEASURES OF STOCK AND BOND PRICES

It is meaningless to compare the prices of different securities, or of the same security over time, in absolute dollar-and-cents terms. The fact that stock X sells for, say, $50 per share, while stock Y sells for $200 per share, in no way implies that stock Y is "dearer" than stock X. It is necessary to relate price to earnings, or dividends, or interest rate, or book value—in other words, to relate price to a fundamental determinant of value. The key measures are:

1. Price/Earnings Ratio, equal to
   Price divided by Net Available for Common per Share
   (Note: The earnings figure used in the denominator is usually either the sum of the latest four quarters or the analyst's estimate of earnings for the current year. However, if current earnings are greatly influenced by unusual factors, an attempt should be made to determine a "normalized" earnings amount.)
2. Relative P/E, equal to
   Price/Earnings Ratio of a particular stock expressed as a percentage of the Price/Earnings Ratio of a broad market index such as the S&P Index.
3. Price/Book Value, equal to
   Price divided by Stockholders' Equity per Share
   (Note: This ratio is used mainly in appraising the stocks of financial companies and in mergers and acquisitions.)
4. Current Yield, equal to
   Annual Dividend Rate on Stock (common or preferred) as a percentage of Price, or Annual Coupon Rate on Bond as a percentage of Price

5. Yield to Maturity, equal to

   Discount Rate which equates Price with Future Interest and Principal Payments

   (Note: This yield is most readily determined from a set of yield tables. However, it usually can be approximated by applying the following formula:

$$\frac{\text{Coupon Rate} \pm (\text{Discount or Premium} \div \text{Years to Maturity})}{\frac{1}{2}\,(\text{Price of Bond} + \text{Par Value})}$$

Part Three
Timing Aids

Investment decisions usually are classified under two broad headings: *selection* and *timing*. Selection deals with the question: *What* to buy or sell—bond or stocks; which bonds; which stocks? Timing deals with the question: *When* to buy or sell—now or wait? As a practical matter, of course, these two categories are not mutually exclusive. The question of what to buy or sell is not made in a time vacuum. The real question is: *What* to do with my capital *now*? Granting the interlocking nature of selection and timing, however, it is useful to differentiate between them conceptually.

The traditional approach to both the selection and timing aspects of investment has been that of *security analysis*, or *evaluation*. In chapter 5 of this book, for example, it was shown that the goal of common stock evaluation is to determine the approximate trend line around which actual stock prices can be expected to fluctuate. At any given time, according to this approach, investors should have a reasonably clear idea whether stocks generally, and individual stocks in particular, seem underpriced or overpriced. This enables them to come to grips with both the what and when questions. For example, they may seek to buy issues which are relatively most underpriced, at a time when the market in general seems underpriced.

Value analysts assume that underpriced and overpriced situations ultimately will come into better balance. But they typically make little or no effort to predict when the corrective price movement will occur. Their reasons for ignoring efforts to predict are several. First, they argue that it is not possible to make predictions about turning points of prices with a better than chance probability of being accurate. Second, they point out that investors confront "a market of stocks rather than a stock market." By this they mean that efforts to predict the turning points of, say, the Dow Jones Industrial Average are rather futile, since an average can go up or down but there is great disparity in the price movement of the individual component stocks of the average. Furthermore, they note with regard to attempts to predict the averages, most downturns during the postwar period have amounted to only some 10–20 percent. Certainly one cannot expect to be farsighted enough to sell at the very peaks and buy back at the troughs. Assuming that even a good forecaster will make his or her sales at least 3–5 percent below the peaks, and that repurchases will be made 3–5 percent above the troughs, and making allowance for brokerage commissions and taxes of several percent on combined sale-repurchase transactions, the average price decline of 10–20 percent doesn't leave much, if anything, for profit. Moreover, there are very real dangers of being "whipsawed" by selling in anticipation of a price decline which fails to occur.

So strong is the antipathy of many value analysts toward price prediction efforts outside of the value context that it seems important to comment on the logic of their position. In the first place, it is hoped that the following chapters will demonstrate that predictive tools are available which can produce better than chance results if utilized properly. It will not be argued that these tools are at all perfect or that they can be employed with little effort. But neither are the tools of security valuation perfect or easy to utilize.

The claim that the stock market is *selective*—that is, that individual stock prices do not all move in tandem—is quite correct. But inappropriate implications seem to have been drawn from this observation. Major upward and downward swings of *the averages* usually do reflect the overall tone of the market rather well, as is shown in the accompanying tabulation. The tabulation indicates that when the averages fall, stocks in most industries fall also. Likewise, when the averages rise, the majority of stock groups rise also.

Selectivity means that in a bull market different stocks rise by very different percentage amounts, and in a bear market they fall by very different amounts. Nor do all stocks make their highs and lows at the same time. Therefore, the investor's attention should not be focused exclusively on the averages. But neither should the averages be ignored. For once a major trend in the averages gets under way, it is extremely difficult to select the issues that will resist the trend. The true significance of the existence of disparate price movements among different stocks would seem to be that value analysis and price forecasting approaches should be considered powerful allies rather than opposing philosophies.

Industry Group Price Changes during Bear Markets*

Peak Month†	*6/48*	*1/53*	*7/56*	*7/59*	*12/61*	*1/66*	*12/68*	*1/73*
Trough Month†	*6/49*	*9/53*	*12/57*	*10/60*	*6/62*	*10/66*	*5/70*	*12/74*
Percent Change S&P Composite..	−17	−11	−17	−10	−23	−17	−28	−43
Percent Change S&P Industrials..	−18	−12	−17	−11	−23	−18	−28	−44
No. of groups with price changes of:								
+10.1% and over	2	1	8	18	0	1	0	4
+ .1 to +10.0%	4	6	9	13	0	5	2	2
0 to −10.0	20	37	13	12	8	9	3	4
−10.1 to −20.0	18	29	24	12	23	25	18	3
−20.1 and over	39	10	31	33	57	55	74	76

Industry Group Price Changes during Bull Markets*

Trough Month†	*6/49*	*9/53*	*12/57*	*10/60*	*6/62*	*10/66*	*5/70*
Peak Month†	*1/53*	*7/56*	*7/59*	*12/61*	*1/66*	*12/68*	*1/73*
Percent Change S&P Composite	+87	+110	+48	+34	+68	+38	+56
Percent Change S&P Industrials	+93	+125	+48	+33	+70	+41	+59
No. of groups with price changes of:							
+100.1% and over	21	29	11	4	24	28	18
+ 50.1 to +100.0%	26	20	38	21	29	29	33
+ 25.1 to + 50.0	20	21	29	32	19	24	26
0 to + 25.0	14	12	8	27	12	13	19
− .1 to − 10.0	2	1	1	4	0	1	2
− 10.1 to − 20.0	0	1	0	0	1	0	5
− 20.0 and over	0	0	0	0	2	0	2

* The industry groups covered in the analysis are as classified by Standard & Poor's. Excluded are various "composites"—for example, Food Composite, Machinery Composite—and also various redundant groupings—for example, Autos, ex. GM. The number of groups has changed over the years.

† The peak and trough dates are based on monthly average prices of the S&P Stock Price Indexes. Daily high and lows may not have taken place in precisely those months. For example, the 1974 daily low occurred in October, although the low month was December.

The argument that the mildness of postwar bear markets reduces the importance of timing also has flaws. First, as the value analysts themselves admit, *selectivity* means that some stocks may have quite severe downturns even when the averages decline only moderately. Second, venturesome investors can enhance the rewards of correct forecasts of downturns by *short* selling over and above their sales of existing holdings. Third, although most postwar bear markets have been milder than in the prewar period (for example, stocks declined 40 percent in 1920–21, 80 percent in 1929–32, and 40 percent in 1937), the severity of the 1969–70 and 1973–74 drops should give pause to those who feel certain that major collapses are rare occurrences. And the difficulty is that the early warning signals prior to major collapses are not really different from the warning signals prior to moderate downturns. In other words, it can be argued that it pays to sell (or at least to stop buying) even in anticipation of a moderate downturn, as insurance against the possibility that the downturn will be very sharp.

The opportunity to improve investment yield by improving one's timing is greater during the more volatile type of stock market experienced in the past decade, and quite possibly to be experienced in the future, than was the case in the 1950–65 period. But even if price-value divergences once again become short-lived and mild, the position that only *in-and-out traders* should attempt to forecast these swings and act accordingly is unconvincing. Merely consider the impact of an extra 1 percent per annum rate of return on the results of a lifetime investment program. If an individual of 35 invests $1,000 a year in a cross section of common stocks which produce an annual rate of return of, say, 8 percent in dividends plus capital appreciation, upon retirement at age 65 a portfolio worth $122,000 will have been accumulated. If, through more appropriate timing of investments, the annual rate of return can be raised from 8 percent to 9 percent, at retirement the portfolio will be worth $148,000, a 20 percent advantage.

Finally, a psychological observation is in order. Focusing on long-term values is supposed to enable investors to weather the cyclical storms of the capital markets—to enable them to avoid being overwhelmed emotionally by cyclical swings. Unfortunately, human beings are not as strong willed as they should be for their own good. Even institutional investors, who are professionally trained and in an eminent position to take a long-term view of things, have a tendency to get carried away by the market's gyrations. It is only too common for members of bank and insurance company investment committees to change their minds about *values* because of the incessant pronouncements of the ticker tape. Would they not have a better frame of reference if they understood the causes of divergences from value, as well as the causes of value itself?

In the chapters which follow, two basic approaches to the problem of forecasting turning points of security prices are examined. One approach—the *fundamental* approach described in Chapter 10—relates security price changes to general business cycle developments and to the economic cycles of specific industries. The other approach—the *technical* approach described in Chapter 11—focuses attention on internal developments within the securities markets themselves.

10

Business Cycle Analysis

Better is one fore thought than two after.
Erasmus

This chapter is divided into two sections. The first section surveys the relationships between stock prices, interest rates, and the broad movements of economic activity which are referred to as the business cycle. The survey suggests that an ability to anticipate forthcoming changes in business conditions can be used to improve the timing of security purchases and sales.

The second section of the chapter follows logically from the first. If economic forecasting can be helpful to the investor, how should the investor go about making or using such forecasts? Obviously, in a single section of a single chapter we cannot present all there is known about the subject of economic forecasting. But we can encourage investors to gain familiarity with some of the most useful tools of the forecaster.

CAPITAL MARKET INFLUENCES OF BUSINESS CYCLES

BUSINESS CYCLES AND STOCK PRICES

There is substantial evidence suggesting that an ability to foresee business cycle turning points for several months improves the ability to foresee major turning points in the general level of stock prices. The evidence does not imply that *every* bear market *must* be accompanied by an economic recession, or vice versa. However, the tendecy for this relationship to exist has been so pronounced, and the lead-lag relationship between the stock market and the business cycle has been so persistent, that if a recession or a slow-down of economic growth appears to lie ahead, the investor should consider that the odds are high it will be preceded by a significant stock market downturn some months in advance. Let's look at the record.

1947–1965. Figure 10–1 compares Standard and Poor's Industrial

Figure 10–1
Stock Prices and Industrial Production, 1947–1965

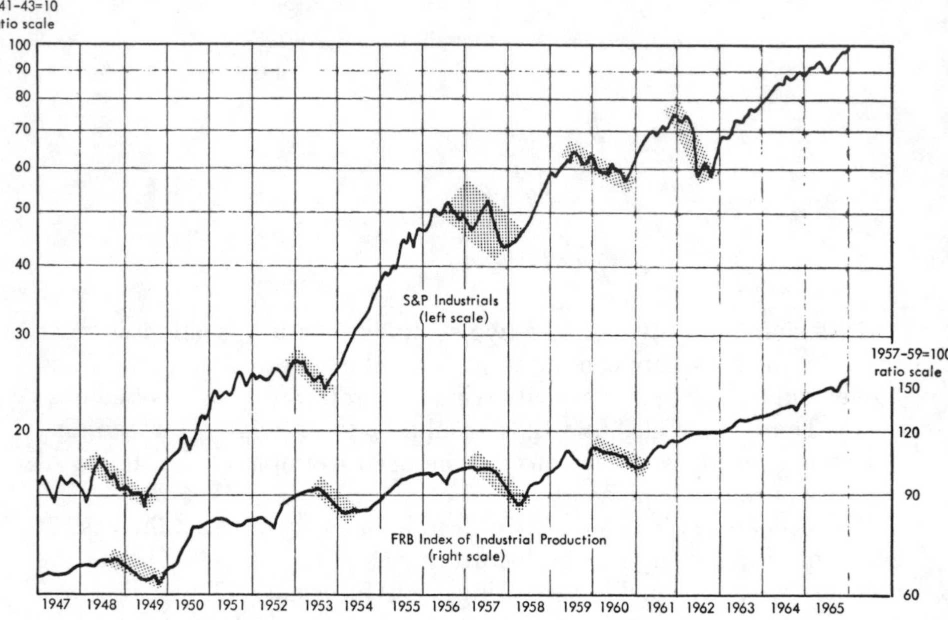

Stock Price Index with the Federal Reserve Board Index of Industrial Production from 1947 through 1965. Examination of the chart reveals that:

1. Both series exhibited uptrends, with stock prices rising more steeply than production.

2. There were five extended reversals in the stock price uptrend. In 1948–49, prices declined 18 percent; in 1953, they declined 12 percent; in 1956–57, 17 percent; in 1959–60, 11 percent; and in 1962, 23 percent. (All percentages are based on *monthly average* prices at the beginning and end of the reversal periods. See tabulation in introduction to Part Three for the monthly dates used.)

3. Four of these five stock price reversals began several months prior to extended periods of declines in industrial production, and ended shortly before the start of renewed advances in production. The 1962 stock price decline did not precede an actual slump in industrial production, but rather a seven-month period of no growth. The end of the stock price decline occurred a few months prior to a strong resumption of growth.

1966–1975. Figure 10–2 compares stock prices and industrial production from 1966 to 1975. Some differences during this period may be noted versus the relationships described above, but the overall picture leads to similar conclusions.

Figure 10–2
Stock Prices and Industrial Production, 1966–1975

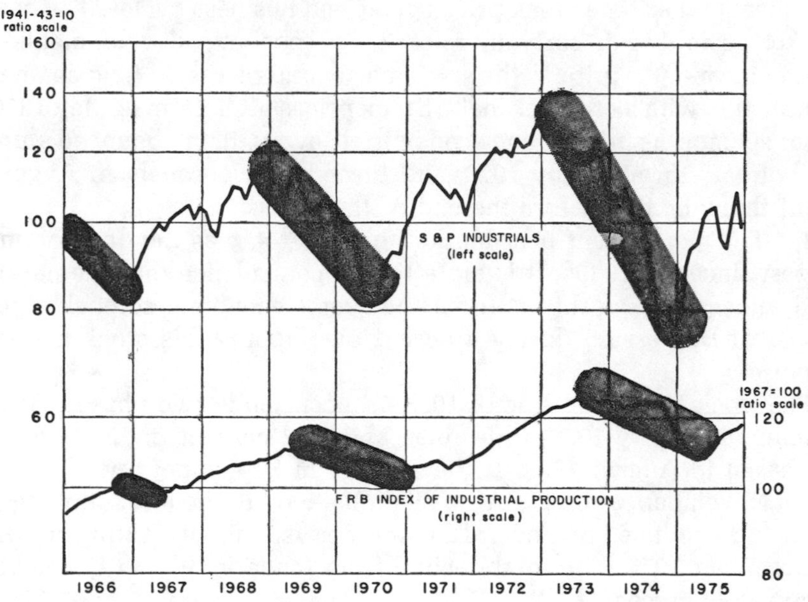

1. Both stock prices and industrial production had exhibited strong uptrends from 1947 to 1965. During the 1966–75 period, on the other hand, stock prices churned violently up and down, with no real trend. But this pattern did not occur in isolation. It seemed to reflect the slower and more volatile growth path of industrial production.

2. Industrial production staged a "mini-recession" from the fall of 1966 to the spring of 1967. But the associated stock price decline began earlier than would be expected on the basis of prior postwar

experience—fully nine months before the slowdown in industrial production began. Moreover, a renewed bull market started up in late 1966, just when industrial production started down. Although this timing sequence was unusual compared with earlier precedent, it seems clear that the 1966 bear market *was* related to forthcoming economic difficulties. If one recollects that during the early months of 1966 there was a *credit crunch,* which led many observers to anticipate a recession, the tie between stock price cycles and the overall business cycle becomes obvious.

3. The 1969–70 bear market lends further support to the notion of a connection between stock price cycles and business cycles. The bear market again began early in relation to economic developments—about nine months prior to the start of a general recession (and again in conjunction with a *credit crunch*). Stock prices hit bottom in May 1970, about six months prior to the economic recovery, then "bounced along the bottom" through July 1970, and turned up vigorously in August, about three months before the end of the recession.

4. The most recent bear market, in 1973–74, was the deepest and longest since the 1930s. It is more than a coincidence that the nation (and, indeed the world) suffered the worst economic setback since the Great Depression during a period overlapping this stock market collapse.

The stock market decline of 1973–74 occurred in two phases. After peaking in January 1973, it declined about 12 percent (monthly average basis) to August 1973. It then rallied in September and October but in November, when the Arab oil embarago hit, the market plunged again and continued downward for another year, finally hitting bottom in December 1974. The total decline from January 1973 to December 1974 was 44 percent.

What was happening to industrial production at this time? It had started to flatten out in July 1973, six months after the stock price peak, and from July to November rose at an annual rate of only 2 percent—not a recession, but a marked economic slowdown. After the embargo, industrial production moved horizontally until September 1974. It then began a full-fledged decline which did not end until April 1975, four months after the stock price trough and a year-and-a-half after the production peak. Measuring from the November 1973 peak to the April 1975 trough, industrial production declined over 15 percent. This compares with a 2 percent decline during the 1966–67 mini-recession, and 8 percent during the 1969–70 recession.

Conclusion. It is essential to stress the fact that stock price peaks and trough typically have *preceded* turning points of general business activity. Many investors are invariably surprised when, in the midst of rather dreary business news, stock prices rise, and in the midst of prosperity, stock prices fall. But such is the nature of the stock market.

Several theories have been offered to explain the stock market's apparent forecasting ability. One is that investors, collectively, have good foresight, and that they act on the basis of what they think is *going to happen* to business activity rather than on the basis of what they currently see happening. Another argument is that investors act on the basis of current rather than anticipated future developments, but that the chief current indicators they watch—corporate profits and profit margins—tend to turn in advance of general business activity. Therefore, profit-oriented investors coincidentally bid stock prices up and drive them down in advance of general business activity. Yet a third theory is that stock price reversals help *cause* subsequent economic reversals by affecting consumer and business confidence and spending decisions. Finally, various monetary explanations for the stock price lead have been offered, as will be noted in later sections. Perhaps the truth lies closest to a combination of all these hypotheses.

From the General to the Particular. Since an ability to foresee business cycle turning points normally would improve one's ability to foresee major turning points in the stock market as a whole, would it also improve one's ability to select the particular stocks to be most affected by the change in overall trend? The answer to this question is "sometimes yes, sometimes no." The relative price changes of individual stocks over short periods of time reflect many factors. These factors include relative changes in company sales, earnings, and dividends, but they also include the degree to which different stocks had been overpriced or underpriced prior to the turning point of the general market. To the extent that accurate forecasts of the overall economy can improve forecasts of relative changes in the prosperity of different industries, forecasts of relative price changes of stocks in different industries should be improved. Examples of this statement are contained in Figures 10–3 and 10–4.

The first set of three charts (Figure 10–3) covers years prior to the severe stock market decline of 1973–74. The charts reveal a fairly close relationship between the relative production in three major sectors of the economy—consumer durable goods, business capital goods, and construction—and the relative price movement of the common stocks of companies operating in those economic sectors. (Relative production data are composites of Federal Reserve Board production indexes for each sector, expressed as a percentage of the aggregate FRB Industrial Production Index. Relative stock prices are composites of the

Figure 10–3
Relative Production versus Relative Stock Prices: Consumer Durables, Business Capital Goods, and Construction

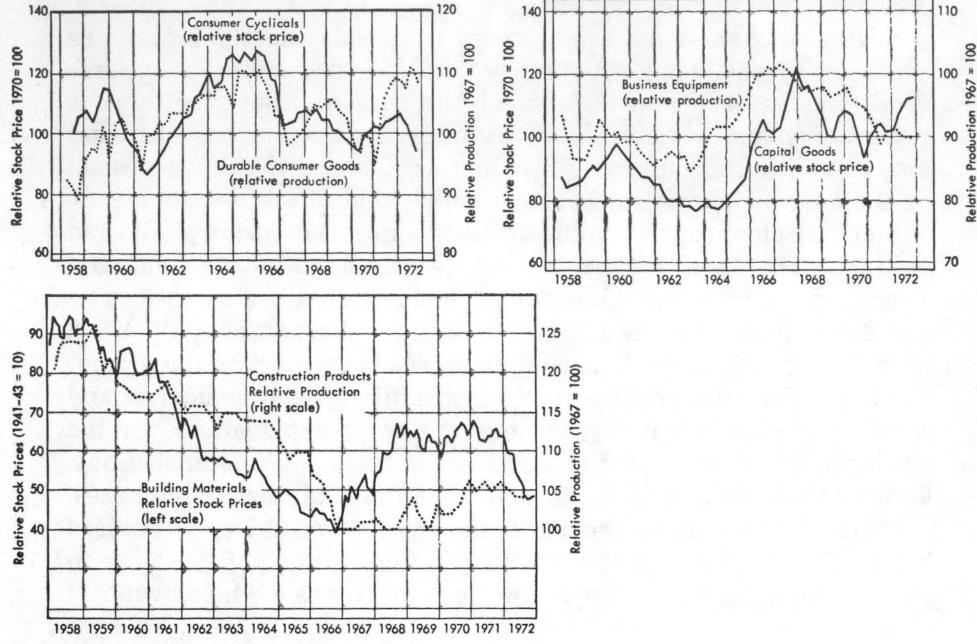

Source: William W. Witter, Inc.

appropriate Standard & Poor's industrial group prices indexes, expressed as a percentage of the aggregate S&P Stock Price Index.)

Few industry groups withstood the 1973–74 bear market. However, as can be seen in the right hand panel of Figure 10–4, one industry whose stocks held up reasonably well was the copper industry. The left panels of the chart, and the accompanying commentary, suggest that the reason was a tremendous surge in the price of raw copper, which became reflected in the earnings of cooper companies.

BUSINESS CYCLES AND BOND YIELDS

Until the mid-1960s, the timing of interest rate cycles, like stock prices, was rather closely related to the upturns and downturns of general economic activity. However, there was one notable difference between the two relationships. Whereas stock prices typically turned well ahead of production, interest rates typically turned at about the same time as production. Thus, the best time to buy bonds was when

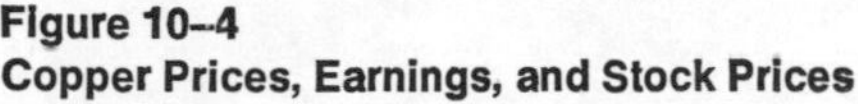

Figure 10–4
Copper Prices, Earnings, and Stock Prices

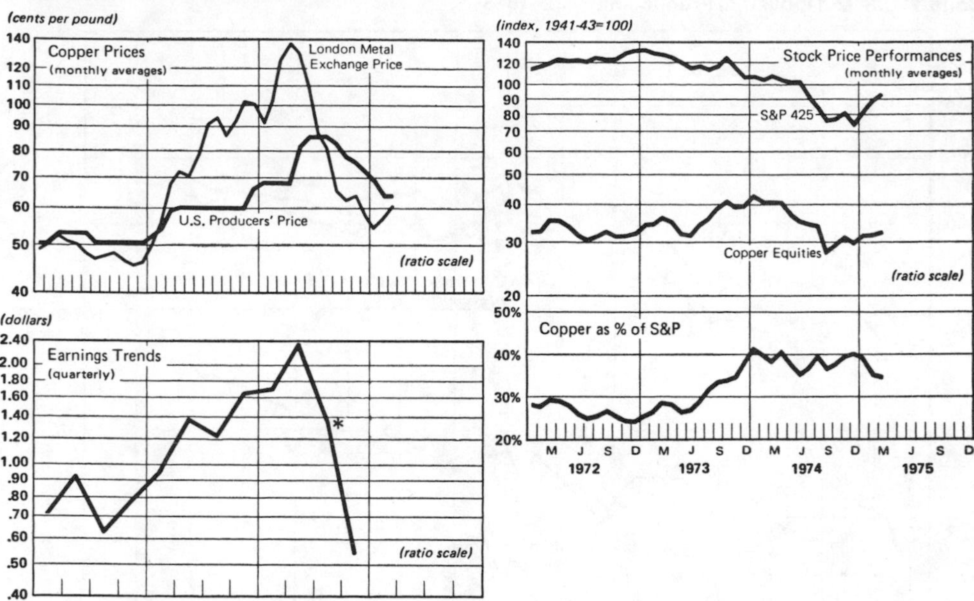

Not terribly surprising, over a long period of years there has been a fairly close correlation in the fluctuations in the price of copper, earnings of copper companies, and the price performance of copper shares. The top left chart displays the more recent relationships that have existed. The mid-1974 industry strike, as well as government price controls earlier in the year and their subsequent demise, distorted the relationships a bit. Moreover, since the Standard & Poor's Indices are weighted by share capitalization, Kennecott represents almost 40 percent of the copper price index, and interest in this equity for some time has focused more on its ownership of Peabody Coal rather than on copper fundamentals. Therefore the S&P copper index appears to have performed somewhat better than would have been expected by observing copper prices or quarterly earnings trends. Nevertheless, the coincident patterns are still evident.

* Reflects strike in July and August.
Source: Loeb, Rhoades & Co.

the peak of economic activity had been reached, not before. Bond prices then were at their lowest point (interest rates were highest). The best time to sell bonds was when a new economic advance began following a recession. At such time, bond prices usually were highest (interest rates lowest). Figure 10–5 compares the movements from 1952 through 1965 of yields on long-term U.S. government bonds and Moody's Aaa corporate bonds with the FRB Index of Industrial Production.

Although the relationship between stock price cycles and business

Figure 10–5
Bond Yields and Industrial Production, 1952–1965

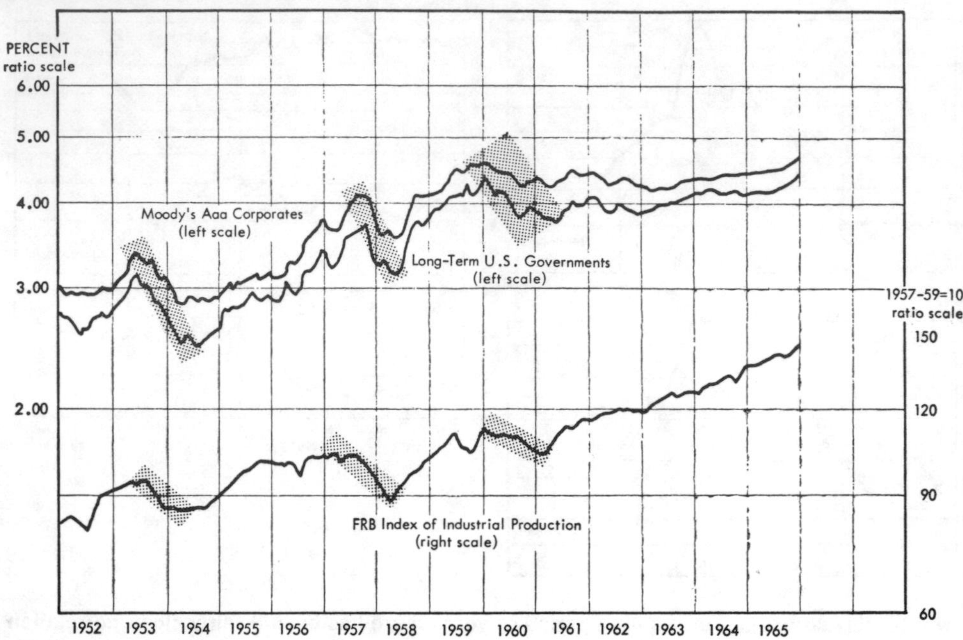

cycles in more recent years has conformed fairly well to the traditional pattern, this has been much less true of bond yield behavior. In the past, as noted above, peaks and troughs of bond yields corresponded fairly closely to peaks and troughs of industrial production. Let us consider, in this context, the movement of bond yields during the mini-recession of 1966–67, the recession of 1969–70, and the major economic downturn of 1974–75.

As shown in Figure 10–6, prior to the onset of the mini-recession in the fall of 1966, yields on new issues of high-grade corporate bonds had risen to a postwar high of almost 6 percent. As industrial production slipped, bond yields declined about 0.75 percent over a three-month period. Before industrial production turned up again, however, the rise of bond yields resumed, and by the summer of 1967 bond yields once more were setting new highs.

By the time the recession of 1969–70 began, high-grade corporate bond yields had reached the 8 percent level. While industrial production declined during the fall of 1969, bond yields *rose* another 0.5 percent. And as the recession cumulated in the first half of 1970, bond yields continued to rise and passed the 9 percent level. It was not until

Figure 10–6
Bond Yields and Industrial Production, 1966–1975

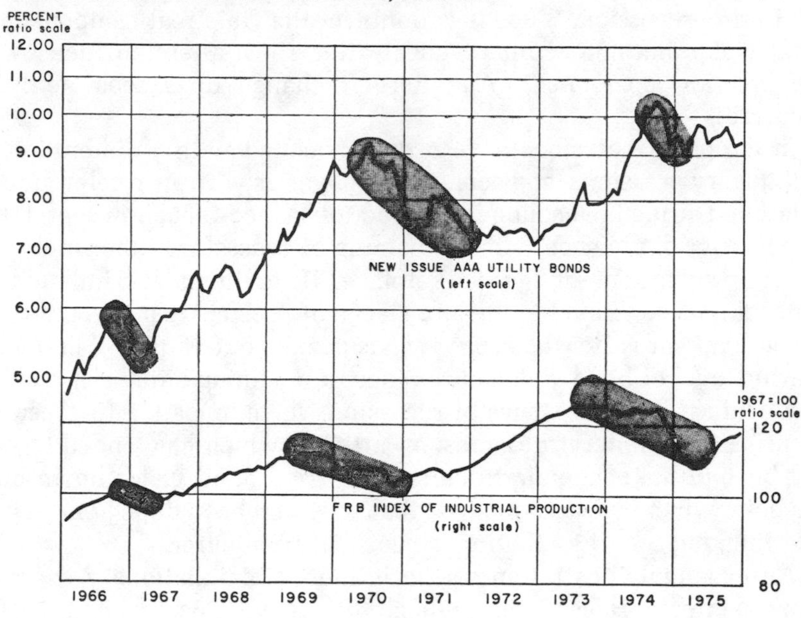

late 1970 that such yields began to decline. Once the decline began, however, it continued (with a notable reversal in the second quarter of 1971, to be discussed below) despite the fact that industrial production had resumed an uptrend. By the end of 1971, high-grade bond yields had reached a 7.25–7.50 percent level, and they were still at that level in the summer of 1972 although a vigorous economic expansion was in progress.

The same pattern recurred in 1974 and 1975. Bond yields rose to unprecedented heights well after the point at which economic activity had peaked. And when interest rates finally turned down, they continued in that direction well beyond the point at which a renewed economic expansion had gotten under way. Early in 1976 (not shown in Figure 10–6), bond yields dropped to significantly lower levels than had been reached in 1975, despite the fact that economic activity was improving steadily.

An explanation for this atypical, almost *countercyclical*, relationship between bond yields and industrial production may be found in the theory which views interest rates as having two components—a *real rate of return* and a premium for anticipated inflation. Most students of the subject believe that the *real* corporate bond yield tends to be fairly stable over time, fluctuating in a range of about 3–4 percent, with some tendency toward procyclicality—that is, to rise during prosperity and fall during recession. Since it is doubtful that this real component of bond yields became countercyclical after 1965, attention focuses on the inflation component. And here a change does seem to have occurred.

In the past, recessions have been associated with a diminution of inflationary pressures, and economic recoveries with an acceleration of inflation. During the economic contractions since 1965, however, inflation has not diminished with the coming of recession, either in fact or in the expectations of the marketplace. If anything, the inflationary expectations generated in the late stages of prosperity have continued to spiral upward after the economy has peaked out, thus explaining the soaring level of bond yields in the face of declining industrial production. Only in the late stages of recessions have investors foreseen diminished inflationary pressures, an attitude which has tended to persist beyond the economic trough and carried bond yields down until the point when investors realized that they had been duped once again into thinking that the inflation cancer had been cured.

An excellent illustration of the influence of inflationary expectations on interest rates was provided in the early 1970s. By late 1970, the inflationary spiral seemed to be easing, and bond yields began to drop. But fears of renewed inflation gripped the market again in the spring of 1971, and a sharp upward movement of bond yields took place. The renewed inflation psychology was a major cause of the national program of economic controls announced on August 15, 1971. The controls program was at least partially successful in dampening inflation expectations, and this was reflected in lower bond yields side-by-side with rising industrial production, until the end of 1972.

Again in 1974, in the midst of severe recession, bond yields rose sharply because of rampant inflation fears. In 1975, each month's price index announcements by the Department of Labor were eagerly awaited by the bond market. When the announcements were favorable (slower inflation), interest rates softened. When the announcements were grim (faster inflation), interest rates rose.

Conclusion. It should be clear from recent history that in order to forecast peaks and troughs of bond yields it is no longer sufficient to concentrate mainly on forecasting industrial production. One must also try to forecast the rate of inflation and inflation expectations. And as we emphasize later in this chapter, economists' tools for making such forecasts are by no means as good as their tools for forecasting real output.

BUSINESS CYCLES, YIELD CURVES, AND YIELD SPREADS

The term *structure of interest rates* describes the relationship between bond yields and bond maturities. A pictorial representation of this relationship is known as a *yield curve.* As described in chapter 7, the shape of the curve changes in response to changing expectations about future interest rates, as well as other supply/demand conditions. Figure 10–7 is a schematic diagram of the typical behavior of yield

Figure 10–7
Typical Yield Curves as Business Cycle Unfolds

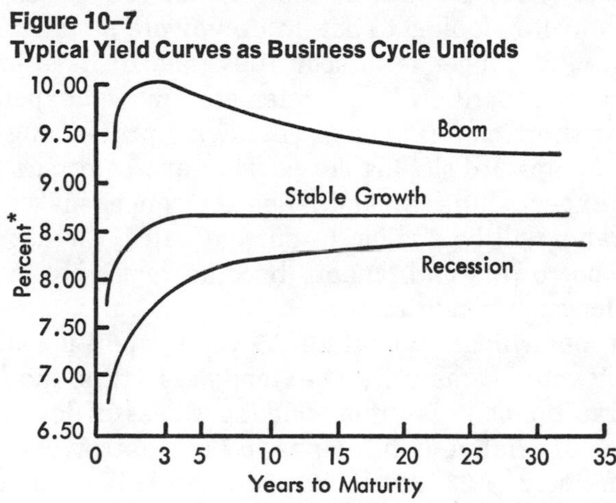

* The interest rate levels are merely illustrative.

curves during recession–recovery–boom periods (the diagram is applicable both to U.S. government obligations and corporate bonds; the yield curve of tax-exempts seldom departs from an upward slope). The bottom curve tends to occur in the midst of a recession, the middle curve during a noninflationary recovery phase of the economy, and the top curve during months of very high business and financial activity.

Note that when the *level* of rates rises as the tempo of business activity speeds up, the shape of the yield curve takes on certain characteristics. These characteristics can be outlined as follows:

1. Up to maturities of about three years—the "short end" of the yield curve—longer term securities tend to have higher yields than shorter term securities whether the level of the yield curve is high or low. This is the area of the maturity spectrum in which investors seek to satisfy their liquidity needs. The shorter the maturity, the greater the liquidity, the greater the demand from liquidity-seeking investors,

and therefore the lower the yield. The upward slope of the yield curve within this maturity range reflects the increments in interest which borrowers have to pay to persuade lenders (investors) to accept lesser degrees of liquidity. Since demands for liquidity tend to be higher in recessions than in booms, the slope is steepest during recessions.

2. From 3 years to about 20 years, that is, between the boundaries of relatively short-term and relatively long-term securities, the yield curve gradually changes shape as the level of rates rises. The curve moves from *upward sloping*, to *flat*, to *downward sloping*. Downward sloping means that longer term securities tend to have lower yields than shorter term securities. When rates are low and expected to rise, lenders prefer short maturities and borrowers prefer long maturities. This leads to an upward sloping curve. The reverse occurs when rates are high and expected to fall. And when the concensus expectation is that future rates will be similar to current rates, the curve tends to flatten since borrowers and lenders become relatively indifferent to maturity under such conditions.

3. Beyond maturities of about 20–25 years, yield usually does not change significantly as maturity is extended. That is, the *long end* of the yield curve typically is rather *flat* regardless of level. It appears to be a matter of relative indifference to both borrowers and lenders whether a maturity is 25, 30, or 40 years, regardless of their expectations about the level of rates.

4. Yield volatility is inversely related to maturity. When the general level of rates rises or falls, short-term rates change much more sharply than long-term rates. (On the other hand, *price volatility* is *directly* related to maturity so far as effects of changes in the level of interest rates are concerned.)

Yield Spreads. The business cycle can have a significant effect on the interrelationships of yields on securities of different types and quality as well as on securities of different maturity. There is a general tendency for yield spreads on different types of long-term fixed-income investments to narrow during the major portion of prosperity periods and to widen as the prosperity reaches a peak and the economy turns down. As an economic advance progresses, investors' confidence in the nation's ability to avoid a severe recession is bolstered. They are, therefore, increasingly reluctant to pay relatively high prices (accept low yields) for high-quality securities, and increasingly willing to raise their bid prices for lower quality issues relative to high-quality issues. If interest rates on both types of securities rise, those of highest quality and lowest yield will tend to have the most rapid increases, and yield spreads therefore will narrow. Conversely, as the boom ends and turns into recession, investors' confidence tends to wane and high quality becomes more important to them. If fixed-income securities of most quality grades are characterized by declining interest rates, those of highest quality will tend to decline most rapidly in yield, and yield spreads will widen.

There also is an interesting relationship between stock yields and bond yields during the course of the business cycle. Generally speaking, as an economic advance progresses, rising stock prices cause dividend yields to fall while bond yields rise. The spread between the two gradually begins to attract income-minded investors away from stocks and into bonds. In addition, capital-gains-minded investors begin selling stocks as corporate profit margins narrow and economic recession begins to threaten. The proceeds of these sales are put either into the bank or into fixed-income securities. The shifting of funds out of the stock market weakens stock prices prior to the peak of business activity, but dividends are still high or rising. Therefore, stock yields begin to reverse their downward movement prior to the business peak.

Eventually the economy reaches a peak and turns down. Interest rates ultimately move down as well. Dividends reach a plateau or decline, but stock prices decline faster, and stock yields therefore rise. The yield spread thus becomes gradually less favorable to bond investment. Income seekers begin switching back into stocks, and bargain hunters do likewise in anticipation of eventual recovery. The expansion process begins anew shortly thereafter.

BUSINESS CYCLE FORECASTING

A BUSINESS CYCLE CHRONOLOGY

For more than 50 years, the National Bureau of Economic Research, a private nonprofit organization, has sponsored the research efforts of America's leading students of the business cycle. Among the products of their efforts are techniques for measuring economic fluctuations and identifying major turning points of overall economic activity. Focusing on the period since the end of World War I, and omitting the years of the Great Depression and World War II, Table 10–1 presents a chronology of American business cycles, based on the National Bureau's identification system.

Examination of the table suggests that the "average business cycle" consists of an expansion lasting about two-and-one-half years and a contraction lasting about a year. But even though the table excludes the atypical years of world war and catastrophic depression, consider-

Table 10–1
A Calendar of Major Economic Expansions and Contractions, 1920–1929, 1946–1975

Dates of Turning Points			*Duration (in months)*	
Peak	*Trough*	*Peak*	*Contractions*	*Expansions*
Jan. 1920	July 1921	May 1923	18	22
May 1923	July 1924	Oct. 1926	14	27
Oct. 1926	Nov. 1927	Aug. 1929	13	21
Nov. 1948	Oct. 1949	July 1953	11	45
July 1953	May 1954	Aug. 1957	10	39
Aug. 1957	April 1958	April 1960	8	24
April 1960	Feb. 1961	Dec. 1969	10	106
Dec. 1969	Nov. 1970	Nov. 1973	11	36
Nov. 1973	Mar. 1975		16	
		Median:	11	31

Source: U. S. Department of Commerce, *Business Conditions Digest*.

able diversity of duration remains. These findings suggest that the timing of American business cycles has not been consistent enough to warrant purely calendar-oriented judgments as to the probability of a peak or trough occurring at any given time. Nevertheless, practicing economists do find it helpful to use historical analogies in their work. The more the present resembles the past, the more likely is the forecaster to assume that the future also will be similar to historical precedent.

Leading Economic Indicators

It is a common observation that no two business cycles are exactly alike. Indeed, most modern business economists have become increasingly impressed with the almost endless variety of the cyclical fluctuations they are trying to forecast. Nevertheless, the unique aspects of each individual cycle usually fit into a common framework which has been referred to as the *cumulative process* or the *self-generating cycle*. The essential characteristics of this framework can be described briefly.

If we look into the business cycle as economic activity is beginning to revive, we see that sales and inventories are at a depressed level and considerable excess plant capacity exists in the manufacturing system. As sales begin to rise and profit expectations improve, business leaders start planning for production increases. They expand working hours, and gradually rehire previously laid-off workers. This increases employee incomes and stimulates personal consumption expenditures. With sales and profits rising, the managers begin to expand

and modernize production facilities. These purchases from the capital goods industries create still more jobs and incomes and more consumption by workers in those industries. And so the expansion *cumulates*.

Workers, machines, and materials eventually become utilized at or near capacity levels, and increased demand exerts upward pressure on prices and wages. Business leaders go increasingly into debt to finance expanding inventories, receivables, and fixed assets. Interest rates rise. Soon costs are rising faster than prices, and profit margins deteriorate. This coincides with the gradual realization that productive capacity has outstripped potential sales. Business executives become uneasy and pull in their reins. They reduce their orders for heavy equipment, cut back on the rate of inventory accumulation, repay loans, lay off marginal personnel, and even sell some of their personal common stock holdings. Caution spreads as incomes are reduced. Consumers postpone purchases of durable goods, business executives slash inventories sharply, and the cumulative process is at work in a downward direction.

As the downturn continues, credit terms ease and interest rates fall. The monetary authorities usually reinforce the ease. Housing construction often picks up as reduced mortgage rates, lowered down payments, and extended maturities bring monthly carrying charges to a level which buyers are willing to undertake despite the recessionary atmosphere. Government spending acts as a strong prop to the economy. The stock market, after a sizeable shake-out, stabilizes and begins to move up. Soon consumers realize that the worst is over and begin to unloosen their purse strings. A new revival is in the making.

It should be clear from this brief *physiology of a business cycle* that fluctuations of the whole of economic activity reflect fluctuations of the economy's many parts. Moreover, while the parts tend to move in unison, there is a sequence to events. When one part changes direction, it pushes another part, which pushes still another. It is logical, therefore, that if we wish to predict turning points of the whole economy, we should try to isolate and study those parts which usually turn *before* the whole.

The search for *leading, coincident,* and *lagging* indicators of general economic activity has been one of the major continuing projects of the National Bureau of Economic Research. In its most recent reappraisal of economic indicators, the NBER has selected 12 *leaders* which come closest to meeting ideal characteristics, such as smoothness of movement from month to month, and consistency and logic of relationship to the general business cycle. These 12 are identified in Table 10–2 which also shows the median number of months by which

Table 10–2
Leading Indicators of Economic Activity

	Median Lead (in months) Peak	Trough
1. Average hours in workweek of manufacturing production workers	12	2
2. Layoffs of manufacturing workers (per 1,000)	11	1
3. New orders of consumer products (in constant dollars)	6	1
4. Vendor performance (i.e., percent of companies reporting slower deliveries)	6	5
5. Net new business formations	11	2
6. Permits to build new private housing units	13	8
7. Contracts for new plant and equipment (in constant dollars)	9	2
8. Change in business inventories on hand and on order (in constant dollars)	5	4
9. Common stock prices (S&P 500)	9	4
10. Change in wholesale prices of industrial raw materials	15	5
11. Money supply (in constant dollars)	10	8
12. Change in total liquid assets	6½	6
Average lead of 12 indicators	9½	4

Source: *Business Conditions Digest,* May 1975, p. xv.

the indicator historically has turned in advance of general economic peaks and troughs.

Professional economists carefully study the monthly movements of these indicators, as well as dozens of others. Their effort is facilitated by the Department of Commerce, which publishes charts and data on a wide variety of economic indicators in a monthly publication, *Business Conditions Digest.* Figure 10–8 is a key to help read the charts published each month by the Department of Commerce, and Figure 10–9 shows the postwar behavior of each of the twelve leading indicators noted in Table 10–2.

As a valuable supplement to the individual indicators, there is a composite index which combines the leading indicators into a single statistical series. There also are composites of the coincident and lagging indicators. The composites are used as checks on the validity of turns in the leading index. That is, if the leading indicator index seems to have turned down, that fact should be confirmed by subsequent downturns of, first, the coincident index, and next, the lagging index. Figure 10–10 displays these composite indexes.

Of course, the investor cannot wait until all the confirming signals

Figure 10–8
How to Read Charts

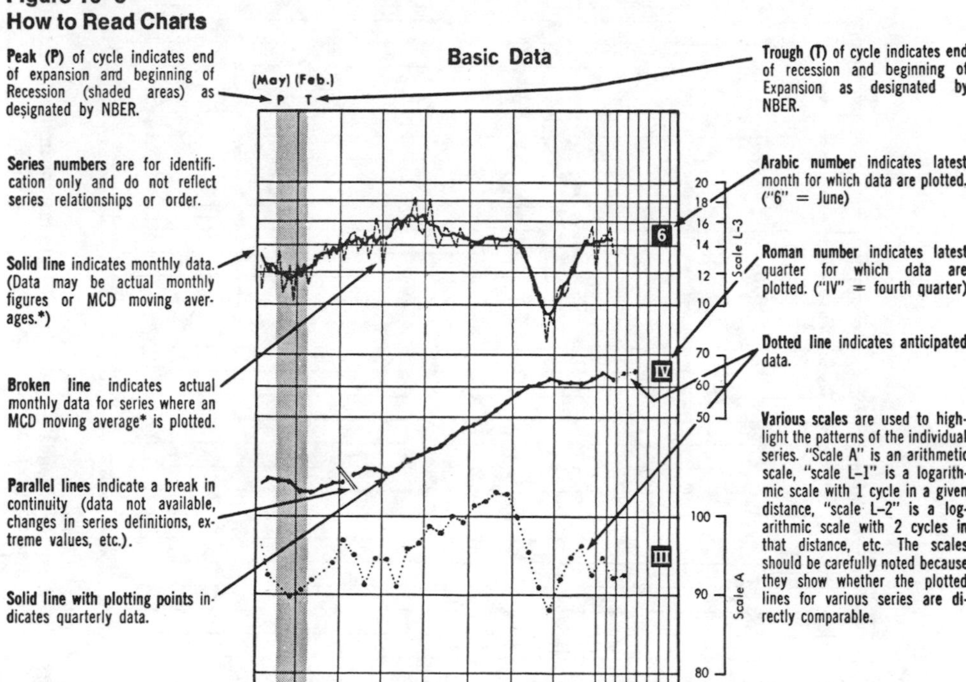
Basic Data
(May) (Feb.)
P T
Peak (P) of cycle indicates end of expansion and beginning of Recession (shaded areas) as designated by NBER.
Series numbers are for identification only and do not reflect series relationships or order.
Solid line indicates monthly data. (Data may be actual monthly figures or MCD moving averages.*)
Broken line indicates actual monthly data for series where an MCD moving average* is plotted.
Parallel lines indicate a break in continuity (data not available, changes in series definitions, extreme values, etc.).
Solid line with plotting points indicates quarterly data.
Trough (T) of cycle indicates end of recession and beginning of Expansion as designated by NBER.
Arabic number indicates latest month for which data are plotted. ("6" = June)
Roman number indicates latest quarter for which data are plotted. ("IV" = fourth quarter)
Dotted line indicates anticipated data.
Various scales are used to highlight the patterns of the individual series. "Scale A" is an arithmetic scale, "scale L-1" is a logarithmic scale with 1 cycle in a given distance, "scale L-2" is a logarithmic scale with 2 cycles in that distance, etc. The scales should be carefully noted because they show whether the plotted lines for various series are directly comparable.
6
IV
III
20
18
16
14
12
10
Scale L-3
70
60
50
100
90
80
Scale A

Source: U.S. Department of Commerce, *Business Conditions Digest,* November 1975, p. 4.

have been given before taking action to sell or buy stocks and bonds. It will be too late. But if quick action is taken, say, by selling stocks when the composite *leading* index looks like it is turning down, but the composite *coincident* index subsequently fails to turn down, the investor would be well advised to conclude that a mistake has been made and should buy back into stocks. We do not mean to imply, of course, that stocks should be sold just because a single economic indicator turns down. Indeed, a whole variety of factors should be reviewed and action should be taken when a consensus emerges. Nevertheless, it must be emphasized that if you wait until "all the evidence is in hand," the market's move will have passed you by.

Monetary Indicators. Among the NBER's selected list of leading indicators is the *real* money supply (that is, demand deposits plus currency held by the nonbank public, deflated by a price index). The influence of money on economic activity is at the center of a good deal of dispute among economists. Some view money as a prime mover of

Figure 10–9
Twelve Leading Indicators Selected by NBER

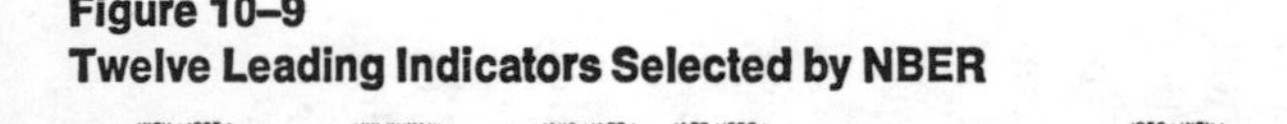

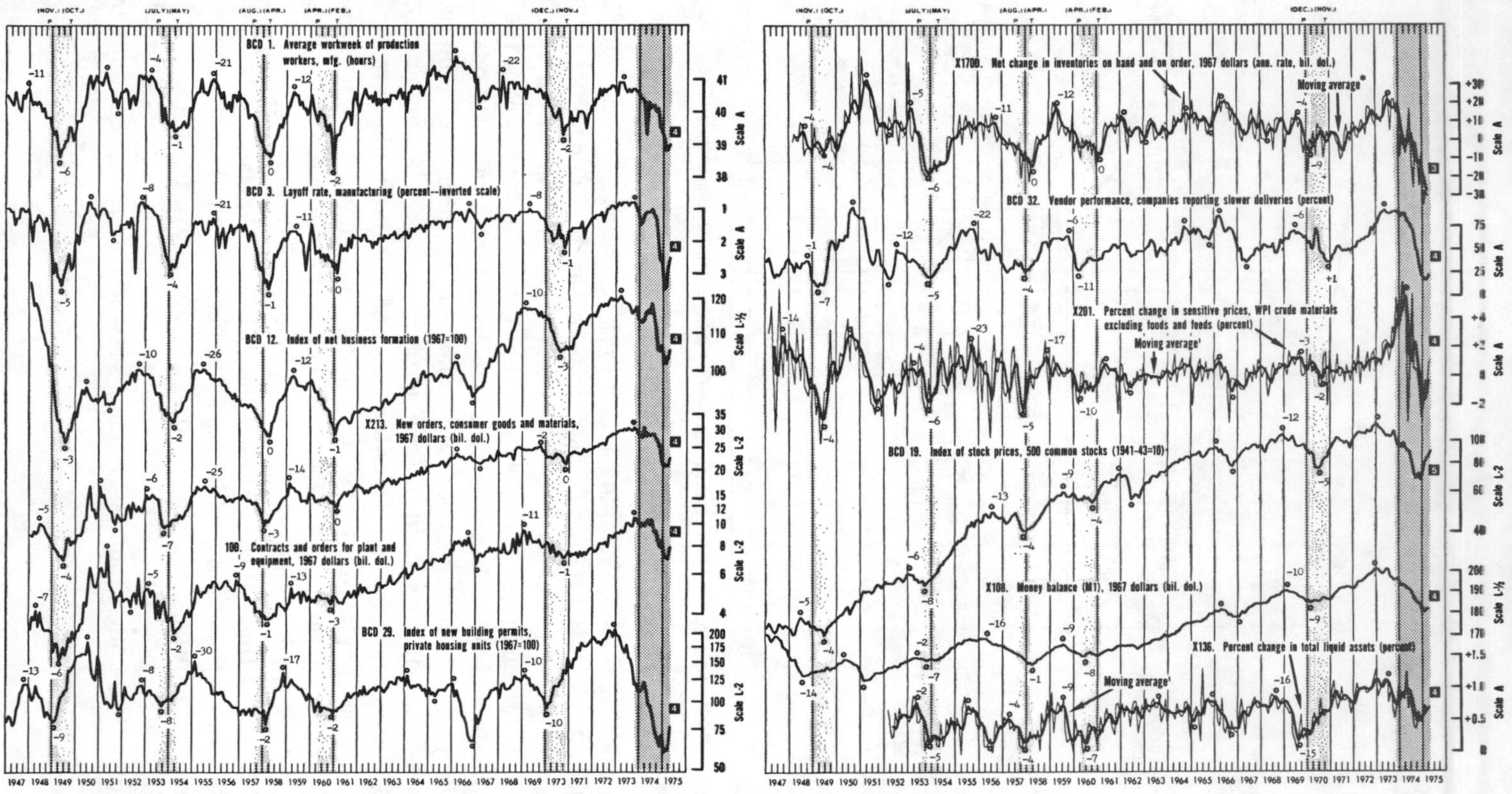

* Weighted 4-term moving average (with weights, 1,2,2,1) placed at the terminal month of the span.

Note: Circles entered on the chart indicate specific turning points; numbers indicate length of leads (—) and lags (+) in months from reference turning dates. Shading for 1973–75 recession was not in original but has been added for greater perspective.

Source: U.S. Department of Commerce, *Business Conditions Digest*, May 1975, pp. xi–xii.

Figure 10–10
Composite Indexes of NBER Indicators

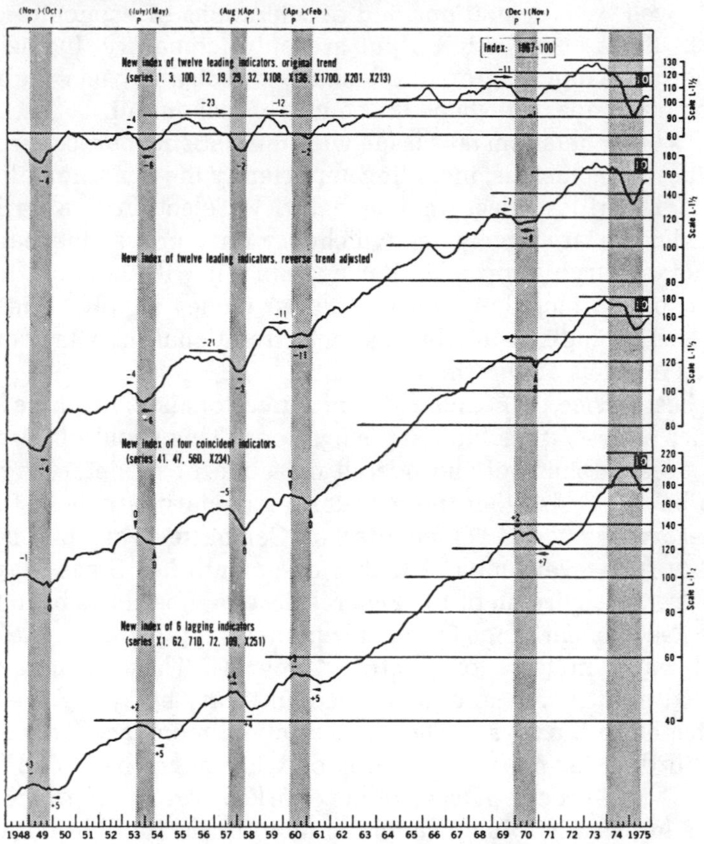

* Numbers entered on the chart indicate length of leads (—) and lags (+) in months from reference turning dates. Reverse trend adjusted index of 12 leaders contains the same trend as the index of 5 coincident indicators.

Note: Shading for 1973–75 recession was not in original but has been added for greater perspective.

Source: U.S. Department of Commerce, *Business Conditions Digest*, November 1975, p. 37.

the economy, as a causal factor of business cycles. Others see money as a sort of lubricating oil—a good supply is necessary to keep the economic engine running, but it doesn't cause movement by itself.

In addition to their theoretical disputes, economists also argue about the empirical evidence. For example, the research staff of the Federal Reserve Bank of St. Louis has argued in numerous articles in that bank's monthly *Review* that:

1. Short-term accelerations and decelerations of monetary growth are followed by accelerations and decelerations of economic output.

2. But these changes in output are only temporary. In the longer run, the trend rate of growth of money directly impacts the rate of inflation but it does not shape the course of real output.

Critics of monetarism take issue with the statistical procedures leading to these conclusions, including importantly the definition of money supply. The critics allege that monetarists select from a variety of so-called monetary aggregates whichever ones proves the particular case they are trying to make. For example, it will be noted that the NBER chose to include a *constant dollar* money supply series in its list of leading indicators whereas most traditional monetary analysis has been in terms of *current dollar* data.

The best advice that can be given to investors is to examine several monetary series rather than any single one. This should improve the investor's awareness of the overall direction of monetary trends. It should be noted also that the near-term monetary targets of the Federal Reserve System's "Open Market Committee" are published in summary form every month, with a one-month lag. Since May 1975, moreover, the chairman of the Federal Reserve Board has been revealing the Fed's longer range targets for money supply growth (defined in several ways) in testimony before Congress. These statements are subjected to intensive scrutiny and commentary by Wall Street firms.

Anticipation Surveys. The economic and monetary indicators referred to thus far all are measures of what might be called accomplished facts—orders *placed,* hours *worked,* prices of *transactions,* changes in *existing* money supply, and so forth. In addition to these accomplished facts, economists have available for analysis a group of surveys of spending *intentions* of business leaders and consumers. These surveys are conducted by various governmental and private organizations, and the investor should be familiar with at least some of them.

Probably the most widely used group of surveys are those relating to business spending for plant and equipment. In October each year, the economists of McGraw-Hill conduct a survey of business capital expenditure plans for the year ahead. The results are published in *Business Week* during the month of November. In December, the Department of Commerce publishes (in the *Survey of Current Business*) an estimate of capital spending in the first quarter of the coming year based on a survey conducted through government auspices. By March, the Department of Commerce has run another survey, this time covering expectations for the first and second quarters and for the full year. In April, McGraw-Hill publishes the results of a follow-up to their October survey, and in June and September, Commerce provides estimates for the current and succeeding quarters based on still more surveys. In addition to this abundance of data, the Conference Board compiles a quarterly record of budgetary appropriations for future capital spending by the boards of directors of America's largest corporations. These findings are discussed and interpreted in the Conference Board's monthly publication, the *Record.*

Since capital spending plays such an important role in our economy (many economists believe it is the single most important generating factor in the business cycle), a successful forecast of such spending obviously is desirable. While the surveys do not have a perfect record, use of the data usually results in a correct forecast of the direction of capital spending, although not necessarily in a correct forecast of magnitude.

During recent years, consumers have joined business executives as objects of economic surveyors' attentions. While no one claims that consumers "plan" their future spending in the same sense as business leaders do, it seems reasonable to hypothesize that families "talk things over" some time prior to purchasing major items such as automobiles, houses, home furnishings and appliances, and perhaps even some nondurables such as clothing. Surely "impulse buying" cannot be the only driving force behind consumer spending, particularly on expensive durable goods. Although consumer spending intentions are subject to swift revisions due to unexpected changes in employment conditions, fluctuations in purchases of consumer durables are such a key element in the business cycle that all available evidence should be brought to the fore in an attempt to forecast these fluctuations.

Since 1952, the Survey Research Center of the University of Michigan has conducted several nationwide surveys each year in an attempt to determine changes in consumer attitudes and in their intentions to purchase durable goods. The findings are made public via books and press conferences. Other organizations, notably the Bureau of the Census and the Conference Board have built upon the work of the Survey Research Center.

It may seem as if there is no efficient way to organize this mass of survey data, monetary data, and other leading indicators in such a way as to derive an overview of what is developing in the nation's economy and a forecast of what is to come. But there is. Economists approach the problem by utilizing what is known as a *GNP model.*

The GNP Model

The word *model* in the context of economic forecasting often refers to a complex set of mathematical equations. But it also may be used simply to convey an impression of *structure*. The gross national product (GNP) is a framework within which economic information may be arranged in an orderly fashion. Analysts can bring to bear whatever amount of mathematics they desire in their attempt to gain insight from this information.

Gross national product, simply defined, is the market value of the nation's output of goods and services. Its measurement can be approached from either of two directions: (*a*) by adding up the incomes generated by the economy—wages, salaries, profits, interest, and rent; or (*b*) by adding up the expenditures of consumers, businesses, and governments (plus net exports). For short-term forecasting purposes, the expenditure approach is more useful than the income approach. What one does is to forecast each major expenditure component of GNP, add up the component forecasts, and thus forecast the movement of aggregate economic activity as measured by GNP. This is why GNP model building is often referred to as *sector analysis*.

GNP data are compiled by the Department of Commerce every quarter (on a seasonally adjusted annual rate basis), and are published in most complete detail in the *Survey of Current Business*. The data are revised frequently as new information becomes available, and the analyst must be careful to work with the most up-to-date statistics. Extensive revisions usually are published in each July issue of the *Survey*, and historical data running back to 1939 on a quarterly basis and to 1929 on an annual basis have been published in a supplement entitled *The National Income and Product Accounts of the United States, 1929–1965: Statistical Tables*. Detailed descriptive material on the conceptual underpinnings of national income accounting have been published in supplementary volumes entitled *National Income* and *U.S. Income and Output*. An analytically convenient statement of the U.S. GNP accounts is shown in Table 10–3.

As noted previously, the economic forecasters' tasks are to enter the numbers they believe are most realistic for each calendar quarter of the period they are forecasting. To do this, they make use of any and every piece of evidence they think is pertinent. This point should be stressed. Sector analysis permits a maximum degree of analytical flexibility and ingenuity. As one analyst has put it, a GNP model has "a ravenous appetite for any data, evidence, or insight concerning the current situation and outlook."

Price versus Output. Perhaps the most difficult aspect of economic

Table 10–3
Major Components of Gross National Product, 1975 (in billions of dollars)

Personal consumption expenditures		
Durable goods	$132	
Nondurable goods and services	841	
Total		$ 973
Gross private domestic investment		
Residential construction (including farm)	51	
Business capital spending	147	
Business inventory accumulation	− 14	
Total		184
Government purchases of goods and services		
Federal	124	
State and local	215	
Total		339
Net exports of goods and services		20
Gross national product		$1,516

Source: *Survey of Current Business,* August 1976.

forecasting, especially since 1965, has been the decomposition of a GNP forecast into its *real* and price components. For example, analysis of the forecasts of the President's Council of Economic Advisers and of private economists reveals a rather good "batting average" on forecasts of real output, both in direction and magnitude, but a very poor record on price forecasts. Few economists have correctly foreseen the enormous inflationary spiral which has plagued the United States, Europe, and Japan during the past decade.

One approach to price forecasting is that of the monetarists, who believe that the price trend, at least in the long run, is a function of the trend rate of growth in money supply relative to the capacity for growth in real output. But, as noted earlier, there are many critics of this view. Moreover, even if it is correct, it leaves open two serious problems: (1) we do not know how to forecast the growth of money, and (2) long-run trends do not tell us much about the shorter run developments we are concerned with in investment timing.

Another approach, which appears more promising, begins with the recognition that the broadest price index—the so-called GNP deflator—can be decomposed as follows:

	Approximate Weighting
Private sector unit labor costs	45%
Government sector wage costs	20
Raw materials and other costs	30
Profits per unit	5

Utilizing this analytical framework, in late 1975, the New York investment firm of William D. Witter predicted that in 1976 the GNP deflator would rise by 5.3 percent. This figure was derived as follows:

1. Based on a study of trends in wage settlements of key industries, average wage gains in 1976 were expected to be about 8 percent. Offsetting this wage gain was an expected productivity gain of about 4.5 percent (based on analogies with historical changes in productivity at similar stages of the business cycle). Therefore, unit labor costs were expected to rise 3.5 percent (8.0 − 4.5).

2. Government wage gains were predicted to be somewhat higher than in the private sector, about 9 percent versus 8 percent. Moreover, in national income accounting there are assumed to be no productivity gains in government.

3. Changes in materials and other costs are estimated on the basis of what the Witter firm refers to as the Pressure Index. This index represents percentage changes in the ratio of manufacturing and trade sales to inventories. When the ratio rises, sales are rising in relation to inventory stockpiles, putting upward pressure on prices; and vice versa when the ratio falls. Empirical evidence supporting this argument is shown in Figure 10–11. With this type of analysis, materials and other costs were predicted to rise 5 percent in 1976.

4. Profit margins per unit of output typically rise in the early stages of economic recovery, then flatten and fall as the prosperity ripens and then turns into recession. Given this pattern, the firm predicted a 10 percent rise in 1976 profit margins.

5. Putting its component forecasts together, the result was:

(a) Factor	*(b)* Predicted Change	*(c)* Weight	*(b × c)* Contribution to Price Change
Unit labor costs	3.5%	.45	1.5%
Government wages	9.0	.20	1.8
Materials and other costs	5.0	.30	1.5
Profit margins	10.0	.05	0.5
			5.3

SUMMARY

Historical evidence suggests various investment strategies which may be employed profitably if investors develop an ability to forecast

Figure 10–11
Relationship between Price Changes and *Pressure Index*

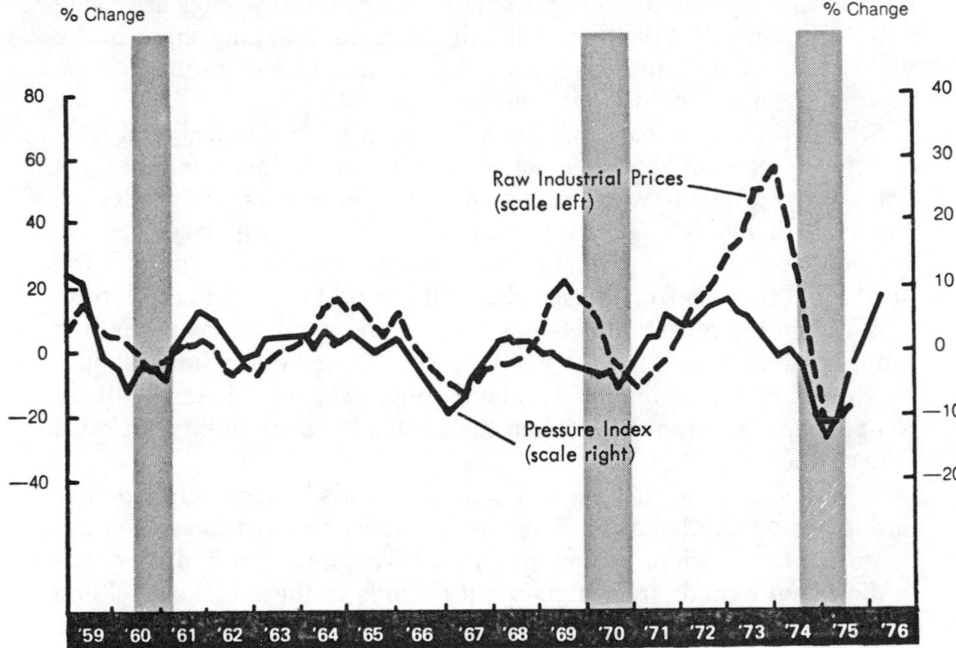

Source: William D. Witter, Inc.

major economic turning points about four to six months in advance—or if they rely on the counsel of others who have such an ability. (Of course, many investors will adopt a "buy-and-hold" strategy which ignores cyclical swings.) The precise implementation of these strategies depends on how aggressive, self-confident, and *flexible* an investor is. For example, large institutional investors are much less flexible than individual investors. Nevertheless, the general nature of the strategies are as follows:

1. If investors suspect that the prosperity phase of the business cycle is coming to an end but are not yet firmly convinced of the fact, they might continue buying common stocks but confine purchases to companies whose sales are likely to be least vulnerable to recession and whose stocks' price-earnings ratios still seem relatively attractive.

2. When investors become convinced that a recession lies shortly ahead, even though the stock market is still strong, they should have the courage to stop making new common stock commitments. Invest-

able funds should be kept liquid at this stage, however—that is, in bank time deposits or in short-term securities. Long-term bond investments probably are not yet appropriate, since interest rates are likely still to be rising. But the typical flat or downward-sloping shape of the yield curve at such times suggests that a good rate of return will be secured even on liquid investments.

3. When stock prices begin to weaken, in their classical lead relationship to general economic activity, it is time to institute quickly a net selling program with regard to common stocks. In particular, stocks of highly cyclical companies and stocks whose price-earnings ratios have risen to unrealistic levels should be eliminated from the portfolio. Proceeds from these sales still should be kept in liquid form.

4. When the recession gets under way, and stock prices are falling rapidly, interest rates are likely to be at a peak, and liquid funds should be shifted into high-quality bonds of long maturity. These are likely to appreciate most in value when the cyclical decline in interest rates takes place.

5. In the midst of the recession, yield spreads between high-quality and lower-quality bonds, and between bonds and mortgages, may become relatively wide. Income-oriented investors often find it worthwhile to shift funds from high-quality bonds to these higher yielding investments at such times.

6. When investors perceive the forthcoming end of the recession, a renewed stock buying program is in order—particularly the stocks of cyclical and *glamour-growth* companies which probably were severely depressed during the bear market. Profits on long-maturity bonds can be realized through sales, although some further rise in bond prices can be anticipated, with the proceeds of the sales to be invested in common stocks.

It must be recognized, of course, that the *business cycle approach* to investment timing has faults as well as virtues. First, since many full-time professional economists have only mediocre forecasting records, investors who are not economists cannot be expected to do very well in forecasting on their own—or in evaluating the forecasts of professionals. Second, even a consistent record of perfect six-month forecasts is unlikely to result in consistently correct investment timing. For although the timing relationships among stock price, interest rate, and business cycle turning points have been reasonably stable, they have not been, and doubtless will not in the future be, unchanging. Consequently, many investors supplement business cycle analysis with the tools of *technical analysis* described in the next chapter.

SUGGESTED READINGS

Butler, William; Kavesh, Robert; and **Platt, Robert** *Methods and Techniques of Business Forecasting.* Englewood Cliffs, N.J.: Prentice-Hall, 1974.

Council of Economic Advisers *Economic Report of the President.* Washington, D.C.: U.S. Government Printing Office, annually.

"Economic Analysis and Timing," *Financial Analyst's Handbook.* Vol. 1, part 5. Homewood, Ill.: Dow Jones–Irwin, 1975.

Katona, George *Psychological Economics.* New York: Elsevier Scientific Publishing Co., 1975.

11

Technical Analysis

There is nothing so disastrous as a rational investment policy in an irrational world.
John Maynard Keynes

The business cycle approach to common stock timing deals with factors outside the stock market itself—for example, industrial production and money supply. The technical approach, on the other hand, seeks to improve the basis of timing decisions by studying phenomena which are an integral part of the market mechanism—for example, prices and volume of trading. For this reason, technical analysis is often referred to as internal analysis or market analysis.

Technical analysts study internal stock market data in an attempt to gain insight into the supply and demand pressures for a stock or for the stock market as a whole. They do this by looking for recurring patterns of price movement or recurring interrelationships between stock price movements and other market data. Since price movements reflect the opinions of millions of different people about everything having a bearing on stocks, it is unlikely that "technicians" can know in all cases *why* the discovered patterns occur. They may try to learn why—including in this effort an examination of relevant external information in addition to internal data—but the probability remains that many patterns and relationships will be unexplainable. Nevertheless, if the patterns are known to recur consistently, it seems sensible to take advantage of this knowledge even though the explanations remain unknown. After all, physicians do not know why aspirin works as well as it does, but they prescribe it nonetheless.

Technical analysts who are intellectually honest will be quick to admit that they have no hope of discovering foolproof methods of forecasting stock prices. Mistakes are bound to be made, often severe mistakes. But they also will argue that as long as their methods improve the *probabilities* of investment success, as long as they reduce the margin of error, they are worthy of serious consideration.

It should be noted that technical analysis is not a new or even recent development. In fact, it is considered by many to be the original form of investment analysis, dating back to the late 1800s. It came into widespread use before the period of extensive and fully disclosed financial information, which in turn enabled the practice of so-called fundamental research to develop. Its principal purpose was to help market technicians monitor the actions of informed investors. Many of the techniques used today have been utilized for over 50 years, although the use of computers has given rise to substantial modification of established methods.

The purpose of this chapter is to examine the usefulness of some of the most widely used technical tools. We shall try to point out the basic strengths and weaknesses of each tool and in doing so to note whether it is applicable to an analysis of the market as a whole, of individual securities or of both.

GENERAL MARKET ANALYSIS

General market analysis covers a very long list of tools and techniques designed to determine the basic, general trend of stock prices. Technicians, and in fact most investors, consider it easier to select "up" stocks, that is, stocks which are expected to rise in price, if they have confidence that the general trend is favorable (bullish) as opposed to unfavorable (bearish).

Breadth of Market

Breadth of market analysis is one of the most popular techniques used to study major turning points of the market as a whole. It is based on a theory of the nature of stock market cycles. Bull markets are viewed as being long drawn-out affairs during which individual stocks reach peaks gradually, with the number of individual peaks accelerating as the market averages (for example, the Dow Jones Industrials) rise toward a turning point. Bear markets, on the other hand, are viewed as concentrated collapses of a large number of stocks in a short period of time. Accordingly, to detect a condition of internal market weakness before it is generally recognized that a bull market tide has turned, evidence is sought to determine whether large numbers of stocks are falling while the averages rise. And to detect the approaching end of a bear market, technical analysts consider how widespread the selling pressure is. In short, what is being examined is the dispersion of a general price rise or decline; thus the phrase *breadth of market.*

There are many ways of measuring breadth of market. The easiest to apply, and probably the most widely used, is a daily cumulation of the net number of advancing or declining issues on the New York Stock Exchange. The daily newspapers publish a table showing the number of issues traded on the previous day, the number which advanced in price, the number which declined, and the number which were unchanged. If the declines are subtracted from the advances, a net positive or negative figure results (described as net advances or net declines). For example, a week's market activity might produce the following data:

	Number of Issues Traded	*Advances*	*Declines*	*Unchanged*	*Net Advances or Declines*
Monday	1,301	530	535	236	− 5
Tuesday	1,310	464	597	249	−133
Wednesday	1,323	303	739	281	−436
Thursday	1,295	607	453	235	+154
Friday	1,308	807	241	260	+566

The next step is to cumulate the net advances and net declines, thus constructing a measure of a breadth. Cumulation simply means the successive addition of a series of numbers. In the above example, cumulation of the final column of data would produce the following:

	Breadth of Market
Monday	− 5
Tuesday	−138
Wednesday	−574
Thursday	−420
Friday	+146

The cumulation is continued ad infinitum. Obviously, over a period of many years of generally rising stock prices the absolute *level* of the breadth measure can become very high. Moreover, if different analysts begin their cumulations on different days, the levels of their breadth series will differ. However, breadth analysis focuses on *change* rather than on level, and the change during any given time period will be the same no matter what the original starting date of the cumulation.

Having measured breadth, the next step is to chart it in conjunction with one of the market averages, such as the Dow Jones Industrials. Normally, breadth and the DJI will move in tandem. What the analyst must be wary of during a bull market is an extended divergence of the two lines—that is, a breadth line which declines to successive new lows while the DJI makes new highs. Such a divergence indicates that an increasing number of issues are turning down while the *blue chips,* which weigh heavily in the DJI and in most other market averages, continue to rise. According to the theory underlying breadth analysis, this suggests an approaching peak in the averages and a major downturn of stock prices generally.

This theory has considerable historical validity. Price-breadth divergences preceded the major market downturns of 1929, 1936–37, 1948–49, 1956–57, 1960, and 1962. On the other hand, the 1953 stock price decline was not preceded by a price-breadth divergence. Moreover, there often may be room for differing interpretations of the movement in breadth. For example, looking at Figure 11–1, some observers claim that the 1966 stock market downturn was preceded by at least a mild price-breadth divergence, since breadth in January 1966 was little different from its level in May 1965, while the market averages were at record highs. However, others counter that this really wasn't a divergence since breadth did not make a series of *new lows* during the intervening months.

Breadth of market was not very helpful in timing some recent general market downturns. The advance-decline line shown in Figure 11–1 "topped out" coincident with, rather than ahead of, the 1968 peaks in both the DJI and S&P 500. Furthermore, from April 1971 throughout 1972 the advance-decline line was in a general downtrend but the broad market averages were able to record successive new highs despite the deterioration in breadth. Market breadth deteriorated even further in conjunction with the 1973–74 bear market, reaching a low in December 1974, when the market averages also bottomed. Since then, breadth improved as the market averages moved higher.

Overall, the evidence suggests that breadth of market may be a useful advance indicator of major stock price declines but that, like any other indicator, it is by no means infallible.

Once the market has entered its declining phase, breadth also can be useful in detecting an impending recovery. It will be recalled that a major premise of breadth analysis is that large numbers of stocks turn-

Figure 11–1
Stock Prices and Breadth of Market

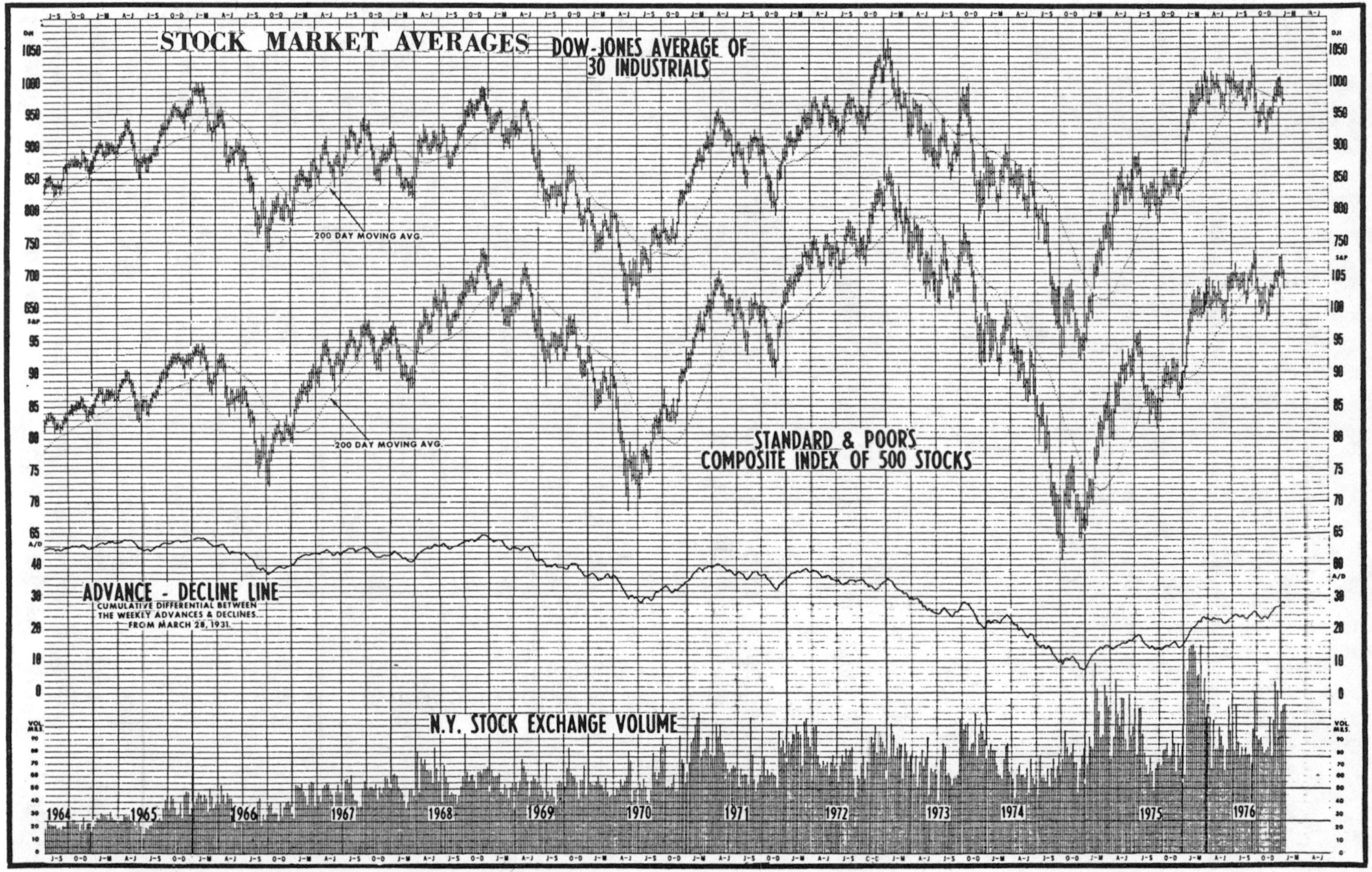

STOCK MARKET AVERAGES

DOW-JONES AVERAGE OF 30 INDUSTRIALS

200 DAY MOVING AVG.

200 DAY MOVING AVG.

STANDARD & POOR'S COMPOSITE INDEX OF 500 STOCKS

ADVANCE - DECLINE LINE

CUMULATIVE DIFFERENTIAL BETWEEN THE WEEKLY ADVANCES & DECLINES. FROM MARCH 28, 1931.

N.Y. STOCK EXCHANGE VOLUME

1964 1965 1966 1967 1968 1969 1970 1971 1972 1973 1974 1975 1976

Source: Trendline's *Current Market Perspectives*, January 1977, p. 7.

ble in price in a short period of time during bear markets. Therefore, the end of a bear market is likely to be near when all anxious and panicky investors rush to sell out at once. Evidence of a so-called selling climax may be obtained by examining the movement of breadth in conjunction with prices and the volume of trading. Typically, for a number of weeks during the latter stages of a bear market the cumulative net advance-decline line will fall by several thousand, the Dow Jones Industrials will fall several percent, and trading volume will be substantially higher than in previous weeks. Prices will not necessarily begin rising immediately after such a selling climax—indeed, they typically bump along the bottom for a few months—but the worst is usually over.

Volume of Trading

Since at least the turn of the century, technicians have followed volume data closely in order to gain perspective on the general health and trend of the market. While there are many ways to measure and interpret volume trends, the underlying principle is quite simple—volume is supposed to indicate the strength or weakness of a given price movement.

Given this principle, volume of trading is expected to provide a clue to the end of a *bull* market by falling in advance of major declines in the stock price averages. And, as noted previously, volume data also can help in detecting the end of a *bear* market, since volume rises sharply during selling climaxes.

Figure 11–2 indicates that the volume-price characteristics of the four market cycles from 1956 through 1962 were remarkably similar. In each cycle, volume and price experienced a steady buildup until the midpoint of the cycle. Then, volume peaked and declined to a relatively low level until the next cycle began. Indeed, for most of the postwar period, new volume highs were always accompanied by new highs in price.

Starting in 1965, however, changes in the price-volume relationship developed. Prices failed to show any further significant increase despite a persistent uptrend in volume. Peaks in volume no longer led peaks in price, but coincided with them. Finally, volume trends became highly erratic.

A third application of volume data is in the study of individual stocks. Prices obviously do not move steadily in the same direction every day. Even if a stock's price is in a major uptrend, it frequently will decline. It does not move up like an arrow, but zigzags up. Many

Figure 11–2
Stock Prices and Volume of Trading, 1956–1975

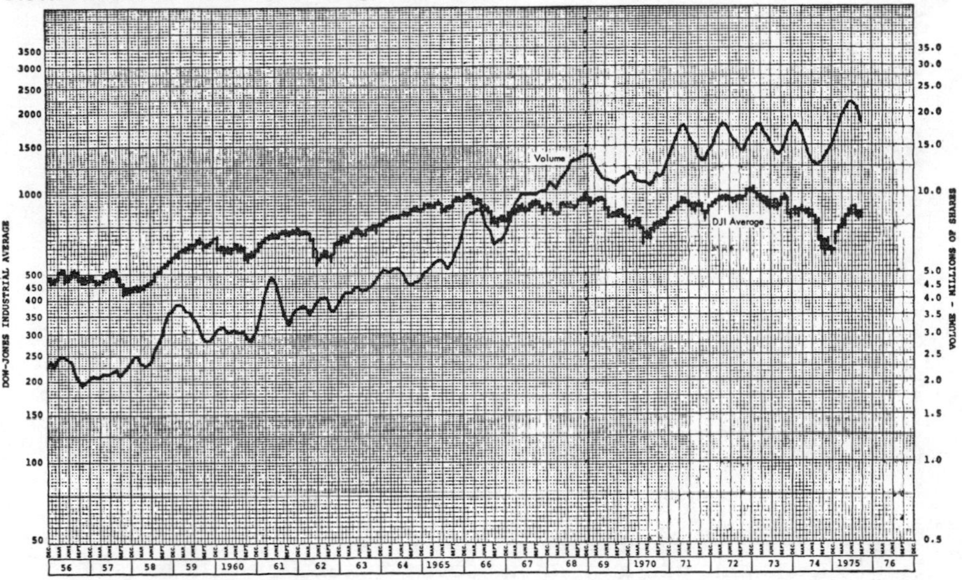

Source: Stone & Mead, Inc.

technical analysts believe that if the volume of trading in a stock rises on the days when its price rises during the course of this zigzag movement, and then falls off when price recedes temporarily, the overall pattern is bullish. On the other hand, if volume rises when price falls, and falls when price rises, the overall pattern is believed to have bearish connotations (unless the volume rise and price decline are of such magnitude as to suggest a selling climax).

The idea behind this application of volume data to the analysis of individual stocks is that volume of trading varies directly with the intensity of emotion on the part of stock buyers and sellers. When anxious buyers outnumber anxious sellers, they bid aggressively and push prices up on heavy volume. When anxious sellers come to dominate events, they offer stock in increasing volume at markdowns in price. Volume therefore becomes a clue to shifts in the supply and demand schedules for a stock.

THEORY OF CONTRARY OPINION

Contrary opinion in the stock market is actually an attitude or intellectual process, not a tool of technical analysis. Further, it is difficult to define *precisely* the general theory without the use of ludicrous or silly-sounding statements. However, the *general* concept is to "go against the crowd." Humphrey Neill, generally considered the father of the theory, put it this way—"When everyone thinks alike, everyone is likely to be wrong," or "The crowd is usually wrong, at least in the timing of events."

This does not mean to imply that the majority is *always* wrong. Rather, that the majority is *likely* to be wrong when there is no real difference of opinion. Therefore, technicians have developed a series of tools and techniques designed to measure the status of popular opinion regarding the trend of stock prices, to determine when popular opinion is becoming "too uniform," and, at that time, to take the opposite position in the market.

Odd-Lot Trading

Odd-lot trading (transactions involving less than 100 shares) is engaged in primarily by the proverbial man in the street. It is assumed that by examining odd-lot trading data in conjunction with the stock market price averages a useful composite picture of popular opinion can be obtained. (Aggregate odd-lot trading data are published in the newspapers on a daily and weekly basis.)

Most analysts of odd-lot data place primary emphasis upon the ratio of odd-lot selling volume to odd-lot buying volume. Usually volume is expressed in number of shares rather than dollar amounts, although dollar amounts are published in the monthly SEC *Statistical Bulletin* and are used by some analysts. Some analysts also use ratios of odd-lot short sales to total odd-lot sales, and total odd-lot volume (purchases plus sales) to round-lot volume on the New York Stock Exchange. But these latter ratios can be viewed chiefly as devices to confirm the indications of the sales-to-purchases ratio, rather than as indicators in their own right.

The general theory is that sophisticated investors should begin to consider selling when the public markedly increases its buying relative to its selling, and vice versa. The underlying assumption is that small investors buy most heavily at market tops, and sell most heavily at the bottom. They seem to reverse Wall Street's golden adage: "buy low—sell high." Much of the historical data supports this theory of the small investor's behavior. The perverse timing of the odd-lotter is usually reflected in the sales-to-purchases ratio diverging in direction from the market just as the latter is reaching a peak or trough. But there also have been periods when the small investor's behavior has been quite astute, particularly in recent years.

The contemporary value of tracking changes in odd-lot activity patterns has been questioned recently since the small investor has steadily reduced participation in the market, while, at the same time, institutions have become an increasingly dominant force. Nevertheless, most technicians still believe that odd-lot indicators are valid for two principal reasons. First, odd-lot statistics are not analyzed to determine small investors' potential market impact, but rather their existing psychology. The only requirement for the determination is the availability of data on a numerically representative sample of this type of investor, and, while diminishing, there are still enough less-than-100 share investors to meet this requirement. Second, by determining the prevailing market psychology of the odd-lotter, investors can hopefully gain some insight into the feelings of professional portfolio managers by assuming, not always correctly as we shall soon see, that they are holding contrary attitudes.

Thus while the odd-lotter may have become increasingly astute in timing purchases and sales, technical analysts still consider their timing to be sufficiently wrong to have some predictive value.

Short Selling

Short selling activity is another widely used barometer of changes in investor sentiment. Short sales are made by people who expect stock prices to decline. From the technical analyst's point of view, it makes no difference whether short sellers are right or wrong. The fact is that most short sales eventually must be covered by purchases. Therefore, an increase in the outstanding (meaning uncovered) short interest generally means an increased potential demand for stock. A reduction in the short interest generally means a reduced potential demand.

Actually, the short-interest ratio is more closely followed than the number of shares sold short. This is a ratio derived by dividing the latest reported short-interest position by some current volume figure, usually the daily average of the preceding month. Historically, this ratio for the aggregate of all stocks on the New York Stock Exchange has moved within a range of around 1.0 to 1.75. Technicians generally believe that a low ratio is bearish and a high ratio a positive harbinger of future market action.

Penetrations of the short-interest ratio normal "band" are designated as sell and buy signals. Most, though not all, of the time, these signals have been justified by subsequent market price movements. Short-interest ratios of 2.0 or higher were associated with important market lows of 1962, 1966, and 1970. The 1974 market low was "bracketed" by relatively high short-interest ratios both several months before and after the fact. At the extreme bottom of the market, however, the short-interest ratio was actually fairly low, as can be seen in Figure 11–3. Interestingly, the short interest ratio reached a very low level early in 1976, but the market, as measured by the Dow Jones Industrial Averages, remained fairly stable. Thus, as with most indicators, the short-interest ratio is by no means an infallible guide.

The data needed to calculate short-interest ratios are readily available. The New York and American Stock Exchanges make public, around the 20th of each month, aggregate short-interest figures plus a detailed list of all issues in which a sizeable short-interest existed as of the middle of the month or which showed a sizeable increase in short interest from the previous month. These data are published in whole or part by the financial press. Volume of trading data, of course, are published daily, and can be averaged by the analyst. Thus, when you are trying to judge whether the time is ripe to purchase or sell a stock, it may be helpful to record its short interest outstanding each month relative to the average daily trading volume for the month. When this ratio rises steadily, it implies that a larger and larger percentage of future trading activity is likely to be represented by anxious buyers, the short coverers. A steady decline in the ratio implies that the price cushion to be had from the short sellers is deflating. Of course, a high short interest should lead investors to double-check the underlying value of the stock. They should try to ascertain whether the short sellers have discovered some critical condition which makes the stock fundamentally unattractive at existing prices.

Some technicians believe that the general character of short-interest activity may have changed in recent years, reflecting the increase in the number of arbitrage situations and the growth of hedge funds. Hedge funds are portfolios, such as mutual funds or private partnerships, which continuously maintain a short position as part of their overall investment strategy. As a result of this suspicion, increased attention is now being directed toward some of the smaller components of total short interest (which are published daily or weekly in the financial press).

One such element which has fascinated market technicians is the trend of odd-lot short sales. The odd-lot short seller is sometimes considered as possibly the least astute of all investors. Thus, changes in

Figure 11–3
Short-Interest Ratio versus Dow Jones Industrial Averages, 1968–1977

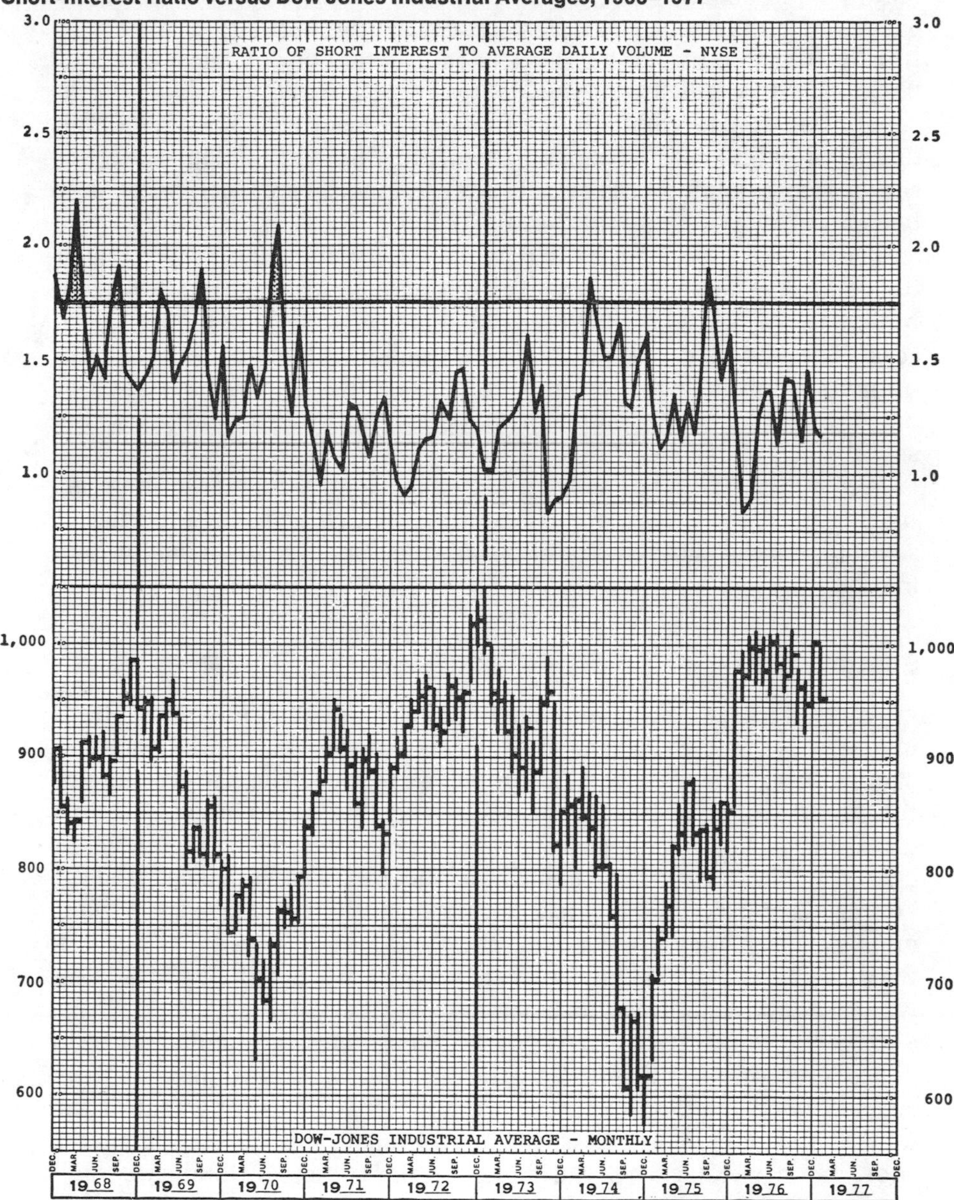

Source: Stone & Mead, Inc.

odd-lot short selling activity is construed by many as one of the better gauges of public sentiment. Historically, an odd-lot short sales ratio (the relationship of odd-lot short sales to total odd-lot sales) of about 0.5 percent has indicated a high degree of public optimism, and, therefore, a *sell* signal; while a ratio of over 3 percent has indicated a high degree of public pessimism, and therefore a *buy* signal. However, observers have pointed out recently that fluctuations in this index have become more extreme since the late 1960s.

The odd-lot short sales ratio reached approximate monthly levels of 6.2 percent, 7 percent, 4 percent and 3 percent at the primary market bottoms of 1962, 1966, 1970 and 1974 respectively (see Figure 11–4). It has been pointed out, however, that one of the major technical abnormalities of the more recent bear market 1973–74 was the failure of odd-lot short sales to build up more sharply than it did given the severity of the decline.

While this indicator has been better in identifying market bottoms than tops, a low level (near 0.5 percent) which lasts for a period of several months has usually signaled the top area of a major bull market.

Specialists' Sentiment

Another interesting component of short-interest activity is the trading behavior of "specialists" on the floor of the New York Stock Exchange; also known as the "informed minority." The short selling of this group, unlike aggregate or odd-lot short selling, is interpreted in a direct rather than a contrary fashion. That is, whereas a high level of aggregate short interest is considered bullish, a high specialist short interest is considered bearish because specialists represent "smart money" and if they are bearish enough to take a large short position we'd better be wary. Likewise, if they cover most of their short sales, we can adopt a similar bullish stance.

Several market technicians have constructed a simple index to gauge specialist sentiment. It is the number of shares sold short by specialists on the floor of the exchange expressed as a percent of the total shares sold short. Thus, if the specialists sell 1.5 million shares short in a particular week during which the volume of total short selling is 3 million shares, the figure is 50 percent. Some technicians believe that when specialists' short sales reach or exceed 60 percent of all short sales, the market is about to peak; when they fall to 40 percent or less, the market is about to develop a new up trend.

Figure 11–4
Dow Jones Industrial Average versus Odd-Lot Short Sales Ratio, 1968–1977

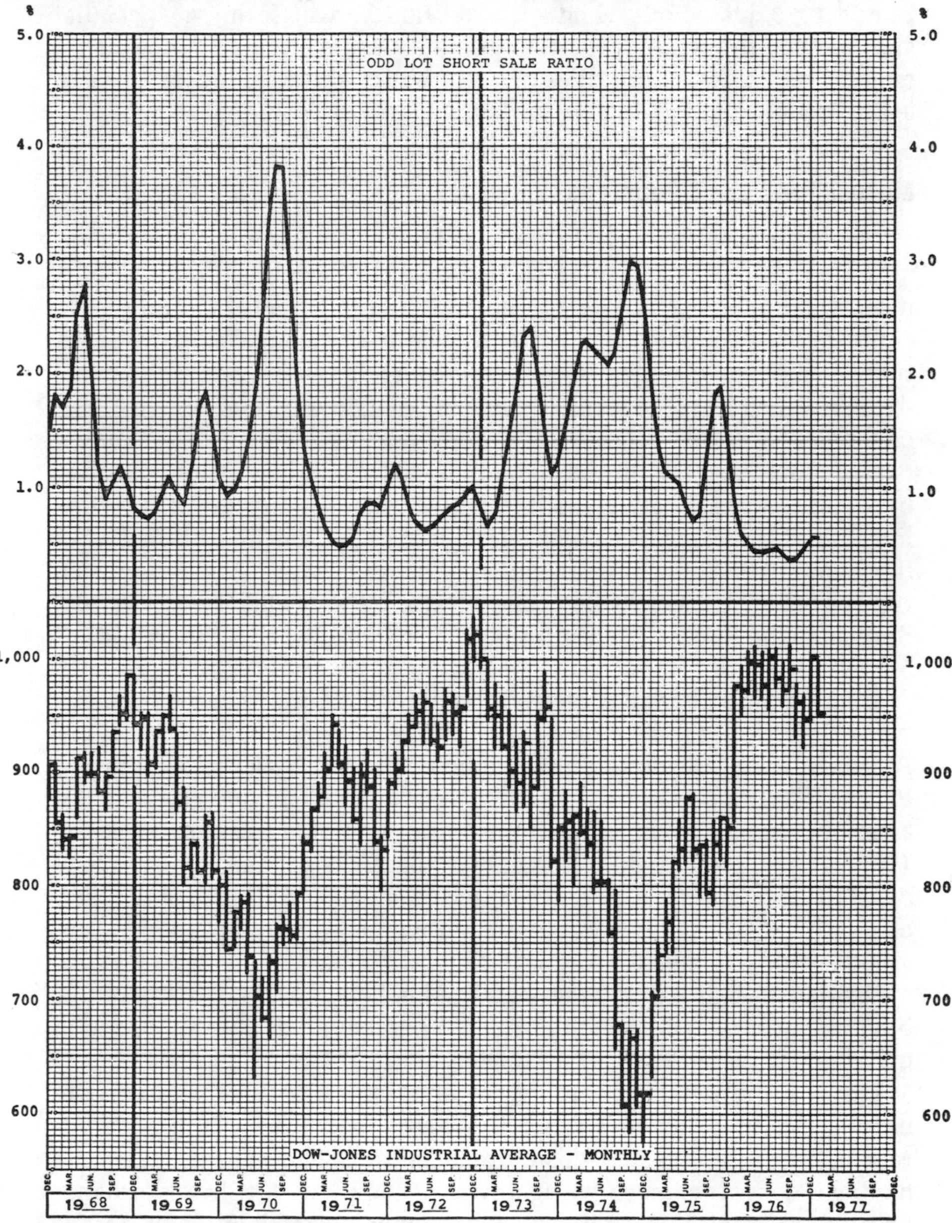

Source: Stone & Mead, Inc.

As an example, in the fall of 1968 the ratio rose to 68 percent, while in early 1972 it reached 62 percent—both times preceding major tops. In mid-1970, just about when a market bottom was forming, specialist short selling dropped close to 40 percent. Again in late 1974, when a major bottom was unfolding, the specialist short-selling ratio once again approached the 40 percent level. (See Figure 11–5.)

Mutual Fund Cash Positions

One of the newer tools in the technician's extensive kit is the analysis of changes in mutual fund aggregate cash positions. This is measured by the percentage of total mutual fund assets held in cash or equivalents, as reported monthly by the Investment Company Institute. Significant changes in this figure are taken by some to reflect overall institutional portfolio management thinking, and not just that of the mutual funds, although this correspondence of views has never been documented due to the lack of consistent and frequent reporting by other segments of the institutional market. In any event, it is believed that, as a general rule, the greater the cash position of the funds, the more bullish the market outlook because when the uninvested funds are put back into the market, stock prices will be driven up. Similarly, the lower the cash position, the more bearish the outlook is believed to be.

Data on mutual fund cash goes back to 1955, and for most of this period has proven to be a useful indicator of future market conditions. A ratio of about 10 percent has usually been bullish, but it is important to note that there appears to be a rising secular trend taking place. For example, the mutual fund cash ratio approximated 9.5 percent at the 1966 market bottom, 12.0 percent at the 1970 bottom, and reached nearly 14 percent in 1974. By comparison, in 1962 an increase to 7 percent, which at that time was regarded as a relatively high level, provided a good buy signal.

Bearish signals have been rendered when the level of available buying power falls to about the 5 to 5.5 percent area. This happened in mid-1965 and late 1967, in late 1968, and in 1974. See Figure 11–6.

Historically, then, institutions, or at least mutual funds, appear to have acted in a fashion generally attributed to amateurs—that is, reaching a fully invested position at the top of a market cycle, and having the most reserve buying power at the bottom. It is understandable, in view of this evidence, why some technicians refer to the mutual fund cash position as the *Institutional Odd-Lot Ratio.*

Figure 11–5
NYSE Specialists' Short Sales versus the DJIA, 1971–1977

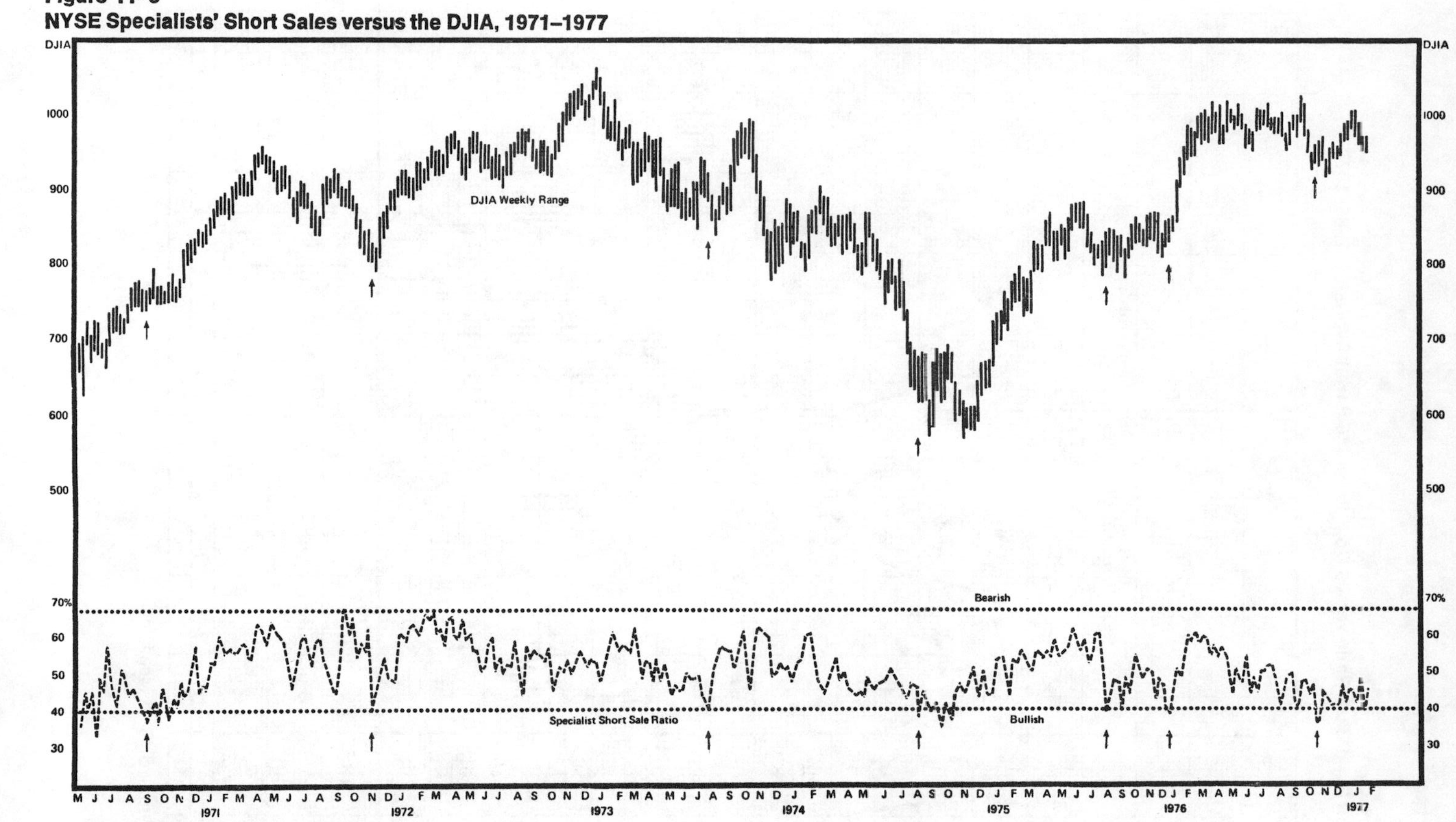

Source: Goldman, Sachs & Co., Inc.

Figure 11–6
Mutual Fund Cash Ratio versus Dow Jones Industrial Averages, 1968–1976

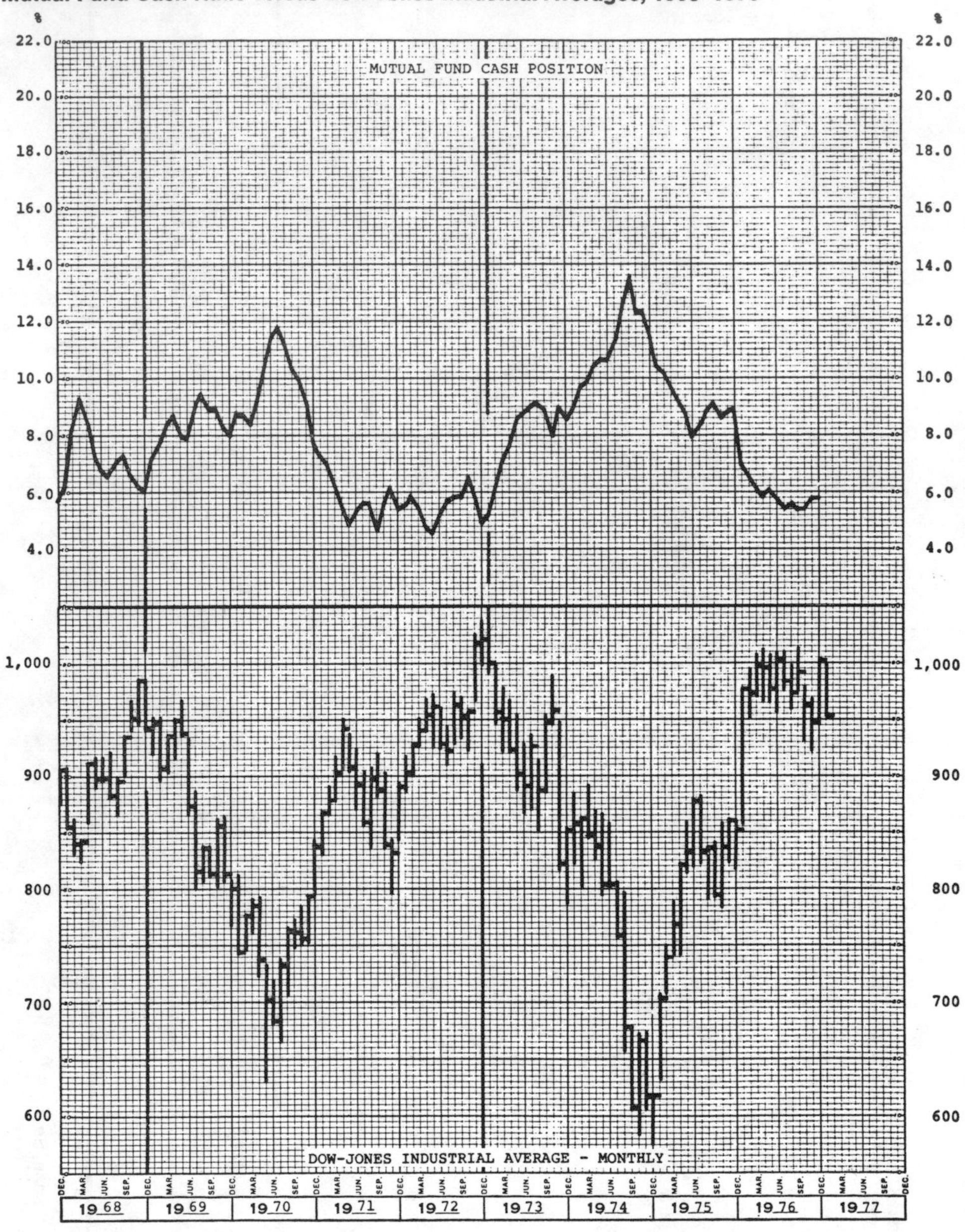

Source: Stone & Mead, Inc.

Investment Advisory Opinion

One of the more interesting contrary opinion indexes has been created by *Investors Intelligence,* an investment advisory service which summarizes the opinions and recommendations of other market letter writers for its subscribers. *Investors Intelligence* began in 1963 to monitor the market trend opinions of a large number of leading investment advisory services, and has found a correlation between the bearish sentiment of the services covered and the Dow Jones Industrial Averages. Typically, the investment services as a group tend to be least bearish at market tops and most bearish at market bottoms. More specifically, when the Bearish Sentiment Index (ratio of services bearish relative to the number of services expressing an opinion) approaches 10 percent, the Dow Jones Industrial Average is usually ready to reverse its trend from bullish to bearish; and, conversely, when the Bearish Sentiment Index goes above 60 percent, the Dow Jones Industrial Average is ready to reverse its trend from bearish to bullish. This is true, according to *Investors Intelligence,* because most of the investment advisory services are trend followers instead of trend anticipators, and this lends itself to contrary opinion—when they are least bearish, the market should go down and when they are most bearish, the market should go up. Figure 11–7 shows the correlation between the Bearish Sentiment Index and the Dow Jones Industrial Averages for the 1963–75 period.

Figure 11–7

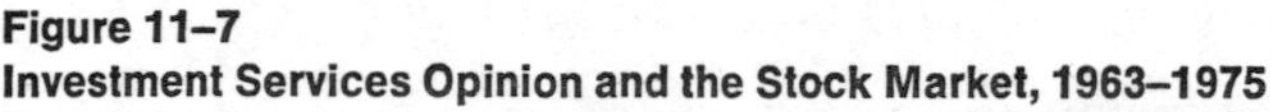

Investment Services Opinion and the Stock Market, 1963–1975

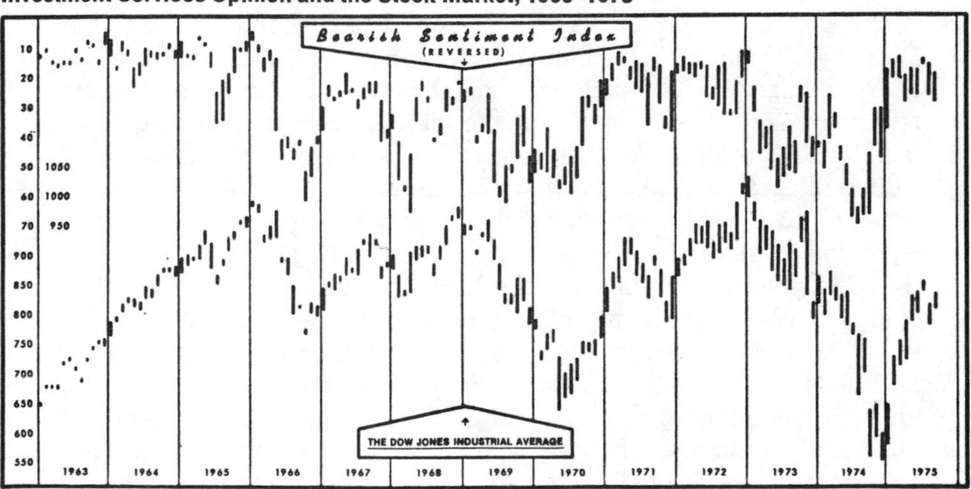

Source: *Investors Intelligence.*

PRICE CHARTS AND STOCK SELECTION TECHNIQUES

Dow Theory

Charles H. Dow is generally recognized as the father, if not the grandfather, of technical analysis. His theories, fashioned in the early 1900s when he was editor of the *Wall Street Journal,* have been used for many years as a means of estimating the general trend of the market. Interestingly Dow originally intended his index of stock prices to serve as a barometer of business trends, not as a stock market timing tool.

Dow's general concept was that market movements should be viewed as having three general components: a primary trend, or main movement, which can last up to four years; a secondary movement, lasting from a few weeks to a few months; and the narrow or short term movements lasting a few days, more or less. The trick, of course, is how to measure and determine each of these movements, assuming some validity of the general premise.

Today, there are many versions of the Dow theory—perhaps as many versions as there are analysts who profess to use it. Therefore, it is unlikely that any description of the technique would command unanimous acceptance of what it *is,* much less how well it works. Nevertheless, aside from certain relatively unimportant details, what seem to be its essential characteristics can be outlined briefly.

As a major (*primary*) uptrend of the market averages proceeds, there are numerous intermediate (*secondary*) downward reactions, each of which retraces a substantial proportion of the preceding rise. After each reaction, price recovers and goes on to surpass the previous high. Dow theorists keep on the alert for a recovery which falls short of the previous high. If, following such an abortive recovery, a downward reaction pierces the low point of the last previous reaction, evidence is at hand that the market has gone into a major (*primary*) downtrend. This is illustrated schematically in Figure 11–8.

Most Dow theorists do not consider a signal of a new primary downtrend to be valid unless the pattern of "descending tops and bottoms" just described occurs in both the Industrial and the Transportation averages. We should point out that the Transportation average used to include only railroads. Insistence on the "confirmation" of a signal by both the Industrial and Railroad averages originally was based on the idea that the Industrials reflect productive processes and the Railroads distributive processes. To have a healthy economy, both types of activities have to be sound. In recent times, the declining importance of railroads in the economy caused many critics to question the signifi-

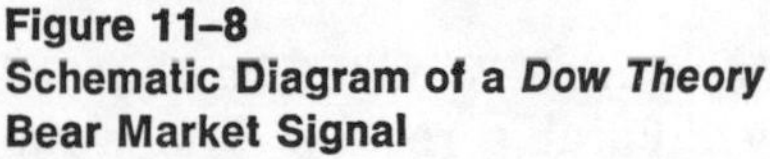

Figure 11–8
Schematic Diagram of a *Dow Theory* Bear Market Signal

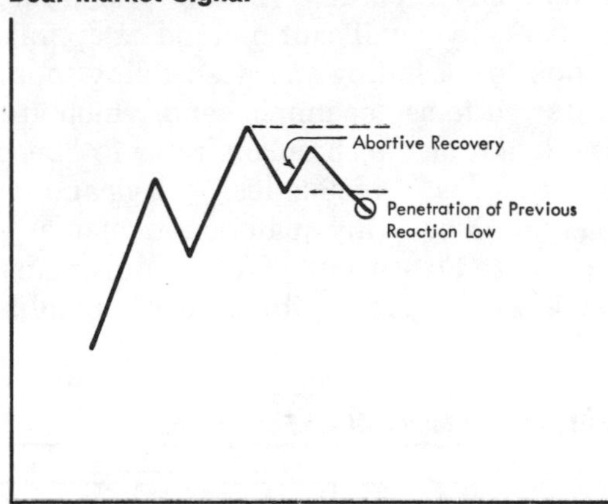

cance of railroad stock prices as a barometer. Even before the change to a more comprehensive Transportation average, however, some technicians argued that railroad stock prices, if not a barometer of economic affairs, are at least a barometer of *speculation* in the stock market and therefore are of legitimate interest.

Since the Industrials and Transportations usually will not form the pattern simultaneously, the market may have a very sizeable decline before a confirmed sell signal is given. Herein lies the principal failing of the technique. In shallow bear markets, the signal usually comes shortly before the downtrend is about to reverse itself. Even this would not be too bad if the Dow theory promptly called the bottom of the market. A few percent saved is better than nothing. But to get a signal of a renewed uptrend the whole pattern previously described must repeat itself in reverse. That is, the Industrials and Transportations must each trace out a pattern of *ascending* bottoms and tops. By the time they do, the investor who has acted upon the signals is likely to have been whipsawed.

Price Chart Patterns

The Dow theory deals with the market as a whole. But the underlying principle of ascending and descending tops and bottoms as symptoms of primary trend reversals also is applied to individual securities. Technical analysts keep hundreds of price charts on stocks in which they have an interest.

Since individual stocks have much more extensive cyclical swings in price than the market averages, it might be that a Dow-type approach produces generally favorable results. The trouble is that we simply have no statistically significant method of appraising the technique. For in addition to ascending and descending tops and bottoms, which are often referred to as "channels" and which are amenable to reasonably precise definitions, technicians refer to "heads and shoulders" formations, "triangles," "rectangles," "flags and pennants," and a host of other configurations with equally exotic names but with quite imprecise definitions (see Figure 11–9). A half-dozen analysts looking at the same chart will rarely give anything near a unanimous interpre-

Figure 11–9
Graphic Illustrations of Major Chart Formations

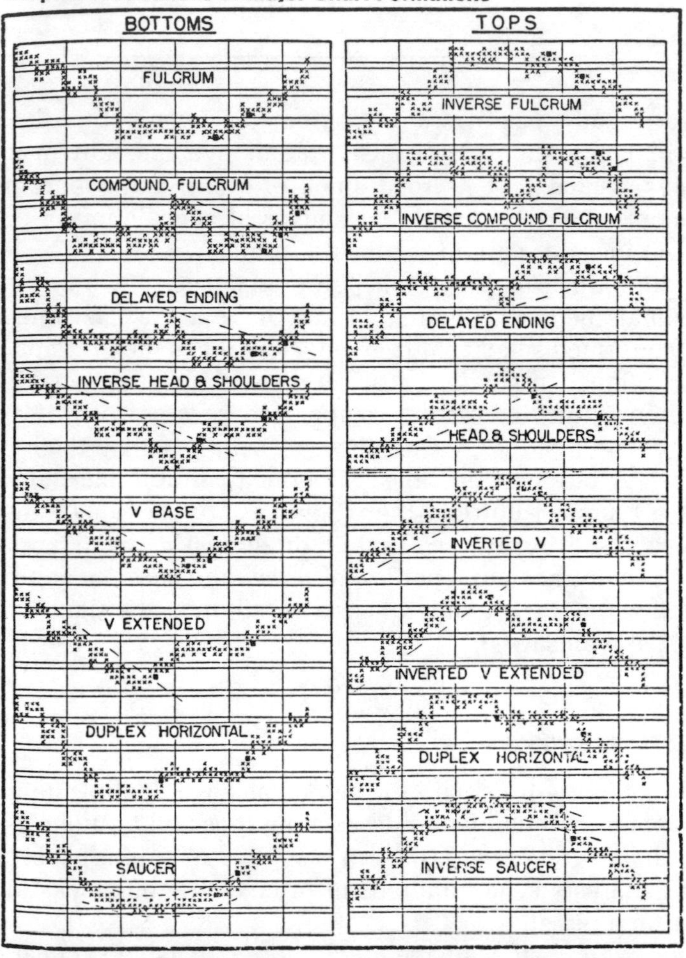

Source: *Commodity Year Book.* Reproduced with special permission of the Commodity Research Bureau, Inc.

tation. We therefore end up testing the performance of the *particular analyst* rather than the *method*.

Of course, somewhat the same comments can be made with regard to "fundamental" value analysis. Given the same information on sales, earnings, and so forth, numerous evaluations are possible. But the lack of clarity seems particularly troublesome in price chart reading.

Bar Charts

Technicians utilize three basic types of price charts: line charts, bar charts, and point-and-figure charts. On both line and bar charts the horizontal axis represents time—days, weeks, or months—and the vertical axis represents price. On a line chart, the closing prices of successive time periods are connected by straight lines. On a bar chart, vertical lines are drawn at each time period, with the top and bottom of each bar plotted at the high and low prices for the period. A small horizontal line is drawn across the bar at the closing price level. Bar charts of various market averages are published regularly in the financial sections of the newspapers. Most such charts include a vertical scale at the bottom of the chart against which are drawn bars representing the volume of trading during each time period. Figure 11–10 contains examples of this type of chart, each of which also shows a

Figure 11–10
Illustrative Bar Charts of Stock Prices

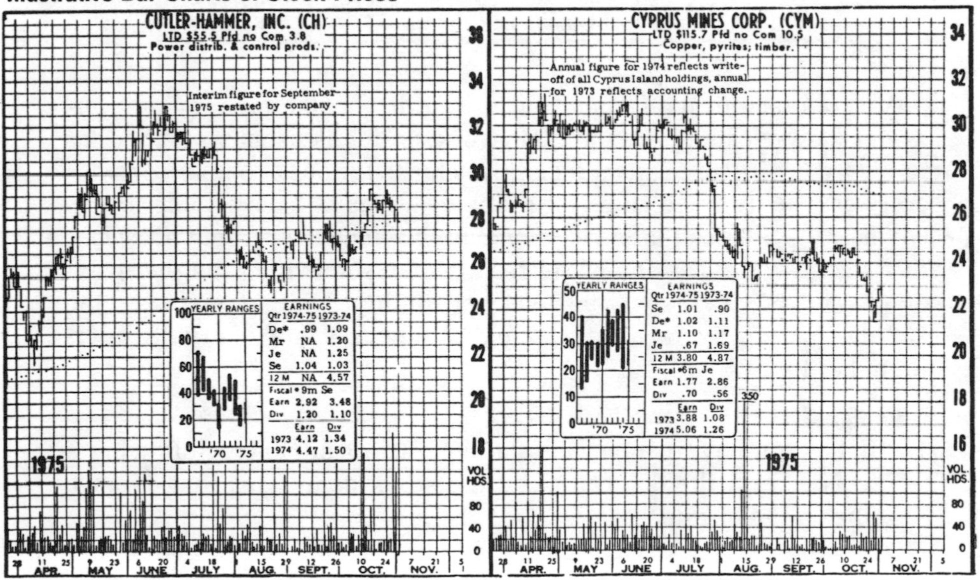

Source: Trendline Corp., *Daily Basis Stock Charts.*

200-day moving average of the daily closing price of the stock together with summary data on earnings, dividends, and capital structure.

Moving Averages

Many technical analysts believe that a reversal in a major uptrend of the price of an individual stock, or of the market in general, can be detected in advance, or at least confirmed shortly after its occurrence, by studying the movement of current prices in relation to a long-term moving average of prices. A moving average is designed to reveal the underlying direction and rate of change of a highly volatile series of numbers. It is constructed by averaging a portion of the series and then successively adding the next number of the series to the numbers previously averaged, dropping the first number, and securing a new average. For example, we could construct a five-day moving average of the daily closings of the Dow Jones Industrials as shown in Table 11–1.

Table 11–1
Five-Day Moving Average

Trading Day	*DJI*	*Five-Day Moving Total*	*Five-Day Moving Average*
1	900		
2	902		
3	899		
4	894		
5	897	4,492 (sum of items 1–5)	898.4
6	896	4,488 (sum of items 2–6)	897.6
7	898	4,484 (sum of items 3–7)	896.8

Veteran technical analysts generally utilize a 200-day moving average of daily closing prices in their work, which is usually graphed (as in Figure 11–10) on regular stock price charts for easy comparison with daily or weekly price changes. Frankly, we have been unable to discover any evidence that a 200-day average—covering about 40 weeks of trading—produces any better results than some other long-term average, say 250 days (covering a year of trading). Be that as it may, the 200-day moving average is a usable technical tool, and is usually interpreted as follows:

Buy signals:

1. If the 200-day average line flattens out or advances following a decline, and the daily price of the stock penetrates that average line on the upside.

2. If the stock price is above the 200-day line and declines toward it, but fails to go through and instead turns up again.

Sell signals:
1. If the average line flattens out or declines following a rise, and the daily stock price penetrates that line on the downside.
2. If the stock price is below the average line and rises toward it, but fails to go through and instead turns down again.

Point-and-Figure Charting

Of all the techniques described thus far in this chapter, not one attempts to forecast how far a price swing will carry. They all have sought to answer such questions as: Are we in a major uptrend or downtrend? Is the trend about to reverse itself? Point-and-figure analysts ask these questions and one more: What price is likely to be achieved by a particular stock or by the market averages?

A point-and-figure chart is quite different in concept and design from a line or bar chart. First, there is no time scale on such a chart—only a vertical price scale. Second, plots are made on the chart only when price moves up or down by a predetermined amount—typically 1 or 2 points in the case of medium-priced stocks, ½ point in the case of low-priced stocks, and 3 or 5 points for high-priced stocks. In addition to these differences, a point-and-figure chart provides no volume data unless the analysts work out some intricate schemes of their own, such as making their plots in different colors to represent different volumes. Most point-and-figure chartists take volume into account only indirectly.

The purpose of point-and-figure charting is to show a compressed picture of *significant* price changes. The analyst decides in advance that all movements of, say, ⅞ of a point or less will be considered as irrelevant. Thus, if price changes by ½ during a given day, no entry will be made on the chart. On the other hand, if price changes by 3 points in one day, three entries will be made on a 1-point chart. If time and facilities are limited, the analyst may work only with closing prices, but most serious chartists work with intraday prices as revealed by the ticker tape.

To illustrate the point-and-figure method of charting prices, let us assume that we are constructing a 1-point chart of a particular stock on the basis of the following closing prices (ignoring, for the sake of simplicity, any other intraday price changes):

December 29	45
January 2	46⅛
January 3	45¾
January 4	48⅛
January 5	46½
January 8	45⅞
January 9	47⅛

Here are a few simple rules to follow:

1. Put an X in the appropriate box each time the price rises to or through a round number, and a O each time it falls to or through a round number.
2. Do not allow gaps. If successive closing prices are, say, 45 and 47, make entries for 45, 46, and 47.
3. Move to a new column each time the *direction* of price *reverses*, except if there is only one entry in a column at the time of reversal.

Figure 11–11 is the resulting point-and-figure chart for these data.

Figure 11–11
Illustration of Point-and-Figure Method of Charting

50					
49					
48	X				
47	X	O	X		
46	1	O			
45	X				
	197X				

The first entry of a new month (46 for January 2, in this example) is designated by a number (1 through 12) instead of by an X or *O*, in order to give some idea of time for future reference. The new year also is indicated for this reason. There is no entry for January 3, because price did not change by a sufficient amount. Two entries (47 and 48) are made for January 4, as price went through two round numbers beyond the previous entry. The January 5 entry (47) calls for a new column because the direction of price reversed by more than a point from the previous entry (48)—and so forth.

Point-and-figure analysts examine their charts to discover areas of "congestion," also called "upside resistance areas," "downside support areas," "tops," "bases," "lateral trends," and so forth. Essentially, these are extended narrow horizontal bands of price fluctuation, indicating a standoff between relative supply and demand pressures. Point-and-figure charting technique, by condensing many months of price fluctuation within a limited space, is uniquely designed to reveal such congestion areas. Since a breakdown of price from a congestion area very often seems to be symptomatic of a new trend, point-and-figure technique can be said to have merit in making detection easy. Figure 11–12 illustrates upside and downside breakouts from congestion areas.

Figure 11–12
Point-and-Figure Upside and Downside Breakouts

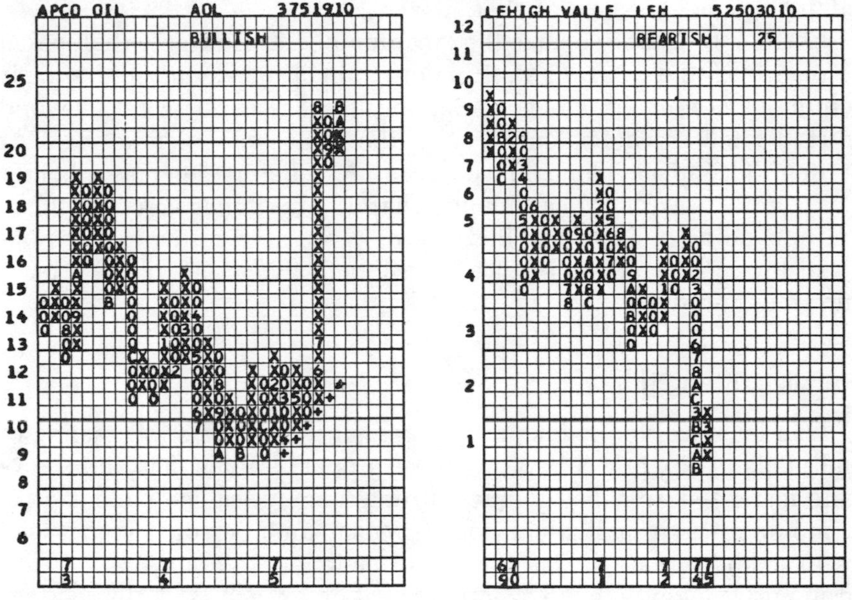

Source: Chartcraft, Inc.

Having detected what appears to be a new trend, the point-and-figure chartist measures the width of the band of congestion by counting horizontally the number of columns covered. If the price breakout has indicated an uptrend, the *horizontal count* is added to the price level of the congestion area, and the resulting price is said to be the level toward which the new uptrend is heading. In a downtrend, the horizontal count is subtracted from the price level of the congestion area to determine the likely stopping point of the decline.

The reader may wonder why on earth price potentials so established should be reliable. It is a fact that most point-and-figure analysts haven't the vaguest notion why, although a few have tried to give an explanation. But explanation or no, they all claim that the technique produces good results on balance. Pressed for some proof of this claim, however, they respond unsatisfactorily.

Indeed, the proof or disproof of the claim is an extremely difficult task. In the first place, several price potentials can be read from the same chart, depending on which price level is chosen for the horizontal count. In most cases, the choice of level is not clear-cut, and analysts use several levels to arrive at a range of possibilities. This complicates the problem of testing the accuracy of the technique. Further complicating testing is the fact that a 1-point chart often produces quite different target prices from a 3-point chart, and many stocks are equally adaptable to either type of chart.

Even more troublesome is the meaning of the price potential which is read from the chart. First, it is not made clear whether the price is a *minimum* or an *absolute* goal. Suppose price rises 50 percent beyond an indicated upside potential. Was the indicated potential right or wrong? Second, how long do we have to wait before deciding whether it was right or wrong? Bear in mind that no time dimension is attached to the reading of the chart. Because of these ambiguities, we are obliged to regard point-and-figure technique, as well as bar chart technique, as unproven.

Relative Strength

One technical tool which deals exclusively with the forecasting of individual stock prices (and industry groups), rather than the aggregate market, is so-called relative strength analysis. The method is to compute ratios of individual stock prices to an index of "the market," or to an appropriate industry group price index, and ratios of industry group price indexes to the overall market index. For example, suppose that we are analyzing Eli Lilly & Co. We could investigate the relative strength of the company's common stock as follows:

1. Obtain a record of the monthly average price of Lilly common stock (the means of the monthly high and low prices are usually adequate). There are numerous sources of such data—for example, *The Bank and Quotation Record*. Set these data up in column (1) of a work sheet, as shown in Table 11–2.

2. In columns (2) and (3) of the work sheet, list the monthly averages of Standard & Poor's Drug Price Index and S&P Industrial Stock

Table 11–2
Work Sheet for Relative Strength Analysis

	(1) Mean Price*	(2) S&P Drugs	(3) S&P Ind.	(4) Lilly/ Drugs	(5) Lilly/ Market	(6) Drugs/ Market
August 1975	65	202.1	103.84	32.2	62.6	194.6
September 1975	57	177.6	96.07	32.1	59.3	184.9

* Average of high and low price.

Price Index (or Composite Price Index). Historical data are available in Standard & Poor's *Security Price Index Record,* and current data appear in the weekly *Outlook.*

3. Divide column (1) by column (2), column (1) by column (3), and column (2) by column (3), and plot the resulting ratios on a graph.

Several brokerage firms prepare just such output for a wide variety of industries and stocks on a monthly basis, although some vary slightly in format from our illustration. For example, Figure 11–13 is from Mitchell, Hutchins, and includes relative price-earnings ratios and relative earnings along with relative price trends. The top panel covers their own ethical drug group composite (Abbott Labs, Eli Lilly, Merck, and Upjohn), while the bottom panel indicates the same relative information for Eli Lilly alone.

These graphs indicate, among other things, how Eli Lilly has fluctuated relative to the market, and how a cross section of drug stocks have also moved relative to the market. The Mitchell, Hutchins service does not include a graph indicating how Eli Lilly has fluctuated relative to the drug group, as we calculated in our example. However, by providing information on the trend of relative earnings and relative price-earnings ratios, they facilitate comparisons of price behavior and *the fundamentals.*

A rising relative price line (for example, Eli Lilly relative to the market during 1974) means that the numerator of the ratio is outperforming the denominator—rising faster or falling slower. A falling ratio (for example, as the drug group displayed in 1975 relative to the market) means that the numerator is not doing as well as the denominator—it is rising slower or falling faster.

Knowledge of whether a stock or industry group is outperforming or doing worse than the market may have forecasting value. Some investors even pursue a "relative strength" investment philosophy which is essentially predicated on the theory that strong (relative) stocks and groups will get stronger, and weak stocks and groups will get weaker. Robert J. Farrell of Merrill Lynch lends support to the

Figure 11–13
Example of Relative Strength Charts

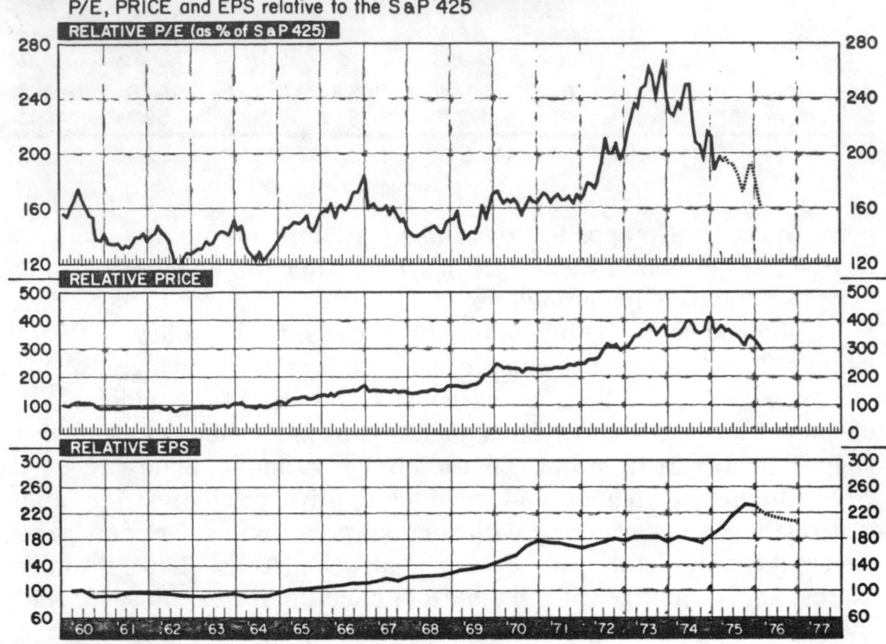

ELI LILLY

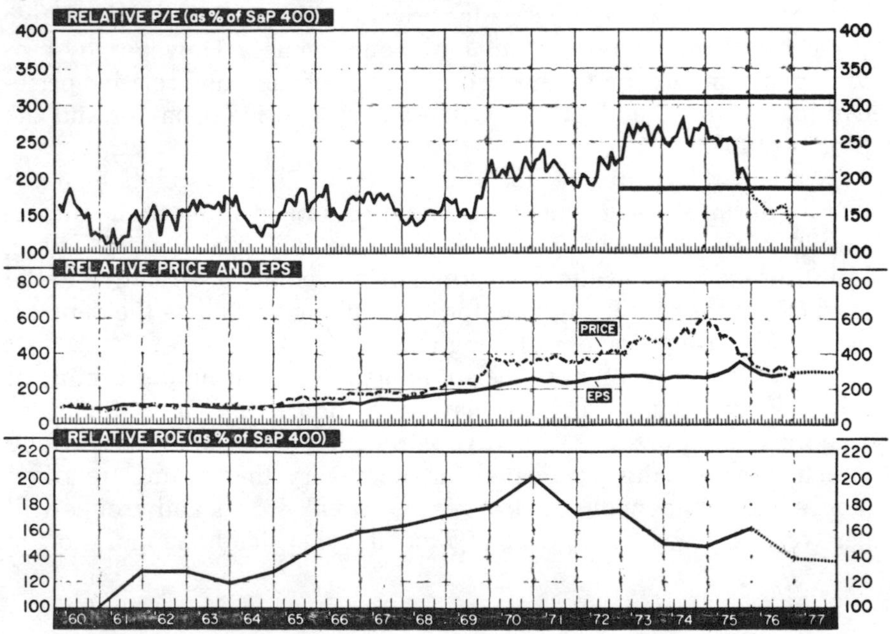

Source: Mitchell, Hutchins, Inc.

general theory by noting that historical studies show that any industry group underperforming the market in the first six months of a bull market is statistically unlikely to have a superior (relative) performance at a later stage of the cycle.

On the other hand, some technicians believe that there is a difference between relative strength during a decline and relative strength during an advance. A group outperforming a major stock average in a general advance may be expending its energy and be about to reverse itself. During a decline, however, we may often get a clue to future leadership by observing those groups (or stocks) which are resisting the decline relatively.

Of course, these are only general tendencies, not invariable rules. However, the tendencies are strong enough to suggest that by coupling relative strength analysis to techniques for analyzing overall market trends and turning points, investors should be able significantly to improve their results. Additionally, a change in relative price action of an industry or stock often reflects some new fundamental development. Thus, a monitoring of relative price behavior can also serve to indicate areas requiring new or additional basic research.

CRITIQUE AND CONCLUSIONS

Many investors think of stock market technicians in much the same way as scientists think of astrologers. To be sure, some technical analysts do seem merely to be "crystal-ball gazers." But to generalize is to cast aside the good with the bad. The more scholarly and sophisticated technical analysts use their tools with a proper sense of proportion. Typically, they use technical analysis as a guide to further study. If a stock looks attractive to them on technical grounds they probe into its *fundamentals.* While their decisions may be more heavily influenced by technical considerations, they are certainly not unmindful of earnings growth, of *values,* or of the impact of business cycles.

The honest technical analysts know that their approaches will not solve all investment problems. But they also know that no other single approach will either. They believe their tools can reduce the margin of error.

Moreover, while no single technical indicator can be expected to "work" every time, a useful picture may emerge when one follows several indicators which appear to be reasonably reliable, particularly in conjunction with the various economic indicators which have been discussed. Indeed, just as a diffusion index of a large number of economic indicators can be created, so too can a composite index of many technical indicators be constructed. A major advantage of a composite index is its stability, or infrequency of giving new signals. Hopefully, this lessens the chance of a whipsaw.

There are several commercial investment services which publish such a composite index on a subscription basis. Figure 11–14 shows the buy and sell signals that would have been given since 1965 by a composite of 12 technical indicators prepared by *Indicator Digest*. While we do not necessarily endorse the particular choice of indicators on which the chart is based, the results are quite intriguing.

Figure 11–14
***Indicator Digest* Composite Index, 1967–1976**

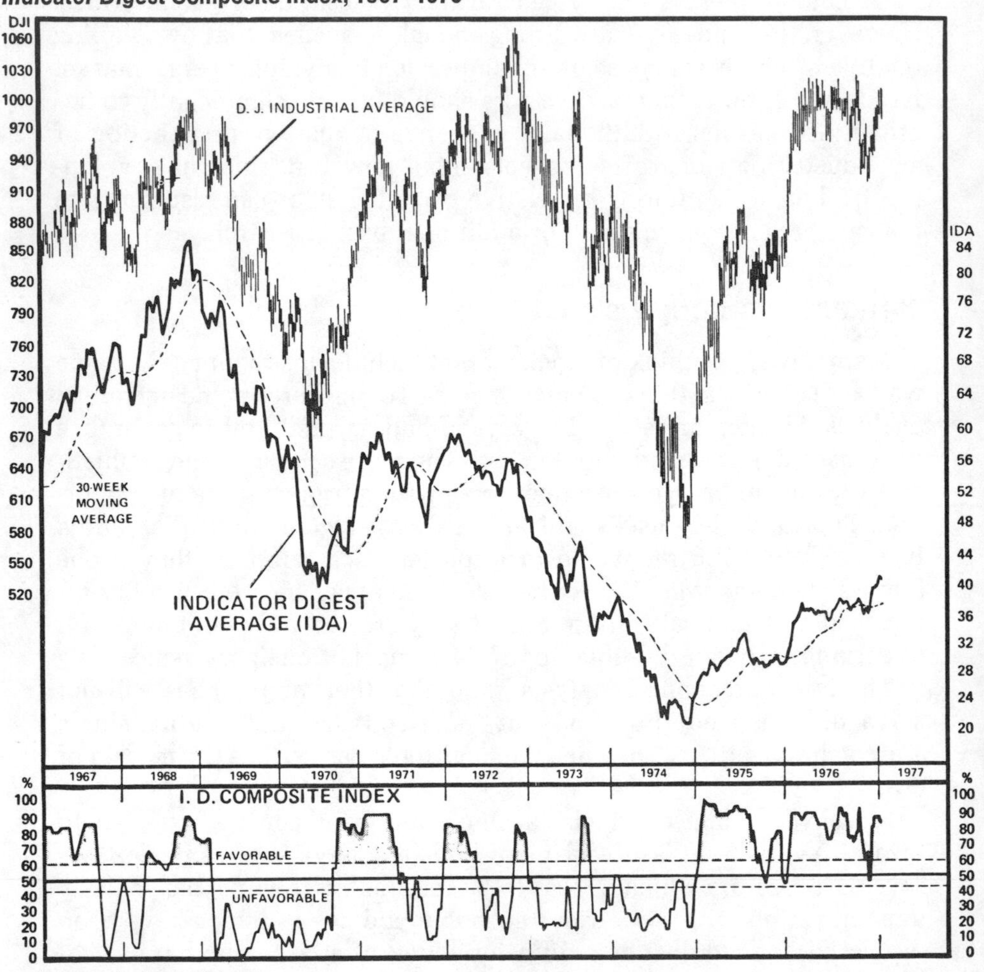

Source: *Indicator Digest*.

We would conclude this chapter by suggesting that the key impediment to investment success is inflexibility of approach. There is no method which is appropriate under all situations. Thus let the intelligent investor discard unjustified biases and consider the possibility of using any and all methods from which there is a theoretical or empirical reason to expect assistance.

SUGGESTED READINGS

Dines, James "How the Average Investor Can Use Technical Analysis for Stock Profits." New York: Dines Chart Corporation, 1974.

Edwards, R. D., and **Magee, John, Jr.** *Technical Analysis of Stock Trends.* Springfield, Mass.: Stock Trend Service, latest edition.

Indicator Digest "The Directory of Indicators." Palisades Park, N.J., latest edition.

Investors Intelligence *Encyclopedia of Stock Market Techniques.* Larchmont, N.Y., latest edition.

Jiler, William L. *How Charts Can Help You in the Stock Market.* New York: Commodity Research Publications Corp., latest edition.

Epilogue

Intelligent Investing in a Random World

These are sweeping changes, and those who are committed to traditional theories and practices naturally resist them.

B. F. Skinner

Effective investing is the art of handling a pool of funds so that it not only preserves its original worth but also yields an adequate return, consistent with the level of risk assumed.

Investors, in their pursuit of this all too often elusive goal, employ a wide variety of investment philosophies and procedures. In fact, it has been frequently noted that there are perhaps as many methods of investing as there are investors.

Some investors base their actions on business cycle analysis or the identification of technical trends, as described in chapters 10 and 11. Others confine their efforts almost entirely to individual stock or bond selection techniques, the subject of Part Two. Some, we are sure, listen to "tips" from brokers and other investors, giving scant thought to the appropriateness of a new "hot" stock for their own particular needs.

Whatever the case, most investors do not practice integrated decision making—that is, a systematic effort to determine their specific objectives, establish a portfolio designed to meet those objectives, provide for the realignment of holdings as conditions change, and monitor their performance. Instead, most investors, professional and amateur alike, act as if each of these tasks is separate and unrelated.

These shortcomings in investment practices have not gone unnoticed. There is now a widening recognition that a haphazard approach to portfolio planning fails to reward investors sufficiently. At the same time, the notion that sound investing only means picking "good" stocks, and avoiding "bad" stocks is fading. However, despite this awareness that there is a need for investors to adopt new approaches to the conduct of their stock and bond affairs, most participants in the market tend to reject new ideas and remain committed to their traditional but often unsuccessful ways.

This is not too surprising. Like most other human beings, investors resist new ideas. Fear of being proved wrong influences the way they react to new information about their holdings. But errors of judgment are inevitable, and intelligent investors must accept this as a fact of life. They must constantly question the reasonableness of their behavior. In fact, a good rule for investors to follow is that the more they believe their own expectations mirror those of other investors (that is, represent "conventional wisdom") the more they should seek out other, less popular, ways of looking at things.

The purpose of this final chapter is to describe some of the newer theories sweeping the investment world and to assess their relevance to the individual investor. We recognize that you may find some of what follows "tough going." But it should be worth the effort. For even if you finish this chapter still practicing your old investment habits, a seed of doubt will have been planted. And as that doubt leads to periodic questioning of old habits you will be on your way to improved performance.

Setting Investment Objectives

To help investors better organize their investment thinking, we present, in Figure E–1, a checklist of the basic elements comprising an integrated decision-making process. Each of the items on this checklist call for difficult decisions, and all of them are to a large extent interrelated. For example, if the objective is to earn a high rate of return, the investor must be able (financially and emotionally) to make a commitment to securities which will permit that magnitude of return. The investor seeking to preserve capital and earn a modest return should not expect to do as well as *the market,* or more aggressive investors, during bull periods. Of all the determinations required, perhaps the most important, and most difficult, is to de-

Figure E–1
Basic Elements of an Investment Decision-Making Process

Decision	*Description*
Investment Objectives	What is expected to be achieved from portfolio investments? Usually expressed as a rate of return expectation, either in absolute terms or relative to some standard of measure.
Time Horizon	Over what time period are current judgments expected to prevail?
Asset Alternatives	What types of assets are to be considered for investment by the investor? Traditionally the mix has been confined to stocks, bonds and cash and equivalents, but real estate is gaining in popularity. A few portfolios now seriously consider works of art, coins, rare metals, furniture, and stamps as viable alternatives.
Expected Rates of Return	What rate of return is expected to be earned by each class of investment to be considered over the investment horizon? What are the likely variances in expected rates of return? Are historic relationships between asset classes expected to prevail? What about inflation and expected returns?
Risk Tolerance Levels	What variance in expected rates of return can be tolerated by the investor? What is the impact, good or bad, if these limits are exceeded?
Security Selection Criteria	What types of stocks will be purchased? Growth stocks, cyclical issues, speculative, low P/E, high P/E? What quality and maturity bonds will be selected? Have the types of securities chosen historically provided the desired rates of return?
Diversification Limits	How much of the portfolio will be invested in stocks, bonds, etc? What limits are to be placed on the amounts to be invested in a single issue or a single industry?
Performance Measurement Standards	How will performance success or failure be measured? Against what yardsticks will investments be judged? Time horizon must be subdivided into interim measurement periods.
Criteria for Changing Decisions	When and why will previous judgments be reassessed as to their appropriateness? Most investors overlook this aspect of the process.

cide what the investor actually expects to achieve from his or her investments. In other words, what are the investment objectives?

Determining one's objectives should be the first step in the development of any soundly conceived investment program. For without first determining the final purpose of investing, it will be impossible to judge effectively the success of investment decisions or the appropriateness of the particular strategies employed. Unfortunately, both individual and institutional investors have found it difficult to articulate their investment objectives with any degree of precision. Even where an effort is made to be precise, most of the more widely adopted goals are simple expressions of a desire to outperform some stock market index or to achieve some absolute annual rate of return, without an accompanying expression of willingness to tolerate losses or of willingness to devote the effort needed to achieve the goals.

Investment objectives are a highly personal affair. They cannot be set in a vacuum. They must reflect both investment market conditions and the particular requirements and constraints of the investor (such as those discussed in chapter 1). While many investors share certain broad goals, each individual investor also has more personal, specific requirements that must be considered. Thus, the companion first step is to identify your particular needs, and to analyze them carefully.

As one goes about this process, it is important to recognize that two of every investor's broad objectives are inherently in conflict: the desire to minimize risk and the desire to maximize return. Investors must work out the appropriate balance between the level of risk which can be tolerated and the rate of return desired to be earned from investing. Personal factors must be considered as carefully as economic ones: your place in the life cycle and your psychological inclination and capacity to carry the burden of risk.

This last point should not be minimized. Most investors fail to appreciate sufficiently the pressures created by a high risk portfolio that falls short of its return expectations. High return goals, hence heavily risky portfolios, require an attitude rare among investors.

When these factors are fully understood, then risk–reward expectations can be specified, and investment policy, strategy and tactics decided. But even this is only a beginning. An investor's circumstances and ambitions change; so do investment market conditions and opportunities. Investment objectives must be reviewed and reappraised on a continuing basis. Successful investing is a process, not a destination. It is also understood better when placed in the perspective of modern portfolio theory, the subject to which we now turn.

MODERN PORTFOLIO THEORY

Efficient Frontiers

The basic elements of modern portfolio theory emanate from the work of Dr. Harry M. Markowitz in the 1950s. Markowitz saw the function of investment management as one of portfolio composition, and not individual security selection—as it is more commonly practiced. He insisted that decisions as to individual security additions to and deletions from a portfolio should be based on the effect such maneuvers have on the delicate diversification balance rather than as good or bad actions in and of themselves.

A central premise of Markowitz's work is that investors avoid increased risk without compensation by an adequate increase in expected return. For example, if Portfolio A is expected to produce a return of 10 percent plus or minus 2 percent (that is, it may yield as much as 12 percent or as little as 8 percent during the forecast period), Markowitz asserts that Portfolio A is clearly more desirable than Portfolio B, whose expected yield is the same 10 percent, but plus or minus a range of 4 percent. The greater range of uncertainty, the greater the risk, and therefore the less the attractiveness of the portfolio, other things being equal.

Starting with this conception of risk, and the investor's aversion to risk, Markowitz urged investors to minimize the deviations from the expected portfolio rate of return by "diversifying" their portfolios, holding different types of securities and/or securities of different companies. But he importantly pointed out that simply holding different issues would not significantly reduce the uncertainty of the portfolio's expected rate of return if the income and market prices of these different issues contained a high degree of positive "covariance." That is, if the timing, direction, and magnitude of their fluctuations were similar. Effective diversification is only achieved if the portfolio is composed of securities that do not fluctuate in a similar fashion, so that the uncertainty of the portfolio's rate of return becomes significantly less than the uncertainty of the individual components of the portfolio.

This important principle can be more easily understood by considering a simple two-stock portfolio, with equal amounts invested in each issue. Let us first assume that both securities are perfectly, and positively, correlated with respect to their price movements. When one moves up, the other does the same in exactly the same proportion;

and a similar relationship exists on the downside. For the sake of simplicity, let us also assume that each security fluctuates in a perpetual up and down pattern of equal dimensions, as exhibited in Figure E–2A. In this case therefore, the fluctuations of portfolio return will be the same as the fluctuations in the return of either, or both, of the two securities. Consequently, combining the two into a portfolio does not reduce the fluctuation in total return.

Figure E–2

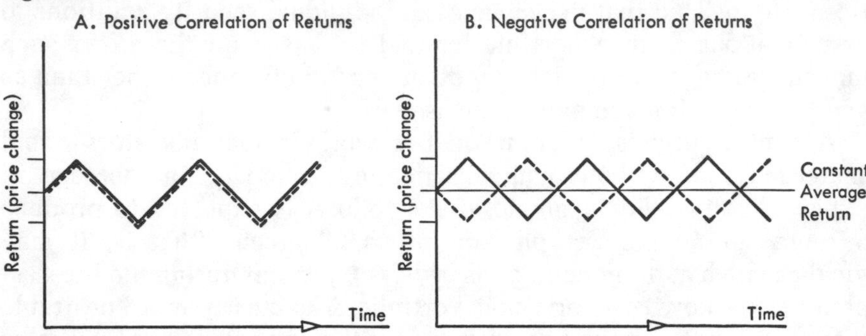

Now, let's assume that the two securities are negatively related to each other. When one moves up, the other moves down in exactly the same proportion, and vice versa, as exhibited in Figure E–2B. By combining these two issues into a portfolio, one completely eliminates fluctuation in the portfolio's return.

Obviously, practical problems go far beyond the consideration of two-stock portfolios. Therefore, this basic principle must be expanded to include all of the possible portfolio combinations available for selection. For each portfolio considered, Markowitz showed how to calculate the expected return and the possible variation in this return, over the time period under review, and how to focus on "the best" portfolios, which Markowitz termed "efficient." Consider the Portfolios A, B, and C in Figure E–3, for example.

Portfolio A is "inefficient" because Portfolio B produces the same expected return but at a lower risk level, while Portfolio C has the same degree of risk but affords a higher expected return. On the other hand, Portfolio B cannot be called more or less efficient than Portfolio C. Portfolio C has a higher expected return, but also a higher risk. The *curve* on which B and C lie was called *The Efficient Frontier* by Markowitz. Each portfolio on the curve offers the highest expected return *for its level of risk.*

Figure E-3
Efficient and Inefficient Portfolios

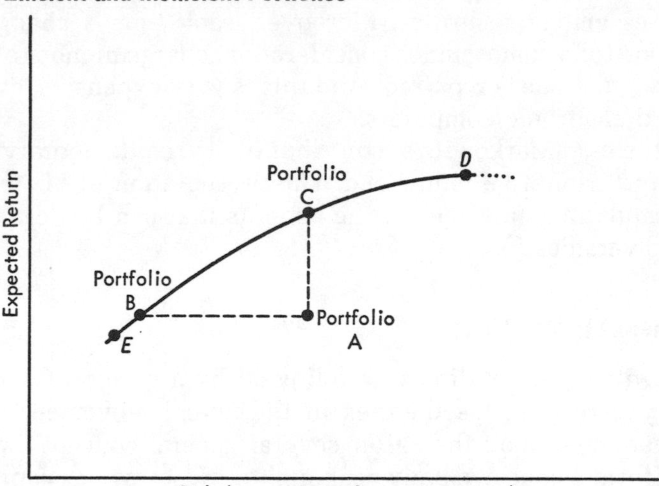

In order to determine the composition of these "efficient portfolios," Markowitz's computer program requires the following input:

1. Projections of the expected rate of return, including both current income and capital gain or loss, to be earned on each security that might be considered for inclusion in the portfolio.
2. Estimates of the possible range of error of each rate of return projection—for example, 15 percent plus or minus 8 percent.
3. An indication of the interrelationships (covariances) of the error ranges among securities. That is, if something happens to cause security A's rate of return to be, say 2 percent, higher than the "most probable" projection, what is the likelihood that the return on security B will be similarly higher than its most probable return? What about securities C, D, E, and so forth?
4. An indication of any constraints placed upon the portfolio manager, such as maximum percentage of the portfolio to be invested in any one security, and minimum number of different securities to be included in the portfolio.

Clearly, this list of required information presents some formidable obstacles to the application of Markowitz's ideas. For while investors are accustomed to thinking about expected rates of return, they are much less comfortable in assessing the possible ranges of error in their expectations, and are generally totally unaccustomed to estimating covariances among securities. Moreover, each time a change in an existing portfolio comes under consideration, a large number of mathematical calculations is required. And this is very expensive, even with high-speed electronic computers.

Nevertheless, Markowitz's contribution to contemporary investment theory cannot be minimized. The presentation of his technique was a stimulating statement of the benefits that can be derived from efficient diversification.

Capital Asset Pricing Theory

Markowitz's presentation was followed by a period of active academic study relating his theories to the actual movement of stock prices over time. Soon thereafter several general concepts were collected to form a cohesive body of thought now known as capital asset pricing theory, also referred to as capital market theory or modern portfolio theory. In essence it basically describes the relationship between risk and return (more precisely, the relationships between *assumed* risk and *expected* return) and seeks to explain stock price movements based on the assumptions that:

1. Most investors are risk averse, as Markowitz described the term, and seek to "optimize" their portfolios through efficient diversification.
2. Investors tend to have similar time horizons and similar views as to the probable range of returns of each security in the marketplace.
3. Investors are able to lend or borrow unlimited funds at the prevailing risk-free rate (for example, the rate on 91-day Treasury bills), and can buy and sell securities in any amount they choose without substantially affecting market prices.

These assumptions need not exactly coincide with the actual state of the security market pricing mechanism. However, it is believed by the theorists to represent a reasonable approximation of real-world investor activity and of the market's pricing behavior. As such, the price of an individual security, and of the market as a whole, is seen at any point in time as being the composite view of interested investors, balanced to reflect differences in existing opinions and preferences. While these differences may be large on occasion, security prices are seen as being basically in equilibrium. That is, each security, and the market as a whole, is seen as being, on balance, priced "fairly" in relation to the risk associated with its ownership. That being the case, the market as a whole is believed to be the closest possible approximation of an "optimal portfolio."

Given this equilibrium assumption about the market, capital asset pricing theory departs somewhat from the Markowitz presentation. As noted above, the Markowitz scheme encourages investors who have different risk attitudes to adjust for their differences by moving up or down an efficient frontier of *alternative portfolios of different individual securities.* Under capital asset pricing theory, on the other hand, risk adjustments should be made by borrowing or lending against the overall market rather than by tailoring individual securities to individual needs. In other words, investors wishing to maintain an "average" risk position should own a portfolio that has the same expected rate of return and probable fluctuations as the market does as a whole. Those wishing to be "more risky" than the market will borrow funds, but will invest their loan proceeds in the same "market" portfolio. Investors desiring a less than market risk profile will keep some of their investable assets in Treasury bills or some other relatively conservative investment but still will invest the balance of their funds in the "market" portfolio.

Since it is virtually impossible for most investors to purchase anything approaching the universe of all risky investments (that is, *the market*), it is much more practical to use a "proxy" for the market universe. The Standard & Poor's 500 Stock Price Index has been most frequently suggested for large institutional investors, and a package of no-load mutual fund shares for individual investors, although the choices are certainly not limited to these.

Random Walk and Efficient Markets

One should immediately question at this point why daily stock market trading activity is actually so hectic if the market mechanism even approximates a condition of price equilibrium. The answers most often given are, first, that investors' risk-return preferences are constantly changing, which gives rise to a frequent need to adjust the composition of their holdings to reflect these changes. Second, different investors are continually revising their anticipations about the expected risk and return associated with the holding of particular securities in response to new events. These new events are held to occur in a random fashion, a tenet of another and related aspect of modern portfolio theory, namely, the random-walk theory of stock price movements.

The random-walk theory is based on the assumption that the security markets are populated by a large number of rational, profit-seeking, risk-averting investors who compete freely with each other in their efforts to predict the future value of individual securities. Information significant enough to affect any security's future value is held to be quickly available to knowledgeable investors. As a result, new information affecting a stock's value becomes quickly reflected in the price of the issue. Consequently, a new investment decision, made after the information becomes widely known, is believed to carry the risk-reward potential of a randomly selected purchase (or sale). This is because the next piece of information is believed to bear no necessary relationship to the prior information. That is, new information is believed to enter the marketplace in random fashion.

This general premise flies in the face of what many investors consider their greatest strength—the ability to benefit from quick action taken after some new important event occurs which substantially affects the value of a particular stock, or occasionally the market as a whole. Most investors still accept what can be considered the "sociology of information recognition." This is a principle indicating that the movement of new information and its proper interpretation flow from the intelligent, well-informed, and sophisticated members of the market, who do tend to act quickly, to the lesser informed, slower moving elements at the other end of the spectrum. This, in turn, is believed to cause a sequence of interim stock price movements to develop, which reflects the accompanying gradual discounting of new information as it moves through the investor system.

Thus, the random-walk theory presents an important challenge to investors following the fundamental or technical techniques described in previous chapters. It might be well to note again that fundamentalists try to predict price changes through the analysis and interpretation of new developments or basic trends such as changes in profits and market share, which affect the value of the underlying common stock. Technicians, on the other hand, believe that predictions can be made by carefully observing stock price and volume movements of one sort or another.

To the chartist, or technician, the threat is simple. If the random-walk theory does, in fact, describe reality, perusing past price data with the hope of identifying future value points is a worthless effort.

The concern of those following a "fundamental" investment analysis approach is somewhat more involved. As noted, the random-walk theory holds that stock prices at any point in time represent the best estimate of intrinsic or basic value. Therefore, additional research efforts of a fundamental nature are of value only when such undertakings can uncover new information which is not part of the body of knowledge or anticipations forming prevailing market prices. Unfortunately, as James H. Lorie noted some time ago, "most analysts (and investors) are usually capable of knowing only what is generally known." But here lies the real challenge. The random-walk theory does not deny the possibility of accurately predicting future stock price changes. It clearly accepts the principle that if investment research techniques can lead to accurate forecasts of future company earnings they should result in better price forecasts. What the random walkers have done is put the burden of proof on those who claim to have such abilities.

Investment Risk

We have established that modern portfolio theory rests on, among other things, the investor's concern over the relationship between risk and return. We have not, as yet, however, precisely defined how to measure risk. There is still substantial controversy over exactly how investment risk is to be measured, and the techniques described below are not likely to represent the final solution.

Most students of the subject agree that investment risk is related to price fluctuations of the securities under consideration. The reason for this linkage of risk to price fluctuation is that such fluctuations reflect investors' uncertainty about the future. That is, current prices change when investors change their ideas about probable future prices (whether for logical or for purely emotional reasons). Therefore, investments whose future prices are highly uncertain are the object of frequent revaluation by the investment community, and their current prices change frequently as a result. Less risk is generally associated with decisions where expected return is more predictable, and conversely greater risk is associated with decisions surrounding less confident expectations.

Alphas and Betas. Portfolio theorists suggest that each security's price movement can be related to a common broad-based stock price index, such as the Standard & Poor's 500 Stock Price Index. In this way, price fluctuation, the chosen measure of risk, can be separated into two distinct elements. The first, identified as the *market* risk (also called *systematic* or *nondiversifiable* risk), is that portion of a security's price movement which can be attributed to movement of the market as a whole. The second element of risk is that portion of price movement unique to the specific security, and is defined (for reasons to be discussed below) as *nonsystematic* or *diversifiable* risk. This, in turn, might be further subdivided into some part attributable to industry characteristics and the balance distinct to the issuing company itself.

Obviously, not all companies are positioned to respond to broad market movements with the same degree of sensitivity. Important market events change the value of some companies more than others. This may reflect the relative degree of financial, operating or earnings leverage; comparative capitalization rates (price-earnings ratios); competitive industry conditions; patterns of earnings instability (or stability); or endless other considerations.

Research studies have shown that, in the general case, the overall market influence accounts for between 20 percent and 30 percent of an individual stock's price change over time, while specific company and industry factors contribute the remainder. The research used to determine these percentages utilizes a procedure illustrated in Figure E–4.

Assume that we are measuring a stock's returns monthly for a one-year period. Each X on the chart represents a particular month's gain or loss in the stock (measured on the vertical axis) and the corresponding gain or loss on the *market* during the same month (mea-

Figure E–4
Measurement of Market Sensitivity

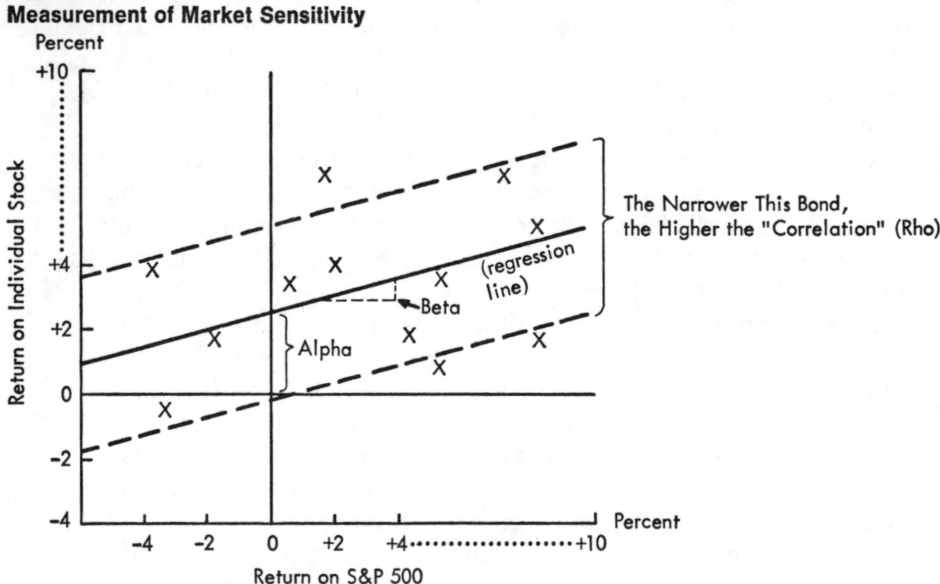

sured on the horizontal axis and using the S&P 500 Index as representative of the overall market).

Using a statistical technique known as "regression," a line is drawn through the 12 monthly observations. This regression line is a description of the relationship between the returns on the stock and the returns on the market. It provides the following information:

1. Beta is the *slope* of the regression line, the amount of vertical movement (stock return) per unit of horizontal movement (market return). If the slope were at a 45° angle, beta would be 1.0, meaning that *on average* every 1 percent return on the market was associated during this period of time with a 1 percent return on the stock. A shallower slope would be represented by a beta of less than 1.0. Suppose that it worked out to 0.8. This would mean that, *on average,* a 1 percent return on the market was associated with a return on the stock of 0.8 percent. Likewise, a steeper slope —a beta of say 1.4—would mean an average relationship of 1.4 percent on the stock per 1 percent on the market. Note that the beta relationship applies to negative as well as to positive returns; that is, it indicates what will happen to the stock, *on average,* if the overall market *declines.* High-beta stocks are said to be highly *volatile,* and low-beta stocks are said to be very *stable.* Thus, beta measures the market component of a stock's returns.
2. Alpha is the *intercept* of the regression line, the point at which the line crosses the vertical axis and zero on the horizontal axis. It represents the amount of return produced by the stock, *on average,* independent of the return on the market. It measures the specific component of a stock's returns.

   Suppose, for example, that alpha is 1 percent and beta is 1.5. If, in this case, the market's return for a particular month was, say, 2 percent, the most likely return on the stock that month would be 4 percent. The 4 percent is derived as follows: a 2 percent market return is, *on average,* associated with a 3 percent stock return (2 percent multiplied by the 1.5 beta equals 3 percent); in addition, and independent of the market, the stock tends to produce a return of 1 percent; thus 3 percent plus 1 percent equals 4 percent. Alphas can be positive, negative, or zero. (Beta can be negative as well; that is, a stock could rise when the market falls, and vice versa, but this is highly unusual, gold stocks being the leading example.) Notice the words *on average* have been stressed. This is because the relationship between the returns on the stock and the returns on the market is not perfectly consistent in each and every month. If it was, all of the Xs would fall on the line of regression. But, clearly, they do not. Indeed, none do in this case. The line of regression merely represents the average relationship. Statisticians have a measure of the extent to which the individual observations deviate from the line of average relationship. It is called *rho*, the correlation coefficient, or rho-squared, the coefficient of determination.

Rho is equal to 100 percent when all the observations fall on the line of regression. This would mean that all of the variability in the return on the stock is explained by the returns on the market. As the observations deviate from the line, rho declines. A total absence of any (linear) relationship between the stock's returns and the market's returns would be indicated by a rho of zero percent.

At this point, modern analysts take a giant step. They recognize that any one stock can have a substantial positive or negative alpha, and can have a fairly low rho. But they argue that as we combine many stocks into a portfolio—that is, as we *diversify*—the relationship between the portfolio's returns and the market's returns becomes much closer than the relationship between the returns on any individual stock in that portfolio and the returns on the market. In other words, rho moves toward 100 percent. Moreover, they argue, the positive alphas of some of the individual stocks in the portfolio tend to be offset by the negative alphas of other stocks in the portfolio. As a result, the alpha of the total diversified portfolio tends toward zero. Thus, we previously referred to research which indicates that the overall market's movements explain only 20 or 30 percent of an individual stock's price movement, with the balance attributable to specific company and industry factors. But in a diversified *portfolio* of 30 or more stocks, so much of the specific element is eliminated that roughly 85–95 percent of all the price fluctuations of the portfolio is market related and only 5–15 percent is attributable to the unique characteristics of the particular stocks in the portfolio. Therefore, beta, the measure of a stock's or a portfolio's price fluctuations relative to the market, is viewed by modern theorists as being an excellent measure of risk.

Thus far, the major lines of thought presented in this section have been as follows:

1. *The Efficient Frontier* is a risk/return trade-off curve. This is a set of alternative portfolios each of which is most *efficient* in that it

provides maximum expected return at its level of risk. The investor's own risk attitude dictates precisely what point on the curve is best for him or her.

2. *The Efficient Market* concept builds upon the random-walk theory of stock price movement. This theory views the security trading mechanism as a highly efficient processor of new information, which enters the marketplace in random fashion. In this type of environment, the market is the optimal risky portfolio. Consequently, the investor's risk attitudes should be reflected by borrowing or lending against this optimal risky portfolio rather than by creating different risky portfolios for different investors.

3. Finally, theorists selected *beta* as the principal measure of investment risk. Beta reflects that part of a portfolio's returns, and variation in returns, which is attributable to the overall movement of the market rather than to any unique characteristics of the portfolio.

Some Questions. Before you begin to alter your own conceptions of how the stock market works, in favor of these new views, we feel obliged to point out that some limitations exist in the theory. One aspect of the theory which has come into serious question is the assumption that all investors can borrow or lend unlimited sums at equal rates of interest (the risk-free rate). In the real world, this assumption simply is untenable.

Furthermore, it is possible that risk-oriented investors tend to exaggerate in their minds the opportunity for gain from high-risk stocks. Certainly, the speed with which *hot new issues* frequently are distributed, despite the high mortality rate of new companies, suggests that this may be so. If it is so, then the prices of high-risk stocks may, in general, be *too high*—that is, investors may *overpay* for them—thus causing ultimate realized returns to be incommensurate with the risks involved.

Another open question is: What are the risks of bonds, mortgages, and real estate in relation to common stocks: For example, are *triple-A* bonds really less risky than *A* bonds and, if so, how much less risky? How does one compare the risks of stocks and bonds in the presence of inflation? And, is real estate a good equity substitute for common stocks? There are two serious obstacles to efforts to answer these questions within the framework of capital market theory.

First, there are simply no large-scale price data banks available on investment assets other than common stocks. Second, even such fragmentary price data as are available do not provide very useful rate of return data because most assets other than common stocks are not readily marketable in large quantities. Therefore, some portion of their rate of return is, presumably, a *premium for lack of marketability*. Yet there is no accepted measure of marketability which can be used to estimate the size of this premium.

The lack of a good measure of marketability is also an obstacle to progress in common stock risk/return analysis. Obviously, some stocks are more marketable than others, small portfolios are more marketable than large portfolios, a 100 share holding is more marketable than a 100,000 share holding of the same stock. Thus, comparisons of the returns against the betas of different stocks or different portfolios may be quite muddied up by differences in their marketability.

Aside from these academic questions, which have been raised by both professors in colleges and investors in the marketplace, there exists an even more basic and fundamental concern. As we pointed out early in our discussion, a major premise of capital market theory is the assumption that most investors react similarly to expectations about the future. Recently, however, evidence has been developed which indicates quite clearly that individual investors, if not professionals, exhibit distinctive groupings with regard to their investment behavior.

The general pattern is that conservatism increases with age. As one proceeds across the age spectrum, from youngest to oldest, short-term capital gain goals diminish as the primary investor objective with increasing emphasis being placed on current income. At the same time, investor portfolios become more diversified. Quite interestingly, female investors have tended to be especially conservative, diversified, and income oriented.

INVESTMENT TACTICS

So what is one to do? Modern portfolio theory argues that there is an *optimum portfolio* which is good for everyone, and all one need do is borrow or lend against it to adjust for risk. Yet real-world evidence suggests that (*a*) such lending and borrowing is quite impractical; (*b*) rightly or wrongly, people differentiate sharply between capital gains and income from interest or dividends; and (*c*) people, at least while they are fairly young, get a kick out of looking for unique investment opportunities. Given these conflicting views, how should an investor go about the tough business of investing and deciding which stocks and bonds are to be bought and sold?

Figure E–5 is a *decision matrix*, designed to place in perspective the investment tactics best suited to the forecasting and security selection abilities of the individual investor. If investors believe they are

Figure E–5
Portfolio Strategy Decision Matrix

Ability to Select Undervalued Securities \ Ability to Forecast Overall Market	Good	Poor
Good	1. Concentrate holdings in selected undervalued securities rather than diversify broadly. 2. Shift beta above and below desired long-term average, based on market forecasts.	1. Concentrate holdings in selected undervalued securities rather than diversify broadly. 2. Keep beta stable at desired long-term average.
Poor	1. Hold a broadly diversified list of securities. 2. Shift beta above and below desired long-term average, based on market forecasts.	1. Hold a broadly diversified list of securities. 2. Keep beta stable at desired long-term average.

Source: Adapted from Keith Ambachtsheer, "Portfolio Theory and the Security Analyst," *Financial Analysts Journal,* November/December 1972, p. 33.

good market forecasters, they should vary the stock/bond proportions of their portfolios quite often, in line with their forecasts. If they believe they are good stock or bond selectors, they should depart from the principle of broad diversification. If they are doubtful that they possess a high degree of either ability, they should concentrate on determining the most appropriate overall risk level for their portfolio and should proceed to create broadly diversified portfolios with constant risk (beta) levels that conform to their appraisals. The point of the matrix is that you must decide what you think you're good at and what you're not good at.

Active or Passive?

Most investors engage in active investing. That is, they attempt to profit from stock selection, market timing, or both.

According to Russell J. Morrison, a leading Canadian portfolio manager and frequent writer on investment techniques, two ingredients are necessary for success in active portfolio management. First, one must have a good idea of how others view alternative investments.

Second, one must disagree with the concensus—disagree as to direction or disagree as to amplitude of price movement. Thus, the task of the active investor is not to forecast returns accurately, but to forecast *more accurately* than the market. Moreover, the difference in expectations must be of sufficient magnitude to cover transaction costs and to allow for the error factor.

Unfortunately, historical evidence suggests that most investors are not very successful in these efforts, and there is now a serious trend toward *passive* portfolio management. This term implies the creation of a well-diversified portfolio at some predetermined risk level, usually not much different from 1.0 beta, and holding it relatively unchanged for the long run. Index funds are one form of passive portfolio management. They are characterized by very low turnover, minimum transaction costs, reduced management expenses, and low levels of specific risk.

Index Funds. An index fund is a portfolio designed to mirror the movement of a selected broad market index by holding commitments in the same proportions as those which comprise the index itself. For example, if IBM accounts for 7 percent of the S&P 500, and the desire is to match the S&P 500, then the portfolio would have put 7 percent of its assets in IBM, and so on. Once the portfolio is established, it need not be disturbed except to accommodate cash flows (in and out), to reinvest dividend income, and to adjust for issues added to, or deleted from, the market index.

An index fund, by definition, has a beta of 1.0. Beta can be adjusted down or up from 1.0 by adding risk-free assets to the portfolio or leveraging it. However, the most popular motivation for index portfolios, at least to date, is the desire to *match the market* over long periods of time with at least some portion of a portfolio's assets.

Unfortunately, as of this writing, there are few market funds (index funds) readily available to individual investors. However, this is really not the problem it may appear to be, as the same level of diversification can be easily achieved by combining several large, no load mutual funds into one portfolio. Such a portfolio can be counted upon to mirror the market's movements very closely, if not exactly.

To go further with this approach, consider how four different individual investors might allocate their funds using this concept. To do so, it is necessary to assign *beta,* or risk levels, to the conventionally used terms which describe investor attitudes. It is clear, from looking at Table E–1, that portfolios with a *beta* (risk) level of 1.0 or less are easier to construct and supervise than those carrying higher beta, or

Table E–1
Individual Portfolios and Risk

	Type of Investor			
	Conservative	*Average*	*Capital Gains Oriented*	*Speculator*
Desired beta	0.75	1.0	1.2	1.5
Percent portfolio in risk-free assets	25%	0%	−20%	−50%
(Borrowed funds per $100 of own funds)	—	—	($20)	($50)
Percent of own funds in a package of large no-load mutual funds	75%	100%	120%	150%

risk, levels. Those in the former category merely require the purchase of several no-load mutual funds and the periodic reinvestment of risk free holdings when they mature. Borrowing, to achieve greater than market exposure, is a more difficult task. But it is not so difficult as to negate the entire concept, particularly for larger sized portfolios. One of the fringe benefits of borrowing is the *reinforcement* of risk actually undertaken. That is, the loan against the portfolio may make investors think twice about their *risky* investment policy.

But Index Funds Are No Fun. Notwithstanding the intellectual appeal of passive portfolio management, we would expect most individuals to follow tradition by selecting a few stocks which hopefully will achieve their investment goals. However, in pursuing this approach, individuals should at least recognize the value of viewing *risk* as consisting of two parts, market risk and specific risk. They should recognize that all stocks are not equal in risk, particularly market risk. Therefore, their stock selections should consider the expected return as consisting of a market-related reward and a specific selection reward.

This means that individuals should select issues for their portfolios which will, in the aggregate, create an average beta value in line with their own investment attitude. It is not necessary that each and every issue resemble, in risk, each other, but that the portfolio's *center of gravity* should fall on, or near, a risk level which approximates the willingness to assume market exposure. For example, a conservative investor would presumably hold primarily international oil stocks, tobacco issues, natural gas distributors, and the like. These industry groupings typically have beta values such as .77, .87, .89 respectively, as shown in Table E–2. As the mix is altered with other holdings, the

Table E–2
Recent Industry Beta Values

Industry	*Beta*	*Industry*	*Beta*
Aerospace	1.04	Oil—domestic	.94
Aluminum	.99	Oil—international	.77
Automobiles	.93	Paper	1.17
Brewers	1.17	Photography	.83
Soft drinks	1.02	Publishing	1.25
Building materials	1.26	Restaurants	1.50
Chemicals	1.10	Radio and television	1.37
Coal	1.08	Retail stores	1.22
Containers	.92	Soaps	1.02
Copper	1.01	Steel	.95
Cosmetics	1.15	Textiles	1.13
Drugs	.92	Tobacco	.87
Electric	1.18	Air transport	1.55
Electronics	1.23	Railroads	1.12
Entertainment	1.37	Electric utilities	1.01
Foods	.95	Natural gas distributors	.89
Hotel and motel	1.57	Natural gas pipelines	1.09
Machinery	1.23	Banks—New York	1.09
Office and business equipment	.76	Banks—other	1.13
Offshore drilling	1.51	Insurance	1.40

Source: Prepared by First Boston Corporation based on material supplied by Barr Rosenberg and Associates.

individual must recognize that the risk level will shift, usually upwards. On the other hand, aggressive investors need not be confined only to risky holdings but can temper their beta level by combining their usual selections with several conservative issues.

Coping Better

Let's ponder the question: Why are so many investors wrong so much of the time?

Surely, one reason is that they accommodate change poorly. More for emotional than logical reasons, investors tend to base their expectations on visible and prevailing trends and patterns. But all too often, expectations based on such patterns fail to materialize. John Maynard Keynes, an outstanding investor of his day, put it this way: "The facts of the existing situation enter, in a sense disproportionately, into the formation of our long-term expectations: our usual practice being to take the existing situation and to project it into a future modified only to the extent that we have more or less definite reasons for expecting a change."

Investors compound the problem by tending to become overly protective of their own judgments. Not because they are right, or even likely to be right, but because they are their own. This in turn leads to an unwillingness to accept new information for what it's really worth. Frequently, it's worth a great deal and the reluctance to consider new information (change) with an open mind makes it harder to recognize the flaws which may exist in their operating investment premise.

Many investors work themselves into a significant loss position by failing to appreciate that a loss taken quickly is usually a minimal loss. Intelligent investors must learn to avoid the defensive rationalization of past bad judgments. They should recognize, rather, that when things change, they change. It is better to take the new events into consideration, admitting error and shifting investment posture, rather than fighting reality until conventional opinion converges on the new view and sweeps the old one away and with it the opportunity to prevent great loss.

In other words, information must be regarded by investors as a perishable commodity. The life cycle of new ideas steadily grows shorter. Change must be placed into its proper perspective much more quickly than heretofore. New developments are usually recognized, appreciated, and acted upon by a few. The new trend enjoys progressively wider recognition until it finally becomes the conventional wisdom, when it is extrapolated beyond its reasonable horizon. The First National City Bank Monthly Economic Letter recently noted: "The temptation to extrapolate events of the recent past into the indefinite future is strong, but it will lead to the wrong conclusion if the fundamental conditions that created these events are changing rapidly and significantly." The point is, they usually are.

Random Walk Revisited. What we are suggesting is that the market is not totally efficient in its response to new developments. First, new and important information simply is not available simultaneously to all who might recognize or use it. Second, not all who have the information recognize it. Third, not all who recognize it are able immediately to translate that recognition into an evaluation of its worth in the market. That is, in any group of investors, some will exhibit the capacity to recognize and use information faster than others, and that capacity puts them at a competitive advantage.

The principal evidence supporting the random-walk hypothesis has been based on the market's reaction to new information as supplied via corporate announcements such as earnings and dividends, stock splits, or secondary distributions; changes in Federal Reserve data; recommendations by brokerage firms and advisory services; and the periodic announcements of industry data. Little, if any, scientific testing has been conducted on the market's response to less obvious developments which affect the fortunes of a particular company or industry. Let us explain further.

The Market Is a Mirror. Generally speaking, the market is a mirror reflection of the forces that weave their way through our social, political, and economic systems. But the market—like the mirrors at amusement parks—tends to create distortions of the truth. These distortions create investment opportunities.

Long-term investment cycles in fact reflect structural economic shifts. For example, one can correlate the entire postwar bull market, up until the mid-1960s, with a persistent buildup of capital and the ability over the years to create wealth sufficiently in excess of basic needs to give rise to speculative tendencies. For most of the postwar period, an increasing number of families and corporations developed very large increases in their discretionary income.

Within that very long cycle, there have been fairly long subperiods which further illustrate the basic premise. The period 1946 to the mid-50s was primarily one in which concern focused on corporate strength and on those strongly financed companies in basic industries capable of generating earnings progress; in other words, a period of industrial expansion. After the consumer and capital goods boom of the mid-50s, investor emphasis shifted toward those companies which were considered *impervious* to the business cycle (the first of several *growth stock* phases). That period was followed by one in which investment attitudes began to concentrate on the maximizing of long-term returns in the new technologies.

Consider the *two-tier market* of late 1972–73. It made sense as a legitimate response to a series of new problems—the much higher than anticipated inflation rate, a more competitive position of fixed income securities via long-term equity rewards, international balance of payments problems, and, perhaps most importantly, greater involvement by the government in heretofore private enterprise decisions. It became part of the conventional wisdom to assume that one way of avoiding these problems was to concentrate on those equities with a much higher than average growth rate, a much higher than average return on investment capital, a much lower labor content, and so forth. Common stocks in the *first tier* were held to have *one dimension*. That is, they required only a *buy* decision in order to provide above average long-term rewards; they would not ever be considered for sale.

At this point the mirror became distorted. Investor response to new economic realities was overdone, and the opportunities that were so obvious to the early investors were not there for those who arrived late on the scene. Just about the time that *one-decision* growth stock investing reached its zenith of acceptance, fundamental business patterns changed dramatically to the detriment of investors following that approach. First, and perhaps most importantly, the economy started to shift from a consumer to a capital goods orientation. The market mechanism began to reallocate resources to those companies that needed capital to relieve shortages building up in the economic system—basic industries, whose stocks had not only been overlooked by investors, but actually were held in such low regard that many leading Wall Street research firms refused to cover these companies as part of their normal analytical effort.

Second, rapidly increasing worldwide inflation rates began to shrink consumer discretionary spending for nonessential items. Unit sales growth around the world declined (investors had forgotten that most growth companies earn much of their net income from foreign markets) and profit margins were squeezed as raw material companies were able to raise prices, due to shortages, faster than consumer oriented businesses. In short order, the worldwide inventory panic created by spiraling energy and other raw material costs produced the inevitable recession. Growth stocks proved to be particularly vulnerable to price weakness in a market made more nervous by increasing regulatory and legislative scrutiny of bank trust department investment practices. Bank trust departments, it may be recalled, had been the really big *one-decision* stock buyers of the period.

At the same time, some investors were rediscovering *value*. Their attention was directed to stocks of companies with highly depreciated plant being operated at high rates of utilization, selling at 5–6 times earnings, producing high current return from well-covered dividends and selling at substantial discounts from artificially low *book values*. The focus shifted to current dividend return from long-term price appreciation. Investors—large and small—began (and still are, as of this writing) selling the *old-fashioned* growth stocks at substantial losses to buy long ignored investment values. And is it not equally predictable that the time will come when *growth* stocks are the rage once again?

Now, why did and why do investment trends change over time? Simply, or perhaps not so simply, because they reflect the changing needs, priorities, and requirements of an economic system in constant evolution. Over the longer-term, stock prices correlate with earning progress. Corporate earnings, in turn, are largely a function of the opportunities provided by changes in the overall economic system. Each new phase of economic movement creates earnings growth opportunities for some companies, while at the same time offering new problems for others. Stock price cycles, long and short, are a reflection, with varying lead and lag times, of these wavelike movements.

Critical Factors. Every industry, company, and economic sector responds to a different set of business phenomena, forces, and critical factors. Any sound analytical approach requires that these factors be identified, isolated, and followed on a consistent basis.

Change in these elements alters the profits outlook and immediately affects investment expectations. Consequently, stock price movements start to mirror these new developments long before it is generally recognized that they have taken place. Every effort must be made to interpret change swiftly and accurately. In today's market environment, the life cycle of a "new idea" is very brief, often as short as the first telephone call.

Early warning signals calling attention to a possible change may take the form of a new trend in a significant statistical indicator or a shift in the attitude of industry participants close to the point of critical action.

Critical factors are not limited to cyclical considerations nor confined to short-term movements, but include slower moving basic trend changes, social and environmental developments as well as internal corporate adjustments, the adoption of new management techniques, new product introductions, changes in market share, and so on.

These critical factors are not always, or even for the most part, obvious, or anyone could run a business. But they exist, are demonstrable, and, when properly understood, yield foresight. They may in some cases seem frivolous or seem in themselves to be the result of irrational behavior—say by the consumer or the government—but they submit to rational analysis.

Avon Products is a good case in point. Throughout 1972, the shares of this outstanding company moved in the forefront of the developing *two-tier* market. By early 1973, the price of Avon common stock had risen to $140 per share, from a low of $60 in 1970, and carried a price-earnings ratio (on estimated 1973 earnings of $2.45–$2.50 per share) of over 55. Institutional investors and research analysts alike were generally secure in their belief that earnings would continue to compound at a 15 percent annual rate and such a performance was adequate compensation for the *lofty* multiple on current earnings. In fact, so strong was the belief in the persistency of past earnings growth, that when the stock declined 40 points from its high, many regarded the development as another buying opportunity. Typical commentary ran as follows: "At its current price of $108, Avon common offers well above-average longer-term appreciation potential. Chiefly responsible for our favorable opinion regarding Avon common is our optimism that over the foreseeable future the company's traditional business can record revenue gains of 14 percent to 16 percent annually."

Despite the prevalence of such views, largely based upon traditional analysis, the stock continued to drop and closed on December 31, 1973 at a little over $60 per share. Why? During the third quarter, management felt obliged to announce that the company was beginning to experience a sales slowdown in the United States. Contributing factors behind this *unusual* development can be cited in the words of management: "Dramatic increases in the price of food and other basic items and the prospects of further increases of this kind in the future have imposed a squeeze on the family's budget." As a visiting Englishman put it, "It was really quite predictable, if one had thought about it that way."

The point is, stock price movements will begin reflecting new developments long before it is generally recognized that they have taken place. In this regard, it has frequently been noted that new investment trends start with the belief of a few and end with the conviction of the many. In other words, some investors do recognize change more rapidly than others. How do they do it? A couple of rules are clear:

1. The ability to recognize an important change stems from an understanding of the fundamentals of a business and not from the gathering of statistical minutia.
2. The fundamentals of a business have to do with customer needs and desires, on the one hand, and the methods employed to satisfy those needs—the key demand factors and the key supply factors.
3. Investors must conquer the urge to learn everything before making a decision.

Let's illustrate with a relatively simple example. In mid-1971, Gerber Products was selling between $45 and $50 a share, approximately 19.5 times the earnings of $2.40 per share reported for the March, 1971 fiscal year. The stock had risen almost 60 percent during the prior 12 months (see Figure E–6). On September 7, 1971 several leading newspapers carried headlines indicating that the "U.S. Birthrate Falls 15 Per Cent," after the stock had already experienced a significant, but unexplained, correction. Sixteen months later the stock dropped to $24½, its lowest price since 1966, after management reported a sharp decline in quarterly profits. The accompanying commentary indicated that the lower earnings reflected price competition and a decline in the number of births.

Now, the point of this narrative is not to elaborate on the obvious

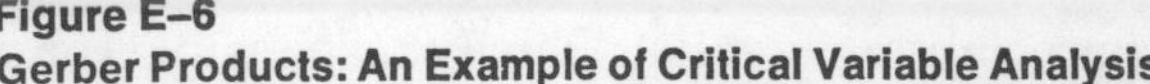

Figure E–6
Gerber Products: An Example of Critical Variable Analysis

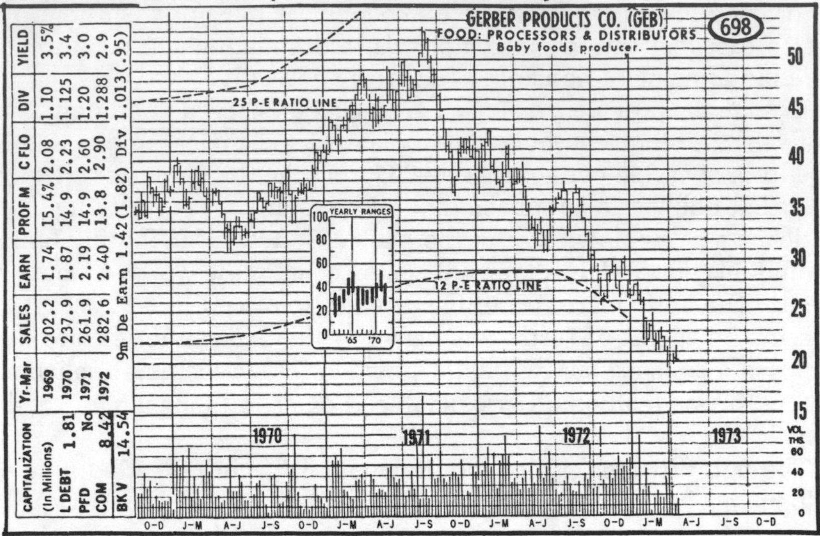

Source: Standard & Poor's Corp.

cause and effect relationship of the birthrate on Gerber's earnings. Rather, it is to support our view of how new information, which affected the stock's value, entered the marketplace's information system and started to change investor expectations of the future. Was it in September, 1971, when a new study on birthrates received substantial publicity, or was it when the company's reported earnings finally reflected a trend that had been in force for some time? Furthermore, and also of importance, was the new information immediately discounted in the price of the stock? We think the answers to both questions are obvious.

As we all know, only too well, good investment decisions are rarely so easy, even in retrospect. The facts that govern the price action of securities are usually much more complex and much less easy to identify. Therefore, the general concept is worth exploring further with two additional illustrations.

1. American Broadcasting Companies had long been regarded as a poor third against its two major TV competitors. The evidence given for this position was that its *ratings* usually were much lower and therefore its ability to price programs competitively was diminished. Also, better ratings feed on themselves, in that good ratings attract good programming which attracts better pricing

which improves profits. In early 1976, *Business Week*—an unusually good source of new investment information—noted "ABC–TV suddenly seems to be making no mistakes. After scrambling for two decades to achieve some sort of equal footing with its older and wealthier rivals, the network this season passed NBC–TV for second place in the season-long prime-time averages." Trade papers, we assume, carried news of this unfolding development long before. A stock price chart (Figure E–7) illustrates the subsequent price action of ABC common on the New York Stock Exchange following the *Business Week* article.

Melville Shoe is one of the nation's largest manufacturers and retailers of men's and women's shoes. The common stock rose from $5 a share at the beginning of 1975 to 17¾ early in November of the same year. Most investors tend to shy away from a stock after such a dramatic price rise. On November 11, 1975, the *Wall Street Journal* carried a relatively lengthy article detailing very favorable industry conditions under the heading "Retailers of Shoes Are Feeling the Pinch of Higher Demand and Lower Inventory." An executive of a major shoe manufacturer was quoted as stating "Our major problem is getting the shoes out the door fast enough." Production, he said, was up 50 percent from February (1975) and still climbing. Another shoe executive noted that retail sales took off last May (1975) at a time when inventories were low. Comments by other executives in the article were equally informing. Furthermore, it is doubtful that investors could have received a better analysis of industry conditions from any professional Wall Streeter. This one was available almost free of charge, providing investors were looking for such information. By early 1977 the stock had risen to 27½, over 50 percent from the time of the *Wall Street Journal* article, and professionals were commenting most favorably on the attractiveness of the shares.

Perhaps the correlation between the items we have selected and the subsequent price action of the underlying common stock is accidental. Perhaps other factors were at work; they probably were. But we think there is a link between stock prices and basic information. These examples also stress another point. Intelligent investors must learn to make better use of widely available, low cost, but important information. In addition to the daily media, there are many publications in each industry which, if read and interpreted correctly, yield accurate accounts of new industry and company developments. Generally speaking, insufficient use is being made of them. Investors also have to

Figure E–7
Stock Prices, Critical Variables, and Public Information

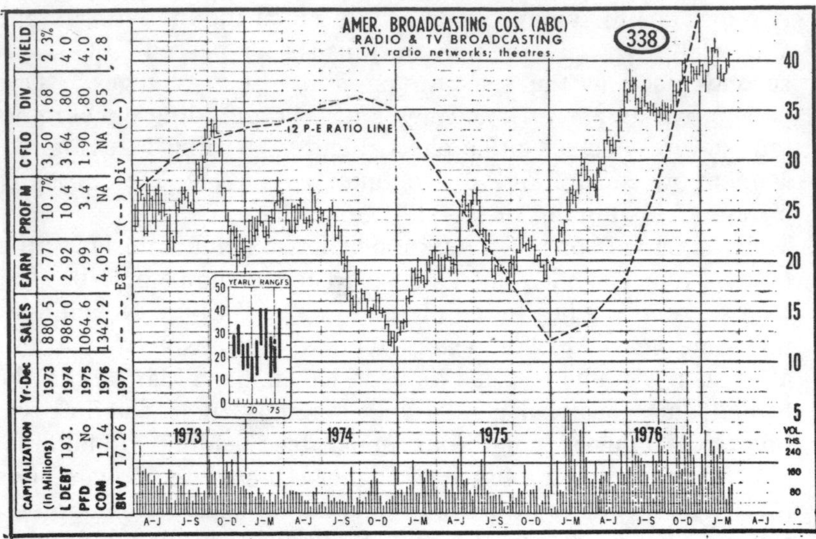

"ABC Cuts Its Losses to Insure Its TV Gains"

Source: *Business Week*, March 15, 1976.

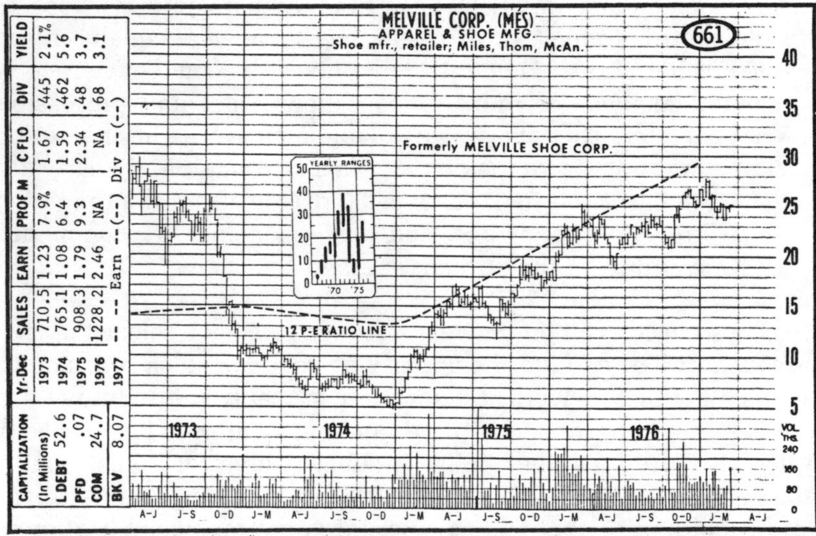

"Retailers of Shoes Are Feeling Pinch of Higher Demand and Lower Inventory"

Source: *Wall Street Journal*, November 11, 1975.

develop a willingness to act on common sense and sometimes instinct, rather than on complete knowledge, when a change occurs. Henry Kissinger once remarked that foreign policy was "the need to gear action to the assessment that cannot be proved true when it is made." Often, investing is no different.

Investors—both stock investors and bond investors—must keep in mind, as they go about the problem of assessing change, that it is not whether conditions *are* good or bad that's important, but whether they are *changing* for the better or worse, relative to expectations, and whether the prospect is for recent trends to continue, or to change once again.

In the final analysis, investment success is not as much a function of intelligence and ability but of personal conviction. Are you willing to back your own judgment, especially if it means going against the crowd?

SUGGESTED READINGS

Baruch, Bernard M. *My Own Story*. Henry Holt & Company, New York, 1957.

Cohen, Jerome B. *Personal Finance: Principles and Case Problems*. 5th ed. Homewood, Ill.: Richard D. Irwin, 1977.

Ellis, Charles D. "The Loser's Game." *Financial Analysts Journal*, July–August 1975.

Klein, Roger, and **Wolman, William** *The Beat Inflation Strategy*. New York: Simon & Schuster, 1975.

Malkiel, Burton G., and **Firstenberg, Paul B.** *Managing Risk in an Uncertain Era*. Princeton, N.J.: Princeton University, 1976.

Index

Index

D

E

F

G

J

K–L

S